INTERNATIONAL MONETARY AND FINANCIAL ISSUES FOR THE 1990s

Research papers for the Group of Twenty-Four

VOLUME VIII

UNITED NATIONS
New York and Geneva, 1997

Note

Symbols of United Nations documents are composed of capital letters combined with figures. Mention of such a symbol indicates a reference to a United Nations document.

*

The views expressed in this compendium are those of the authors and do not necessarily reflect the views of the UNCTAD secretariat. The designations employed and the presentation of the material do not imply the expression of any opinion whatsoever on the part of the Secretariat of the United Nations concerning the legal status of any country, territory, city or area, or of its authorities, or concerning the delimitation of its frontiers or boundaries.

* *

Material in this publication may be freely quoted; acknowledgement, however, is requested (including reference to the document number). It would be appreciated if a copy of the publication containing the quotation were sent to the Editorial Assistant, UNCTAD, Division on Globalization and Development Strategies, Palais des Nations, CH-1211 Geneva 10.

UNCTAD/GDS/MDPB/1

UNITED NATIONS PUBLICATION
Sales No. E.97.II.D.5
ISBN 92-1-112409-3   ISSN 1020-329X

Contents

MANAGING FOREIGN CAPITAL FLOWS: THE EXPERIENCES OF THE REPUBLIC OF KOREA, THAILAND, MALAYSIA AND INDONESIA

THE NEW CONDITIONALITIES OF THE INTERNATIONAL FINANCIAL INSTITUTIONS

Abbreviations

ADF	African Development Fund
ADR	American Depositary Receipts (Chile)
AfDB	African Development Bank
AFESD	Arab Fund for Economic and Social Development
ALADI	Association for Latin American Integration
AMF	Arab Monetary Fund
APEC	Asia-Pacific Economic Cooperation
BADEA	Arab Bank for Economic Development in Africa
BIBF	Bangkok International Banking Facilities
BIS	Bank for International Settlements
BNB	Bank Negara Bill
BWIs	Bretton Woods institutions
CABEI	Central American Bank for Economic Integration
CBFER	Central Bank Foreign Exchange Regulations (Chile)
CFA	Communauté Financière Africaine
DAC	Development Assistance Committee
EBRD	European Bank for Reconstruction and Development
EC	exchange certificates
EDI	Economic Development Institute (World Bank)
EEF	Exchange Equalization Fund
EPF	Employee Provident Fund
ESAF	Enhanced Structural Adjustment Facility
FDI	foreign direct investment
FEMA	Foreign-exchange Management Act
FSO	Fund for Special Operations (IDB)
FY	Fiscal Year
GAB	General Arrangements to Borrow
GDI	gross domestic investment
GEF	Global Environment Facility
GNP	gross national product
HIPCs	highly indebted poor countries
IBRD	International Bank for Reconstruction and Development
IDA	International Development Association
IDB	Inter-American Development Bank
IFIs	international financial institutions
IMF	International Monetary Fund
LDCs	least developed countries
LIBOR	London Interbank Offered Rate
MDBs	Multilateral Development Banks
MDF	Multilateral Debt Facility
NAFTA	North-American Free Trade Area
NDA	net domestic assets
NEAPs	national environmental action plans

NFA	net foreign assets
NGOs	non-governmental organizations
NID	negotiable instruments of deposits
NIEs	newly industrializing economies
ODA	official development assistance
OECD	Organization for Economic Co-operation and Development
PERs	public expenditure reviews
RBZ	Reserve Bank of Zimbabwe
SAF	Structural Adjustment Facility
SCA2	Special Contingency Account II
SDR	Special Drawing Right
SET	Stock Exchange of Thailand
SILCs	severely indebted low-income countries
SSA	sub-Saharan Africa
UMDF	Uganda Multilateral Debt Fund
UNCTAD	United Nations Conference on Trade and Development
UNDP	United Nations Development Programme
VDR	variable deposit requirements
WTO	World Trade Organization

The authors

- **Carlos Budnevich L.,** International Director, and Manager of Financial Analysis, Central Bank of Chile

- **Rudi Dornbusch,** Ford Professor of Economics and International Management, Department of Economics, Massachusetts Institute of Technology, Cambridge, Massachusetts

- **Gerald K. Helleiner,** Professor of Economics, University of Toronto, Canada

- **Devesh Kapur**, Program Associate, The Brookings Institution, Washington, D.C.

- **Louis Kasekende,** Executive Director, Policy and Research, Bank of Uganda, Kampala

- **Damoni Kitabire,** Commissioner, Macro-Economic Policy Department, Ministry of Finance and Economic Planning, Kampala, Uganda

- **Guillermo R. Le Fort V.,** Deputy Director of Research, Central Bank of Chile

- **Matthew Martin,** Director, External Finance for Africa, London

- **Aziz Ali Mohammed,** Special Adviser to the Governor, State Bank of Pakistan

- **Peter Murrell,** Department of Economics, University of Maryland, United States

- **Yung Chul Park,** President, Korea Institute of Finance, Seoul, Republic of Korea

- **Chi-Young Song,** Research Fellow, Korea Institute of Finance, Seoul, Republic of Korea

Preface

The Intergovernmental Group of Twenty-Four on International Monetary Affairs (G-24) was established in November 1971 to increase the negotiating strength of the developing countries in discussions that were going on at that time in the International Monetary Fund on reform of the international monetary system. Developing countries felt that they should play a meaningful role in decisions about the system, and that the effectiveness of that role would be enhanced if they were to meet regularly as a group, as the developed countries had been doing for some time in the Group of Ten (G-10).

It soon became apparent that the G-24 was in need of technical support and analysis relating to the issues arising for discussion in the Fund and Bank, including the Interim and Development Committees. In response to representations by the Chairman of the G-24 to the Secretary-General of the United Nations Conference on Trade and Development (UNCTAD), and following discussions between UNCTAD and the United Nations Development Programme (UNDP), the latter agreed in 1975 to establish a project to provide the technical support that the G-24 had requested. This was to take the form, principally, of analytical papers prepared by competent experts on issues currently under consideration in the fields of international money and finance.

Mr. Sidney Dell, a former Director in UNCTAD's Money, Finance and Development Division and subsequently Assistant Administrator of UNDP headed the project from its establishment until 1990. During this period, some 60 research papers were prepared by the Group of Twenty-Four. The high quality of this work was recognized by the Deputies and Ministers of the Group and the reports were given wide currency, some being published in five volumes by North-Holland Press and others by the United Nations.

The project work was resumed in 1990 under the direction of Professor G.K. Helleiner, Professor of Economics, University of Toronto, Canada. The UNCTAD secretariat continues to provide both substantive and administrative backstopping to the project. Funding is currently being provided by the G-24 countries themselves, the International Development Research Centre of Canada and the Governments of Denmark, the Netherlands and Sweden. As a result, it has been possible to continue to provide the Group of Twenty-Four timely and challenging analyses. These studies are being reissued periodically in compendia. This is the eighth volume to be published.

CAPITAL ACCOUNT REGIMES AND THE DEVELOPING COUNTRIES

G. K. Helleiner*

Abstract

Private portfolio capital flows to developing countries have expanded rapidly in recent years and created macroeconomic management problems for some countries. The benefits and costs of capital-account liberalization are considered, together with analysis of the purposes and efficacy of capital controls. The results of a series of country studies done for the Intergovernmental Group of Twenty-four are summarized and conclusions drawn. Direct and indirect controls over external capital flows, by influencing their volume and composition, are found to have been valuable macroeconomic policy instruments in selected Asian and Latin American countries, complementing the traditional monetary, fiscal and exchange-rate instruments. The IMF should take an active role in international capital market surveillance and the provision of liquidity where necessary, but should not require all its members to introduce convertibility to the capital account. Further areas for international action and research are suggested.

*   For comments on an earlier draft, and without implicating them in the contents of the current version, I would like to thank Andrew Cornford, Roy Culpeper, Dinesh Dodhia, Rumman Faruqi, Eric Helleiner, Louis Kasekende, Guillermo Le Fort, Azizali Mohammed, Chi-Young Song, and John Williamson.

I.   Introduction

Debate over the role of volatile private capital flows in international payments and appropriate government policies relating to them has a long history. The League of Nations produced an influential study of exchange-rate experience in the interwar period that addressed some of these issues (Nurkse, 1944); policy debate thereon sharpened in the preparations for (and at) the Bretton Woods conference in 1944; and it resurfaced repeatedly as current and capital-account convertibility was restored to an increasing number of developed countries in the post Second World War period (Helleiner, 1994).

In the developing countries, the early discussions tended to centre upon the benefits and costs of foreign direct investment and the problems of "capital flight" rather than those of the volatility of (then virtually non-existent) portfolio financial flows. With the dramatic expansion of commercial bank lending to the developing countries in the 1970s and the subsequent debt crisis of the 1980s, attention shifted to analysis of sovereign debt, default, emergency lending, and possible "workout" schemes, with particular reference to the respective roles of Government, banks and the international financial institutions. The difficulties encountered with financial liberalization and the "opening" of external capital accounts in the Southern Cone of Latin America in the late 1970s generated a burst of research and discussion of necessary prerequisites or concomitants of a liberalized capital account and related issues of optimal sequencing (e.g. Diaz-Alejandro, 1985; McKinnon, 1991; Corbo and DeMelo, 1986). With the sharp increase in private international portfolio capital flows to developing countries in the 1990s, particularly to countries in Asia and Latin America, interest in the problems and possibilities they create began to accelerate, as did discussion of the appropriate external capital-account regime for these countries.

By the early 1990s several general analytical studies of these questions had already been undertaken (e.g. Williamson, 1991; Akyüz, 1992; Reisen and Fischer, 1993). In the past few years, however, there has been an unprecedented burst of books, papers, and conferences on the problems created for developing countries by massive and volatile international flows of private capital, larger for them than ever before, and appropriate policy responses.[1] Both the IMF and the World Bank have directed a great deal of further attention, during this period, to

the problem of volatile private capital flows and the management of capital surges (notably in IMF, 1995b and 1995d; EDI, 1995; Corbo and Hernandez, 1996). Indeed, in some respects, as will be seen, IMF documents have altered their message over this short period as analysis and experience accumulated. Not only has the IMF directed increased research attention to capital-account issues in recent years but, in 1995, its Executive Board also authorized increased attention to them in its surveillance activities. Of course, none of this recent experience or the analysis thereof has altered the prime need for macroeconomic policy to create a sound framework for private domestic savings and investment decisions, which remain at the core of successful long-term development.

Among those who first directed G-24 attention to these problems were Calvo (1996) and Mohammed (1996) whose papers at the G-24 technical conference (in Cartagena) in early 1994 stimulated lively debate there. A modest research programme was launched by the G-24 shortly thereafter to attempt to shed greater light on the policy issues raised by emerging capital-account experience. In the meantime, the Mexican crisis of late 1994 and early 1995 stimulated further public debate and policy discussion. Many other new studies have since been published, as already noted, some of them overlapping those of the G-24 project.

The G-24 project included case studies of a number of Asian and Latin American countries (Park and Song, 1997; Le Fort and Budnevich, 1997), and one of the first research efforts to consider sub-Saharan African experiences in this sphere (Kasekende, Kitabire and Martin, 1997).[2] It also included a paper on the possibility of an IMF financing role in financial crises (Williamson, 1996a) and a general paper on alternative capital-account regimes (Dornbusch, 1997). The five papers prepared under this programme were completed in 1995/1996. The purpose of this paper is to summarize their major results, place them into the context of ongoing debate, consider some of their policy implications at national and international levels, and suggest further research requirements.

This paper surveys the current state of knowledge as to the new forms, and roles, of private capital flows to developing countries in the 1990s and appropriate national and international policy responses to the problems and possibilities they create. Section II describes the growth of these flows in the 1990s, and some of their effects in recipient countries. Section III addresses the question of alternative capital-account policies for developing countries, including the rationale and efficacy of various kinds of direct and indirect controls over international capital flows. In section IV, the possibility of improved international arrangements is considered, including the provision of increased liquidity, better procedures for orderly debt workouts, and clarified international regimes. Section V presents issues deserving further research. There follows a brief conclusion.

II. The new private capital flows to developing countries in the 1990s

A. *Increased size and altered composition*

Private capital flows to developing countries, after slumping in the 1980s, increased dramatically, and to unprecedented levels, in the first half of the 1990s. According to the IMF, net private flows in the 1989-1995 period were, on average, about ten times those of the 1983-1988 period, whereas net official flows had fallen by more than half (see table 1). According to the World Bank, between 1990 and 1993 private capital flows to developing countries rose nearly fourfold, before stabilizing at about $160-170 billion in 1994-1995 as United States interest rates rose and the Mexican crisis hit (World Bank, 1996, pp. 10-11). These private flows remain, however, highly concentrated. Only about twenty developing countries are today considered creditworthy by international capital markets and banks (World Bank, 1996, p. 11). Foreign direct investment is almost equally concentrated. In recent years, the African continent has received only 4 per cent of total net private flows.

In the 1990s there was a sharp increase in international portfolio investment, both in debt instruments and in equity, in developing countries. The relative importance of bank lending to developing countries fell drastically; that of foreign direct investment also fell, although its absolute size grew very rapidly. Much higher proportions of external capital were also now directed to private-sector borrowers than to Governments in developing countries. Tables 2 and 3 summarize the overall composition of capital flows to the major developing areas and selected countries (studied in the G-24 project) in recent years. Private flows have accounted for very substantial percentages of individual recipient countries' GDP in the 1990s (e.g. 6 to 8 per cent in Colombia and Chile, respectively; 10 to 13 per cent in Thailand and Malaysia, respectively). Foreign direct investment has been relatively more important in Asia

than elsewhere but the relative contribution of portfolio flows has risen nearly everywhere. In some of the sub-Saharan African countries, "private transfers" have reached remarkable levels (e.g. 9 per cent in the United Republic of Tanzania, 4 per cent in Uganda), although knowledge as to what they really are remains sparse.

These new flows can be partly explained as a once-for-all (permanent) stock adjustment on the part of the world's investment community (notably insurance companies, mutual funds and pension funds) to newly liberalized international financial markets, both in developing countries and in the industrialized world, and the perception of new profit opportunities in emerging markets, particularly in countries that have achieved sound macroeconomic fundamentals and a receptive environment for foreign capital. (Other capital flows may also be of such a "one-off" portfolio adjustment nature, e.g. returning flight capital or purchases of privatized assets.) Since global investors still allocate small fractions of their portfolios to developing countries and capitalization in emerging markets can still expand, such flows may continue for some time. Once such stock adjustment has been completed, however, the flows resulting from it can be expected to fall to more "normal" levels (around which they will continue to fluctuate). It would be helpful, in such circumstances, to address the possibilities for smoothing the macroeconomic adjustment in recipient countries to these one-off shifts in global portfolio choices.

The new private capital inflows to developing countries can also be seen, however, in terms of an *ongoing* and perfectly normal response on the part of more globally oriented investors to changing incentive structures - including relative rates of interest, exchange-rate expectations, political volatility, etc.. Private capital inflows may also be procyclical, increasing in "good" times and falling, even reversing in direction, in "bad" times; such flows, often found in primary exporting countries and in part essentially speculative, create obvious extra problems for attempts at macroeconomic stabilization. If recent international capital flows (into developing countries) are *not* significantly the product of "one-off" stock adjustment, but reflect normal response to changing incentives, their surge in one direction is likely to be reversible.

In any case, newly liberalized international and domestic financial markets certainly create new opportunities for international incentive-responsive private capital flows and short-term volatility in such flows. When large institutional investors alter their overall

Table 1

DEVELOPING COUNTRIES: CAPITAL FLOWS^a

(Annual average, $ billion)

	1973-1977	1978-1982	1983-1988	1989-1995	1994	1995
All developing countries						
Net private capital flows^b	10.2	26.0	11.6	114.3	149.0	166.4
Net direct investment	3.6	9.0	12.6	39.8	61.3	71.7
Net portfolio investment	0.2	1.7	4.3	41.5	50.4	37.0
Other net investments	6.4	15.3	-5.2	33.1	37.3	57.8
Net official flows	11.0	25.5	29.5	11.7	2.6	27.3
Change in reserves^c	-20.2	-21.7	-9.6	-56.8	-57.9	-75.7
Africa						
Net private capital flows^b	4.5	4.3	0.5	4.9	11.9	9.8
Net direct investment	1.0	0.3	1.1	2.1	2.2	2.1
Net portfolio investment	0.1	-0.3	-0.4	-0.3	1.1	0.1
Other net investments	3.4	4.3	-0.1	3.0	8.6	7.6
Net official flows	2.4	7.2	6.6	2.0	1.5	2.8
Change in reserves^c	-1.4	0.4	-0.4	-2.1	-5.1	-1.4
Asia						
Net private capital flows^b	4.3	13.9	11.2	45.7	75.1	98.2
Net direct investment	1.4	3.0	5.6	24.4	41.9	52.4
Net portfolio investment	0.1	0.2	0.9	10.1	16.0	18.5
Other net investments	2.8	10.7	4.7	11.2	17.1	27.3
Net official flows	4.0	7.4	6.4	7.2	6.0	5.9
Change in reserves^c	-6.9	-7.0	-18.0	-38.9	-61.6	-50.0
Middle East and Europe						
Net private capital flows^b	-10.3	-21.1	1.9	29.7	11.4	19.0
Net direct investment	-1.3	-0.1	1.2	0.9	-0.5	0.0
Net portfolio investment	0.0	-0.2	5.0	13.6	15.9	8.4
Other net investments	-9.1	-20.8	-4.3	15.2	-4.1	10.5
Net official flows	2.3	6.6	6.6	-2.6	-1.4	-3.8
Change in reserves^c	-14.2	-17.6	9.5	-1.4	-0.2	-2.6
Latin America and the Caribbean						
Net private capital flows^b	11.7	28.9	-2.0	34.0	50.7	39.5
Net direct investment	2.5	5.8	4.7	12.4	17.7	17.1
Net portfolio investment	0.0	2.0	-1.2	18.1	17.4	10.0
Other net investments	9.2	21.1	-5.6	3.6	15.6	12.3
Net official flows	2.3	4.4	9.8	5.1	-3.5	22.4
Change in reserves^c	2.2	2.5	-0.7	-11.4	9.0	-21.7

Source: IMF, 1996.

a Net capital flows comprise net direct investment, net portfolio investment and other long- and short-term net investment flows, including official and private borrowing.

b Because of data limitations, other net investments may include some official flows.

c A minus sign indicates an increase.

Table 2

PERCENTAGE COMPOSITION OF EXTERNAL LONG-TERM CAPITAL FLOWS TO DEVELOPING COUNTRIES, 1994

	Private			Official	Total	Total flows
	Net debt flows	FDI	Portfolio equity flows			*in per cent of GDP*
All developing countries	21.1	38.6	16.8	23.4	100	3.9
East Asia	25.4	50.5	14.8	9.4	100	5.6
Indonesia	17.9	23.2	40.4	18.5	100	5.2
Republic of Korea	64.4	10.9	33.9	-9.2	100	2.0
Malaysia	14.4	63.2	19.2	3.2	100	9.7
Thailand	87.5	13.9	-11.7	10.3	100	3.2
South Asia	-0.4	9.0	45.1	46.3	100	3.5
Latin America and the Caribbean	30.7	40.7	25.7	2.9	100	3.2
Chile	39.8	43.6	21.1	-4.4	100	7.9
Colombia	38.9	62.6	21.1	-22.5	100	2.2
Europe and Central Asia	19.7	31.2	7.2	41.8	100	2.6
Middle East and North Africa	3.1	35.8	1.0	60.1	100	2.4
Sub-Saharan Africa	4.4	14.8	4.3	76.5	100	5.1
Kenya	-260.4	3.8	0.0	356.6	100	1.5
Zambia	-13.5	12.6	0.0	100.8	100	13.6
Zimbabwe	-45.6	10.3	14.7	120.6	100	6.3

Source: Calculations by the author, based on World Bank, 1996, pp. 84-85.

international portfolio composition only marginally (for them) they can have dramatic consequences for individual national asset markets and exchange rates. Some of the surge towards developing countries' financial markets in the early 1990s *is* undoubtedly attributable to the low interest rates in the United States (and other industrialized countries) at that time (Calvo et al., 1993).

External circumstances have always been understood to play an important role in setting the context for national macroeconomic management, particularly in small open economies. Shocks in the external terms of trade have long been recognized as a particular problem for developing countries. Now

changes in global interest rates, and their effects upon private international capital flows, are revealed as a further *major* source of exogenous shocks. "Contagion effects" from financial events elsewhere (e.g. "tequila effects") are also now an important additional source of exogenous shock; of the countries studied in this project, the "tequila effects" of the Mexican crisis were most notable in Thailand, Malaysia and, to some extent, South Africa. Policy changes - particularly in exchange regimes - in geographically contiguous countries are another potentially significant source of exogenous influence upon domestic macroeconomic experience, as shown in some recent African experience (e.g. Kenya and Uganda, and the CFA franc zone and its neighbours). Realignments of major

Table 3

MAJOR TYPES OF PRIVATE CAPITAL INFLOW TO SELECTED DEVELOPING COUNTRIES, 1990-1994

(Per cent of GDP)

		FDI	Net flow of short-term debt	Net flow of long-term debt[a]	Private transfers[b]	Total private flows
Latin America						
Chile	(1990-1994)	2.4	3.1	1.2	-	7.7
Colombia	(1993-1994)	3.0	-0.3	3.8	-	6.3
East Asia	(1990-1994)					
Indonesia	(1990-1993)	1.3	-	4.1	-	5.5
Republic of Korea	(1991-1994)	0.2	0.4	1.8	-	2.4
Malaysia	(1991-1993)	7.7	4.7	0.4	-	12.8
Thailand	(1990-1994)	1.7	6.1	2.6	-	10.5
Sub-Saharan Africa	(1990-1993)					
Kenya		0.3	0.4	0.2	1.9	2.8
South Africa		0.0	0.3	0.0	0.0	0.3
United Republic of Tanzania		0.3	-0.4	0.0	9.1	9.1
Uganda		0.1	-0.2	0.0	4.7	4.7
Zambia		2.9	-0.9	0.0	-0.3	1.7
Zimbabwe		0.2	0.8	0.8	0.3	2.0

Source: Kasekende, Kitabire and Martin, 1997; Le Fort and Budnevich, 1997; Park and Song, 1997.

    a   Including net portfolio equity flows, except in Malaysia.

    b   Shown only for sub-Saharan African countries.

currency exchange rates can also profoundly affect developing countries' real effective exchange rates and hence their prospects for external balance, e.g. the nominal appreciation of the yen against the dollar in the 1990s brought depreciation of many East Asian currencies vis-à-vis the yen (Park and Song in this volume).

B. Impacts and responses

Capital inflows are generally welcome in developing countries for their role in financing investment, and thereby assisting in long-term development, and/or in shorter-term smoothing of consumption. It has long been recognized, however, that where there are significant domestic micro-

economic "distortions", profit-motivated inflows can be immiserizing. Prior to and during the debt crisis of the 1980s there was a great deal of discussion as to how the proceeds of external bank lending (mainly to Governments) had been used, and whether they had contributed to development. Always there has been appropriate concern as to whether the Government had its economic policy fundamentals "right". There is obviously a continuing need to understand how capital inflows are ultimately used, and whether recipients' national policies may contribute to any "misdirection".

Concern with the potentially undesirable *macro-economic* consequences of private inflows, even when policies in the recipient country are basically sound, is much more recent. Surges of inflowing private capital create macroeconomic problems, above all, through their effects on either the exchange rate or the domestic money supply, together with the risk of their abrupt cessation or capital outflow.

If the central bank attempts to maintain stability in the exchange rate, private capital inflows will expand the monetary base (as the central bank increases its foreign exchange reserves). To prevent consequent overheating of the domestic economy, and a real appreciation of the currency, the central bank may seek to sterilize the domestic monetary consequences, through open-market operations - in Government securities or in the interbank market (as in Malaysia) or, more usually, through the issue of its own securities; or through increased reserve requirements; or via the redeployment of Government deposits from the commercial banks to the central bank.

Tightened domestic monetary policy may, however, involve significant quasi-fiscal losses for the central bank as it pays higher interest rates on its domestic liabilities (including those earned by foreigners) than it earns on its foreign-exchange reserves. To the extent that interest rates increase in consequence of such sterilization policies, they may induce a further fillip to external capital inflows. (Interest rates are presumably lowered through private capital inflows in the first place, however, and inflows will, in any case, cease once a new portfolio equilibrium is reached).

Increasing bank reserve requirements may also "redirect capital flows to domestic borrowers through channels other than the domestic banking system - such as through domestic markets for equity and real estate. If this disintermediation is effective, the macroeconomic stabilization problem would remain" (Fernandez-Arias and Montiel, 1996, p. 73). Domestic agents may also resort increasingly to offshore borrowing. Clearly the structure of the domestic financial system and, in particular, the interest of foreign investors in other domestic assets and their access to them are important to overall macroeconomic outcomes.

One obvious additional (or alternative) possible response to surging capital inflows is to tighten the fiscal regime, and this is frequently appropriate, particularly in countries previously running large fiscal deficits. But recent experience indicates that many countries experiencing monetary and exchange-rate pressures from private capital inflows had already achieved fiscal balance or even surpluses (e.g. Chile, the Republic of Korea and others). In any case, as a recent IMF paper argues, "In most countries ... it is difficult to use fiscal policy as a short-run response, and it may also exacerbate the problem of unsustainable inflows if confidence in economic policy grows strongly" (IMF, 1995d, p. 5). Thus macroeconomic policy instruments other than or additional to fiscal ones must usually be deployed to respond effectively to capital surges.

If the central bank instead allows the value of the domestic currency to appreciate in response to capital inflows, this will have undesirable consequences for the overall incentive structure. The current account of the balance of payments is likely to deteriorate in response to currency appreciation, and the economy will become increasingly vulnerable to a sudden reduction or reversal of the capital inflows. (The same results follow from real currency appreciation stemming from domestic price inflation with a stable nominal exchange rate, such as may follow from unsterilized central bank intervention in the foreign exchange market.) The critical question is whether the capital inflows that are associated with such an increasing current-account deficit are likely to be sustainable and, if so, at what level. Countries operating a pure floating exchange-rate system (in some African countries, they seem to have had few options) are consequently faced with a major set of problems: appreciating and potentially unstable currencies, rising current-account deficits and rising external debt.

In the many developing countries where there are relatively weak domestic financial markets, there are likely to be further difficulties created by surges of external private capital, either inward or outward. They can easily spark increased volatility in domestic markets for financial assets and real estate. Capital surges have been associated with stock market and property market booms; and outflows with corresponding busts. Where domestic financial markets are thin and/or weakly supervised, even modest inflows of external private capital can overwhelm both local financial institutions and their regulatory authorities, and create additional macroeconomic management problems. Even in relatively strong financial systems, deposit insurance, whether explicit or implicit, creates moral hazard that may encourage overenthusiastic foreign depositing in domestic banks, and overenthusiastic (and, particularly when there is rapid expansion, inadequately supervised) bank lending to domestic agents.

Although the increased inflow of foreign portfolio capital in the 1990s did not destabilize national financial markets in the four Asian countries studied in this project in the sense of increasing average weekly exchange rate, interest rate, or stock market volatility, these countries did experience episodes of extreme stock market volatility which appeared to be associated with foreign capital flows - e.g. a stock market boom in late 1993 and early January 1994 in Malaysia, followed by rapid decline again in the first half of 1994; and sudden stock market declines in early 1995 in Thailand and Malaysia in response to the Mexican crisis in early 1995, and the Gulf War in the second half of 1990. Similarly, there were at the same times sharp interest rate changes in response to the same external capital surges, and the pressures on policy that they created.

Many developing countries maintain various forms of control over external capital-account transactions. The ease and speed with which private capital can flow internationally depends partly on the nature of the capital asset or liability, but, no less importantly, on the costs of the flows to private transactors, as influenced by such capital controls - in the form of restrictions, regulations and taxes, both direct and indirect. To an analysis of such policies for the capital account we now turn.

III. Policies for the capital account in developing countries

A. *Benefits and costs of international financial integration, and the rationale for controls*

Capital flows internationally with or without governmental controls over the capital account. Increasing numbers of countries have opted for full capital-account convertibility and integration with global capital markets. This is a clear policy option for all developing countries today.

The principal gains from capital-account liberalization at the national level and from global financial integration more generally are those deriving from the increased efficiency of both national and global capital markets that they can create. By easing or removing constraints on private decision-making, Governments permit private agents to make savings and investment decisions on a freer basis. The result should be less "distorted" intertemporal decision-making both within individual liberalizing nations and

at the global level. Within the (relatively capital-scarce) developing countries, no less than elsewhere, this can be expected, in the best-case scenario, to include greater international portfolio diversification for their own investors; greater diversification of capital sources on the part of their public and private borrowers; greater competition and thereby increased efficiency for their financial services sectors; deeper financial markets and the increased efficiency of intermediation that it brings; and greater domestic savings and investment. These potential advantages are great enough to motivate open capital accounts in the OECD and to inspire most countries to declare capital-account liberalization to be an ultimate objective, whatever their current practices. But none of these potential gains are assured, and capital-account liberalization also involves risks and potential costs.

Capital controls have traditionally been employed to permit domestic monetary authorities to pursue monetary policies more independently of international interest rates than they otherwise could do (frequently, although not so much in recent years, within the context of a fixed-exchange-rate system). Such measures are both easier to make effective and theoretically more defensible on a temporary basis than as a long-run system for maintaining a fundamentally inappropriate exchange rate. Domestic interest rates have typically (although not universally, e.g. not in Indonesia) been deregulated in financial reforms associated with capital-account liberalization. Total capital-account openness would generate, in equilibrium, domestic nominal interest rates equal to the "world" rates plus a premium reflecting the market's exchange-rate expectations and its assessment of other country risks associated with imperfect enforceability of international contracts.[3] Since the resulting domestic interest rates could be inappropriate to domestic needs, there has been interest in policies that could drive a (variable) wedge between domestic rates and these fully market-determined rates. Stated differently, the unwanted private capital flows engendered by official efforts to set domestic rates that are "appropriate" for domestic needs create an obvious interest in policies that could reduce such flows. In some instances, where Governments were using the inflation tax and/or reducing domestic debt service costs via *lowered* domestic interest rates, controls over outflows carried primarily a fiscal purpose. In Chile and the Republic of Korea, on the other hand, domestic interest rates have been maintained at rates *above* those in the major financial markets in industrial countries by means of controls over capital inflows.

Controls over outflows, notoriously difficult to enforce, have also traditionally been motivated by a desire to utilize domestic savings for the purpose of domestic investment. An older literature has long argued that the potential vulnerability of developing countries' external payments positions or exchange rates to volatile private expectations legitimate controls over capital outflows, and should make capital-account outflows the very *last* to be liberalized (e.g. Williamson, 1991).

In the 1990s, however, capital controls have frequently been motivated by the desire to stabilize the domestic economy in a world of volatile private capital surges, either inward or outward. There is by now plenty of evidence that developing countries can encounter severe macroeconomic management problems, even financial crises, in consequence of surges of private capital flow. Such surges are presumably easier and therefore both more likely and more frequent when capital flows are "freer".

According to much current wisdom, it is critically important for development that countries maintain a stable and appropriate real exchange rate, and thus a stable and sustainable current account, and a reasonably stable macro economy. Such stability is seen by many as more important for the achievement of an adequate level and efficiency of investment than the details of incentive structures which purport to have microeconomic efficiency benefits. For this purpose, it may be desirable to moderate overall capital flows that are not driven by long-term economic fundamentals. From this motivation it is but a small further leap to the objective of attempting to influence the *composition*, as well as the overall size, of capital flows so as to achieve more stable and more productive inflows.

In the face of the limits to the efficacy, in terms of macroeconomic management objectives, of the available fiscal, monetary and exchange-rate policy instruments, the monetary authorities of many developing countries have sought to deploy direct and indirect controls over private international capital flows as additional macroeconomic policy instruments. Such capital controls typically seek to reduce the level, slow the pace or alter the composition of private capital flows.

Further measures to restrain expansion of consumer expenditures which might otherwise be associated with capital inflows (and, in many cases, with import liberalization) may also be considered appropriate, e.g. limits upon domestic consumer and mortgage credit, or compulsory private savings programmes (McKinnon and Pill, 1995). These may be able to reduce the prospect of credit-driven booms in private consumption of the recent Mexican type.[4]

There are also prudential grounds for controls over international capital flows in the developing country context. Increased openness in the capital account may involve domestic banks and other financial institutions in increased risks, both because of increased deposit volatility and because of increased foreign exchange risk. Capital-account liberalization therefore is likely to require strengthened prudential supervision and information disclosure. According to some, prudential requirements or market "standards" relating to a country's international financial transactions are separate issues, not strictly part of the issue of capital-account convertibility (IMF, 1995d, p. 11); others, however, prefer to consider these issues more holistically, evidently finding it difficult to distinguish control measures purely on the basis of their purported or presumed motivation (IMF, 1995b, pp. 13-16).

Capital-account convertibility is obviously not a matter of all or nothing. Some types of transactions may be free while others are not; and the tightness of restrictions may vary in the same country over time. In this respect, as in trade policy and the analysis of the current account, "openness" can have a variety of interpretations. There is as yet no agreed way of measuring the degree of openness in the capital account (Montiel, 1994).[5] For the present, there seems little alternative but to rely on descriptive accounts, such as the IMF offers in its *Annual Reports on Exchange Restrictions*, for data on the extent of capital-account convertibility and changes therein.

Direct regulation of international capital flows, both inward and outward, has evidently been common in developing countries. A summary of existing capital controls in 155 developing countries, based on IMF data, is given in table 4. Of the 155 developing countries surveyed by the IMF, 119 employ some form of control over international capital flows, although 75 have accepted Article VIII obligations in respect of the current account. (For further discussion of the IMF Articles, see section IV.C.) The forms of these controls are numerous and the degree of their use varies greatly both across countries and over time. Some may be motivated more by the need to monitor than the desire to restrict. Table 4 shows that regulation of outward flows has been considerably more frequent than that of inward flows. Regulation of outward flows also has a longer history and remains fairly pervasive.

Table 4

CAPITAL CONTROLS IN DEVELOPING COUNTRIES

Category	Number of countries maintaining controls
Any form of capital control	119
Comprehensive controls	67
on outflows	67
on inflows	17
Foreign direct investments	107
of non-residents	84
of residents	35
Profit repatriation and capital liquidation	34
Taxes on capital transactions	9
Non-resident-controlled enterprises	6
Portfolio investments	61
of non-residents	30
of residents	33
Security issuance by non-residents	15
Security issuance abroad by residents	6
Debt-to-equity conversion	2
Financial transactions	78
of non-residents	41
of residents	66
Trade-related financial transactions	7
Deposit requirements for borrowing from abroad by residents	2
Deposit accounts	83
of non-residents in foreign exchange	37
of non-residents in local currency	52
of residents abroad	29
of residents in foreign currency with domestic banks	23
Other capital transfers	70
Personal capital transfers	34
Blocked accounts	24
Real-estate transactions	
of non-residents	23
of residents	30

Source: IMF, 1995e, p. 35.

Restrictions on residents' external investments and holdings of foreign currencies are frequent, at least in the form of upper limits, often based purely on prudential objectives, on the proportion of total assets that financial institutions may place abroad. Of inward flows, FDI is much more frequently regulated than purely financial flows. But there is evidently increasing interest in and resort to controls over the latter. In general, positive lists (in which only those transactions listed are "free") are more restrictive than negative lists (in which only those activities listed are restricted, regulated or prohibited).

B. *Influencing the composition of inflows*

There seems to be general agreement that some forms of external private capital inflow are more attractive to the recipient country than others. From the standpoint of future macroeconomic stability, the longer-term and the more stable are inflows of capital, the better. This would suggest a preference for longer-term investments - in long-term loans, equity and/or in the form of foreign direct investment,[6] particularly that which takes the form of physical flows of capital goods. Such flows are more likely to be based on long-term economic fundamentals and should be less susceptible to short-term volatility. (Some "reliable" development assistance may also carry these desirable attributes.)

If it is possible to distinguish between long-term and short-term investments, long-term ones are clearly preferable. Categorization of portfolio capital flows, however, is often difficult. In some sub-Saharan African countries, for instance, the authorities have little idea about the detailed composition of such capital flows. Informed analysts conjecture that much of what is at present recorded as private "transfer" in some African countries is actually more appropriately categorized as private capital flow, quite probably quickly reflected in real investment (Kasekende et al. in this volume). If the authorities do not know which flows are which, they will obviously face great difficulties in developing appropriate controls or macroeconomic stabilization policies. Indeed, in some developing country circumstances, authorities are said to be inhibited in their attempts to collect more accurate information on private capital flows by their fear of frightening market participants, discouraging real investors and stimulating undesired outflows (*ibid.*).

1. *Short-term versus long-term flows*

Short-term capital inflows (and outflows) have been an important element in the recent experience of many developing countries (including Thailand, Malaysia and several sub-Saharan African countries, where such flows have dominated). These include:

- short-term external borrowing (lending) by domestic commercial banks or other local firms,

- increased (decreased) non-resident holdings of domestic currency deposits in local banks,

- sales (purchases) of short-term money-market instruments to (by) non-residents,

- reduced (increased) resident holdings of foreign-currency deposits (where these are allowed), and

- swap transactions - sales (purchases) of foreign currency simultaneously unwound by forward market contracts.

Some of these flows may be directly related to real international trade in goods and services. A high proportion, however, may be unrelated to any real transactions, whether international or domestic. If so, they may be highly volatile. In Zambia in the late 1980s, for instance, there were sharp reversals in the direction of such flows involving year-on-year changes amounting to 6-8 per cent of GNP (Kasekende et al. in this volume).

Unfortunately, it is often difficult to distinguish flows that are related to real transactions from purely financial ones, or short-term from long-term flows. The Republic of Korea *has* consciously tried to treat capital-account transactions related to real investments differently from (more liberally than) purely financial transactions but this is inherently very difficult. Over many years, it has proven difficult even to distinguish current from capital transactions.

Long-maturity external obligations may seem, in principle, less vulnerable to volatility than short-maturity ones; but if there are active secondary markets, long maturities may be highly liquid. Longer-maturity instruments are thus not necessarily less volatile in their short-term behaviour than nominally short-term ones (Claessens et al., 1995). According to the IMF, "financial asset flows have become increasingly fungible ... [making it] more difficult for ... countries ... to maintain the effectiveness of their controls" (IMF, 1995d, p. 18). Indeed, OECD and European Union codes on capital flows have abandoned efforts to distinguish short-term capital flows from others and this indicates that others may eventually be forced along the same route (IMF, 1995d, p. 9). Monetary authorities in Chile, among other countries, have nonetheless found it possible to encourage longer-term bank deposits and longer-term credits via carefully structured bank reserve requirements and "minimum stay" regulations respectively (Le Fort and Budnevich in this volume).

2. FDI versus portfolio capital

Foreign direct investment is generally believed to be motivated differently, to behave differently, and to create different macroeconomic (and developmental) effects from portfolio capital flows. Foreign direct investors are presumed to base their decisions on longer-term economic and political fundamentals and thus to be less volatile in their short-term behaviour. FDI also often takes the form of real flows of capital equipment and brings technology and/or managerial and marketing skills along with its capital.

As far as stability and macroeconomic consequences are concerned, however, these presumed differences can be overdone. Foreign direct investment flows can also be volatile. Transnational corporations manage liquid funds as well as flows of real goods and services, and they usually do so very effectively. Foreign direct investors can also, when appropriate, borrow from foreign or domestic financial institutions in pursuit of their international financial flow objectives. FDI can therefore be associated with higher, rather than lower, variability in capital flow, reflecting TNCs' capacities for managing international intrafirm financial transactions to respond quickly to changing national circumstances (Dooley et al.,1995). Some of these FDI-related flows may be recorded as portfolio flows in traditional statistical systems.

The regimes for foreign direct investment in developing countries are usually quite different from those for portfolio capital, and they are not typically primarily motivated by short-term macroeconomic management considerations. In many ways, FDI inflows are treated more liberally than foreign portfolio capital because of the presumed advantages brought by its longer-term motivation, and the potential managerial, technological and export market-opening attributes associated with it. On the other hand, there are often selective prohibitions, controls and approval procedures - designed to protect strategic sectors or to ensure national benefits of various kinds - that are more stringent for FDI than for "arms-length" portfolio capital (IMF, 1995d). Although controls over inward foreign direct investment are not usually primarily directed at reducing the volatility of capital flows, they can be. Chile has instituted "minimum stay" regulations for direct investors to complement its reserve requirements for portfolio investors, in pursuit of its macroeconomic stabilization objectives.

3.   Debt versus equity

External portfolio investment in domestic equities clearly involves fewer risks to the borrowing country than debt. External debt requires servicing regardless of domestic economic circumstances and the roll-over of its principal can never be assured. Foreign owners of equity can, of course, choose to exit at any time, but when they do so as a group they must first find domestic buyers and, when they do so, they may be forced to take capital losses that ease the blow to the capital-losing country. There is therefore a risk management rationale for developing countries to favour portfolio equity inflows over debt-creating ones (although they may, on average, be more expensive). It can be argued that the shift toward equity borrowing in the 1990s has already imparted an important stabilizing influence on developing country borrowers, relative to their variable-interest bank borrowing in the 1970s (Williamson, 1996b).

C.   *Efficacy of controls*

According to some analysts, direct controls (and, for that matter, sterilization) can only be effective in the short-run:

> ... given the worldwide integration of financial markets and the sophistication of financial intermediaries, *such policies do not seem to work in the long run.*
>
> (Corbo and Hernandez, 1996, p. 84)

It is well-known that controls over capital outflows are difficult to enforce and that considerable capital flight will occur when market participants deem it warranted, even in the tightest of control regimes - via misinvoicing of trade transactions, leads and lags in external payments, alterations in the terms of trade credit, changes in overseas workers' remittances, etc.. Expectations effects, as always, can also generate unexpected results. The tightening of controls may constitute a signal to investors, generating greater net outflows than before; similarly, liberalization of out-flows may trigger more inflows.

But it would be a considerable logical leap to the conclusion that controls are *always totally* ineffective. Particularly in the large-scale formal financial sector, they are likely to have *some* effect. The issue is usually, rather, whether the actual social benefits of such controls warrant their administrative and other (including efficiency) costs; and, more

fundamentally, whether domestic macroeconomic management is, or is about to become, sound.

Controls over capital outflows are *not* universally associated, as some seem to imply, with payments crises or preludes to currency devaluation and payments liberalization. Many developing countries have maintained such controls over outflows over *very long* periods of time, and varied them in response to their external payments positions (e.g. IMF, 1995d, p. 21). ·

Controls over capital inflows are inherently easier to make effective than controls over outflows. Foreign owners of capital are likely to be concerned to hold legal title to their financial assets in the country, providing them with motivation to abide by domestic regulations where they exist. At the same time, the domestic monetary authorities, not usually facing crises in the circumstances of surging inflows, are in a much stronger bargaining position in seeking compliance with the rules. Needless to say, it will still be impossible to prevent the usual range of evasions through leads and lags, misinvoicing in the current account, and the like. (Similar argument is now made by the IMF in 1995b, p. 108.) Needless to say, it would be easier to make controls work if the monetary authorities at both ends of the flows cooperated - as they rarely do at present except with reference to the "laundering" of illegal funds.

Dooley's recent survey (1995) of the academic literature on capital controls (which has mainly been addressed to attempts at control of unwanted *out*flows) concludes that they *have* often successfully driven wedges between domestic and international interest rates, thereby generating Government revenue and reducing the costs of public domestic debt servicing (pp. 29-32); but in developing countries, contrary to the evidence for developed countries, they have not succeeded in influencing the volume or composition of capital flows, or exchange-rate levels (pp. 34-35). This study is also sceptical, in view of the distortions they create, of their overall benefit-cost ratio. (See also Mathieson and Rojas-Suarez, 1993.)

Analyses of recent developing country experience in the G-24 project, by those closer to policy-making, however, suggest more optimistic conclusions regarding the efficacy of capital controls, particularly those relating to *in*flows (Le Fort and Budnevich, and Park and Song, in this volume). Many developing country macroeconomic managers evidently believe it *is* possible to influence not only the pace but also the composition of external private capital inflows.

D. Recent policy response to capital surges

As has been seen, many developing countries have encountered large surges of capital inflow in the 1990s, surges which have significantly complicated the tasks of macroeconomic policy-makers in recipient countries. Analysts have noted the contrast between the Latin American and Asian experiences with private capital inflows in the early 1990s: in Asia, foreign direct investment played a greater role, investment rates typically rose more, and the real appreciation of currencies was more limited than in Latin America (e.g. Calvo et al., 1996; Corbo and Hernandez, 1996). The G-24 studies confirm these results (Le Fort and Budnevich, and Park and Song, in this volume). They also found that in some sub-Saharan African countries, private capital inflows began to increase noticeably in the 1990s, to the point where their size relative to GDP was as large as in Asia and Latin America (Kasekende in this volume).

How can the policy responses of the countries studied in this project be briefly summarized? In the sub-Saharan African countries studied, such as Uganda, Zambia and the United Republic of Tanzania, macroeconomic policy response has consisted primarily in letting the exchange rate reflect the increased capital flows; and this has not yielded results with which policy-makers can be fully content. In the East Asian countries studied (Indonesia, the Republic of Korea, Malaysia and Thailand), on the other hand, strenuous efforts were made by macroeconomic policy-makers to preserve incentives for their tradable goods sectors by preventing too much real currency appreciation. Inevitably this involved the use of activist policies in currency and financial markets, and pragmatic resort to direct and indirect capital controls that varied in their intensity in response to changing external circumstances. In Chile and Colombia, too, policy-makers sought to moderate the exchange-rate effects of the new capital inflows by "managing"exchange rates, monetary sterilization and judicious resort to capital controls, principally in the form of indirect taxes (via reserve requirements).

The experience reviewed and the analysis conducted in these studies suggests that the vigorous use of market-friendly policy instruments - particularly official participation in financial markets, and direct and indirect taxes (rather than direct controls) on certain international capital flows - has helped many developing countries in their pursuit of traditional macroeconomic objectives in the context of volatile international flows of private capital and could help more. The most important such instruments are:

- flexible central bank intervention in the foreign-exchange market, with varying limits and "bands", and without overly rigid adherence to nominal exchange rate targets;

- flexible intervention by the monetary authorities in domestic financial markets and/or provision to them of new financial instruments for purposes of monetary sterilization;

- maintenance of fiscal discipline;

- use of reserve requirements (deposits in foreign currency in the central bank) on domestic bank deposits of non-residents, domestic foreign currency deposits, and all external borrowing, bond issues or lines of credit. (These deposits have sometimes included a minimum time period, sometimes varied with the maturity, and have typically been designed to discourage shorter-term flows.)

The "successful" managers of capital surges in East Asia and Latin America also often buttressed their more "market-friendly" instruments with more direct regulations.

Regulation of *inward* flows of portfolio capital has involved:

- overall quantitative restrictions or even prohibitions on some types of flows (e.g. some short-term flows in Malaysia in early 1994);

- regulation or restrictions on borrowing or issuance of securities abroad by residents;

- restrictions on access by foreigners to domestic stock and financial markets, or limits on foreign ownership of shares of domestic corporations (which often vary with the sector of activity);

- restrictions and conditions on (and sometimes incentives for) foreign direct investment, varying with different kinds and sectors, including minimum length of stay (e.g. in Chile, one year).

Obviously, such controls on capital flows can be liberalized or tightened over a wide range of restrictive possibilities. Governments have often varied their capital-account regulations so as to pursue their macroeconomic objectives as external circumstances changed. The Republic of Korea systematically tightened or eased restrictions on both capital inflows and outflows in response to developments in the current account of its international payments. To counter excessive inflows, some Governments have at times eased regulations only on outflows (e.g. Thailand). They have also varied their reserve requirements on foreign borrowing.[7]

The East Asian and Latin American countries studied in this project thus appeared remarkably successful in responding to surges of private capital inflows in the 1990s through a judicious combination of exchange-market intervention (to moderate real currency appreciation), monetary sterilization, fiscal discipline, and the careful and changing use of direct controls on both inward and outward flows to dampen volatile short-term movements.

It is always difficult to assess the effects of policy in the absence of clarity as to the relevant counterfactual. Those with faith in the perfectibility of markets may argue that the provision of greater information is always more socially efficient than governmental interventions. Still, Government interventions, including direct controls, did frequently seem to be effective in terms of their own declared (and limited) macroeconomic objectives. It is important to recognize that the purpose of controls in the more "successful" cases was generally *not* to maintain a fundamentally unsustainable exchange rate, but to assist in *real exchange rate stabilization*. In some cases, there may also have been a longer-run concern to prevent undue real currency appreciation and its detrimental effects for the tradables sector. The policy objective was always a stable and appropriate overall incentive structure, and thus effective macroeconomic management for development.

Capital controls or taxes, whether direct or indirect, are not a panacea. If used to support weak macroeconomic policy they can even be harmful. Nor are they without difficulties or costs. In Dornbusch's words, however, "while a near-perfect system of managing capital flows would be desirable, something that falls even far short may still do the job much better than doing nothing" (p. 28 of this volume). There are many recent examples of reasonable success with their use in developing countries and many more examples of recent developing country difficulties with capital surges that might have been eased through greater use of such controls.

Policy-makers should draw pragmatic conclusions from these recent experiences, like those of a recent literature survey of the same subject:

In view of the multiplicity of factors that should in principle influence the response of macroeconomic policies, no single combination of policies is likely to be optimal in all cases.

(Fernandez-Arias and Montiel, 1996, p. 76)

E.   New policy instrument: a cross-border transactions tax?

There are strong theoretical and practical grounds for relying on *taxes on* international transactions rather than direct controls. Such taxes (often known as a "Tobin tax") are likely to interfere less with the allocative efficiency of the relevant capital markets, and to be administratively no more (and maybe even less) demanding. They overcome the difficult administrative task of distinguishing long-term from short-term flows by leaving market agents to decide what types of flows will be altered. They also have the important side-benefit of raising fiscal revenues (some of which can be used to fund their own administrative costs). Some developing countries have levied taxes on international financial transactions, most notably Brazil from 1994 onwards; and their experience deserves more study. Obstfeld is among those who have argued that: "A coherent case can be made for a Tobin tax in the context of stabilizing developing countries, which need to manage exchange rates and have relatively shallow financial markets, and where the cost of failed stabilization is extremely high" (Obstfeld, 1995, p. 188). Such taxes have also been advocated for OECD countries (Eichengreen et al., 1995) and active professional debate continues over the merits and feasibility of a worldwide Tobin tax (e.g. Felix, 1995; Kenen, 1995; Frankel, 1995; Spahn, 1995; ul Haq et al., 1996).

In his paper for the G-24 project (included in this volume), Dornbusch argues for a (small) tax, levied by individual countries, which could be varied over time, on all international (cross-border) transactions so as to discourage short-term capital flows and lengthen investor horizons. Such a tax, he argues, is superior to administrative controls in that "a maximum of market choice and discipline is maintained and a minimum of bureaucratic control intrudes" (p. 31).

He suggests that most of the relevant problems of tax evasion could readily be overcome by imposing the tax on *all* transactions in foreign exchange, whether for trade in goods or services, or for international capital movements. Since the tax applies to all cross-border flows rather than only to financial transactions and since its object is to moderate instability in cross-border flows not financial asset markets, the arguments concerning the ineffectiveness of financial transactions taxes, he argues, are irrelevant. There could be some negative effects on international trade but, at the tax rates contemplated, they would be minimal. Rather, he argues, the tax would smooth the process of national integration into the world economy.

IV. Improving international arrangements

A. *The provision of liquidity in response to capital surges*

To the extent that private international capital flows are subject to volatile and herd-like ("disequilibrating") behaviour that does not accurately reflect "fundamentals" there is a case for official intervention. As has been seen, this may involve efforts to slow the pace or change the composition of these flows. But official intervention more frequently is a matter of *responding* to capital flows which have not been, and probably could not be, controlled.

Recent analysis has not said much about the possibility of increased direct cooperation, for the purpose of more effective macroeconomic management, between the monetary authorities of the capital-losing and capital-gaining countries. This is somewhat surprising since there are evidently considerable underexploited opportunities for such mutual assistance (see, for instance, Felix, 1993). Some such cooperation takes place bilaterally on an ad-hoc basis and, among the central banks of the major industrial countries, in the activities of the Bank for International Settlements (BIS). Except in emergencies, such as those of Mexico in 1982 and 1994/95, however, little direct cooperation normally is found between Northern and Southern monetary and financial authorities.

For some years there has been discussion of means for the provision of emergency credits to developing countries facing large and sudden capital outflows that are not associated with changes in domestic economic fundamentals. It is easy to envisage circumstances in which the changes in interest rates and/or exchange rates that would be required in the capital-losing developing country to restore capital market stability are impossible or undesirable; or in which there is a prospect of major defaults on external debt; or in which there is a risk of inappropriate and internationally damaging intervention via controls or taxes on international transactions. In such circumstances, there is a strong case for official intervention in the form of the provision from abroad of official credit to offset the disequilibrating flows.

In order to be effective and, in particular, to serve as credible "signals" to markets and as catalysts for other official sources, such credits would have to be provided in very large amounts and at very short notice. The 1994/95 Mexican crisis, described by the IMF's Managing Director as "the first financial crisis of the twenty-first century", and generating the largest IMF loan to a member in its history (both absolutely and in relation to its quota), demonstrated the urgent need for significantly improving upon current arrangements. During the past year progress has been made towards improving "early warning systems" via sharpened data systems, and towards the significant expansion, principally for this purpose, of the IMF's General Arrangements to Borrow (GAB).

The key issues for the construction of an effective mechanism for the provision of official finance in response to the problems created by disequilibrating private capital flows were identified by Williamson in his G-24 paper as follows: (i) the criteria for judging the eligibility of countries for such assistance, including, for instance, upper bounds on prior current-account deficits (expressed as percentages of GDP) adjusted to reflect different means of financing, previous debt loads, etc.; (ii) the need for speed in response, and therefore prior authorization of later "automatic" access; (iii) the necessary size of the resources to be supplied, where they might come from, and through which channels; (iv) the appropriate maturity on the credits, the upper limits upon individual country access to them, and the need, evident in the Mexican case, to provide them on a longer-term basis in some instances (Williamson, 1996a).

Such credits are best provided, Williamson also argued, through the IMF, rather than through the BIS or the G-7, so as to preserve a fully multilateral approach to such crises, which could quickly generate systemic consequences, and so as to buttress the role of the Fund in international monetary and financial affairs. They should also rely on "special financing" for such credits, including the possibility of SDR creation, in order not to risk "crowding out" other IMF lending.

The new arrangements being constructed in this sphere build upon the GAB. As long as they do not reduce the prospect for an IMF quota increase (and they might), these financing arrangements are likely to be additional. Developing countries have reasons for concern, however, as to many elements of the emerging scheme for the provision by G-10 and other countries of increased IMF finance for crisis lending. In particular, there are grounds for doubt as to whether its resources will be sufficient, whether its procedures for determining eligibility and activation will be appropriate, or whether the new arrangements are likely to succeed in achieving their stated objectives. Developing countries have also expressed their concern over the unrepresentative decision-making processes outside the IMF employed in setting up the new arrangements (G-24 Communiqué, April 21, 1996, para. 11). It is not surprising, therefore, that further regional financing mechanisms are being actively discussed, most notably in the Asian context with the active participation of the Bank of Japan.

What is clear is that in the new world of volatile private capital flows, traditional measures of the adequacy of international liquidity, based primarily upon the relationship between owned foreign-exchange reserves and imports of goods and services, are obsolete. Appropriate guidelines for reserve management in a world of large and volatile capital flows are unfortunately still nowhere to be found. Presumably new guidelines would have to take account of stocks (of external debt, domestic money supply, etc.) as well as flows. The capacity of the IMF, with current resources, to address the likely liquidity requirements of emerging markets in coming years remains very much in doubt. IMF quota increases and further SDR issues are minimum necessary steps in the rebuilding of a credible multilateral liquidity system.

B.   Orderly debt workouts

The experience of the 1980s has demonstrated that financial crises in developing countries may also reflect more fundamental problems, problems of "solvency" that cannot be addressed solely by the provision of increased liquidity. In the absence of an agreed international framework for dealing with these more fundamental solvency problems, the "workouts" have been slow, ad hoc, and consequently socially costly and often inequitable.

Whereas within national jurisdictions, bankruptcy procedures provide the legal means for reducing the inefficiencies and inequities that can be associated with such workouts, there are no such agreed arrangements for sovereign debtors in international financial markets. There has been increasing governmental realization that improvements in current international arrangements are both desirable and possible (e.g. Sachs, 1995a and 1995b; Eichengreen and Portes, 1995; Group of Ten, 1996). Many private financial institutions continue to oppose such reforms, no doubt believing that eventual governmental bailouts are a brighter prospect for them than officially sanctioned write-down of sovereign debt.

Where financial crises have "fundamental" origins, there can be no substitute for reform, restructuring and improved (and usually changed) management. External financial support can be essential for the success of efforts to reform and restructure fiscal, financial and macroeconomic management systems. Its objective must be to assist Governments and countries to restructure themselves with minimum social cost and to do so in such a way as to minimize moral hazard. Sachs has stressed the need for financial assistance at three critical points in a debt workout: a standstill on debt servicing obligations at the outset; "fresh working capital during restructuring, so that critical governmental functions don't collapse" (1995a, p. 20); and eventual debt reduction to assist in the restoration of solvency (1995a and 1995b). At each of these points there are severe collective action problems in that individual creditors have little incentive, by themselves, to assist. Hence many see the need for a significantly enhanced role for a multilateral financial institution like the IMF to establish appropriate principles, set the conditions, and organize the financing for more orderly and efficient sovereign debt workouts.

The recent report of the Group of Ten (G-10) sides with those (like Eichengreen and Portes, 1995) who have argued for the incorporation of new provisions in international loan contracts and bond covenants that clarify the means for collective representation and decision-making on the part of lenders and bondholders in (what they hope is the unlikely) event of future difficulties with debt servicing. How such provisions are to be pushed upon unwilling market participants remains a question.

The G-10 report also suggests that the IMF could both signal its approval of a (unilateral) cessation of external debt servicing and assist in the provision of working capital by conditional lending to Governments that have entered into external arrears. There is already a precedent for such IMF practice in the case of arrears on bank loans. The new IMF financing arrangements discussed in the previous section can clearly be deployed in support of orderly workouts of sovereign debt problems as well as to provide emergency liquidity. As noted above, the details of such arrangements remain to be negotiated. Adding the support of orderly debt workouts to the financial responsibilities of the IMF, however, can only raise further doubts as to the adequacy of IMF resources for the effective performance of its twenty-first century role.

The longer-term nature of the reform and restructuring processes involved in orderly debt workouts and the potential need for more sizeable external resources than the IMF, by itself, is able to suggest an important complementary role for the World Bank. In low-income countries, the development of joint IMF-Bank programmes based upon ostensibly locally developed policy framework papers already has a considerable history. Analogous approaches would seem to be appropriate for future debt workouts in middle-income countries.

C. The IMF and capital controls

Under the IMF Articles of Agreement (Article VIII),[8] members are required to seek current-account convertibility though by no means all have done so. Of the 125 low- and middle-income countries with populations of over one million, 51 have accepted the obligations of the IMF's Article VIII (see table 5). Under Article VI, however, members are permitted to retain capital controls[9] and, as noted above, about three-quarters of them (119 of 155) do so.

An obvious difficulty in making the current Articles function is distinguishing between international flows in the capital account and international flows in the current account. Where there is convertibility in the current account it is likely to be extremely difficult to exercise fully effective control over international capital flows. The desire for effective capital-account controls may therefore generate pressure for the maintenance or reintroduction of controls in particular types of current-account transactions, notably in financial and other services. Where the domestic administrative and managerial capacity is particularly weak, as in some sub-Saharan African experience, the decision to "free" international payments on current account is likely to imply freedom for both current and capital

transactions; it is simply impractical to attempt to make fine distinctions in the context of weak administrative and statistical systems (Kasekende et al.).

In recent years, the IMF has actively promoted capital-account convertibility as well as current-account convertibility for all of its members, and it now reports upon capital controls in its surveillance of members' exchange-rate policies and exchange restrictions. In a series of speeches in 1994 and 1995, the Managing Director of the IMF vigorously advocated capital-account convertibility and floated the idea of revising the Articles of Agreement to promote that end, an idea considered in more detailed fashion in a recent Fund paper (1995d).

In Article IV consultations with industrial countries the IMF has generally been strongly supportive of capital-account liberalization. In those with developing countries, according to a recent IMF survey of this subject (1995d), it has approached the issue of capital controls on a case-by-case basis; however, "the tightening of controls over capital movements ... was generally discouraged ...". The IMF survey speaks of "a general distaste for such controls as a way of addressing balance of payments difficulties", although "prudential limits on foreign exchange risk exposure have been endorsed" (1995d, p. 6).

In its technical assistance, the IMF appears frequently to have been more forceful. "Traditionally, the IMF's technical assistance in the area of foreign-exchange systems focused on efforts to facilitate current-account convertibility in its member countries; however, from the mid-1980s the focus shifted toward encouraging the adoption of full capital-account convertibility. Common themes in technical assistance supporting a move to capital convertibility have included the ineffectiveness of existing controls, improved transparency associated with a free exchange system, the benefits of recognizing an informal market through which a significant proportion of transactions was already taking place, and the need to develop a competitive and efficient exchange system" (*ibid.*).

In 1995-1996, the IMF appeared to modify its approach. A series of research papers and conferences have portrayed a more nuanced IMF position - to the effect that controls may serve some useful purposes, in particular circumstances, and when employed on a temporary basis (IMF, 1995d, pp. 4, 6, and 22-23; IMF, 1995c). In late 1995, an IMF report argues:

Table 5

DEVELOPING COUNTRIES THAT HAVE ACCEPTED IMF
ARTICLE VIII OBLIGATIONS[a]

Argentina	Jamaica	Papua New Guinea
Bangladesh	Jordan	Paraguay
Bolivia	Kenya	Peru
Chile	Kyrgyz Republic	Poland
Costa Rica	Latvia	Republic of Korea
Croatia	Lebanon	Saudi Arabia
Dominican Republic	Lithuania	Singapore
Ecuador	Malaysia	South Africa
El Salvador	Mauritius	Sri Lanka
Estonia	Mexico	Thailand
The Gambia	Moldovia	Trinidad and Tobago
Ghana	Morocco	Tunisia
Guatemala	Nepal	Turkey
Haiti	Nicaragua	Uganda
Honduras	Oman	Uruguay
India	Pakistan	Venezuela
Indonesia	Panama	Zimbabwe

Source: IMF, 1995e.

a Low and middle-income countries with population of one million or more.

... during times of surges in inflows a country might consider measures to influence the level and characteristics of capital inflows, such as taxes on short-term bank deposits and other financial assets, reserve requirements against foreign borrowing, and limits on consumption credit. In this regard, the experiences of Chile, Colombia, and Malaysia have been revealing .... In countries facing large and potentially unsustainable capital flows, a mix of intervention, sterilization, fiscal consolidation, *and some direct measures to discourage short-term portfolio flows or to influence their composition may be appropriate.* The mix of policies will, naturally, vary from country to country.

(IMF, 1995b, p. 27; my italics)

In its background paper (in the same document) it concludes, "In light of the recent experiences of countries that adopted measures designed to curb short-term capital inflows, it appears that, at least in the short run, the policies were effective in either reducing the volume of capital inflows or affecting their composition, or both" (*ibid.,* p. 108). Even in the longer term, there seems to be IMF acceptance that liberalization of the capital account serves no purpose if it must subsequently be reversed.

In places, these same IMF documents still state strong caveats:

It should be noted, however, that comprehensive restrictions on capital flows can be highly distorting and their effectiveness tends to erode over time. Capital controls on outflows are generally viewed as confiscatory taxes and, if applied during periods of exchange market stress, may aggravate a crisis of confidence.

(IMF, 1995b, p. 27)

That it feels it necessary to include caveats does not alter the fact that the IMF has made an important shift in its overall approach. Thus, the proposition that the IMF stands for an open capital account, plain and simple, is no longer correct (see also Dornbusch, p. 32 of this volume).

Whatever the eventual advantages of an open capital account, it is generally agreed that there may be difficulties in the transition and that some sequences of policy reform make more sense than others. Generally, there seems to be agreement that *domestic* stabilization and financial reforms (particularly the strengthening of prudential regulation and the creation of solvent and sound banking and financial institutions) are a prerequisite, or at least a corequisite, for successful external capital-account liberalization (IMF, 1995d). If domestic banks or other financial institutions are fragile and weakly supervised, a large inflow of funds can be very inefficiently intermediated with the prospect of bubbles and future crises. It is also generally agreed that trade liberalization should precede or, at least, accompany liberalization of the external capital account. In some cases, reforms may move concurrently and with speed; but experience in the Southern Cone and elsewhere in the late 1970s and early 1980s illustrates the danger that underlying weaknesses in the financial sector can be aggravated and further problems created by premature and overly rapid capital-account opening.[10]

On the basis of the experience to date, reviewed in the G-24 papers and elsewhere, one must conclude that capital controls - both indirect and direct - have played an important positive role in the macroeconomic management of a great many developing countries. Some see such controls as purely temporary or transitional, pending the liberalization and strengthening of domestic financial markets and/or the achievement of domestic macroeconomic stability. But such temporary or transitional conditions are likely to continue for a considerable period in most developing countries. Moreover, private capital surges have continued to create severe macroeconomic problems in countries that have ostensibly already come through such reforms, and controls, albeit usually temporary, have been an important part of the policy armoury for responding to them. It would certainly seem premature at this time, and, quite possibly, inappropriate for a much longer time, to consider an amendment to the IMF Articles of Agreement that required all members to commit themselves to the achievement of an open capital account.

If an amendment relating to capital-account issues is required, it is most urgent in the anomalous provisions describing the IMF's authority, under Article VI, to lend in Mexican-type circumstances. Section 1 of Article VI prohibits the use of the Fund's general resources "to meet a large or sustained outflow of capital" and authorizes the IMF to require members "to exercise controls to prevent such use". The capital outflows to which future IMF loans are likely to have to respond may be "large", "sustained" or both. It would be wise to attempt to clarify the IMF's role and responsibilities in future "twenty-first century" financial crises. This may also involve, as argued by some in the IMF, expansion of its jurisdiction over "payments and transfers and multiple currency practices related to international capital movements. No other international agency exercises jurisdiction over such transactions" (IMF, 1995a, p. 32). In light of the declining share of current transactions in total exchange transactions and the difficulty in distinguishing current from capital transactions, some argue, the IMF may be unable to pursue its broader responsibilities without such a modification of its formal jurisdiction (*ibid.*, pp. 31-32).

D.   Other international regimes

International regimes relating to capital-account transactions can have a variety of purposes, e.g. facilitation of cross-border transactions (including harmonization of accounting, disclosure or other regulatory standards), encouragement of competition in financial services, achieving and maintaining financial stability, etc. (White, 1996). Controls and regulations relating to international capital flows are not the same thing as controls relating to foreign financial institutions or the services they provide. The IMF has rules relating only to the former. The World Trade Organization (WTO) is among the multilateral bodies striving to develop a regime for the latter (Zutshi, 1995), but also active in these issues are the BIS, OECD, the European Union, NAFTA, and other regional bodies. There is evidently considerable clutter, confusion and overlapping jurisdictions in the international regimes for capital flows and financial transactions. Are these various regimes mutually consistent? Are the needs of the developing countries different and are they taken into account? Is the march toward liberalization of financial services in developing countries any more defensible than the arguments for the total liberalization of their external capital accounts? Many emerging market policymakers will identify readily with the Dornbusch assessment that: "Liberalization of world trade in financial services is the most fiercely lobbied issue of the day" (p. 34 of this volume). These issues urgently require more detailed and comparative analysis.

A further (sub)question relates to the potential role of regional agreements and institutions. Freedom of portfolio capital flows and (most) FDI is central, for instance, in the NAFTA. It is also obviously a key feature of the CFA franc zone. If the world economy evolves on a regionalized basis, as some predict it will, one could easily envisage large regions within which capital, as well as trade in goods and services, would flow relatively freely but between which some controls remained. Negotiations concerning future capital-account regimes and supportive financial arrangements among central banks may thus be at their most vigorous on a bilateral or plurilateral (regional) basis, e.g. in the Free Trade Area for the Americas, or the APEC, or the successors to the Lomé Convention.

In some cases, as has been suggested for sub-Saharan Africa, such arrangements might increase the credibility of governmental policy commitments by providing an "agency of restraint" on Governments with deficient "track records" (Collier, 1991). But such "opening", as has been seen, may be inappropriate or premature. It is also quite possible that the United States (or other reserve-currency countries) might attempt to "link" future trade policies to capital-account regimes in much the same manner as they now link them to intellectual property ones. As always in these matters, and other things being equal, the interests of smaller and less developed countries are more likely to be protected in fully multilateral arrangements than in discriminatory ones.

E.   *Global macroeconomic management*

Implicit in the increased sensitivity to international interest rates of private international capital flows to (and from) developing countries is the need for greater consideration of the fairly immediate consequences for these flows of the macroeconomic policies of the major industrialized countries. Many analysts argue, with the wisdom of hindsight, that the Volcker anti-inflationary "shock" of 1979 was a major contributor to the international debt crisis of the 1980s. Yet the links between interest rates in the United States (and, to a lesser extent, Germany, Japan and other industrial countries) and macroeconomic developments in developing countries are much tighter today, by virtue of the increased integration of their capital markets, than they were then. Those who model the functioning of today's global economy must take account of these new linkages through the capital account and the increasingly important potential feedback effects from

the economic performance of the developing countries to that of the high-income countries. Macroeconomic policy-makers in the major industrial countries, and those who assess or advise them (including the IMF), must recognize, as never before, the potential *global* economic consequences of their policy choices.

V.   Issues requiring further research

A.   *Efficacy of alternative policy instruments*

Evidently the countries of Asia and Latin America studied in this project considered that a degree of exchange-rate management, within the context of a generally flexible regime, was critically important to the provision of adequate incentives to their tradables sectors. To this end, they found a variety of policy instruments to reduce the incentives for unwanted capital flows and to sterilize the domestic monetary consequences of such flows as nevertheless took place. Rather than continuing the quasi-theological debate over the efficacy of capital-account convertibility, the most useful research and policy debate would therefore now seem to concern the relative efficacy of these various instruments. The issues surrounding the choice of policies of exchange-rate management and sterilization are, by now, fairly well understood. The experience with various policies relating directly to the capital account, many of recent origin, however, has not as yet been as widely shared. In particular, there would seem to be a need for more comparative research and discussion on the most cost-effective instruments for influencing the volume, composition and productive usage of capital flows in countries with thin and vulnerable foreign exchange and financial markets.

B.   *Behaviour of agents in financial markets*

Much of the policy debate seems to hinge on the assumed behaviour of different agents in financial markets. Imperfect substitutability between domestic financial assets (including those denominated in foreign currencies) and otherwise identical foreign assets implies that either foreigners or nationals (or both) see differences between them. But do foreigners and nationals behave similarly in their substitution of one for the other? It is often implied that OECD investors are sluggish in their response to new opportunities where they require entry into unaccustomed areas like developing country markets; and they are skittish and prone to early departure at the first hint of potential trouble. On the other hand, it is also often said, for instance in discussions of the 1994/95 Mexican crisis, that because domestic residents of developing countries are so much better informed about national affairs than foreigners, they will be the first to move their funds in or out in response to changing domestic circumstances; some domestic holdings of Government debt may therefore be inherently more unstable than foreigners' holdings. Can these alternative hypotheses be tested? Do such ownership traits offer any presumptions as to the likelihood that capital flows may be volatile? Do they offer guidance as to the efficacy of alternative kinds of taxes or controls on international capital flows?

In the same vein, do large institutional investors like pension funds, mutual funds or insurance companies - the new external investors in developing countries' bonds and equities - typically take a longer view than commercial banks as they construct their international investment portfolios? Might they be persuaded, through incentives or suasion, to do so?

C. Interaction between domestic financial markets and external convertibility

Where domestic financial liberalization and macroeconomic stabilization create, for a time, high real and nominal interest rates, there are strong incentives for short-term capital (not least in the form of trade credit) to move in. Where capital controls are inoperative or where they have been abandoned, as in some of the African cases studied in this project, very large capital flows (relative to GDP) can result. More generally, external capital flows (inward or outward) of even quite modest size can easily "swamp" the relatively thin and fragile financial markets and financial institutions of individual developing countries. Where such flows are relatively "free" and where, as in the majority of developing countries, business "confidence" is subject to some uncertainty, the domestic financial environment is inherently volatile. Statistical reporting systems have often failed to keep up with the new monitoring requirements: foreign purchases and sales of domestically issued financial instruments require new reporting arrangements beyond those already in place for internationally issued ones. The interactions between domestic reforms and external capital-account regimes demand more careful study than they have so far received.

D. The impact of "dollarization"

The implications of liberalizing the financial system to the extent of authorizing domestic residents to hold foreign currency deposits and domestic financial institutions to do local business (offering deposit facilities and loans) in foreign-currencies was not fully explored in the G-24 studies. Changes of this kind have been prominent in recent developing country reforms, and they have profound implications for macroeconomic management.

Where foreign-currency denominated financial transactions (notably bank deposits and loans) are permissible, further problems of macroeconomic management may arise. As long as there are no reasons for doubt about the value of the domestic currency, particularly if there is a peg to the currency of a major trading partner, there need be no such problem. Speculation against the national currency, however, may work extremely rapidly in the context of a partly "dollarized" system. Pressure on the exchange rate via "capital flight" does not then require that financial assets, whether owned by foreigners or nationals, actually leave the country; they need only leave the national currency. Even if the domestic currency is fully backed by foreign-exchange reserves, in a currency-board system, difficulties may arise as the values of longer-term domestic currency financial assets fall. (Where there is a loss of confidence in the soundness of domestic banks and/or the domestic financial system, of course, investors *will* seek to leave the country, or more properly, the country's financial institutions, wherever located. These issues are elaborated in Rojas-Suarez and Weisbrod, 1995.)

Even if banks' dollar assets and liabilities are balanced (as often required), their dollar liabilities are likely to be shorter-term than their dollar assets, such transformation being the essence of successful commercial banking. The central bank cannot act as a (dollar) lender of last resort, beyond early limits set by its own foreign-exchange reserves, if there should be a "run" on the banks' dollar deposits. The Mexican example showed a similar problem with over-reliance by the Government on short-term dollar-denominated (or dollar-indexed) debt. Although *tesobono* debt was not large, in terms of the visual indicators, it exceeded dollar foreign exchange reserves, preventing the central bank from rescuing the Government once panic set in. The need for an *external* lender of last resort in domestically dollarized systems has frequently been noted (e.g. by Calvo, 1996).

In light of G-24 members' expressed interest in these and related policy issues during their earlier discussion of the papers in this research project, they merit further analysis.

E.   *The potential of Tobin-Dornbusch taxes*

The G-24 project has not seriously explored the benefits and costs of a globalized version of the taxes on cross-border transactions advocated by Dornbusch for individual nations or other related schemes such as the Tobin tax. Others have recently explored these issues surrounding the Tobin tax (e.g. Felix, 1995; Frankel, 1995; Kenen, 1995; Spahn, 1995; ul Haq et al., 1996) and more work in this sphere, particularly on the Dornbusch variant, would be appropriate.

VI. Conclusions and recommendations

Private international capital flows have become a much more important and potentially volatile element in many developing countries' economies. Their macroeconomic policy-makers must acquire accurate and timely information as to their size and composition. The IMF should do all in its power to assist member countries with weak data on these flows to improve them. Monetary authorities in the developed countries should also actively assist and cooperate with those in developing countries in the collection of data, monitoring of developments, and, in some cases, implementation of controls on international private capital flows. Global macroeconomic modellers and macroeconomic policy-makers in the major industrial countries must take account of the increased sensitivity to interest rates of private capital flows to (or from) developing countries, and the potential for significantly increased feedback effects from the developing countries' performance to the global economy, in their models and policy decisions.

The IMF should be encouraged to recognize capital-account controls, direct and indirect, as important macroeconomic policy instruments in most developing countries for the foreseeable future. A revision in the IMF Articles of Agreement to require capital as well as current-account convertibility of all its members would be inappropriate at this time. The IMF should be encouraged, however, to expand its role, in conjunction with other relevant bodies, in the surveillance of international capital markets. (This would be facilitated by an amendment to its Articles of Agreement.) Early efforts should be made to clarify

rules and jurisdictions relating to international capital-account transactions and international financial institutions in the many areas in which there are potential overlaps, e.g. those of the IMF, the WTO and other international and regional institutions or agreements.

The IMF should be formally mandated to lend into financial crises in developing countries, both to provide emergency liquidity and, in conjunction with the World Bank and others, to support orderly workouts of sovereign debt problems. (This may also require amendments to its Articles of Agreement.) Decisions as to the appropriate procedures for activating such lending and the decisions actually to lend should be taken via the fully multilateral decision-making mechanisms of the IMF. To permit it to perform its role, the IMF will have to be provided with significantly expanded resources, particularly through quota increases and SDR issues.

More understanding is required of the behaviour of agents in financial markets, and the efficacy of alternative policy instruments in the capital account and in financial markets more generally. Strengthened research could be helpful in such other areas as: the implications of dollarization, interactions between domestic financial markets and external convertibility, the potential of Tobin/Dornbusch taxes, and appropriate measures of reserve adequacy.

Notes

1   These include Calvo, Leiderman and Reinhart, 1993, 1994, 1996; Claessens, Dooley and Warner, 1995; Corbo and Hernandez, 1996; Dooley, Fernandez-Arias and Kletzer, 1996; Dornbusch and Park, 1995; Edwards, 1995; Fernandez-Arias and Montiel, 1996; Ffrench-Davis, Titelman and Uthoff, 1994; Ffrench-Davis and Griffith-Jones, 1995; Grilli and Milesi-Ferretti, 1995; Hausmann and Rojas-Suarez, 1996; IMF, 1995a, 1995b, 1995c, 1995d; Quirk, 1994; Rojas-Suarez and Weisbrod, 1995; Schadler *et al.*, 1993; UNCTAD, 1994; EDI, 1995).

2   The countries for which these studies present data are: in Latin America, Chile and Colombia; in Asia, Indonesia, Malaysia, Thailand and the Republic of Korea; and in Africa, Kenya, South Africa, Uganda, Zambia, Zimbabwe and the United Republic of Tanzania. The case studies do not include any countries that adopted currency board arrangements like those of Argentina. Nor do they include Eastern European or other economies in transition.

By now there have been numerous other published studies of Asian and Latin American experiences in the IMF and elsewhere. IMF accounts of some of these countries' practices (Chile, Colombia, Indonesia, Malaysia, Thailand and the Republic of Korea) may be found in a recent paper (1995b, pp. 80-94) and summary versions of three of them (Chile, Colombia and Malaysia) in another (1995e, pp. 38-44).

3   In a recent study of nine Latin American and Asian countries with liberalized capital accounts in the 1987-1994 period, exchange risk was far more important than country risk (or remaining capital controls) in "explaining" such premia (Frankel and Okongwu, 1996).

4   Mexican private savings fell from 15.5 per cent to 7.7 per cent of GDP in the 1989-1993 period (Schadler *et al.*, 1993).

5   There is no agreed method in the current or trade accounts either, but there is a much more extensive empirical literature on the subject, including an important (and remarkably under-cited) one that finds little correlation among alternative such measures (Pritchett, 1991). There seems to be some consensus on the use of the percentage premium on the black market as against the principal official exchange rate as a measure (at least in an ordinal sense) of the strength of *overall* foreign-exchange controls or official currency misalignment.

6   There may be significant differences, however, within items which are categorized similarly. Under the heading of long-term loans, for instance, East Asian borrowers averaged bond maturities of nearly twelve years in 1995 whereas Latin American borrowers averaged only three years; and Latin American spreads over comparable government benchmark bonds were nearly three times as high as East Asia's (World Bank, 1996, p. 11).

7   Where they exist, they could also vary their taxes on foreign exchange transactions, as advocated by Park and Song in this volume.

8   Under Article VIII: "no member shall, without the approval of the Fund, impose restrictions on the making of payments and transfers for current international transactions" (section 2) or "... engage in any discriminatory currency arrangements or multiple currency practices" (section 3). These Articles have never been amended.

9   Section 3 of Article VI of the IMF's Articles of Agreement states that "members may exercise such controls as necessary to regulate international capital movements, but no member may exercise these controls in a manner which will restrict payments for current transactions or which will unduly delay transfers of funds in settlement of commitments."

10 The World Bank has adopted quite similar approaches (see, for instance, World Bank, 1996, p. 11).

References

AKYÜZ, Y. (1992), "On Financial Openness in Developing Countries", in UNCTAD, *International Monetary and Financial Issues for the 1990s*, Vol. II (New York and Geneva: United Nations).

CALVO, G.A. (1996), "The Management of Capital Flows: Domestic Policy and International Cooperation" in G. Helleiner (ed.) *The International Monetary and Financial System: Developing Country Perspectives* (London: Macmillan).

CALVO, G.A., L. LEIDERMAN, and C.M. REINHART (1993), "Capital Flows and Real Exchange Rate Appreciation in Latin America, The Role of External Factors", *IMF Staff Papers*, Vol. 40, March (Washington, D.C.: International Monetary Fund).

CALVO, G.A., L. LEIDERMAN, and C.M. REINHART (1994), *The Capital Inflows Problem, Concepts and Issues* (San Francisco: International Centre for Economic Growth).

CALVO, G.A., L. LEIDERMAN, and C.M. REINHART (1996), "Inflows of Capital to Developing Countries in the 1990s", *Journal of Economic Perspectives*, Spring.

CLAESSENS, C., M.P. DOOLEY, and A. WARNER (1995), "Portfolio Capital Flows: Hot or Cold?", *World Bank Economic Review*, Vol. 9, January.

COLLIER, P. (1991), "Africa's External Relations: 1960-1990", *African Affairs*, July.

CORBO, V., and J. DeMELO (eds.) (1986), "Liberalization with Stabilization in the Southern Cone of Latin America", *World Development*, Vol. 13, No. 8 (August).

CORBO, V., and L. HERNANDEZ (1996), "Macroeconomic Adjustment to Capital Inflows: Lessons from Recent Latin American and East Asian Experience", *World Bank Research Observer*, Vol. 11, No. 1, February.

DIAZ-ALEJANDRO, C.F. (1985), "Goodbye Financial Repression, Hello Financial Crash", *Journal of Development Economics*, September/October.

DOOLEY, M.P. (1995), "A Survey of Academic Literature on Controls Over International Capital Transactions", *NBER Working Paper Series* 5352, November.

DOOLEY, M., E. FERNANDEZ-ARIAS and K. KLETZER (1996), "Is the Debt Crisis History? Recent Private Capital Inflows to Developing Countries", *World Bank Economic Review*, Vol. 10, No. 1, January.

DORNBUSCH, R. (1997), "Cross-Border Payments Taxes and Alternative Capital Account Regimes", in UNCTAD, *International Monetary and Financial Issues for the 1990s*, Vol. VIII (New York and Geneva: United Nations).

DORNBUSCH, R., and Y.C. PARK (eds.) (1995), *Financial Opening, Policy Lessons for Korea* (Seoul: Korea Institute of Finance and International Centre for Economic Growth).

DOWLING, J. M., and N. RAO (1995), "External Capital Flows and Policy Challenges in the ASEAN Economies", *Research Paper*, Economics and Development Resource Center, Asian Development Bank.

EDI (Economic Development Institute, World Bank), (1995), "Managing Economic Reform under Capital Flow Volatility", Selected Readings for First Annual Seminar on Managing Economic Reform in an Uncertain World.

EDWARDS, S. (ed.) (1995), *Capital Controls, Exchange Rates and Monetary Policy in the World Economy* (Cambridge and New York: Cambridge University Press).

EICHENGREEN, B., and R. PORTES (1995), *Crisis? What Crisis? Orderly Workouts for Sovereign Debtors* (London: Centre for Economic Policy Research).

EICHENGREEN, B., J. TOBIN, and C. WYPLOSZ (1995), "Two Cases for Sand in the Wheels of International Finance", *Economic Journal*, Vol. 105, January.

FELIX, D. (1993), "Suggestions for International Collaboration to Reduce Destabilizing Effects of International Capital Mobility on the Developing Countries" in UNCTAD, *International Monetary and Financial Issues for the 1990s*, Vol. III (New York and Geneva: United Nations).

FELIX, D. (1995), "Financial Globalization versus Free Trade: The Case for the Tobin Tax", *UNCTAD Discussion Papers*, No. 108, November.

FERNANDEZ-ARIAS, E., and P.J. MONTIEL (1996), "The Surge in Capital Inflows to Developing Countries: An Analytical Overview", *World Bank Economic Review*, Vol. 10, No. 1 (January).

FFRENCH-DAVIS, R., D. TITELMAN, and A. UTHOFF (1994), "International Competitiveness and the

Macroeconomics of Capital Account Opening", *UNCTAD Review*.

FFRENCH-DAVIS, R., and S. GRIFFITH-JONES (eds.) (1995), *Coping with Capital Surges, The Return of Finance to Latin America* (Lynne Rienner, International Development Research Centre).

FRANKEL, J. (1995), "How Well Do Foreign Exchange Markets Function: Might a Tobin Tax Help?", *Working Paper C'95-058*, Centre for International and Development Economics Research, University of California at Berkeley.

FRANKEL, J., and C. OKONGWU (1996), "Liberalized Portfolio Capital Inflows in Emerging Markets: Sterilization, Expectations, and the Incompleteness of Interest Rate Convergence", *International Journal of Finance and Economics*, Vol. 1, No. 1, January.

GRILLI, V., and G. M. MILESI-FERRETTI (1995), "Economic Effects and Structural Determinants of Capital Controls", *IMF Staff Papers*, September.

GROUP OF TEN, *The Resolution of Sovereign Liquidity Crises*.

GOLDSTEIN, M. (1995), "Coping with Too Much of a Good Thing: Policy Responses for Large Capital Inflows in Developing Countries", *Policy Research Working Paper*, No. 1507, September (Washington, D.C.: World Bank).

HAUSMANN, R., and L. ROJAS-SUAREZ (eds.) (1996), *Volatile Capital Flows, Taming Their Impact on Latin America* (Inter-American Development Bank, distributed by Johns Hopkins University Press).

HELLEINER, E. (1994), *States and the Reemergence of Global Finance, from Bretton Woods to the 1990s* (Ithaca and London: Cornell University Press).

IMF (1995a), *Issues in International Exchange and Payments Systems*, April 1995 (Washington, D.C.).

IMF (1995b), *International Capital Markets*, August 1995 (Washington, D.C.).

IMF (1995c), Roundtable on Responses to Sudden Capital Inflows, reported in *IMF Survey*, 22 May 1995.

IMF (1995d), *Capital Account Convertibility, Review of Experience and Implications for IMF Policies*, Occasional Paper 131, October 1995 (Washington, D.C.).

IMF (1995e), *Annual Report on Exchange Restrictions* (Washington, D.C.).

KASEKENDE, L., D. KITABIRE, and M. MARTIN (1997), "Capital Inflows and Macroeconomic Policy in sub-Saharan Africa", in UNCTAD, *International Monetary and Financial Issues for the 1990s*, Vol. VIII (New York and Geneva: United Nations).

KENEN, P.B. (1995), "The Feasibility of Taxing Foreign Exchange Transactions", *Working Paper*, No. 29, Centre for Economic Policy Studies, Princeton University.

Le FORT, G., and C. BUDNEVICH (1997), "Capital Account Regulations and Macroeconomic Policy: Two Latin American Experiences", in UNCTAD, *International Monetary and Financial Issues for the 1990s*, Vol. VIII (New York and Geneva: United Nations).

MATHIESON, D.J., and L. ROJAS-SUAREZ (1993), "Liberalization of the Capital Account: Experiences and Issues", *IMF Occasional Paper*, No. 103, March (Washington, D.C.).

McKINNON, R. (1991), *The Order of Economic Liberalization, Financial Control in the Transition to a Market Economy* (Johns Hopkins)

McKINNON, R., and H. PILL (1995), "Credible Liberalizations and International Capital Flows: The 'Over-Borrowing' Syndrome", Department of Economics, Stanford University.

MOHAMMED, A. (1996), "Implications for IMF Policies arising from Effects on Developing Countries of Industrial-Country Macroeconomic Policies", in G. Helleiner (ed) *The International Monetary and Financial System, Developing Country Perspectives* (London: Macmillan).

MONTIEL, P. (1994), "Capital Mobility in Developing Countries: Some Measurement Issues and Empirical Estimates", *World Bank Economic Review*, September.

NURKSE, R. (1944), *International Currency Experience* (League of Nations).

OBSTFELD, M. (1995), "International Currency Experience: New Lessons and Lessons Relearned", *Brookings Papers on Economic Activity*, No. 1 (Washington, D.C.).

PARK, Y.C., and C.-Y. SONG (1997), "Managing Foreign Capital Flows: The Experiences of Korea, Thailand, Malaysia and Indonesia", in UNCTAD, *International Monetary and Financial Issues for the 1990s*, Vol. VIII (New York and Geneva: United Nations).

PRITCHETT, L. (1991), "Measuring Outward Orientation in Developing Countries: Can It Be Done?", *Policy Research Working Paper*, No. 566 (Washington, D.C.: World Bank).

QUIRK, P.J. (1994), "Capital Account Convertibility: A New Model for Developing Countries" in T. Balino and C. Cottardli (eds.), *Frameworks for Monetary Stability* (Washington, D.C.: International Monetary Fund).

REISEN, H. (1993), "Capital Flows and their Effect on the Monetary Base", *CEPAL Review*, No. 51, December.

REISEN, H., and B. FISCHER (eds.) (1993), *Financial Opening, Policy Issues and Experiences in Developing Countries* (Paris: OECD).

ROJAS-SUAREZ, L., and S. R. WEISBROD (1995), *Financial Fragilities in Latin America, The 1980s and 1990s*, IMF Occasional Paper, No. 132 (Washington, D.C.).

SACHS, J. (1995a), "Do We need an International Lender of Last Resort?", Frank D. Graham Lecture, Princeton University, 20 April, mimeo.

SACHS, J. (1995b), "Alternative Approaches to Financial Crises in Emerging Markets", November, mimeo.

SCHADLER, S., M. CARKOVIC, A. BENNET, and R. KAHN (1993), *Recent Experiences with Surges in Capital Inflows*, IMF Occasional Paper, No. 108 (Washington, D.C.).

SPAHN, P.B. (1995), "International Financial Flows and Transactions Taxes, Survey and Options", *Working Paper 95/60*, IMF, Fiscal Affairs Department.

UL HAQ, M., I. KAUL, and I. GRUNBERG (eds.) (1996), *The Tobin Tax: Coping with Financial Volatility* (Oxford University Press).

UNCTAD (1994), "Controls on International Capital Movements" in *Trade and Development Report, 1994* (New York and Geneva: United Nations Publication Sales No. E.94.II.D.26), pp. 95 115.

WHITE, W.R. (1966), "International Agreements in the Area of Banking and Finance: Accomplishments and Outstanding Issues", Bank for International Settlements, mimeo.

WILLIAMSON, J. (1991), "On Liberalizing the Capital Account" in R. O'Brien (ed.) *Finance and the International Economy*, Vol. V (Oxford, for the *Amex Bank Review*).

WILLIAMSON, J. (1996a), "A New Facility for the IMF?" in UNCTAD, *International Monetary and Financial Issues for the 1990s*, Vol. VII (New York and Geneva: United Nations).

WILLIAMSON, J. (1996b), "Prospects for Avoiding Crises with Liberalized Capital Flows", Institute for International Economics, Washington, D.C., mimeo.

WORLD BANK (1996), *Global Economic Prospects and the Developing Countries* (Washington, D.C.).

ZAHLER, R. (1992), "Monetary Policy and an Open Capital Account", *CEPAL Review* No. 48.

ZUTSHI, U. (1995), "Aspects of the Final Outcome of the Negotiations on Financial Services of the Uruguay Round", *UNCTAD Discussion Papers*, No. 109, December.

CROSS-BORDER PAYMENTS TAXES AND ALTERNATIVE CAPITAL-ACCOUNT REGIMES

Rudi Dornbusch

Abstract

The paper reports on managing international capital flows by means of explicit taxes or restrictions. The IMF has already issued a verdict: there is a problem with the untamed flow of capital to emerging economies, something ought to be done.

A number of questions can be posed that highlight the problem of international capital flows for emerging economies: as an individual country opens up, how can it avoid that large capital inflows lead to an excess appreciation? In the course of the waves of lending and credit rationing, what is a good regime to stabilize capital flows? What is a good capital-account regime to deal with the ebb and flow of capital movements driven by country-specific news, good or bad? What is the advice to countries receiving too little capital?

The paper develops the following policy prescriptions:

- *Capital controls are in no way a panacea. In fact, they are undesirable if their purpose is to support and sustain mismanagement of exchange rates.*
- *While a near-perfect system of managing capital flows would be desirable, something that falls even far short may still do the job much better than doing nothing.*
- *Experience with the management of capital flows is not uniformly negative - Chile is an outstanding example of stellar performance and managed capital flows.*
- *A cross-border transactions tax is a plausible measure for any individual country even if there is no global move to such a scheme. The author advocates a specific variant, a cross-border payment tax.*
- *There are other ways of segmenting capital markets, ranging from strict exchange control to reserve deposits on selected or all cross-border transactions.*
- *It is useful to distinguish various contexts in which a cross-border transactions tax might be useful: as a* transitory *device in the context of stabilization or in the process of opening-up or, less plausibly, as a* permanent *feature of a country's payments regime.*
- *No system is effective unless it is comprehensive in its coverage and moderate in its ambitions. Failure on either count will lead to troublesome distortions. Managing the capital account decidedly does not provide coverage for bad macroeconomic policies. But it may give the window for sequencing the opening of domestic financial markets or trade in a way that is not dominated or even swamped by cross-border capital flows.*

I.   Introduction

This paper reports on the scope for managing international capital flows by means of explicit taxes or restrictions. This is an area of hot debate ever since the Mexican crisis and the resulting contagion spread to other emerging market economies. At the same time, it is a topic left over from the 1992 collapse of European economies. The IMF has already issued a verdict: there is a problem, something ought to be done, nothing can be done (IMF, 1995). But the question stays on the agenda simply because it is implausible that countries otherwise well-managed should become exposed to excess capital flows or the accompanying volatility.

Specifically, several points are to be made.

- First, capital controls are in no way a panacea. In fact, they are undesirable if their purpose is to support and sustain mismanagement of exchange rates (see Dornbusch et al., 1995).

- Second, while a near-perfect system of managing capital flows would be desirable, something that falls even far short may still do the job much better than doing nothing.

- Third, experience with the management of capital flows are not uniformly negative - Chile is an outstanding example of stellar performance and managed capital flows.

- Fourth, a Tobin tax is a plausible measure for any individual country even if there is no global move to such a scheme. We advocate here a specific variant, a cross-border payments tax.

- Fifth, there are other ways of segmenting capital markets ranging from strict exchange control to reserve deposits on selected or all cross-border transactions.

- Finally, no system is effective unless it is comprehensive in its coverage and moderate in its ambitions. Failure on either count will lead to troublesome distortions. Managing the capital account decidedly does not provide coverage for bad macroeconomic policies. It may, however, give the window for sequencing the opening of domestic financial markets or trade in a way that is not dominated or even swamped by cross-border capital flows.

II.   The capital flow problem

To prepare the ground, consider the capital flow problem of developing countries. Stated simply, there is either too much capital or too little, and it is mostly hot rather than cold.

Table 1 shows the size and composition of capital flows. Across sub-periods - the build-up of the first debt crisis, the period of involuntary lending, the new boom - the amounts vary sharply across periods and even in sign. In composition, direct investment always is small and portfolio investment large.

More strikingly, the number of emerging market funds increased almost tenfold in the period 1988-1994. For Latin America, the increase in the number of funds was a factor of more than twenty.

Of course, the capital flow issue is not just one of emerging economies and perhaps not even dominantly so. The large swings in the exchange rates of the United States dollar and the Yen clearly have their counterpart in capital flows that are largely unrelated to the financing of current-account balances or the real exchange rate consistent with full employment. Little rhyme or reason can be made, for example, of the strong dollar in 1985 ore the superstrong Yen in early 1995.

In what follows we concentrate on issues raised for emerging economies where the management of capital flows is a problem in several possible ways.

- First, as an individual country opens up, how can it avoid that large capital inflows lead to excessive appreciation. The smaller the country, the larger the risk.

- Second, in the course of the waves of lending and credit rationing, what is a regime that helps stabilize capital flows?

- Third, what is a good capital-account regime to deal with the ebb and flow of capital movements driven by country-specific news, good or bad.

- Fourth, what is the advice to countries receiving too little capital?

The last issue can be dealt with quickly. Clearly, a country has to offer attractive, plausible returns to investors - absent that, why should capital come. Often it may be difficult in terms of social, economic and political trade-offs to offer such returns. It also may

Table 1

NET CAPITAL INFLOWS TO DEVELOPING COUNTRIES

(*Period average, $ billion*)

	1977 -1982	1983 -1989	1990 -1994
All Developing Countries	30.5	8.8	104.9
Asia	15.8	16.7	52.1
Net direct investment	2.7	5.2	23.4
Latin America	26.3	-16.6	40.1
Net direct investment	5.3	4.4	11.9
Other	-11.6	8.7	12.7
Net direct investment	3.2	3.7	3.8

Source: IMF.

be shortsighted because capital flows can potentially make a lot of difference. For countries receiving too little capital, the issue of managing the capital account is just as significant as for those receiving too much. In all likelihood, poor policies toward capital flows are one of the reasons why capital is unwilling to come. These policies might provoke serious questions about property rights or just random behaviour toward convertibility or other issues bearing on the quality of an investment. Predictability and stability of regime is a key aspect. It may not be enough to attract capital, but it certainly is a precondition. Any capital that comes even in the absence of these basics is also likely to leave without much notice.

But the focus today is much more on countries receiving either too much capital or capital that is too erratic, resulting in excess volatility throughout the macroeconomy. Consider then countries receiving too much capital. The most obvious case is a situation of initial opening-up. Or consider a country exposed to volatile capital - say Brazil as a by-stander of Argentine and Mexican instability or Asian countries faced with a Latin-driven sell-off. A financial transactions tax may be a remedy or at least a shock absorber for these problems. We state the case, elaborate some points of cost/benefit and then return to the application.

III. A trading tax

It is useful to state at the outset that the economic contribution of capital inflows varies directly with the commitment of investors. The more the lenders have a mind set of investors rather than traders, the longer the horizon with which they approach a proposition and the more stabilizing and growth-enhancing their contribution. By contrast, the shorter the maturity of loans, the more it is out of tune with development needs and the more risky it is in the perspective of a bank-run syndrome. A financial transactions tax, or more narrowly a foreign-exchange transactions tax, is designed to lengthen horizons and shift agents from trading to investing; if there is too much trading at short horizon, trading should be taxed.

Such a tax has been advocated by Nobel Laureate James Tobin but has also attracted vigorous support from the present Deputy Secretary of the United States Treasury, Larry Summers, in his former academic incarnation. Among industrial countries, it apparently was on the G-7 Halifax menu and enjoys interest, if not support, from Canada. Among emerging economies it has attracted interest in the aftermath of the Mexican crisis or in the context of excessive capital inflows and resulting sterilization problems. Finally, among NGOs it is of interest as a source of world revenue for good causes.

A financial transactions tax heavily penalizes short-run trading but puts virtually zero penalty on the long-term profitability of investment. The reason is that payment of a, say, 0.25 per cent tax on a 10-year investment represents a negligible fraction of the principal earnings. By contrast, on an overnight round trip it would eat up the profits except on investments with extremely high returns. With this tax, the hurdle rate of return for short-term transactions is inversely related to the holding period. A one-night stand would require an annualized rate of return of more than 470 per cent just to pay the tax. For a half-year round trip the hurdle rate is down to almost 1 per cent, and for a 3-year investment the burden falls to less than 0.2 per cent.

Clearly, the tax is not an obstacle to long-term investment. Investors will look for assets that promise serious returns in the long term, not for a way to get overnight returns from the negative-sum game of volatility. Predictably, the round-trip industry will disappear, and good riddance.

The scheme might sound populist - "tax the trader" -, but it is, in fact, in the best tradition of the Chicago School. The economy needs a favourable environment for capital accumulation. Often, chief executives of non-financial businesses divide their time between litigation and speculation, rather than focusing on investment in research and development of technology, products and markets. Capitalism blossoms when business takes the long view, unimpeded by insecurity of property rights or financial fragility. Innovation and competition have undermined the blessings of capitalism by turning financial markets into overly trigger-happy institutions with an emphasis on debt-leverage, capital gains and the short horizon. Liquidity is the buzz-word; the fallacy is that in liquid markets "one can get out" before the curtain goes down.

Keynes, in the *General Theory*, offers a description of the difference between "speculation" - which is geared to making capital gains from uncovering the shifting psychological moods of the market - and "enterprise"- which seeks to earn income from the long-term holding of an asset. He notes the markets' pursuit of short-term capital gains rather than long-term holding yields:

> When capital development of a country becomes a by-product of the activities of a casino, the job is likely to be ill-done. The measure of success attained by Wall Street, regarded as an institution of which the proper social purpose is to direct new investment into the most profitable channels in terms of future yield, cannot be claimed as one of the outstanding triumphs of laissez-faire capitalism - which is not surprising, if I am right in thinking that the best brains of Wall Street have been in fact directed toward a different object.

Keynes concludes with the recommendation of:

> a substantial transfer tax on all transaction ... to mitigate the dominance of speculation over enterprise in the United States.

That advice of 1934 is even more appropriate today. In fact, Nobel Laureate James Tobin has advocated a variant of this scheme to curb excessive zest for speculation in international capital markets. In Tobin's scheme, a tax on international currency purchases should "throw some sand in the wheels" of international markets. Others have gone further to argue that if sand is not enough, use rocks.

Why interfere with short-horizon speculations? It could be argued that financial market participants must know what is best for them. Who is to second-guess that their individual profit maximization does not also lead to the best social use of resources? The short-run focus creates a negative externality in the form of excessive liquidity. An analogy helps build the case. Most sane people agree that gun control is desirable because an uncomfortably large number of people carry guns. Whatever they may be maximizing, it surely is not social welfare. Gun control disarms an overly trigger-happy world, just as speed limits cool overly aggressive driving. Liquidity is of the same nature: it cries out for a tax that curbs the excess. We all want to be totally liquid, all the time; yet the economy's capital must be held. Too sharp a focus on the short run means that the capital stock will adjust; there will be little, and what there is will be short-lived and not the most productive.

If most trading takes a short focus, most actors in the economy cannot but follow the same pattern. If everybody speaks loudly, we have to shout to be heard; if everybody carries revolvers, we have to carry submachine guns to be safe. And if everybody trades by the minute, we have to trade by the second to get ahead. The economy converges to a bad equilibrium, far away from the investment in productive ventures and the building of businesses, totally focused on minute capital gains. Nobody stops us from taking the long view, but that would be a lonely life made far more precarious by the high volatility created by the market's short horizon. Excess liquidity produces an abnormal and counter-productive shortening of the economic horizon; it spreads from financial markets to corporate suites and the shop floor.

A financial transactions tax is no panacea, just as gun control would not stop all murder; poison and knives would make a comeback. And speed limits have not done away with traffic accidents (and not even altogether with speeding). A financial transactions tax will not stop speculation altogether. But it certainly will help lengthen the horizon and focus the mind of capital markets on enterprise and investment rather than trading.

The notion of a financial transactions tax is a much broader ambition to refocus financial markets - it would apply to *all* financial assets rather than only foreign exchange. Here our concern is a much narrower one of lengthening the horizon for cross-border flows. That makes the effectiveness much stronger and limits the costs. Let us consider how such a foreign-exchange tax might work.

Implementation

Suppose every purchase or sale of foreign exchange and every cross-border payment is taxed in a particular country at the rate of, say, 0.25 per cent, irrespective of whether it is a goods transaction, a service deal or a financial operation. Whatever sale or purchase of foreign exchange occurs, participants are required to remit to the Government 0.25 per cent and are jointly liable. (Much like a stamp tax of old. Of course, the payment would only be made by one party, exporter or importer.) This, clearly an exporter on receipt of his proceeds will have to pay; an importer will pay as she acquires foreign exchange for payment. The same is true for tourist operators or insurance brokers, recipients of interest or dividend, buyers of stocks or bonds, or real estate.

The point of the Tobin tax is that the amount paid is independent of the maturity of the project - it is a fixed cost incurred for making cross-border transactions. The profitability of the transactions, however, depends on the maturity. The tax achieves two desirable outcomes: first, unlike in the case of quotas or administrative procedures, investors can self-select as to who wants to invest in what. Thus, a maximum of market choice and discipline is maintained and a minimum of bureaucratic control intrudes. Second, the incentive structure of the tax is to discourage investors who are unwilling to commit. The tax makes it very expensive to stay only for a brief period and thus discriminates against investors who ex ante feel they only want to stay for a short period. This self-selection process lengthens the implicit maturity of the investment.

A Tobin tax does not take investors hostage. In the face of a fundamental and lasting deterioration of prospects they would sell off. But if the deterioration is only temporary, they would weigh hanging in against the extra cost of a round trip. If the uncertainty is limited and the adversity short-lived, on balance they might choose to stay. The discussion highlights that a Tobin tax in no way is a panacea to get by with bad policies; it merely makes capital somewhat less liquid.

Effectiveness

The focus is cross-border payments which lead to reserve losses or gains, exchange-rate movements, inflation or deflation. The focus is not whether off-shore someone buys from someone else a claim on domestic assets. Here is a critical difference from financial transactions taxes. Our focus is not to reduce

the volatility of stock or bond prices but rather to manage the pace of cross-border flows. The prospects of accomplishing this are far better than those of stabilizing asset prices. Hence much of the discussion of why financial transactions taxes cannot work are irrelevant to a foreign-exchange tax. (For a forceful statement of why a financial transactions tax might not work and is definitely undesirable, see Hakkio, 1994.)

How effective would the tax be? Consider implementation in a single country. Can it work? The immediate temptation, not surprisingly, is to ask how the tax can be avoided. It is obvious that unless it applies to all and any cross-border transaction, the untaxed transactions will become vehicles for under- or over-invoicing. Once it is comprehensive, avoidance is difficult unlike in the case of financial transactions taxes. The latter can be avoided by trading outside the jurisdiction where the tax is levied.

A tax that applies solely to cross-border transactions falls fully within the jurisdiction of the levying country. Consider the example of a securities transactions tax designed to reduce short-term speculation in stocks and the resulting volatility. Levying the taxes forces the business offshore and leaves the volatility unchanged. By contrast, cross-border payments by definition cannot be forced off-shore. This difference takes away the central criticism of financial transactions taxes, namely that they cannot work unless they are practised at the world level.

This is an important aspect. Suppose cross-border investments in stocks and bonds are taxed as is bank borrowing abroad. That obviously forces large corporations into borrowing abroad. That does not make a difference because they, too, are taxed upon repatriating their borrowing. If the tax is administered in a comprehensive way, by registration of capital transactions where they do not cross the foreign-exchange market and by stiff penalties, the system is mostly effective.

No doubt, there will be some transactions that might escape. One possibility is obviously fraud, but that is hard for large corporations or financial institutions and hence will not systematically amount to much. The other is the possibility of offshore transactions by domestic agents: rather than exporting capital at the cost of the tax, a Brazilian firm might borrow in New York to finance an investment in Angola. Again this will be hard for large companies, and for small companies it is difficult and hence unimportant. There is always some leakage in taxation; the point of this system is that it is difficult to circumvent it and not really worthwhile since the tax rate is very low except for round-trip financial agents.

Costs

If the tax is effective, what are the costs of applying the system. There are obviously two kinds of costs. First, this *is* a tax on trade in goods, services and assets and as such reduces the level of trade. That is undesirable but also unlikely to be quantitatively of great importance. A tax of 0.25 per cent is so small that, except for the administrative encumbrance, it would practically not matter for any goods or service transaction. And the same is true for long-term investments. For short-term financial transactions, by contrast, it does matter, and in fact is prohibitive, but here is precisely where effect should be.

There is, of course, the additional question of the administrative bureaucracy to implement the tax. Since foreign-exchange transactions mostly go through a relatively concentrated market, there is very little cost in levying the tax. As for cross-border payments that do not go through the local foreign-exchange market, they have to be monitored at the level of tax audits of major firms. Again, this does not appear to be an overriding issue. Auditing will, however, be necessary to avoid such possibilities as offshore clearing of inflows and outflows with taxation only applying to the residual. No doubt, schemes of this kind will come up, but in most countries everybody, including the Government, knows how they work, and it is just an issue of tax enforcement to assure compliance.

IV. IMF arguments

In its important report *International Capital Markets* the IMF (1995) has directly addressed the issue of volatility induced by capital flows, the merits in attempting to shield an economy from capital-account disturbances, and the effectiveness of alternative strategies of sterilization, regulation or a financial transactions tax. The IMF team was sufficiently impressed with the problems raised by capital flows to recognize the desirability of policies to manage the capital account. Postponing liberalization of capital account liberalization is specifically recommended - i.e. financial repression should be continued while other measures of reform go ahead.

The IMF concludes with scepticism on the issue of effective policies to limit capital flows. Policies including selective regulations or reserve requirements can be effective, but not on a lasting basis, not fully, not without important side effects or even perverse results. Its judgment on a financial transactions tax is basically negative.

The IMF discussion of financial transactions taxes picks up the wide range of reactions to such a measure that have been offered specifically in the context of taxes on security transactions rather than cross-border transactions taxes. That discussion need not be entered here because it has little bearing, if any, on the question of a tax on cross-border transactions. There is a reference, however, to capital outflow restrictions practised in the United States in the 1960s which were subsequently repealed because of ineffectiveness due to loopholes. One assumes that this draws attention to the need for comprehensiveness rather than to ineffectiveness *per se*. The IMF report also mentions specifically reserve requirements, at the margin, on capital inflows such as practised by Chile or proposed in the European context by Eichengreen and Wyplosz (1994). No judgment is offered on these proposals; this might be deemed to mean quiet assent for lack of alternatives.

V.   Who should use the cross-border tax?

In the abstract, a cross-border payments tax appears a plausible instrument to domesticate capital flows. But whose problems, specifically, would it solve? To be honest at this point, one has to say that it will do relatively little other than change a bit the temperature of capital flows, and possibly the extent of capital committed to emerging markets.

That the temperature will cool off is not in doubt. By and large, the tax will work and, once in place, it will sort out investments toward the longer end. There will be disappointments and surprises - investors who stay shorter than they had thought or others who stay beyond their expected duration, but on average the maturity is up and that is a stabilizing factor. It is even more stabilizing if Governments respond to the opportunity by shifting to more stable policies which help business take a longer view, and if their own financing takes longer maturities.

The question of what happens to the total capital committed to emerging markets is difficult to assess. The first answer is that volatility is what attracts capital, and less volatility means less lending. That is true for some of the trade-oriented capital, but clearly not for all. It might also be true that the drop-off in trade-oriented investment is offset or perhaps even more than compensated by an increase in longer-term investment, including direct investment. That is not at all excluded. Thus, the presumption that with the tax less capital will be available is simply not warranted. And even if this were warranted, it would still have to be demonstrated that it is harmful.

Consider then specific situations to see how a tax might work or what else is called for. The starting point is a country that has a balanced current account, or some moderate deficit, and experiences recurrent surges and dry-ups of external capital. These would be predominantly reflected in reserves with the accompanying problem of sterilization or of macro-economic adjustment. When money comes, reserves swell and costly sterilization has to offset the inflows; when money goes, reserves fall and restraint has to be practised. Some of these fluctuations measure the productivity of capital throughout the world and should be reflected in the country's external balance and level of absorption: when elsewhere capital is plentiful, that is the time to invest and spend, and when it is scarce, the country should save. But because these swings are expensive due to a number of externalities, a cross-border payments tax will be useful in mitigating at least the short-term fluctuations in capital availability. This is the cleanest case.

The next case involves a country with intrinsic political and economic instability. It is difficult to look ahead and get a clear picture of what will happen. External money is available on occasion, but only on a short-term basis. Hard as it is, the country should screen out the "hot" portion of money and deny itself the temptation. The hot money, more likely than not, exacerbates the instability. A cross-border payments tax is useful in reducing instability. This is a clear-cut case, too.

Consider next the difficult case of a country that is basically closed to foreign capital and is under pressure to open up - OECD membership requires an open current account. Specifically, consider the Republic of Korea. The country practices relatively complete restrictions against the inflow of capital, for three main reasons. First, saving and investment rates are high and hence there is no obvious need for more capital. In fact, how would the country accommodate a major capital inflow other than by an undesired and even troublesome real appreciation? Second, opening-up means exposure to external instability for which

there is little need or tolerance. Third, the domestic financial system is only starting to be deregulated. Accordingly, there is a serious risk in too much cross-border finance as domestic institutions are still learning to practise competition.

The reasons seem highly plausible. Yet, Korean interest rates are far higher than those in the United States and the Won has been appreciating. Clearly, opening-up would increase the supply of capital, push down interest rates and increase lending. In the process, spending would rise and the transfer of resources from foreign lenders to home borrowers would occur via an increased external deficit. Where is the problem in going down to world interest rates?

The Republic of Korea would be well-served to proceed with its inevitable opening in two directions. First, direct investment should be immediately and fully liberalized in both directions. Restrictions in this area merely hamper the effectiveness of the division of labour within firms and across borders. Second, a cross-border payments tax should be introduced and, at the outset, should be quite substantial. That acts as a significant restraint on any but the longest cross-border investments. Over time that tax should be reduced so that five years later it will be very moderate. At the same time, full liberalization of cross-border portfolio flows should take place. The combination of policies allows a gradual internationalization of the financial sector. It assures that flows will be at the outset of very substantial maturity and hence fully impervious to short-term events. Once the internationalization is accomplished, a far more moderate tax is appropriate to provide the minor noise reduction that combines the double objective of substantial openness and short-term stabilization.

The strategy will not help contain altogether net capital inflows. The Republic of Korea may well find that the net direction is still inward and that either a difficult sterilization task or a current-account deficit result. Here the issue is predominantly how long-term capital should be allocated in the world and it is neither operational nor desirable to interfere too much in this respect. The purpose of a cross-border tax is to avoid that countries have precarious financing for large deficits, not to avoid imbalances.

VI. Alternative measures

If the issue is to contain capital flows, a broad array of policies can be thought of. At one extreme, there is full financial repression with a heavy exchange-control bureaucracy. A milder form is a selective control of capital flows by stated criteria such as investment vehicles or maturity or characteristics of financial intermediaries. At the other end of the spectrum, there is a clean, comprehensive, moderate cross-border transactions tax. Controls are strictly undesirable - they involve bureaucracies, corruption and a lack of flexibility in response to economic criteria. The more moderate strategy of selected controls at least allows the prospect of full liberalization for direct investment, possibly the stock market and long-term fixed income. Of course, financial engineering may easily play havoc with such controls.

Then there is the possibility of reserve requirements on cross-border flows, either across the board or at the margin. The trouble here is that these deposits must be fully comprehensive not only for all forms of inward-bound financial transactions but also including reserves on offshore borrowing of non-financial agents. A clean reserve requirement system is effectively the same as a cross-border transactions tax. The only difference is that a cross-border payments tax is more comprehensive and involves less administrative complication. It thus limits from the outset the incentive to invent transactions that could circumvent the tax.

VII. A world system?

A last set of questions concerns the implementation of such a system. Specifically, would it not be a good idea to do this at the world level? And failing that, can an individual country do it?

Opponents of a cross-border financial tax will be quick to claim that it cannot work. Business will simply move offshore, to the islands, where catering to tax evasion is already the chief industry. True, some trading would move offshore. But the risk is easily exaggerated, and in any event it can be checked. As argued above, what is true of a financial transactions tax is much less true of a cross-border tax. Moreover, why not seek international agreement on a world tax since the disease is clearly spreading?

The G-7 has not done anything useful for years; why not surprise the world with a genuine innovation

- an agreement on a world cross-border tax or even a broader concept of a comprehensive financial transactions tax. All Governments want revenue; none believes short-horizon speculation does anyone any good. Liberalization of world trade in financial services is the most fiercely lobbied issue of the day; a financial transactions tax can tame capital flows, thus enhancing their productivity and make the world capital market safe for development finance.

It is clear from the IMF reaction (IMF, 1995, pp.98-99) that this is not about to happen. There is scepticism of the effectiveness and comprehensiveness, and there is an overriding fear of the vehement backlash from Wall Street. That leaves the question whether individual countries, against the background of the difficulties of many emerging economies should not just move ahead individually. The answer here is quite clear. A cross-border transactions tax can definitely be administered unilaterally. It gains relatively little from being the system for all. The experience of Chile indicates that prudent, flexible, moderate management of the capital account is an effective strategy in the opening process and beyond. Once capital has thoroughly become accustomed to a country, markets have deepened and the future has stabilized, there is no reason to tamper with international capital flows. Of course, most emerging economies still have a long way to go before reaching that stage.

An entirely different question about the world system is the discriminatory aspect of cross-border payments taxes. Clearly, such a tax discriminates between internal and international transactions and, in that fashion, results in new barriers. International institutions rightly express concern when new measures of discrimination are introduced. But the point here is that the negative externalities associated with too volatile and large capital flows interfere with the process of opening-up goods and internal financial markets. There is no theory demonstrating that capital liberalization must be phased in on a par with domestic financial deregulation and trade liberalization. In this perspective, cross-border payments taxes, although they are decidedly discriminatory, are an essential instrument in carrying out the successful integration of a country in the world economy. Inability to use such an instrument will be reflected in excess volatility, inefficient controls and financial repression or a reluctance to open up altogether.

References

BOSWORTH, B., R. DORNBUSCH, and R. LABAN (eds.)(1995), *The Chilean Economy* (Washington, D.C.: The Brookings Institution).

DOOLEY, M. (1995), "Transmission of Monetary Shocks to Partially Open Economies", mimeo., University of California, Santa Cruz.

DORNBUSCH, R., and Y.C. PARK (1995), *Financial Opening* (San Francisco: International Center for Economic Growth).

DORNBUSCH, R., I. GOLDFAJN, and R.O. VALDEZ (1995), "Currency Crises and Collapses", *Brookings Papers on Economic Activity*, No. 2, pp. 219-270.

FFRENCH-DAVIS, R., and S. GRIFFITH-JONES (1995), *Coping With Capital Surges* (New York: Lynne Rienner).

GHOSH, A., and J. OSTRY (1993), "Do Capital Flows Reflect Economic Fundamentals in Developing Countries?", *IMF Working Paper*, WP/93/34.

EICHENGREEN, B., and C. WYPLOSZ (1993), "The Unstable EMS", *Brookings Papers on Economic Activity*, No. 1.

HAKKIO, C. (1994), "Should We Throw Sand in the Gears of Financial Markets?", *Federal Reserve Bank of Kansas Economic Review*, No. 2.

IMF (1995), *International Capital Markets* (Washington, D.C.).

LE FORT, G. (1995), "Capital Account Regulation and Macroeconomic Policy in Chile", mimeo., Central Bank of Chile.

McKINNON, R., and H. PILL (1995), "Credible Liberalization and International Capital Flows: The Overborrowing Syndrome", mimeo., Stanford University.

SUMMERS, V., and L. SUMMERS (1989), "When Financial Markets Work Too Well: A Cautious Case for a Financial Transactions Tax", *Journal of Financial Services Research*, Vol. 3, No. 3.

TOBIN, J. (1984), "On the Efficiency of the Financial System", *Lloyds Bank Review* (July).

TOBIN, J. (1993), "International Currency Regimes, Capital Mobility and Macroeconomic Policy" *Greek Economic Review* (autumn).

Wall Street Journal (1995), "Backward at the IMF", Editorial Page, August 24.

CAPITAL-ACCOUNT REGULATIONS AND MACROECONOMIC POLICY: TWO LATIN AMERICAN EXPERIENCES

Guillermo Le Fort V.
Carlos Budnevich L.*

Abstract

Regulations that limit international financial integration have been at the centre of a recent policy debate. Any developing economy can benefit from financial development, but international financial integration implies the risk of macroeconomic instability. The approach that has been favoured in Chile and Colombia is one of gradual and limited financial integration, attempting to increase the effectiveness of monetary and exchange-rate policies. The reduction in the risk premium demanded by investors have created downward pressure on domestic real interest rates. However, a lower interest rate would increase domestic expenditure, the price level and the current-account deficit. Among the policies put into effect to deal with this problem are increasing exchange-rate flexibility and taxing external financing. Both countries have registered a successful macroeconomic performance, with the success partly owing to effective capital-account regulations. The effectiveness of the regulations is shown by the fact that a once-and-for-all currency appreciation followed by a depreciating trend has been avoided, and that the current-account deficit has been kept at sustainable levels. Using stronger restrictions on capital flows, such as quantitative limits, would not only create very significant microeconomic costs and slow economic and financial development, but would also most likely be ineffective.

* The views presented in this paper represent the opinions of the authors and not necessarily those of the Central Bank of Chile. A first version of this paper was presented at a UNCTAD Conference on Globalization of Financial Markets, held at the Jerome Levy Economics Institute of Bard College, New York, in March 1996. We have benefited from the comments of Y. Akyüz and G. Helleiner and acknowledge the able assistance of O. Landerretche M.

I. Introduction

A new policy debate has arisen in Latin American countries after international investors' recent re-awakening to opportunities in emerging markets. Two polar positions have been defined in this policy debate. On the one hand, the "integrationists" defend financial integration on the grounds that free market operation will always produce the best result for the developing economy. On the other, the "isolationists" consider financial integration dangerous for macroeconomic stability, and prefer a developing world without market-determined international capital movements. The regulations that limit international financial integration have been at the centre of this policy debate, as they define the degree of financial integration and the distance between reality and these two polar positions.

The debate is in itself surprising. An international macro-economist from only five or ten years ago would be extremely puzzled to see that the external financing problems that some Latin American countries are struggling with today relate no longer to the lack, but rather to the excess, of external financing. Colombia and Chile were denied access to external financial markets operating on a voluntary basis during the second half of the 1980s. Many analysts back then considered that market-based external financing was not to be resumed anytime soon. But everything changes, and so did the lenders' perceptions of the risk involved in holding emerging market assets. In the mid-1990s, market-based external financing, including medium- and long-term lending, direct investment, and portfolio investment, have been abundant for both countries.

In our opinion the polar positions are both to be rejected. Any developing economy has the need for international financial integration, not only because of the external financing needs of a rapidly growing economy, but also because of the long-term advantages that can be derived from financial development, including risk diversification and the efficient provision of financial services. Despite these advantages, the immediate and complete opening-up of the capital account implies very significant potential costs for macroeconomic stability in a developing economy. Several experiences with negative effects of excessive spending and external indebtedness prompted by private capital flows have already been recorded.

Thus, the discussion that has been focused on the question of the convenience or inconvenience of opening the capital account should instead be focused on the particular strategy for international financial integration.

The approach that has been favoured in both Chile and Colombia is one of gradual and limited financial integration. Foreign-exchange market regulations and capital-account intervention (including regulations) have been used to limit the secondary effects of international financial integration and to deter interest-rate arbitrage, destabilizing speculation, bubbles and overshooting behaviour of asset prices (including the real exchange rate). The strategies differ in the instruments used and in the emphasis of policies and objectives, but both place particular emphasis on neutralizing the disturbances to the current account and domestic prices caused by net capital inflows. The regulations are not exclusively based on macroeconomic policy considerations. They also relate to the potential problems derived from public insurance of the liabilities of financial institutions, and the need for monitoring and limiting their risk taking. Both deposit insurance and exchange-rate guarantees may encourage over-intermediation of international funds by banks and an increase in systemic risk, expanding therefore the vulnerability of the banking system (see Le Fort, 1994).

This paper describes and analyses the policies followed in Chile and Colombia regarding their external capital accounts during the 1990s. The policies are analysed and assessed in the context of the macroeconomic and financial results obtained in the period. The first section of the paper deals with the main analytical issues relating to international financial integration, its costs and benefits, its implications for monetary and exchange-rate policy, and the main limitations to financial integration. The second section of the paper describes the experience of regulated financial integration in Chile during the 1990s, including a brief historical review, a review of foreign-exchange market regulations and the regulations on capital movements, and the results in the capital account and at the macroeconomic level. The third section of the paper is devoted to an analysis of the Colombian case, including a review of the main regulations and intervention schemes in the foreign-exchange markets and the regulations for different types of capital movements, with special emphasis on the reserve requirement system, and the results obtained. The last section presents our concluding remarks.

II. Major issues in international financial integration

This section analyses some important issues relating to the integration of the so-called emerging markets with the world's financial markets without making reference to specific countries. To some extent, this integration is the result of the change of views of investors regarding the risks represented by emerging markets, and to some extent it is the result of an explicit financial integration strategy pursued by developing countries during the 1990s. The issues discussed include the benefits and costs of financial integration, the implications of integration for monetary and exchange-rate policy, and the policy instruments used to limit international financial integration.

The limits imposed upon the international integration of financial markets should not be seen as a macroeconomic policy objective by themselves, but rather as instrumental to more effective monetary and exchange-rate policies. Given that these instruments have some shortcomings, they should be used only to a certain extent; the need for their use arises mainly from the concern about the effects of abundant external financing on the current-account and debt positions. This concern in general relates to the fact that large current-account deficits and increasing external indebtedness erode a country's creditworthiness, rendering domestic macroeconomic stability vulnerable to external financial turbulence.

A. Benefits and costs of financial integration

1. Benefits

An open capital account has important benefits for an economy with an outward-oriented development strategy, characterized by the growth of the sectors in which the country has comparative advantages. In principle, and perhaps oversimplifying, it can be said that the opening-up of the capital account can be associated with two types of benefits:

(1) Development of the financial services sector: A developing economy may have comparative advantage in the production of financial services; if that is the case, an export sector would develop after the elimination of restrictions to international financial integration. However, it is also possible that foreign competition may take control of this sector, and the

country may become a net importer of financial services. In any case, international integration would imply lower costs and better quality for users of financial services. Financial integration then allows for reduced cost of capital and more efficiently provided financial services to help in the intertemporal stabilization of consumption. Certain comparative advantages for financial development partly stem from the experiences derived from an earlier liberalization attempt, which allow for the development of a regulatory framework that has operated successfully, and the possibility of benefiting from the existence of scale economies. It must be stressed that in developing economies, capital-account openness implies larger net capital inflows on a sustained basis, due to the higher productivity of capital because of the abundance of labour and the availability of natural resources. This capital inflow allows for higher growth and a reduction in the cost of capital.

(2) Greater diversification of the asset portfolio of domestic economic agents can also result from integration, by making the composition of domestic portfolios independent of the composition of domestic production. In a financially closed economy, the composition of domestic asset portfolios tends to be closely related to that of domestic output. After all, domestic financial assets represents rights to domestic income stream, basically determined by production. In a financially integrated economy, foreign securities that derive returns from external productive activities which are independent from those of domestic activities allow for greater domestic income stability through greater diversification. Income of domestic residents becomes more stable to the extent that their portfolios include assets that derive their returns from activities more or less independent from domestic exports. Such diversification may be used to compensate for the (often great) volatility of national income that affects open economies due to the variability of individual export prices.

2. Costs

Financial openness also poses several costs, some of which are only valid during the transition to a fully integrated economy. Among these costs can be distinguished:

(1) Transitional costs: One way of looking at the process of financial integration is that it constitutes a way to overcome a stock imbalance. Financial liberalization allows stock adjustments, directing capital towards regions where the expected

profitability of capital is greatest, or to where opportunities exist for risk diversification at a reasonable cost in terms of profitability. It is clear that in countries like Chile and Colombia, the returns to capital are typically higher than in the developed world, a condition for foreigners to invest and finance investments in these countries. Full integration implies a jump in asset prices within a relatively short period of time, and a massive inflow of foreign capital that lasts until the stock adjustment is completed and risk-adjusted domestic rates of return converge to the levels of foreign rates. If this process takes place in a short period of time, then a source of macroeconomic imbalances can be developed in the form of rapid growth in investment, wealth and consumption, real currency appreciation, inflationary pressures and a widening current-account deficit. It can create destabilizing wealth and expenditure effects, resulting in confusing signals to domestic consumers with detrimental effects on domestic savings, exchange-rate stability and the stability of the growth process (see Budnevich, 1994, for a model of this kind of transition).

(2) *Policy costs*: In a financially open economy monetary policy loses its ability to affect domestic macroeconomic conditions without modifying the external balance. In general, an increase in the real interest rate directed at controlling inflationary pressures will also result in an exchange-rate appreciation, both in nominal and real terms. The appreciation helps in reducing inflation, but may generate a larger current-account deficit. In fact, under some conditions, in a financially open economy monetary authorities may be forced to choose between the inflationary target or the external balance objective. It is true that a tighter fiscal policy may be used in place of monetary restraint under these circumstances; however, real world fiscal policies lack the flexibility needed for short- or medium-term stabilization, particularly when the fiscal accounts are already in balance or in surplus.

(3) *Real costs*: Financial integration leaves the economy exposed to the turbulence of international capital markets, adding a risk factor and volatility to the exchange market which may affect macroeconomic balances. International capital markets can move very rapidly and almost without warning signals, from an optimistic lending phase in which funds are abundant and relatively cheap, to a pessimistic phase in which funds are not available and a sharp adjustment is forced. The recent case of Mexico and that of most Latin American countries in the 1980s come to mind in this respect.

(4) *Systemic risk costs*: Economic agents tend to perceive the existence of publicly provided insurance to liabilities of financial institutions and institutional investors, whether or not it has been explicitly offered. This implicit or explicit insurance requires regulations that limit risk-taking by those institutions. Full and unrestricted international financial integration allows portfolio selection from a wider set of assets, making it more difficult to control and monitor their risk-taking.

B.   Financial integration, and monetary and exchange-rate policy

The perceptions of foreign investors of the risk and returns from investment in the Chilean and Colombian economies have changed significantly following institutional changes and the success of macroeconomic policy. This change has resulted in a very significant reduction in the risk premium demanded by investors in these countries, which in turn has resulted in sizable capital inflows that have modified the degree of integration of the domestic financial markets into the corresponding international markets. It can be said that in economies like Chile and Colombia, the risk-adjusted marginal efficiency of capital has increased to levels above those prevailing in the developed world. As a result, capital tends to move into these economies, reducing the domestic cost of capital and increasing the prices of domestic assets.

Financial integration implies that the integrating economy is fully open to financial arbitrage. Consequently, domestic real interest rates are forced to reflect the external real interest rate and a country-risk premium. Any deviation from this requirement of risk-adjusted international interest rate equalization implies changes in the opposite direction in the real exchange rate.[1] However, the domestic interest rates required to generate domestic macroeconomic equilibrium may be higher than the rates forced by international arbitrage. In these conditions, when domestic interest rates are increased, in addition to the standard closed economy response in terms of a lower expansion of domestic expenditure, in the financially open economy, a real appreciation of the domestic currency takes place. The real exchange-rate adjustment shifts demand towards the rest of the world, alleviating pressure on domestic output but also increasing the current-account deficit.

The size and duration of the arbitrage effect of the domestic interest rate change on the real exchange rate depend on, among other factors, the time-horizon of arbitrageurs and the expected duration of the new interest rate differential. The shorter their horizon, the lower the impact on the real exchange rate. It also depends upon the effect on the country-risk premium of the exchange-rate appreciation. If the increase in the country-risk premium brought about by the real appreciation of the currency is significant, then the impact on the exchange rate is minimized.

International arbitrage may imply that the real exchange rate becomes and remains, for significant periods of time, out of line with respect to the authorities' external equilibrium objective. Consequently, the current-account deficit may exceed, in the medium term, the level that is sustainable over a longer term, rendering the economy vulnerable to a forced external adjustment.[2] This adjustment is triggered if external creditors no longer consider it safe to continue lending to an addictive borrower. The market's automatic correction mechanism is the effect of the larger current-account deficit on the country-risk premium and on expectations of currency depreciation. If larger deficits make the market participants uneasy, then this by itself should stop or even reverse the capital inflows and thus correct the real exchange rate. However, it seems that market participants are not always very sensitive to this risk, and that they typically only react when it is too late, after the external conditions have worsened so much that a very large and painful domestic expenditure adjustment is needed.[3]

A first policy response to the real appreciation of the currency is to try to compensate for the effect of capital inflows on the exchange rate. This has been done through the intervention of the monetary authority in the foreign-exchange market. However, the purchase of foreign exchange by the Central Bank has thereby become the main source of domestic liquidity creation. To limit the effects of exchange market intervention on monetary conditions, the Central Banks have used different forms of sterilization, including the sale of bills or forcing the temporary holding of foreign-currency certificates. However, this sterilization is costly for the Central Bank and losses arise from the international interest-rate differential and the real currency appreciation: the Central Bank acquires assets that yield the international interest rate and that depreciate in real terms, while having to issue liabilities that pay the higher domestic interest rate and keep their real value. As a transitory mechanism, sterilized intervention works; however, over the longer term, its effectiveness is impaired by the resulting financial losses.

A second alternative is to reduce the domestic interest rate. However, this reduction would create an increase in domestic expenditure that would put pressure on the price level, force a real currency appreciation and increase the current-account deficit. An obvious solution is to reduce the interest rate and at the same time compensate for the effect on expenditure via tighter fiscal policy. An austere fiscal policy directed at controlling the expansion of aggregate expenditure, limiting both public and private expenditure expansion, is a must for the final success of any stabilization effort. However, there are political limits to what fiscal policy can deliver, and thus restrictions or limitations to international financial integration may be required to preserve macroeconomic stability.

It is generally suggested that another way to compensate for capital inflows is by opening the economy to capital outflows, allowing domestic residents, firms, and financial institutions to hold assets abroad. Although a valid tool to favour the diversification of domestic portfolios, this is not effective as a tool to reduce net capital inflows. As domestic residents increase their holdings of foreign assets, they reduce their demand for domestic assets. A lower demand for domestic assets, *ceteris paribus*, is reflected in lower asset prices and higher asset returns, which serve as an additional attraction for foreign capital inflows.[4] Furthermore, by making the exit easier, facilitating capital outflows reduces the risks faced by foreign investors (see Labán and Larraín, 1993).

Limitations on international financial integration give additional degrees of freedom to monetary and exchange-rate policies, allowing adjustments in domestic interest rates that cannot be arbitraged to the exchange rate. In practice, these restrictions give room for the use of monetary policy to gradually reduce domestic inflation, while keeping the current-account deficit at reasonable levels.

The problem created by capital inflows for the effectiveness of monetary policy is better dealt with by a flexible exchange rate. In this connection, exchange-rate stability is costly because it facilitates the international arbitrage of interest rates. If the Central Bank actively tries to achieve exchange-rate stability, it faces additional costs in terms of higher reserve purchases, and at the end is forced to accept a more appreciated currency. In this sense, avoiding rules for official intervention, increasing the width of the exchange-rate band, and using a basket of currencies rather than a single currency to peg the reference rate are measures that increase the effectiveness of monetary policy, by helping to insulate against excessive capital inflows. The ex-ante volatility of the exchange rate also tends to deter short-run capital inflows as it removes exchange-rate "guarantees" and thus helps to support a higher real exchange rate (see Sanhueza, 1995).

C.   Limitations to financial integration

In order to reduce the need for sterilized intervention, several restrictions to international financial integration have been used. These restrictions, by limiting the possibilities of financial arbitrage, have given some room for the operation of monetary policy as it seeks to achieve domestic macroeconomic equilibrium. In most cases the restrictions to capital transactions introduce registration procedures for international capital transactions. These procedures can be important sources of information for measuring the external accounts, and also for the tax authorities; but they also involve obvious administrative costs.

The first type of restriction is the use of dual foreign-exchange markets. One market, the formal, is used for current-account transactions and authorized capital flows, and the other, the informal one, is used for other financial flows. In this scheme, financial arbitrage takes place in the informal market, permitting this secondary exchange rate to deviate from the authorities' target rate. Since the formal market is not subject to arbitrage, the current account is isolated from exchange-rate volatility. During the days of scarce foreign financing, the informal rate reflected a more depreciated domestic currency than the rate in the formal market. The opposite should be the case under abundant external flows.

The dual exchange-rate scheme has one serious shortcoming - the existence of leaks that allow for arbitraging the differential between the exchange rates in the two markets. These leaks not only render the exchange restrictions ineffective, creating pressure towards the equalization of the exchange rates, but also imply significant costs. The leaks include the over- and under-invoicing of current-account flows, and they tend to increase in importance as the absolute value of the premium becomes larger. The leaks, in general, result in quasi-fiscal losses and transfer of resources from the central bank to those agents that discover ways to buy foreign exchange in one market and sell it in the other at a premium. Additional costs

of the leaks are the regulations and administrative costs incurred in the effort of preventing them.

A second type of restriction is the imposition of reserve requirements or other more direct measures that increase the marginal cost of external financing. The reserve requirements increase the cost of foreign financing since they demand the use of additional resources to finance the required deposit in the Central Bank. The reserve requirements may relate to all forms of foreign financial flows; however, in practice, they have not generally affected direct investment and other forms of equity financing, suppliers' credits on imports, or advanced export returns.[5]

In general, the financial cost effects of the reserve requirements tend to be stronger for short-term financing and therefore work particularly against short-term arbitrage. In Chile, the required reserves must be kept in the Central Bank for a period of one year, diminishing the relative financial burden for longer-term operations. In the case of Colombia, however, the requirement is variable depending on the maturity of the loan; for longer maturities the reserve requirement ratio is lower, implying discrimination against short-term inflows.

Mechanisms like the reserve requirements have certain limitations. First, they can be avoided by using vehicles that are not affected by the requirement; for example, accelerated export returns, supplier credits, or equity investments. There is a limitation, however, on what can be brought in through these alternative vehicles. The requirements can also be evaded by not registering capital flows, although penalties may be imposed on those who evade the regulations.

The reserve requirements are effective only under expectations of a stable real exchange rate, and thus are unable to stop a speculative attack created by expectations of exchange-rate adjustments. The capital gains that can be made with a discrete exchange-rate jump cannot be sufficiently reduced by the financial cost of the reserve requirement. This implies that, despite the reserve requirement, only exchange rates that are consistent with market expectations can be successfully defended. The equilibrium trend of the exchange rate, even if it represents a significant real appreciation of the currency, cannot be influenced by such policies. An exchange-rate adjustment can be spread more over time, but only to a certain extent. The reserve requirements as well as the other restrictions to financial integration increase financing costs for individuals and firms, limit business opportunities for the financial sector, and reduce portfolio diversification for domestic agents. They also affect the equity-debt mix, and create financial segmentation that tends to favour big over small enterprises, and to encourage informal means of financing. They are thus not free of private and social costs. There are also costs derived from weaknesses of the regulation that make the reserve requirement not completely effective. In a country like Chile, with a long and a deep seated law abiding tradition, these effects are more important than direct evasion.

Other types of restrictions affect the ability of domestic firms and financial institutions to issue debt or stock in international capital markets. These restrictions can take the form of discretional authorization or conditions like a minimum credit rating, minimum amount issued, or others. In this respect, the purpose of the restrictions is not only related to limiting the external capital inflows but also to screening the companies that are authorized to participate in international capital markets. Since the actions of each firm generate externalities to others, in the sense that all of them are seen as firms belonging to a particular country, some type of screening process is required.

Finally, restrictions may be applied to portfolio investors from abroad in the form of quantitative restrictions on entry into domestic markets, or minimum stay (or permanence) requirements.

Restrictions on international financial integration are effective to a certain extent but could not be considered a cure-all or a way to completely isolate the domestic economy from the realities of the international financial markets. There are always ways to circumvent the restrictions, ways that tend to be reinforced the larger the risk-adjusted interest-rate differential. Consequently, only to a certain extent is it possible to use these restrictions to give some room for manoeuvre to domestic monetary policy.

III. Regulated financial integration in Chile

During the 1990s, important policy measures have been taken to regulate the financial integration of the Chilean economy with international markets. These measures, together with the recognition of the Chilean economy in financial centres, have allowed for increasing financial integration and for important changes in the composition of Chilean capital flows during the 1990s. The foreign-exchange market and capital flows regulations existing in the Chilean

economy are briefly reviewed in this section. In addition the results derived from this strategy are presented.[6]

The regulations are directed to reducing potential effects on macroeconomic stability, increasing the effectiveness of monetary policy, and imposing prudential regulations on banks and institutional investors. They have taken the form of exchange-market regulations, capital flows regulations and other related policies.

A. Brief history of regulations

Financial activity, which had been repressed for years by negative real rates of interest and administrative allocation of credit, and with the majority of financial institutions under government control, entered an accelerated liberalization process in the 1970s. After decades of financial repression, the supervisory institutions lacked the experience necessary to impose prudential regulations effectively. The result was a financial system with insufficient capitalization, that went into bankruptcy in the early 1980s. A deep recession, beginning at the end of 1981, eroded the solvency of financial institutions which were in a very vulnerable position. The trigger for the crisis was a sharp reduction in external capital inflows and a deterioration of the terms of trade, causing a sharp adjustment in domestic expenditure. The financial crisis spread throughout the financial system by the beginning of 1983.

The volatility of international capital flows played a very important role in setting off the crisis. A significant proportion of capital flows entering the country in the period prior to the 1982 crisis had been intermediated by the financial system. The removal of restrictions to capital inflows, when domestic interest rates, duly adjusted for exchange risk, widely exceeded international rates, generated a massive capital inflow which financed a strong expansion of domestic spending. The external debt problems provoked a drastic change in the direction of capital flows, forcing an adjustment and contributing to the deepening of the crisis of the financial system.

The financial institutions recovered from the crisis in the second half of the 1980s. Following this experience, a macroeconomic policy characterized by caution and a concern to control the expansion of expenditure has resulted, during the 1990s, in moderate current-account deficits. Macroeconomic policy has defined a target range for the medium-term current-account deficit of between 3 and 4 per cent of GDP. External financing has more than exceeded financing requirements, resulting in significant increases in international reserves. As a result of balance-of-payments flows alone, international reserves increased by almost $10 billion in the period 1990-1995, reaching a level of around $14 billion by the end of that period despite the pre-payment of public external debt of about $1.5 billion.

The policy of external financial opening pursued by the Chilean authorities in the 1990s is characterized by the maintenance of a series of regulations which affect the foreign-exchange market and the capital account, and limit the degree of integration of external and domestic markets.

B.   Foreign-exchange market regulations and intervention

During the 1990s the Chilean foreign-exchange market has evolved from a dual market to an increasingly unified market. The formal foreign-exchange market is affected by regulations and access restrictions, while the informal foreign-exchange market is fully liberalized. Total unification has not been achieved yet, but the exchange-rate differential in both markets is almost non-existent - less than a 0.5 per cent difference on average in 1995. The dual exchange market was conceived as a way to isolate the formal-market exchange rate - the one at which trade flows were carried out - from the volatility of capital flows, particularly portfolio outflows, that must be carried out through the informal exchange market. Over time, however, the duality has lost relevance.

Some transactions must be effected through the formal market: in particular, all foreign portfolio capital inflows must be processed through the formal market. Investors and borrowers obtain, in exchange, the right to access the same market at the time of servicing the debt or remitting profits or capital. Other capital outflows, including foreign direct investment and portfolio investment by residents, cannot be carried out through the formal market. Finally, there are transactions that can be carried out in either of the two exchange markets. These include exports and imports of goods and non-factor services.

The dual-exchange-market approach has been gradually revised. Increasing confidence has allowed the reduction of exchange restrictions, particularly those affecting export proceeds. In several steps, the export surrender requirements were first reduced and then completely eliminated (on June 16, 1995). The exchange-market regulations that remain in place are mostly related to capital flows.

The formal foreign-exchange market operates under a managed float within an exchange-rate band. Intervention by the Central Bank is directed at maintaining the nominal and, through it, the real exchange rate within a range consistent with a sustainable current-account position. In an indexed economy like that of Chile, changes in the nominal rate only affect the level of the real exchange rate for a limited period. It is understood that the real exchange rate cannot be permanently affected through the nominal rate, and that it is necessary to create adequate conditions in terms of real variables to attain that result.

By "external equilibrium" the authorities understand the maintenance of a deficit in the current account of the balance of payments, which, while allowing the use of a reasonable amount of external saving for financing domestic investment, still ensures that the increase in external debt is compatible with the long-term growth of the Chilean economy without introducing a significant source of further external vulnerability for the country. In practice, this means a deficit on current account of the order of 3 to 4 per cent of GDP. Obviously this target is interpreted as an average since in any given year the current-account deficit must be permitted some divergence from the average.

Since the market has been at, or close to, the more appreciated end of the exchange-rate band, the Central Bank, as noted above, has accumulated a significant amount of net international reserves, while a significant portion of the external public debt has been pre-paid. The monetary impact of official intervention in foreign-exchange markets has been sterilized through the issuance of central bank debt.

C.   Regulations on capital movements

The regulation of capital movements differentiates between direct investment and debt flows. Direct investment is favoured due to the presumed positive externalities associated with it, including access to international markets and the transfer of management techniques and technology.

As a consequence, the direct-investment regime is fairly liberal, while the regulations are designed to limit foreign indebtedness, particularly that of a short-term nature. The only important restriction for direct investment is the one-year minimum stay. Portfolio investment through American Depositary Receipts (ADRs) placed in New York is limited by credit-rating and minimum-amount conditions.

Direct investment inflows[7]

Direct investment is subject to a minimum stay of one year for the principal. Profits, with the single exception of investment performed through debt conversions, are not subject to time limitations. The rules that allowed for foreign investment through debt conversions were eliminated in mid-1995.

Portfolio investment inflows and ADRs[8]

Procedures relating to bonds and ADRs - which represent the acquisition of shares of domestic companies by foreigners - set limits on the right to issue these types of instrument in terms of minimum amount and risk classification. Initially the minimum amount demanded for the issuing of non-financial firms' ADRs was $50 million. As of September 1994 this was reduced to $25 million. At the same time it was decided to reduce the issuers' long-term debt risk rating to BBB or better for non-financial companies, and to BBB+ or better for banking institutions. This rating has to be granted by three internationally recognized risk-rating agencies.

Since July 1995, the secondary ADR inflows have been subject to the 30 per cent reserve requirement that relates to most forms of foreign indebtedness. In addition, in November 1995, for those companies that have at least one previous issue, the minimum amount for primary issues of ADRs (not subject to the reserve requirement) was reduced to $10 million. A condition imposed on the new primary issues is that all previous issues of the same company become subject to the same regulations as the last issue.

Other portfolio capital inflows

Regulations on debt-related capital flows and on deposits of non-residents are tighter. Instead of minimum-stay or credit-rating requirements, these types of flows are influenced by a reserve requirement. The purpose of the reserve requirement is to increase the cost of external financing, and consequently increase the level of the domestic interest rate at which international arbitrage results in external inflows. At present, the reserve requirement ratio is 30 per cent of the value of the loan, bond or deposit, and the reserve deposit must be placed at the Central Bank in United States dollars.

Loans and bonds[9]

External loans and bonds issued abroad are subject to a 30 per cent reserve requirement, to be kept in the Central Bank for a period of one year, irrespective of the maturity of the loan or bond. In all cases, the reserve deposit must be constituted in United States dollars; however, an alternative to the deposit is the payment, in advance, of the financial cost implied by the reserve requirement. In addition, bonds are subject to regulations similar to those that affect ADRs. There is a minimum amount of bonds to be issued ($25 million for corporate bonds), and a minimum risk rating of BBB for non-financial issuers and BBB+ for banks.

Deposits and credit lines[10]

External credit lines, used mainly to finance trade operations, are also subject to the 30 per cent which is applied on the average balance of the month. Foreign-currency deposits are treated similarly; like placements in foreign currency they are also subject to the reserve deposit of 30 per cent, applied on the average balance of the month.

Capital outflows

With respect to the acquisition of foreign assets by Chilean residents, regulations are rather liberal with the sole exception of prudential restrictions imposed on banks and institutional investors.

Foreign investments by the Chilean non-financial private sector[11]

Foreign investments carried out by individuals and by non-financial companies are not in practice subject to any restrictions. The only limitation is related to access to the formal foreign-exchange market, which is not always granted. In any case, the informal market is readily available at a rate roughly the same as in the formal market. This measure has greatly facilitated Chilean investment abroad, which has boomed since 1990. Chilean investment abroad is concentrated mainly in the financial services, electrical, and transportation and telecommunications sectors.

Foreign investments by Chilean institutional investors[12]

Foreign investments by pension funds, mutual funds and life-insurance companies are subject to certain limits as to the amounts and types of foreign assets that they can hold. These restrictions were recently upgraded by the Central Bank after the

Table 1

CHILE AND COLOMBIA: BALANCE OF PAYMENTS, 1990-1994

(Per cent of GDP in dollars)

	Chile			Colombia		
	Balance of payments	*Capital account*	*Current account*	*Balance of payments*	*Capital account*	*Current account*
1990	7.7	9.4	-1.7	1.2	-0.3	1.5
1991	3.5	3.2	0.3	4.2	-2.1	6.3
1992	5.8	7.4	-1.6	2.2	0.0	2.2
1993	1.2	5.7	-4.5	-2.1	2.4	-4.5
1994	6.1	7.5	-1.4	0.3	4.6	-4.3

Source: Calculations by the authors, based on data of the Banco Central de Chile, Banco de la República de Colombia, IMF and DANE, Colombia.

Note: A minus sign indicates a deficit.

approval by Congress of a new capital market law. Pension funds are authorized to hold up to 9 per cent of their total funds in foreign assets, which may include a variety of fixed-income assets and company shares; the latter are limited to 4.5 per cent of the fund. Life-insurance companies are limited to investments of up to 10 per cent of their funds in foreign assets. The limit on general-insurance companies is 15 per cent of their reserves, and for mutual funds the limit is 30 per cent of the fund.

Foreign investments by banks

Regulations on foreign asset holdings by commercial banks are associated with the problem of systemic risk and deposit insurance affecting the banking system. Foreign financial investments by commercial banks are limited to 25 per cent of the bank capital and reserves, and restricted to bills and bonds issued or guaranteed by foreign Governments or central banks. Banks are also authorized to use foreign-currency deposits and credit lines to finance trade within the Association for Latin American Integration (ALADI). In addition, commercial banks can acquire stock of foreign banks or establish branches abroad provided that the domestic banks have a capital-adequacy index of 10 per cent or more. (This index, based on the Basle Convention, measures capital as a proportion of the value of total assets adjusted by credit risk.) Only to the extent that bank

supervision can be effective in monitoring the risk of foreign assets is further liberalization possible in this area.

D. Capital-account and macroeconomic results

The international perception of the reduction of the risk of Chilean investment is reflected in several indicators. The investment-grade rating for Chilean public debt, equivalent to Standard & Poor's A-, which is given by the most prestigious international agencies, is the highest in Latin America and comparable to that of some countries in Southern Europe and South-East Asia.

The reduction in the international perception of risk in the Chilean economy has resulted in a substantial increase in the supply of external funds available for the country. Net capital inflows have been significant over the last five years, averaging 6.6 per cent of GDP over the period 1990-1994, with a maximum of 9.4 per cent of GDP in 1990. With a current-account deficit averaging only 1.5 per cent of GDP, the available external financing has been more than necessary or desired and, as a result, net international reserves increased markedly, by about

$10 billion, to a level equivalent to 26 per cent of GDP which represented more than one year of imports by the end of 1995 (see table 1).

An important question is whether under these circumstances the existing capital-account regulations have been effective. Particularly the reserve requirement has been under scrutiny. If the effectiveness of this measure is judged against its success in checking overall capital flows, the regulations have not been effective since inflows have continued at a significant pace. However the effectiveness of regulations should be measured only in terms of their objectives, which do *not* include drying-up the capital account. The first objective is to favour equity over debt financing and long-term financing over short-term financing. The second is to give more freedom for monetary policy which can be tightened without resulting in large current-account imbalances.

As a consequence of the capital-account regulations, a significant change in the composition of the capital account occurred in the 1990s. Foreign direct investment and longer-term portfolio investment (associated mainly with the placement of ADRs) grew in importance relative to external indebtedness (see table 2). Indeed, net foreign investment plus portfolio investment grew from about 3 per cent of GDP in 1990 and 1.2 per cent of GDP in 1991, to 2.5 per cent in 1993 and 4 per cent in 1994.[13] In recent years there has also been a change in the composition of external borrowing, with a trend towards a larger share of medium- and long-term debt and a consequent reduction in external short-term financing. In fact, in 1990 external short-term debt financing amounted to 4.6 per cent of GDP, while in 1994 short-term financing was equivalent to 2.4 per cent of GDP (see table 3).

Monetary policy has been tight, with the short-term real interest rates averaging 6 per cent per annum while inflation came down from almost 30 per cent in 1990 to 9 per cent in 1994. This reduction has been based on the control of expenditure expansion. Expenditure control has paid off not only in terms of lower inflation but also in that the current-account deficit has averaged less than 2 per cent of GDP in the 1990s. Expenditure control has been achieved through interest rates that were higher than the standards in the developed world. Despite strict monetary policy, the economy has been able to grow at an average of close to 7 per cent per year in 1990-1995. Exports have led the expansion; for example, during 1995 real GDP grew by 8.5 per cent, and exports by 11 per cent in real terms.

Table 2

CHILE AND COLOMBIA: CAPITAL ACCOUNT BALANCE AND FOREIGN DIRECT INVESTMENT, 1990-1994

(Per cent of GDP in dollars)

	Chile		Colombia	
	Capital account balance, excl. net FDI	Net FDI	Capital account balance, excl. net FDI	Net FDI
1990	6.4	3.0	-1.6	1.3
1991	2.0	1.2	-3.2	1.1
1992	5.9	1.5	-1.8	1.8
1993	3.2	2.5	0.8	1.6
1994	3.9	3.6	2.4	2.2

Source: See table 1.
Note: See table 1.

Expenditure control would not have been possible if capital-account regulations had not been effective, because otherwise capital inflows would have made it impossible to keep rates above international levels (see table 4). It is possible to conclude that reserve requirements have been effective in limiting the international integration of fixed-income markets. The international interest-rate differential

Table 3

CHILE AND COLOMBIA: TIME STRUCTURE OF NON-INVESTMENT CAPITAL FLOWS, 1990-1994

(Per cent of GDP in dollars)

	Chile		Colombia	
	Medium- and long-term capital	Short-term capital	Medium- and long-term capital	Short-term capital
1990	2.2	4.6	0.5	-0.5
1991	-0.2	1.4	0.3	-2.5
1992	0.6	4.5	0.4	0.4
1993	1.1	2.4	1.9	2.1
1994	2.5	2.4	5.7	-1.1

Source: See table 1.

Table 4

CHILE AND COLOMBIA: MACROECONOMIC INDICATORS, 1990-1994

		Real exchange rate	GDP growth	Rate of inflation	Fiscal balance	Real interest rate
		(Dec. 1989=100)[a]	*(per cent)*	*(per cent)*	*(per cent of GDP)*	*(per cent)*
Chile	1990	112.8	3.3	27.3	0.8	9.4
	1991	106.4	7.3	18.7	1.5	5.4
	1992	97.6	11.0	12.7	2.2	5.2
	1993	96.9	6.3	12.2	1.9	6.4
	1994	94.3	4.2	8.9	1.7	6.3
Colombia	1990	101.0	4.2	29.9	-0.3	4.4
	1991	98.0	2.0	26.8	0.2	4.8
	1992	92.0	3.8	25.1	-0.3	0.0
	1993	91.0	5.2	22.6	0.3	2.4
	1994	90.0	5.6	22.6	2.6	4.7

Source: See table 1.

   a An increase denotes a depreciation of the domestic currency.

would not have been possible without this type of restriction. Longer-term markets show, ex ante, a similar spread as short-term markets. The explanation seems to be that for longer terms the insurance premium against country risk is higher, thus offsetting the lower financial effect of the reserve requirement.

At the same time an important segment of the Chilean equity market has been effectively integrated with international stock markets through the ADRs. However, the risks associated with the price of each particular stock, or even with a composite index, make it very difficult to perform international financial arbitrage through this mechanism.

It is important to note that the reserve requirement cannot be used to avoid a trend of real appreciation of the domestic currency. Indeed in Chile the real effective exchange rate has shown an appreciating trend averaging 4 per cent per year during the last five years. The currency appreciation trend has been an equilibrium trend, in the sense that it has been consistent with a sustainable deficit in the current account of the balance of payments of less than 2 per cent of GDP. In the face of expectations of currency

appreciation, the reserve requirement is ineffective in stopping capital inflows. The financial cost implied by the requirement, i.e. 2 or 3 percentage points per annum, can be easily offset by an expected appreciation of 1 per cent or 2 per cent in the following few weeks.

Domestic financial indicators show that the capital-account regulations have not impaired the financial system. In fact, despite the regulations, the financial system and the capital markets have gone through a very significant development in Chile over the last few years. An indication for the rapid development of the banking system is the expansion of total liabilities of the financial system to the private sector, which have increased from 47 per cent of GDP in 1990 to 67 per cent of GDP in 1995. At the same time, the real rate of return on capital of domestic banks has been kept at a high and stable level. On average, between 1990 and 1994 commercial banks earned 20 per cent, in real terms, on their capital and reserves.

The results in the stock market are even more remarkable. On average, the stock market index in terms of United States dollars rose 40 per cent per

Table 5

CHILE AND COLOMBIA: SAVINGS AND INVESTMENT, 1990-1994

(Per cent of GDP in dollars)

	Chile		
	Investment[a]	National savings	External savings[b]
1990	26.3	24.2	2.0
1991	24.5	24.0	0.4
1992	26.8	24.7	2.0
1993	28.8	23.9	4.8
1994	26.8	25.3	1.4

	Colombia			
	Investment[a]	National savings	External savings[b]	External savings[c]
1990	18.5	18.9	-1.5	-0.4
1991	15.9	18.6	-6.3	-2.7
1992	17.2	17.0	-2.2	0.2
1993	20.4	...	4.5	...
1994	...	...	4.3	...

Source: See table 1.
  a Gross capital formation and inventory accumulation.
  b Current-account deficit.
  c Non-domestic savings, defined as investment minus domestic savings over GDP.

year in the period from December 1989 to December 1995. As a consequence, total stock market capitalization towards the end of 1995 reached 125 per cent of GDP, compared to 50 per cent of GDP in 1990.

Moreover, the country shows a strong international financial position. Total external debt net of international reserves is just equivalent to 10 per cent of annual GDP or 35 per cent of annual exports.

IV. Capital-account and exchange-rate policy in Colombia

During the first half of the 1990s, the Colombian economy was engaged in a wide-reaching programme of structural reform. The programme included the opening of the economy to international trade through

the elimination of administrative restrictions to imports and a generalized reduction of tariffs; the subscription to bilateral international trade agreements with Venezuela, Mexico and Chile; the creation of a Ministry of Foreign Exchange and a Foreign Commerce Bank; the introduction of measures increasing the flexibility of the exchange-rate regime; the enhancement of possibilities to acquire external financing for national agents; the removal of restrictions on external investment and the establishment of national treatment for foreign investors; the reduction of the overall taxation rate; labour-market liberalization and partial privatization of the social security system; privatization of some public enterprises; and the reform of the Central Bank Charter to grant its legal independence.

A. Exchange-rate regime and sterilization

Since the end of the 1970s, Colombia had used a crawling-peg exchange-rate regime. The Banco de la República, Colombia's Central Bank, has made a daily announcement of the rate at which the bank was willing to engage in foreign-exchange transactions. Towards the mid-1980s, the rate of currency devaluation had consistently lagged behind inflation differentials, resulting in a sustained real appreciation. The response of the Banco de la República was an acceleration of the devaluation programme, even above the inflation differential, improving competitiveness at the cost of higher inflation.[14]

In 1991, the Banco de la República was granted political independence through a constitutional reform. The new Central Bank Charter formally established a commitment to the reduction of inflation. In a context of stubborn inflationary pressures and a tendency to currency appreciation, the Banco de la República reformed the exchange-rate regime, introducing exchange certificates (EC), aiming at a more flexible and market-oriented exchange rate. In this way, the first formal exchange market in many years was established.

The scope for using sterilization policy hinges on the cross-border mobility of capital. As benefits, one can mention the recovery of monetary control and the avoidance of excessive intermediation through the banking system without increasing intermediation costs associated with a reserve requirement. Among the associated costs, it is worth mentioning that monetary sterilization has implied an increase in interest rates and an increase in the quasi-fiscal deficit.

The intervention mechanism in Colombia combined, in the same transaction, exchange-market intervention and sterilization. The Central Bank purchased foreign exchange with ECs, a dollar-denominated financial instrument issued by the Banco de la República that initially was redeemable in pesos at full value and on demand. The redemption price, in pesos, of these instruments was determined daily by the Central Bank, and corresponded to its liquidation price at the maturity date. This price is similar to the exchange rate and was called "the representative rate".

The maturity of ECs was extended to three months in June 1991, and to one year in October 1991. These financial instruments could be sold at a discount in the secondary market, and the Central Bank opened a discount window to redeem ECs at 87.5 per cent of their value, i.e. at a discount of 12.5 per cent. Foreign exchange was sold to the Banco de la República in exchange for the ECs at the exchange-certificate redemption rate, the official exchange rate fixed by the Central Bank. This rate was adjusted in a crawling-peg fashion, creating a gap with respect to the market rate. This gap was fundamentally determined by domestic interest rates (since the ECs were substitutes for other peso-denominated financial assets) and the expected rate of devaluation of the official exchange rate. When interest rates rose, the gap widened and the market rate appreciated, converging to the exchange-rate floor which was 87.5 per cent of the official exchange rate, the value at which the Banco de la República bought back new ECs.

The nominal value at time T of an "EC-dollar" was equal to the official exchange rate (ER) at time T. The market value of an "EC-dollar" with maturity date of T+1, which claims the right to one dollar, and is bounded by the discount price at which it can be sold to the Banco de la República (the floor), must be determined as a function of the expected official exchange rate (ER) at time T+1, and the opportunity cost given by the interest rate of peso-denominated debt issued by the Banco de la República . The price in pesos could be written as:

$$P_{ecdollar} = \frac{E(ER_{T+1} / ER_T)}{(1+r)} \times ER_T$$

The floor price is determined by the Banco de la República, which buys an "EC-dollar" at a discount of 12.5 per cent of the official exchange rate:

$$P_{ecdollar} = 0.875 \; ER_T$$

If the foreign-exchange market works efficiently, the EC price should correspond to the market exchange rate which depends positively on the level of the official exchange rate and its expected rate of devaluation, and negatively on the interest rate.

The ECs tied the hands of the Banco de la República in the conduct of its monetary policy. If the Central Bank raised interest rates through open-market operations, the market exchange rate (the price in pesos of the EC dollar) would be pushed to the floor, and intermediaries would liquidate their EC stocks. As the stock of ECs in the market fell, the monetary stock would increase, eliminating the initial interest rate rise, unless it was sterilized with peso-denominated debt. The system operated practically as a pseudo flotation-band, given that by arbitrage the market price could never fall below what we have called the floor. If the market rate rose above the official rate, agents would lower their stock of ECs, which is equivalent to buying dollars from the Banco de la República to sell them to the market.

Back in the crawling-peg years, monetary sterilization had been carried out through open-market operations. ECs were introduced with the objective of eliminating the need for such sterilization, or performing it directly in the exchange market. The system was of very limited effectiveness. As long as market operators accumulated EC stocks, the flow of dollars going into the market and, hence, central bank intervention were reduced. At the point when the flow of EC liquidations was equal to the issuance of new certificates, however, the sterilization effect of EC was nullified. The attempts at forcing an increase in the EC stock through longer maturity for the EC were bound to fail.[15]

In January of 1994, the EC system was discontinued, and an exchange-rate band of ±15 per cent around a central parity entered into operation. The Central Bank intervened, within the band, in both the spot and future exchange markets. The Banco de la República announced daily the central parity for the next 10 days, and the rate of devaluation of the central parity was initially set at 11 per cent. Parallel to the band, a "monetary corridor" was established, that is a band for M1 which the Central Bank is committed to maintain through operations in its peso-denominated debt. In December 1994, and as the market rate put pressure on the band, the band's central rate was appreciated by 7 per cent. As a compensation, the rate of subsequent devaluation of the central parity was increased to 13.5 per cent.

B. Foreign-exchange restrictions and public debt policy

In 1991 a formal foreign-exchange market was created, substituting for the previous exchange controls through licenses, a mechanism that had existed since 1967. Resolutions 55 and 57 authorized banks, financial corporations, and to some extent savings funds and commercial financing corporations, to operate as authorized dealers in the exchange market. Resolution 57 stipulated that the more important trade and investment operations, including imports, exports, and foreign investment and loans, must be channelled through the formal exchange market.

The authorized dealers in the market could negotiate foreign-exchange proceeds coming from the activities required to be in the formal market, but also with currency coming from other activities. Dealers were also authorized to trade among themselves and with the Banco de la República. The transactions and the exchange rates were to be reported daily to the Banking Superintendent and the Central Bank. Resolution 55 authorized the Banco de la República to intervene in the exchange market through transaction in ECs, certificates that were denominated in dollars but payable in pesos. They were freely negotiable and could be liquidated at the Banco de la República before their maturity at a discount. The Banco de la República could not negotiate dollars with the public, but only with authorized intermediaries, by means of ECs, or with the Government.

Two measures forced dealers to align their rates with the official exchange rate. In order to sell dollars to the Banco de la República, a domestic agent had to buy ECs through a market dealer. In order to acquire dollars from the Central Bank, the agent had to liquidate ECs, obtaining them in the secondary market. As mentioned above, the principal objective of the new regime was to give more flexibility to the exchange rate, avoiding the important cost of sterilized intervention. This was the first step towards a flexible exchange rate, which allows more flexibility in monetary policy to stop inflationary pressure.

Before the establishment of the EC regime, the Banco de la República had centred its monetary policy on the sterilization of the effects of significant capital flows coming from abroad. This implied a financial burden for the Central Bank as the cost of its domestic debt grew continuously.[16] Inflation continued unabated as the Banco de la República tried to compensate for the observed real appreciation through a more aggressive devaluation calendar that induced additional capital inflows. By 1991, there was a widespread perception that the devaluation programme was not sustainable. The devaluation-intervention-sterilization cycle was too costly for the Banco de la República, and the expectations of real appreciation that ensued generated a more vigorous capital inflow. Exchange-rate flexibility was the only way out of this pervasive cycle.

The EC system produced, in the short run, an effective sterilized intervention. As domestic agents accumulated their EC stocks, the pressure concentrated on the exchange market until the floor was reached and pressure on money creation started. In 1993 though, the ECs started to mature, causing a new impulse for monetary creation that needed to be sterilized through debt issues. The ECs gave some degree of freedom in the short term, but by no means monetary policy independence, as it was not a stable sterilization tool. What appears obvious is that the exchange market was forced to gradually evolve towards a system of managed floating. The EC's term was an adaptation period, thought to create the necessary institutional background for the development of the market. Domestic open-market operations were the principal source of sterilization before, during and after the EC system.

More recently, the exchange reforms contained Resolution 21 had the objective of advancing more quickly than Resolution 57 in facilitating transactions with international markets. The reforms were oriented towards speeding up long-term investment flows and to hold out speculative capital. The reforms applied to the capital market were mainly:

(a) simplification of authorized exchange-market operations;
(b) extension of the types of operations not required to being made through the formal foreign-exchange market;
(c) authorization to make payments for exports and imports in Colombian pesos;
(d) increase in the possibilities of obtaining loans abroad;
(e) liberalization of capital outflows to foreign markets.

The public debt policy, on the other hand, had the following objectives: to diversify internal financial alternatives, to develop the national financial market, to improve the external debt time profile, and to expand the possibilities for public corporations to engage directly in foreign financing. Consequently, during 1993 and 1994, long-term bonds were issued and placed in international markets at interest rates that were more favourable than those of previous issues of external debt. Part of the resources generated were used to pre-pay outstanding debt.

Bonds were issued not only by the Central Government. About 60 per cent were issued by public enterprises, including Ecopetrol, the Financiera Electrica Nacional and the Bank of Colombia. These issues, along with the low international interest rates, helped to improve the liquidity and solvency of Colombia as an international debtor.

C. *Reserve requirements and capital-account regulations*

During the second half of the 1980s, the Colombian current account registered a sustained surplus. At the beginning of the 1990s, the authorities reacted to this surplus with measures to liberalize external trade, consisting mainly of a reduction of import tariffs, a mix of sterilized interventions to neutralize the monetary effects of capital inflows, and reserve requirements to limit the attractiveness of those inflows. Moreover, capital-account liberalization in conjunction with tax forgiveness led to capital repatriation. As a result, the current account went into deficit and a surplus in the capital account was created, which increased further in 1992 and 1993, due to relatively low international interest rates. Net international reserves grew rapidly in 1991 and 1992, but the increase slowed down in 1993 as a result of a reduction in sterilized intervention in the foreign-exchange market.

In 1993, the Banco de la República reformed the exchange ordinance, aiming at making foreign-exchange transactions more flexible but at the same time maintaining some control over speculative capital movements.

In 1993, Article 30 of resolution 21 of the Banco de la República introduced a reserve requirement ratio of 47 per cent on any credit in foreign exchange obtained by a resident that had a total repayment period of up to 18 months. The deposits associated with the reserve requirement were considered as exchange operations and were to be made through exchange-market intermediaries. Upon deposit of the required reserve, the Banco de la República issued a certificate corresponding to the reserve requirement

ratio multiplied by the amount of the loan. The remaining part of the loan could enter freely. The certificate was denominated in United States dollars, was non-negotiable, had a maturity of one year, and was redeemable at its nominal value in pesos at the official exchange rate. It was called "Financial Foreign Currency Title" (FFCT). The Banco de la República could, if considered necessary, acquire the titles before their maturity, applying a discount of 13 per cent over their nominal value at the official exchange rate on the day of issue if the buyback was performed immediately. If redemption was made at a later date, the corresponding official exchange rate had to be applied.

In 1994, the reserve requirements were modified allowing for differentiation according to the maturity of the loan. Resolution 7 of 1994 introduced reserve requirements for operations of less than 36 months, the Banco de la República issuing FFCTs in exchange. For certificates with a maturity of 12 months the reserve requirement ratio was 93 per cent, for a maturity of 18 months 64 per cent, and for a maturity of 24 months it was 50 per cent.

Certificates could be partitioned to the agents' preference, and the Central Bank could buy back only those with a maturity of 12 months, at a 55 per cent discount on the official exchange rate at the day of issue. Finally, Resolution 22 of 1994 established a new schedule of reserve requirements, extended to maturities of up to 5 years (see annex I). This shows that in Colombia there is discrimination against short-run capital inflows; the shorter the maturity, the higher the reserve requirement. The reserve requirement is applied for the duration of the operation. The Colombian authorities have tried to eliminate possibilities for arbitrage, as the reserve requirement ratios were set so as to close the arbitrage gap. The objective was clearly to increase the cost of short-term capital inflows, in parallel with the liberalization of the capital account.

It is important to mention that this system differs from that used in Chile where the reserve requirement has been oriented towards closing the gap of interest-rate arbitrage only for operations of up to one year. For longer maturities, greater uncertainty and risk may act as deterrent to longer-term arbitrage. Annex II, however, shows that under the assumption of risk neutrality and flat term structures of interest rates and expectations of devaluation, the reserve requirement which eliminates arbitrage for different durations increases with the length of the maturity.

D. The capital account and macroeconomics

During the first half of the 1990s, Colombia has experienced a significant accumulation of international reserves, especially at the beginning of the decade. Recently this accumulation has slowed down as a consequence of the movement of the current account from a significant surplus to deficit. We interpret this evolution as a result of the liberalization of external trade which led to an import boom and to a sudden adjustment of the stock of durable consumption goods. We reject the hypothesis that this behaviour was driven by capital inflows. The surplus in the capital account, which at the beginning of the 1990s was moderated, started to increase significantly in the last two years. Our interpretation is that the current-account deficit caused the capital-account surplus to increase. This is because trade liberalization, while generating an expansion in imports which needs to be financed, usually increases the availability of voluntary external financing. Thus, the current-account deficit contributed to balance-of-payment equilibrium through a capital-account surplus, partly generated due to better expectations of the future income stream.

With respect to the composition of the capital account, there is a stable trend towards an increase in foreign direct investment (FDI). Annual FDI flows have accounted for between 1 and 2 per cent of GDP. Capital flows not related to FDI evidenced greater volatility and a steeper trend growth. Debt flows have increased from 1 to 5 per cent of GDP. Short-term financing has oscillated around zero; in some years there was an increase in short-run indebtedness and in others there was a net repayment of external debt. In controlling short-term capital inflows Colombia has been more successful than Chile where such inflows represented, on average, 3 per cent of GDP.

In any event, it is important to recall that the reserve requirement theoretically may not affect the path of the real exchange rate. Without a reserve requirement, it is quite possible to obtain the same path, but with higher public debt and higher losses for the Central Bank. Some authors have argued that the reserve requirement is ineffective. However, the question is how can an authority maintain higher interest rates than the rest of the world without increasing public debt to infinity and without a deep misalignment in the real exchange rate? If the reserve requirement were ineffective, market interest rates should be lower than they are or public debt would be very high. That capital controls have been effective is indicated by the fact that even under high domestic

interest rates and low private disposable income, due to the fiscal surplus and to inflation, there are no big capital inflows into Colombia. Both Chile and Colombia have managed to keep high interest rates without an explosive path of public debt. Moreover, real exchange rates have been aligned with fundamentals. This shows the effectiveness of capital controls. It is important to say that both countries had already attained fiscal equilibrium before the turn of the decade, generating conditions for a sustainable fiscal balance.

During the first half of the 1990s, public finances have been in balance, and in some years there has been a surplus. Nevertheless, inflation has remained at a level of 20 to 25 per cent per annum - another case of chronic inflation. Despite steady inflation and a crawling-peg system without intervention, there has not been undue pressure in the foreign-exchange market. This also indicates the effectiveness of capital controls. The Colombian economy has maintained a moderate growth record during the first half of the 1990s, with a tendency to acceleration in 1993 and 1994.

V. Concluding remarks

In this paper, two successful macroeconomic experiences of Latin American countries during the 1990s have been reviewed. Both Chile and Colombia have registered an impressive performance compared to their historical record and to the contemporary results of other countries in the region. They have been able to achieve sustained growth: Chile at an average rate close to 7 per cent per year, and Colombia at around 5 per cent. The current-account deficit has been kept at reasonable levels in both countries: in Chile at below 2 per cent of GDP, and in Colombia at around 3 per cent. The main difference in terms of macroeconomic performance is that, while Chile has succeeded in gradually reducing inflation to single digits, Colombia has maintained the trends of the past, with moderate inflation of between 20 and 25 per cent per annum.

The capital-account regulations applied in the two countries can take part of the credit for the successful macroeconomic performance. Of course, consistent macroeconomic policies and the right microeconomic incentives are the main reasons behind this success; however, the macro policies would not have been possible without effective capital-account regulations.

The two polar views in the policy debate on international financial integration coincide in their assumptions that reserve requirements and other qualified capital-account regulations, like those used in Chile and Colombia, are ineffective. Some critics (for example Valdés and Soto, 1995) argue that the reserve requirements have been unable to modify the appreciating trend of the currency, and have thus been ineffective in favouring a gradual sectoral adjustment process. Others argue that the regulations have been unable to stop excessive capital inflows and reserve accumulation, thus defending the imposition of quantitative limits on capital flows. We find both types of criticism unfounded.

The fact that the appreciating trend of the Chilean currency has continued at about the same rate after the introduction of a reserve requirement is not an indication of the ineffectiveness of this tool. The reserve requirement allows for maintaining an interest-rate differential in favour of the emerging economy, without having to generate an expectation of currency depreciation to fulfill the arbitrage condition. That is to say, the reserve requirement is successful if a once-and-for-all currency appreciation followed by a depreciating trend is avoided. An appreciating trend could be the result of financial pressures rather than a trend in the equilibrium exchange rate; and rather than indicating weaknesses of the reserve requirement itself, such a sustained trend shows the strength of the existing capital-account regulations, including the reserve requirement.

The effectiveness of the reserve requirement can also be seen from the change of the composition of net capital inflows. Increasingly, external financing has been moving from debt to direct investment and equity-based portfolio investment. This implies a more flexible structure of financing, favouring risk-sharing between domestic and external partners. It also allows the attainment of externalities associated with direct investment, in the form of international market access for exports and an inward transfer of technology and management. At the same time, medium- and long-term forms of debt have gained ground and represent increasing proportions of total debt financing.

While there could be leaks in the reserve requirement and other regulations, they do not seem to be of macroeconomic significance. If the leaks were severe, short-term external financing would be of great importance, but that has been the case neither in Colombia nor in Chile. There are periods, however, when short-term financing is more abundant. These are periods in which the expectations of currency

appreciation are exacerbated. Confronting even a small expected appreciation in a short period of time is an impossible task for the reserve requirement. The gains implied by the change in the value of the currency in a few months, cannot be compensated by the financial cost implied by the reserve requirement.

This opens the possibility of using stronger restrictions on capital flows, such as quantitative limits. In our opinion, quantitative limits not only create very significant microeconomic costs and slow down economic and financial development, but also most likely would be ineffective. Quantitative controls would create a dual exchange market. Officially authorized transactions would take place at the official rate, and unauthorized capital flows would be carried out at the parallel-market rate, which in this case would be higher than the official rate. When the exchange-rate differential becomes significant, the incentives for arbitraging between the two exchange markets would increase, allowing some private operators to make a bundle by buying foreign currency cheap in the informal market and selling it at a higher price in the formal market. Consider, for instance, an exporter who would sell and even over-invoice his proceeds in the official market, but would try to finance all his imports in the parallel market. The Central Bank would then be forced to accumulate reserves purchased at a transitory high exchange rate, and big losses would eventually accrue when the rate has to be adjusted.

Overall, the reserve requirement and other capital-account regulations, with all their limitations, have played a very important role in these two successful experiences. Perhaps the problem of the critics is what they expect from such regulations. One should expect from such measures no more than a contribution to efforts aimed at keeping the current-account deficit within reasonable bounds and at sustainable levels, while domestic macroeconomic targets of growth and price stability are attained.

Notes

1   Throughout this paper we use the Latin American definition of the real exchange rate (RER); that is, the RER increases when the domestic currency depreciates in real terms.

2   It is also possible to explain the dynamics of capital inflows, with booms and busts, in terms of bandwagon effects, yet this model seems not appropriate for the Chilean reality of the 1990s. There is no evidence of a

bubble in asset prices. Asset prices and the real exchange rate appear to be in line with fundamentals.

3 Experiences of the lack of immediate response of market participants in the face of large external indebtedness include the Mexican crisis of the 1990s and the Chilean financial crisis of the 1980s. In both cases, financing was abundant up to a point at which a large adjustment was needed. (See Arellano, 1983; Budnevich and Cifuentes, 1993.)

4 Institutional investors and banks are subject to regulations and supervision of their investments abroad because of the systemic risk and public insurance problem. These restrictions are not related to the regulation of capital flows to preserve macroeconomic stability. It is important to mention that there are regulatory restrictions that limit bank exposure to foreign currency.

5 An exception to this rule is the reserve requirement imposed on secondary inflows of American Depositary Receipts (ADR) in Chile.

6 For a complete description of the regulations and capital-account results in Chile in the 1990s, see Le Fort and Varela (1995).

7 Decree Law 600 (DL-600), and Chapters XIX and XIV of the Central Bank Foreign Exchange Regulations (CBFER).

8 Chapter XXVI of the CBFER.

9 Chapter XIV of the CBFER.

10 Chapters III and XIII of the CBFER.

11 Chapter XII of the CBFER.

12 Chapter XXVIII of the CBFER.

13 If we exclude from total foreign investments those performed through external debt instruments, the change in the composition is still more significant. Net foreign investment as a percentage of net capital inflows rises from 20 per cent in 1990 to 44 per cent in 1994. The remainder is external borrowing which falls from 80 per cent to 56 per cent in the same period.

14 According to Carrasquilla (1995), macroeconomic policy never sought explicitly the reduction of inflation since it constituted an important source of resources for the public sector, characterizing what he calls an accommodative exchange-rate policy.

15 At the end of 1992 and the beginning of 1993, the liquidation of ECs forced the monetary authorities to tighten their market operations. The open-market operations were made through the sale of notes issued by the Banco de la República.

16 Carrasquilla (1995) illustrates this with the alarming statistic that the domestic debt of the Central Bank grew from 1.5 per cent of GDP in 1989 to 7 per cent in 1991.

References

ARELLANO, J.P. (1983), "De la Liberalización a la Intervención: El Mercado de Capitales en Chile 1974-1983", *Colección de Estudios CIEPLAN*, No. 11 (December).

BUDNEVICH, C. (1994), "The Intergenerational and Dynamic Effects of Opening the Capital Account", *Revista de Análisis Económico*, Vol. 9, No. 2 (November).

BUDNEVICH, C., and R. CIFUENTES (1993), "Manejo Macroeconómico de los Flujos de Capitales de Corto Plazo: La Experiencia de Chile", *Colección Estudios CIEPLAN*, No. 38 (December).

CALVO, G., L. LEIDERMANN, and C. REINHART (1992), "Capital Inflows and Real Exchange Rate Appreciation in Latin America: The Role of External Factors", *IMF Working Paper* (August).

CARRASQUILLA B., A. (1995), "Bandas Cambiarias y Modificaciones a la Política de Estabilización: Lecciones de la Experiencia Colombiana", *Revista del Banco de la República de Colombia* (January).

CARRASQUILLA B., A., and C. VARELA (1993), "Apendum al Documento Controles a los Flujos de Financiamiento Externo GT-0893-007-C", Banco de la República de Colombia, Santa Fé de Bogotá, 25 August.

CORBO, V., and R. MATTE (1984), "Capital Flows and the Role of Monetary Policy: The case of Chile", *Documento de Trabajo*, No. 92, Instituto de Economía, Pontificia Universidad Católica de Chile (May).

CUMBY, R.E., and M. OBSTFELD (1983), "Capital Mobility and the Scope for Sterilization: Mexico in the 1970s", in *Financial Policies and the World Capital Market: The Problem of Latin American Countries* (University of Chicago Press for the NBER).

DORNBUSCH, R. (1980), *Open Economy Macroeconomics* (New York).

DORNBUSCH, R. (1983), "Real Interest Rates, Home Goods and Optimal External Borrowing", *Journal of Political Economy*, Vol. 91, No. 1 (February).

EDWARDS, S., and A. COX-EDWARDS (1987), *Monetarism and Liberalization: The Chilean Experience* (Cambridge, Mass.: Ballinger).

FFRENCH-DAVIS, R. (1983), "El Problema de la Deuda Externa y la Apertura Financiera en Chile", *Colección de Estudios CIEPLAN*, No. 11 (December).

FFRENCH-DAVIS, R. (1989), "Debt Equity Swaps in Chile", *Notas Técnicas*, No. 129, CIEPLAN.

FFRENCH-DAVIS, R., and J. P. ARELLANO (1981), "Apertura Financiera Externa: La Experiencia Chilena en 1973-1980", *Colección de Estudios CIEPLAN*, No. 5 (July).

FONTAINE, J.A. (1991), "La Administración de la Política Monetaria en Chile, 1985-89", *Cuadernos de Economía*, No. 83 (April).

KOURI, P., and M. PORTER (1974), "International Capital Flows and Portfolio Equilibrium", *Journal of Political Economy*, Vol. 82, No. 3 (May/June).

LABÁN, R., and F. LARRAÍN (1993), "Twenty Years of Experience with Capital Mobility in Chile", mimeo. (April).

LE FORT, G. (1994), "The Financial System and Macroeconomic Stability: The Chilean Experience", in S. Faruki (ed.), *Financial Liberalization: Comparative Experience in Asia and Latin America* (Washington, D.C.: Economic Development Institute of the World Bank).

LE FORT, G., and C. ROSS (1987), "La Devaluación Esperada: Una Aproximación Bayesiana. Chile 1974-1984", *Cuadernos de Economía*, Pontificia Universidad Católica de Chile (April).

LE FORT, G., and C. VARELA (1995), "The Chilean Capital Account in the 1990s and Regional Origins of Capital Flows", paper presented at the Pacific Economic Outlook Structural Meeting, Osaka, March.

LÓPEZ M., A., and J.P. TÉLLEZ C. (1995), "Una Historia de los Veinte para los Noventa", *Revista del Banco de la República de Colombia* (February) .

MORANDÉ, F. (1991), "Flujos de Capitales hacia Chile 1977-1982: Una Nueva Mirada a la Evidencia", in F. Morandé (ed.), *Movimientos de Capitales y Crisis Económica: Los Casos de Chile y Venezuela* (Ilades-Georgetown University).

POOLE, W. (1970), "Optimal Choice of Monetary Policy Instruments in a Simple Stochastic Model", *Quarterly Journal of Economics*, Vol. 85, No. 2 (May).

SANHUEZA, G. (1995), "Volatilidad vs. Nivel del Tipo de Cambio Real", mimeo., Banco Central de Chile.

RAZIN, A., and E. SADKA (1991), "Efficient Investment Incentives in the Presence of Capital Flight", *Journal of International Economics*, Vol. 31, No. 1-2 (August).

VALDÉS, S. (1992), "Financial Liberalization and the Capital Account: Chile 1974-84", mimeo. (March).

VALDÉS, S., and M. Soto (1995), "New selective capital controls in Chile: Are they effective?", mimeo., Universidad Católica de Chile, Santiago, September.

WILLIAMSON, J. (1991), "Costs and Benefits of Liberalizing the Chilean Capital Account", mimeo., The World Bank.

URIBE, J.D. (1995), "Flujos de Capital en Colombia", *Revista del Banco de la República de Colombia* (January).

URRUTIA M., M. (1991), "La Política Económica en 1991", *Revista del Banco de la República de Colombia* (December).

URRUTIA M., M. (1992), "La Política Económica en 1992", *Revista del Banco de la República de Colombia* (December).

URRUTIA M., M. (1993), "La Política Económica en 1993", *Revista del Banco de la República de Colombia* (December).

URRUTIA M., M. (1994), "La Política Económica en 1994", *Revista del Banco de la República de Colombia* (December).

URRUTIA M., M. (1995), "El Sistema de Bandas Cambiarias en Colombia", *Revista del Banco de la República de Colombia* (January).

ZAHLER, R. (1980), "Repercusiones Monetarias y Reales de la Apertura Financiera al Exterior. El caso Chileno: 1975-1978", *Revista de la CEPAL* (April).

Annex I

Colombia: Maturity of FFCT [a] and Reserve Requirement Ratio, according to Central Bank Resolution 22 of 1994

Maturity of FFCT (days)	Reserve requirement ratio (per cent)	Maturity of FFCT (days)	Reserve requirement ratio (per cent)
1-30	140.0	901-930	76.6
31-60	137.2	931-960	75.1
61-90	134.5	961-990	73.6
91-120	131.8	991-1020	72.1
121-150	129.2	1021-1050	70.7
151-180	126.6	1051-1080	69.3
191-210	124.1	1081-1110	67.9
211-240	121.6	1111-1140	66.5
241-270	119.2	1141-1170	65.2
271-300	116.8	1171-1200	63.9
301-330	114.5	1201-1230	62.7
331-360	112.2	1231-1260	61.4
361-390	110.0	1261-1290	60.2
391-420	107.8	1291-1320	59.0
421-450	105.7	1321-1350	57.8
451-480	103.6	1351-1380	56.7
481-510	101.5	1381-1410	55.5
511-540	99.5	1411-1440	54.4
541-570	97.5	1441-1470	53.3
571-600	95.6	1471-1500	52.3
601-630	93.7	1501-1530	51.2
631-660	91.8	1531-1560	50.2
661-690	90.0	1561-1590	49.2
691-720	88.2	1591-1620	48.2
721-750	86.4	1621-1650	47.3
751-780	84.7	1651-1680	46.3
781-810	83.0	1681-1710	45.4
811-840	81.4	1711-1741	44.5
841-870	79.7	1741-1770	43.6
871-900	78.2	1771-1800	42.8

Note: The required reserve is to be kept for the duration of the investment.
a Financial Foreign Currency Title (Título en Divisas par Financiaciones).

Annex II

International Arbitrage and the Reserve Requirement

1. Investment and required reserves for an equivalent period of one year

Consider the arbitrage condition that equates the rate of return of domestic and international financial investment, in this case for an investment with one-year maturity and where the reserve requirement should be kept at the central bank for the same period. In equation (1), i* is the external interest rate, i the domestic interest rate, ε is the reserve requirement ratio (RRR), and ê is the expected depreciation of the domestic currency.

$$(1) \quad (1 + i^*) = \frac{(1 + i)(1 - \varepsilon)}{(1 + \hat{e})} + \varepsilon$$

The solution for the RRR that fulfills this arbitrage condition, depends on the international interest rate differential, on the expected rate of currency depreciation, and on the level of domestic and external interest rate according to the following expression:

$$(2) \quad \varepsilon = \frac{(i^* - i) + \hat{e}(1 + i^*)}{\hat{e} - i}$$

2. Investment and RRR for an equivalent period of X months

For an investment of X months, with the required reserve to be kept for the maturity of the operation, it is possible to obtain an expression similar to (1). The only difference is that the relevant rate is the compound rate for the period in question.

$$(1') \quad (1 + i^*)^{X/12} = \frac{(1 + i)^{X/12}(1 - \varepsilon)}{(1 + \hat{e})^{X/12}} + \varepsilon$$

and, equivalent to (2):

$$(2') \quad \varepsilon = \frac{(1 + i^*)^{X/12}(1 + \hat{e})^{X/12} - (1 + i)^{X/12}}{(1 + \hat{e})^{X/12} - (1 + i)^{X/12}}$$

It can be shown that the necessary condition for the RRR to increase with the maturity of the operation, i.e. the partial derivative of ε with respect to X to be positive, is fulfilled whenever the domestic interest rate exceeds the external rate adjusted by exchange-rate expectations.

CAPITAL INFLOWS AND MACROECONOMIC POLICY IN SUB-SAHARAN AFRICA

Louis Kasekende
Damoni Kitabire
Matthew Martin*

Abstract

Since 1993, studies on private capital flows to developing countries have proliferated but virtually ignored sub-Saharan Africa. This reflects a perception that capital flows to this region are tiny. However, when the figures are adjusted for poor recording and updating, they reveal that flows to some economies in sub-Saharan Africa are as large in relation to GNP as those to other developing regions. This paper examines the scale, composition, causes, sustainability, macroeconomic effects and policy implications of capital flows to six sub-Saharan countries (Kenya, South Africa, the United Republic of Tanzania, Uganda, Zambia and Zimbabwe). It concludes that:

- *including returning flight capital mis-recorded under "private transfers", some sub-Saharan countries have seen capital inflows relative to GNP larger than developing countries in Asia or Latin America;*
- *the flows have been mainly private transfers and short-term bank loans;*
- *they reflect mainly transitory positive economic developments in the recipient economies, and only secondarily international interest rate differentials and macroeconomic reforms;*
- *there is therefore a high risk of unsustainability and reversal;*
- *capital flows have caused huge rises and volatility in exchange and interest rates;*
- *they were spent mainly on consumption and imports rather than investment or reserves;*
- *they have been procyclical, exacerbating commodity booms and deterring donor aid.*

Several policies are recommended to influence capital flows indirectly and to counter their negative effects (within the limits of economic and administrative capacity). The key priorities are:

- *improving recording mechanisms without driving flows back to parallel markets;*
- *analysing the effects of flows on the real and financial sectors, and on savings and investment;*
- *continuing with sterilized intervention and fiscal tightening, where desirable, without distorting long-term monetary and fiscal policy;*
- *sterilization by using selective reserve requirements and transfers of government deposits where feasible, given the health of the financial sector;*
- *limiting foreign purchases of treasury bills and domestic bonds, and removing distortionary incentives for capital inflows;*
- *liberalizing the capital account only gradually and after careful analysis;*
- *convincing donors to maintain programme aid to safeguard against future outflows.*

All of these issues will be subject to further analysis in a follow-up project by the six Governments, funded by the Governments of Sweden and Denmark.

* The views expressed in this paper are of the authors and do not reflect the views of the Bank of Uganda or the Ministry of Finance and Economic Planning of Uganda in any way. The authors are grateful to Andrew Bvumbe, Ibrahim Elbadawi, Stephany Griffith-Jones, Richard Ketley, Mohsin Khan, Polycarp Musinguzi, Stuart Kufeni, Benno Ndulu, Carmen Reinhart, Charles Ojwiya, Jonathan Leape, Allister Moon, Tim Lamont, Carlene Francis and Daudi Sajjabi for supplying their valuable time, opinions, data and materials during the preparation of this paper; and to the Swedish and Danish Governments for funding earlier work on capital flows to Africa. However, we remain responsible for any errors and misinterpretations in the paper.

I.   Introduction

During the last three years, there has been an increasing literature on private capital inflows to developing countries. In 1992 and 1993, attention focused on the rise in such inflows, their causes and nature. Gradually, it moved to their potential macroeconomic impact and the policy implications. In 1994 and 1995, following events in Mexico, it has concentrated on the sustainability of the inflows, and the policy implications of potential reversal.

Virtually all of the studies have focused on Latin America, though some authors have also examined East Asian experiences. Analysis of Eastern Europe is extremely rare (Calvo, Sahay and Vegh, 1995; Griffith-Jones, 1995), and that of Africa is virtually non-existent (with the notable exception of the excellent study by Asea and Reinhart, 1995). Even the most comprehensive recent analysis and survey of the literature (Fernandez-Arias and Montiel, 1995) has concluded that there is only impressionistic evidence of private capital inflows to sub-Saharan Africa, where "capital inflows have not materialized". Africa has continued to be analysed from the view that most of its capital inflows causing a ":Dutch Disease" effect are aid inflows (see, for example, Younger, 1992). Figures quoted in an UNCTAD document (TD/8/ITNC) indicate that Africa's relative share of inflows to developing countries has declined considerably, from about 14 per cent during 1982-1986 to about 5 per cent during 1992-1994.

The key areas examined in the literature have been the scale and composition of private capital inflow, their causes and sustainability, their effects on macroeconomic stability, and their responsiveness to policy measures. This paper analyses the characteristics of capital inflows to sub-Saharan Africa in each of these areas, showing the similarities and differences with other regions of the developing world. A debate is also developing as to the nature of capital Africa should attract. Scholars have warned that short-term capital inflows, subject to abrupt reversal, will be very disruptive to the domestic financial sector, in particular in the presence of existing weaknesses in the sector (Lipumba, 1994; Calvo, Sahay and Vegh, 1995). Some argue for Foreign Direct Investment (FDI) which is less susceptible to transient financial shocks. But counter-arguments have also been made to the effect that FDI is equally volatile, as dividends and retained earnings will be quickly repatriated during a financial crisis.

It is important to emphasize at the outset that both national and international data on capital inflows to Africa are extremely unreliable. Data issues in other regions have centred on distinguishing between private and official inflows; gross and net inflows; short- and long-term capital; bank and non-bank flows; and between debt and non-debt-creating flows. It has been necessary to rely fairly extensively on data from either the IMF (*International Financial Statistics*), OECD (*Financing and External Debt of Developing Countries*) or the World Bank (*World Debt Tables*) (Fernandez-Arias and Montiel, 1995). For many countries in sub-Saharan Africa the data problems are more fundamental: they have poor recording systems for virtually all capital inflow data, and many inflows are recorded in the current account or under errors/omissions.[1] In addition, even superficial comparison of global and country data indicates huge underestimates and unreliable categorizations of inflows in global data and particularly for sub-Saharan Africa.

These data problems will be addressed in a forthcoming project funded by the Swedish and Danish Governments on *Capital Inflows and Macroeconomic Policy* which will seek to clarify many of these issues. Owing to data and other limitations, the scope of this paper is limited. It focuses on six countries for which reasonably reliable data is available (Kenya, South Africa, the United Republic of Tanzania, Uganda, Zambia and Zimbabwe), with particular emphasis on the experiences of Uganda, Zambia and the United Republic of Tanzania. The latter county witnessed one of the largest surges in capital inflows in the early 1990s with dramatic macroeconomic effects.[2] A brief summary of the liberalization process in the above mentioned countries is given in Appendix 1.

It also has to be recognized that there are diverse experiences in Africa in general. The speed and sequencing of policy reforms has varied across countries (Kasekende and Martin, 1995). Notwithstanding, the policy regime in a number of countries in the region is currently more conducive to both domestic and foreign investment. Foreign-exchange markets have been extensively liberalized to a point where even the capital account has been highly decontrolled. Some countries are currently receiving inflows which are significant relative to GDP, and the less desirable effects of such inflows are emerging. In the recent past, Kenya, Uganda and Zambia have experienced disruptive effects originating from capital inflows. The reform of the policy regime has been frequently credited for the resurgence in capital inflows to selected countries in Africa especially by the IMF and World Bank.[3] While domestic policy reforms have, without doubt, contributed to the marked improvement of capital inflows to Africa, they cannot fully account for the varied country experiences. It would be quite interesting to assess the factors that have played an important role in stimulating private inflows to Africa.

II. Scale and composition of private capital inflows

In absolute terms, the scale of private capital inflows to other developing regions dwarfs inflows to sub-Saharan Africa (SSA). According to the latest World Bank estimates, based on capital-account and equity/debt flows, inflows to all developing countries averaged more than $131 billion a year during 1990-1994, peaking at about $190 billion in 1993 (table 1). Of this amount about $2.1 billion a year went to SSA countries, peaking at about $3.4 billion in 1990. Even in relation to macroeconomic variables such as GDP or exports, inflows to SSA based on capital-account recordings were much lower than those to Latin America, East or South Asia. However, when private transfers are included in these flows, these are comparable or even higher than those to other developing countries in Asia and Latin America.

The main reason for the underestimates of inflows to SSA in published global databases (apart from the fact that they do not show the most recent trends) is the specific composition of inflows to many SSA countries, which makes them much harder to measure, and the absence of recording systems for the main types of inflows.[4]

Firstly, the main inflows to SSA have been difficult to record or classify. With the loosening of borrowing restrictions, short-term bank loans to the private sector for trade financing have grown considerably. At the same time, because it has not historically been an important inflow, virtually no country in SSA has adequate recording systems for monitoring private sector debt, especially short-term debt. Most countries do not even attempt to record inflows, believing that such intrusion may prove counter-productive to the spirit and intent of liberalization. Moreover, large amounts of capital inflows by residents and non-residents are mis-recorded in the current account under a residual item, "private transfers".[5]

These transfers have risen dramatically since SSA countries liberalized their foreign-exchange systems, by introducing, first, "own-funds" imports, where no questions were asked about the source of the funds, and later, foreign-exchange bureaux, where all current-account transactions may be conducted. Originally, it was assumed that the source of funds for the bureau system were unrecorded exports and workers' remittances. However, more recently it has become clear that, due to inadequate monitoring and supervision of bureaux transactions, virtually any capital-account transaction can be conducted through the bureaux.[6] In other words, the current account is entirely porous and the capital account has effectively been liberalized. In some countries, large amounts of flight capital have returned (or left) through the bureaux; and non-residents are thought to conduct frequent, albeit small, capital-account transactions. However, inadequate recording procedures make it impossible to separate out the proportion of bureaux inflows which are capital-related, let alone to distinguish among types of capital-related inflows. In short, inflows related to the current account produce "capital inflows" whose scale in relation to the economy is comparable to, and in some cases exceeds, that of other regions.

The more easily measurable inflows to SSA fell since the early 1990s, from around $5 billion a year to under $1.2 billion. The composition of these inflows evolved somewhat differently from other regions (see table 2):

- Medium- and long-term commercial lending to both the public and the private sector collapsed after the debt crisis as it did in Latin America, but to an even more dramatic degree. In 1978-1982, such lending accounted for around half of total inflows, but in 1990-1993 outflows virtually offset all non-debt inflows.

- Short-term bank loans have always accounted for a larger proportion of inflows than in other regions and became even more pronounced in 1990-1993; even though they were only around 20 per cent of inflows in 1978-1982.

- FDI rose sharply as a proportion of total inflows over the period 1990-1993, but remained relatively small (at around $1.6 billion a year and lower in real terms than in the early 1980s) and confined largely to six SSA countries.

- Portfolio investment has grown recently, with booms in most regional stock markets and the launching of several new regional portfolio funds (with the exception of South Africa), but still remains relatively small; in 1990-1993 it did not exceed $120 million a year.

Table 1

CAPITAL FLOWS TO DEVELOPING COUNTRIES AND SUB-SAHARAN AFRICA

($ billion)

	1990	1991	1992	1993	1994
All developing countries					
FDI	24.10	34.40	45.20	68.50	78.20
Portfolio investment	2.80	7.10	13.90	45.80	34.50
Long-term private flows	5.80	10.30	19.10	23.10	20.40
Private flows (minimum)	32.70	51.80	78.20	137.40	133.10
Short-term flows	17.00	20.90	39.30	33.60	23.70
Private non-guaranted flows (PNG)	9.30	8.40	20.70	19.80	27.40
Private flows (maximum)	59.00	81.10	138.20	190.80	184.20
Long-term official flows	28.40	27.60	23.20	23.40	16.80
Grants	25.10	32.50	27.10	23.60	22.80
IMF credit	0.05	3.20	1.20	0.70	1.60
Total all flows	112.55	144.40	189.70	238.50	225.40
Profits on FDI	-17.70	-18.50	-21.20	-23.10	-25.10
Interest on long-term private debt	-32.50	-30.40	-26.90	-23.80	-28.00
Private transfers (minimum)	-17.50	2.90	30.10	90.50	80.00
Interest on PNG	-4.90	-5.60	-5.90	-6.40	-7.60
Interest on short-term debt	-15.50	-17.60	-15.30	-16.70	-18.10
Private transfers (maximum)	-11.60	9.00	68.90	120.80	105.40
Interest on long-term official debt	-20.40	-22.10	-22.10	-24.20	-26.20
IMF charges	-2.50	-2.50	-2.40	-2.30	-1.80
Total net transfers	19.05	47.70	95.90	142.00	118.60
Sub-Saharan Africa					
FDI	0.90	1.90	1.80	1.90	2.30
Portfolio investment	0.00	0.00	0.00	0.20	0.90
Long-term private flows	-0.03	0.04	-1.40	0.30	-0.40
Private flows (minimum)	0.87	1.94	0.40	2.40	2.80
Short-term flows	2.30	-0.50	1.20	0.80	-1.90
PNG (to private sector)	0.20	0.04	0.10	0.02	-0.20
Private flows (maximum)	3.37	1.48	1.70	3.22	0.70
Long-term official flows	4.70	4.00	4.90	4.10	4.00
Grants	10.40	9.60	9.60	8.50	8.50
IMF credit	-0.30	-0.03	0.00	-0.20	0.45
Total all flows	18.17	15.05	16.20	15.62	13.65
Profits on FDI	-1.70	-1.60	-1.70	-1.70	-1.80
Interest on long-term private debt	-1.30	-1.40	-1.50	-0.60	-0.80
Private transfers (minimum)	-2.13	-1.06	-2.80	0.10	0.20
Interest on short-term debt	-0.70	-0.60	-0.60	-0.50	-0.50
Interest on long-term official debt	-2.40	-2.90	-1.80	-2.10	-2.40
Private transfers (maximum)	-2.73	-5.02	-3.90	-1.68	-4.80
Interest on PNG	-0.30	-0.30	-0.30	-0.30	-0.20
IMF charges	-0.20	-0.20	-0.20	-0.10	-0.10
Total net transfers	11.57	8.05	10.10	10.32	7.85

Source: World Bank IECIF Database, January 1995.

Note: A large portion - but not all - of short-term and private non-guaranted inflows are private. The private inflows/transfers are shown excluding (minimum) and including (maximum) short-term and private non-guaranted flows.

Table 2

COMPOSITION OF PRIVATE CAPITAL INFLOWS TO DEVELOPING REGIONS

(Per cent of total)

	1978-1982			1990-1993		
	Latin America	*Asia*	*Sub-Saharan Africa*	*Latin America*	*Asia*	*Sub-Saharan Africa*
FDI	15.1	15.0	9.8	33.0	37.5	140.3
Portfolio investment	4.9	3.6	0.0	68.1	14.2	10.9
Long-term bank loans	63.6	53.9	53.9	-32.1	21.7	-143.5
Short-term loans	16.4	27.5	36.3	30.5	27.0	92.3

Source: IMF, *International Financial Statistics*, various issues; and World Bank, *World Debt Tables*, various issues.

Aggregate net private capital inflows to the six countries in our sample were greatly influenced by the experience of South Africa. This country was a net exporter of capital in the period 1986-1989. However, the direction was reversed in the period 1990-1993 (see table 3). The huge outflow of private capital from South Africa resulted in the sample countries recording a net export of private capital of $6,195.6 million in the period 1986-1989. This was reversed to a net inflow of private capital amounting to $2,072.6 million in 1990-1993. Excluding South Africa, the five remaining countries received private capital inflows amounting to $851.4 million in 1986-1989 and decreasing slightly to $868.6 million in 1990-1993.

The experience of Zambia also presents some interesting trends in private capital inflows. Net private capital inflows amounted to $714 million in the period 1986-1989 (see table 3). Subsequently, they declined significantly to $240 million. By contrast, the remaining countries in the sample experienced sizable growth in inflows during 1990-1993 compared to the period 1986-1989.

Excluding official inflows, it is estimated that net private capital flows of the six countries as a ratio to GDP moved to an inflow of 0.8 per cent in 1990-1993, from a net outflow of 1.2 per cent in 1986-1989. Zimbabwe and Uganda recorded an increase in net private capital flows from -0.4 and 3.2 per cent in 1986-1989 to 2.0 and 4.7 per cent in 1990-1993, respectively. Similarly, Kenya and the United Republic

of Tanzania experienced an increase in net private capital inflows from 1.7 and 5.5 per cent to 2.8 and 9.1 per cent of GDP, respectively, in the two reference periods (table 4).

By contrast, private capital inflows as a ratio to GDP fell markedly in Zambia, from 6.0 per cent in 1986-1989 to 1.7 per cent in 1990-1993. One distinguishing factor between Zambia and the other five countries is that macroeconomic instability was much greater in 1990-1993 compared to 1986-1989. In particular, inflation increased from an average of about 50 per cent in 1986-1989 to an average of 149 per cent in 1990-1993. In the case of Kenya and Zimbabwe, the moderate increase in inflation between the two periods did not discourage private capital inflows.

Overall, trends in inflows to SSA are similar to those for other small countries relying predominantly on short-term bank loans and FDI rather than medium- and long-term loans or portfolio inflows (S. Calvo and Reinhart, 1995). In terms of their sustainability, it is significant that the less volatile medium- and long-term bank loans and FDI virtually cancel each other out, leaving SSA economies excessively dependent on short-term bank inflows, which could be unsustainable (table 5).

As indicated above, South Africa dwarfs the other five countries as it accounts for about 58 per cent of total net private capital inflows to the six countries in the sample. Apart from the size of inflows,

Table 3

CAPITAL FLOWS TO SELECTED COUNTRIES IN SUB-SAHARAN AFRICA

($ million)

	Including private transfers			Excluding private transfers		
	1986-1989	*1990-1993*	*1986-1993*	*1986-1989*	*1990-1993*	*1986-1993*
Kenya	647.7	779.6	1427.3	327.0	252.0	579.0
South Africa	-6655.0	1243.0	-5412.0	-7047.0	1204.0	-5843.0
United Rep. of Tanzania	765.2	943.9	1709.1	-214.0	-8.0	-222.0
Uganda	450.0	586.7	1036.7	31.0	-20.0	11.0
Zambia	597.0	200.0	797.0	714.0	240.0	954.0
Zimbabwe	-97.7	471.2	373.5	-6.6	404.6	398.0
Total	-4292.8	4224.4	-68.4	-6195.6	2072.6	-4123.0

Source: See table 2.
Note: A minus sign indicates a net outflow.

the nature of inflows to South Africa is quite different from those of the remaining countries in the sample. South Africa received significant resources under the categories of private long-term debt and portfolio investments, equivalent to 0.8 per cent and 0.4 per cent of GDP in the 1990 -1993 period. Of the remaining five countries, it is only Zimbabwe that received meagre inflows under these two categories . The surprising finding is that even for countries that have had stock markets for a relatively long period, e.g. Zimbabwe and Kenya, investors are yet to be significantly attracted to take shareholding in domestic investment.

The other interesting finding revealed by the data is that investor confidence has greatly improved in South Africa. In the period 1990-1992, South Africa received substantial resources under the category of short-term inflows (net), amounting to $2,181 million with a peak in 1991. But since 1992 the shift is in favour of portfolio investment and private long-term debt.

Short-term capital inflows have exhibited a very high degree of volatility. In a number of instances countries have recorded high inflows in one year followed by a net outflow in the subsequent recording period. For example, in 1987, Kenya received net inflows under this account amounting to 2.6 per cent

of GDP but this was followed by an outflow equivalent to -0.8 per cent of GDP. The experience was repeated in 1990-1991, when Kenya allowed holders of foreign-exchange certificates to negotiate premiums in secondary market trading. As a result, Kenya received net short-term inflows amounting to about $300 million (equivalent to 3.2 per cent of GDP) in 1990, but following the reversal of the policy, Kenya experienced an outflow of $273 million (equivalent to 3.6 per cent of GDP) in 1991. Similarly, Zambia has recorded wide swings in net short-term capital inflows. Net inflows equivalent to 4.2 per cent of GDP were recorded in 1988 as Zambia was borrowing short-term for its balance of payments; these were followed by outflows in 1989 and 1990 equivalent to 2.4 and 3.3 per cent of GDP, respectively, when the loans matured and had to be serviced. For most of the countries in the region, short-term capital inflows are accounted for by short-term trade credits.

FDI has been mainly directed to Zambia in the period 1986-1993, equivalent to 3.6 and 2.9 per cent of GDP in 1986-1989 and 1990-1993, respectively. This reflects investments in the mining industries. Kenya, the United Republic of Tanzania, and Zimbabwe have also benefitted from FDI but the inflows as a percentage of GDP have only been between 0.16 and 0.3 per cent. For the six countries aggregated, FDI amounted to $279.8 million in 1986-

Table 4

PRIVATE CAPITAL FLOWS TO SELECTED COUNTRIES IN SUB-SAHARAN AFRICA

(Per cent of GDP)

	Including private transfers			Excluding private transfers		
	1986-1989	*1990-1993*	*1986-1993*	*1986-1989*	*1990-1993*	*1986-1993*
Kenya	1.71	2.75	2.15	0.86	0.89	0.87
South Africa	-2.44	0.29	-0.77	-2.59	0.28	-0.83
United Rep. of Tanzania	5.50	9.05	7.02	-1.54	-0.08	-0.91
Uganda	3.21	4.69	3.91	0.22	-0.16	0.04
Zambia	6.00	1.69	3.66	7.18	2.03	4.38
Zimbabwe	-0.44	2.01	0.82	-0.03	1.72	0.87
Total	-1.16	0.81	-0.01	-1.67	0.40	-0.46

Source: See table 2.
Note: A minus sign indicates a net outflow.

1989, increasing to $475.2 million in 1990-1993, equivalent to 0.09 per cent of GDP (table 6).

The other development that distinguishes South Africa and Zambia from the remaining four countries is that the latter countries receive substantial resources recorded as private transfers. If such transfers are included in the broad assessment of private capital inflows, the six countries exported just over $4,292.8 million in 1986-1989 but received over $4,224.4 million in 1990-1993. Excluding South Africa, the region was a net recipient of private capital during the two sub-periods; private capital inflows increased from $2,363 million in 1986-1990 to $2,981 million in 1990-1993. In the latter period private transfers accounted for over 50 per cent of the total private capital inflows, equivalent to about 0.5 per cent of GDP. Most of the private transfers were accounted for by Kenya, Uganda and the United Republic of Tanzania. These three countries recorded receipts of private transfers equivalent to 2.0, 4.9 and 9.1 per cent of GDP, respectively. Zimbabwe also recorded a marked increase in private transfers during the 1990s, especially in 1992 when it recorded receipts equivalent to 0.6 per cent of GDP.

Finally, it has not been possible to collect data on costs or maturity of inflows, particularly of bonds, or on the sources of inflows (especially the division between domestic and foreign investors). These variables would be expected to have major implications for the sustainability or volatility of inflows and the resulting policy response (see IMF, 1995; and Ffrench-Davis and Griffith-Jones, 1994).

III. Causes for the evolution of capital flows

Having discussed the main features of the capital flows, we now examine the factors that have led to their increase. The factors underlying capital inflows to developing countries tend to be divided into external or "push" factors, on the one hand, and domestic or "pull" factors, on the other.

The "pull" factors include:

- political and economic reforms boosting confidence in the economy;
- debt restructuring to reduce the debt overhang and enhance the sustainability of foreign-exchange inflows;
- liberalization of foreign-exchange markets and the current or capital account of the balance of payments;

Table 5

COMPOSITION OF PRIVATE CAPITAL INFLOWS TO SUB-SAHARAN AFRICA[a]

	$ million			Per cent share in total private capital inflows
	1986-1989	1990-1993	1986-1993	1990-1993
FDI	279.8	475.2	755.0	11.2
Short-term debt, net	-3061.0	1379.0	-1682.0	32.6
Long-term debt, net	-2235.0	-1502.0	-3737.0	-35.5
Portfolio investment	-1179.4	1720.4	541.0	40.7
Private transfers	1902.8	2151.8	4054.6	50.9
Total	-4292.8	4224.4	-68.4	100.0

Source: See table 2.
   a   Kenya, South Africa, United Republic of Tanzania, Uganda, Zambia, and Zimbabwe.

- proliferation of specific incentives and simplification of procedures for direct and portfolio investment (Gooptu, 1994);

- liberalization of restrictions on private sector foreign borrowing;

- very high real domestic interest rates (including the effect of the change in the exchange rate).

The major "push" factors have been identified as:

- the decline in international interest rates;

- the cyclical downturn in developed countries, which reduced economic activity and demand for investment funds;

- the trend towards diversification of assets by portfolio investors, determined by the maximum stock of investments in emerging markets that such investors wish to hold;

- changes in regulations in developed countries which made investment in emerging markets easier and more profitable.

Overall, the literature has concluded that both factors were involved, with some stressing "push" factors, especially interest-rate differentials (Calvo, Leiderman and Reinhart, 1992 and 1994; Asea and Reinhart, 1995; Chuhan et al., 1993; Fernandez-Arias, 1994), and others stressing "pull" factors (Edwards, 1991; Hernandez and Rudolph, 1995; Niehans, 1994).

One of the problems with much of the literature on causes of capital inflows is that it tends to rely on econometric analysis of relative prices (notably interest-rate differentials), which takes too little account of the influence on inflows of structural factors in individual countries or of the subjective "sentiment" factors influencing international capital markets (Fernandez-Arias and Montiel, 1995). As a result, some of the literature has attempted to judge the influence of different "pull" factors by trends in the stock markets of the recipient countries, or in their secondary market debt prices, as if these trends were objective measures of the credibility of the recipient country. This is a particularly dubious method to use for SSA countries, where there are large subjective "risk premia" in all such prices, and where individual distorted trade patterns based on speculative information can determine prices.

There has been little econometric analysis of the causes of capital inflows to SSA countries with the exception of Asea and Reinhart (1995), due partly to lack of data. Given the less "formal" nature of the inflows, "push" factors, especially United States short-term interest rates, have had much less of an impact than in other regions (Asea and Reinhart, 1995), suggesting that inflows might be more sustainable, but African interest rates were highly significant in this study.

As a result of the poor sequencing of adjustment reforms, it seems likely that several transitory "pull"

Table 6

COMPOSITION OF CAPITAL FLOWS TO SUB-SAHARAN AFRICA, BY COUNTRY

($ million)

	FDI		Short-term debt, net		Long-term debt, net		Portfolio investment		Private transfers		Total		
	1986 -1989	1990 -1993	1986 -1989	1990 -1993	1986 -1989	1990 -1993	1986 -1989	1990 -1993	1986 -1989	1990 -1993	1986 -1989	1990 -1993	1986 -1993
Kenya	138.0	84.0	87.0	115.0	102.0	53.0	0.0	0.0	320.7	527.6	647.7	779.6	1427.3
South Africa	-171.0	-26.0	-3416.0	1241.0	-2376.0	-1760.0	-1084.0	1749.0	392.0	39.0	-6655.0	1243.0	-5412.0
United Republic of Tanzania	1.0	31.0	-215.0	-39.0	39.0	205.0	0.0	0.0	979.2	951.9	765.2	943.9	1709.1
Uganda	3.0	7.0	28.0	-27.0	...	...	0.0	0.0	419.0	606.7	450.0	586.7	1036.7
Zambia	360.0	342.0	354.0	-102.0	...	...	0.0	0.0	-117.0	-40.0	597.0	200.0	797.0
Zimbabwe	-51.2	37.2	101.0	191.0	...	...	-95.4	-28.6	-91.1	66.6	-97.7	471.2	373.5
Total	279.8	475.2	-3061.0	1379.0	-2235.0	-1502.0	-1179.4	1720.4	1902.8	2151.8	-4292.8	4224.4	-68.4

(Per cent of GDP)

	FDI		Short-term debt, net		Long-term debt, net		Portfolio investment		Private transfers		Total		
	1986 -1989	1990 -1993	1986 -1989	1990 -1993	1986 -1989	1990 -1993	1986 -1989	1990 -1993	1986 -1989	1990 -1993	1986 -1989	1990 -1993	1986 -1993
Kenya	0.36	0.30	0.23	0.40	0.27	0.19	0.00	0.00	0.85	1.86	1.71	2.75	2.15
South Africa	-0.06	-0.01	-1.25	0.29	-0.87	-0.40	-0.40	0.40	0.14	0.01	-2.44	0.29	-0.77
United Republic of Tanzania	0.01	0.30	-1.54	-0.37	0.00	0.00	0.00	0.00	7.04	9.12	5.50	9.05	7.02
Uganda	0.02	0.06	0.20	-0.22	0.00	0.00	0.00	0.00	2.99	4.85	3.21	4.69	3.91
Zambia	3.62	2.90	3.56	-0.86	0.00	0.00	0.00	0.00	-1.18	-0.34	6.00	1.69	3.66
Zimbabwe	-0.23	0.16	0.46	0.81	0.18	0.87	-0.43	-0.12	-0.41	0.28	-0.44	2.01	0.82
Total	0.08	0.09	-0.83	0.26	-0.60	-0.29	-0.32	0.33	0.51	0.41	-1.16	0.81	-0.01

Source: See table 2.

factors were even more important in SSA countries, notably:

- Extremely high real domestic interest rates on Treasury Bills and Central Bank Bills were a significant factor in capital inflows to Zambia, Kenya, Uganda and Zimbabwe during the initial stages of financial liberalization (see also Asea and Reinhart, 1995). In a number of countries in SSA, financial liberalization was launched at a time when the Government budget still depended heavily on bank financing. Efforts to manage liquidity and at the same time mobilize resources to finance the fiscal deficit through the sale of Government and/or Central Bank paper resulted in high discount rates and caused a self-sustaining cycle through exchange-rate appreciation and even higher interest rates, attracting further capital inflows (see also Galbis, 1993; Montiel, 1994; and Roe and Sowa, 1995). In addition, private sector borrowers were pushed to seek foreign loans in order to avoid high domestic interest rates.

- Temporary booms in export prices which (as in earlier periods - see Hadjimichael et al., 1995) attracted large export pre-financing loans and speculative capital inflows. This was particularly the case in Kenya and Uganda in 1994-1995.

One other factor explored has been the "spillover" effect from the crisis in Mexico on inflows to all developing countries and of inflows from large countries on smaller countries (S.Calvo and Reinhart, 1995). Spillover effects from Mexico on SSA are not thought to have been great, being overruled by regional factors, with the exception of South Africa.

A review of South Africa's international borrowing reveals that delayed entry of South Africa into the international capital markets was to a great extent due to the Mexican crisis. There was a global bond issue by South Africa in December 1994 but this did not perform well as investors shifted to higher quality bonds at the time. Interest in South African bonds was only regained in the second half of 1995. This has been in part influenced by the high yield on the South African bonds and the stable exchange rate. Trends in capital inflows to Kenya and Uganda have also varied sharply with perceptions of relative economic prospects and arbitrage opportunities from relative trends in interest and exchange rates. Similarly, there is growing evidence that capital inflows to South Africa have influenced the entire Southern African region, partly because South African

companies are borrowing for investment in neighbouring countries.

A deeper analysis of the numbers in the sample countries in the study reveals that most short-term borrowing is in the form of trade credit. Following the liberalization of the foreign-exchange markets in these countries, exporters and importers found it cheaper to access short-term trade financing since foreign interest rates were far lower than interest rates prevailing in these countries (see table 7). This is explained by a combination of pull and push factors. Since such inflows are normally for very short periods and are highly volatile, there is need for a rapid restructuring of the financial sectors in the recipient countries to reduce intermediation margins. There is evidence in the numbers presented in table 6 to suggest that countries in the sample received external capital on account of the very high interest-rate differential. In the case of Kenya, this is evidenced by the receipt of short-term debt which shifted from an outflow of about $70 million in 1988 to an inflow of about $350 million in 1989-1990. Similarly, the flow of short-term debt to Zimbabwe shifted from a net outflow of $8 million in 1986-1988 to an inflow of $290 million in 1989-1990. In addition, foreign export creditors have an advantage as it is common for foreign Governments to guarantee such lines of credit. This substantially reduces the risk borne by the creditor agency. The ECGD of the United Kingdom and COFACE of France have actively participated in guaranteeing credit to SSA.

Further analysis of the data on private capital inflows reveals that recent developments, especially in the policy environment, are critical in accounting for the inflows to the six countries in our sample. In the case of South Africa, political factors influenced capital flows to the extent of reversing the outflows that occurred in the 1980s to inflows in the 1990s. In particular, the reforms initiated by De Klerk in 1989 and the release of Nelson Mandela in 1990 improved the credit rating of South Africa, resulting in a resurgence of short-term trade financing. Further, investor risk assessment improved following successful abolition of the Financial Rand in March 1995.[7] The liberalization of the foreign-exchange markets, permitting residents to hold foreign exchange in the domestic banking system, has also played a catalytic role in the return of flight capital and increasing remittances by nationals working abroad in the countries in our sample, excluding South Africa. The countries have attracted private transfers that represented mainly returning flight capital, workers remittances and mis-reported capital-account

Table 7

REAL LENDING RATES[a] IN SELECTED COUNTRIES OF SUB-SAHARAN AFRICA

(Per cent per annum)

	1986	1987	1988	1989	1990	1991	1992	1993	1994
Kenya	10.1	8.8	6.7	6.6	2.4	0.2	-9.5	9.2	-
South Africa[b]	10.0	15.0	18.0	18.0	18.0	17.0	14.0	13.0	13.0
United Republic of Tanzania	-20.4	-20.9	-3.0	0.4	10.3	8.7	8.9	15.6	-
Uganda	-128.0	-238.0	-143.6	-40.2	-119.0	-12.9	-20.9	13.9	-
Zambia	-23.8	-22.0	-38.0	n.a.	-72.0	n.a.	-142.4	-76.0	-
Zimbabwe	-1.3	-0.5	5.6	0.1	-5.4	-7.3	-7.1	8.4	-

Source: IMF, *International Financial Statistics*, various issues.
   a Real lending rates are equivalent to nominal interest rates net of inflation.
   b Figures are for the nominal bank rate.

transactions and short-term inflows, mainly on account of financing trade. The presence of sizeable private transfers in the overall private capital inflows complicates judgement on the volatility of inflows. If these are transformed into holding of real assets, the private transfers will be less susceptible to high volatility. There are chances that private transfers may be sustained as long as attractive policies are maintained such as allowing residents and/or non-residents to open foreign-exchange denominated accounts in the domestic banking system.

As countries reduce their debt burden, improve on import cover and maintain a track record of private sector inflows such as private transfers, their credit rating in international capital markets will improve. This is likely to trigger increased (primarily short-term) capital inflows. One interesting observation from the numbers is that FDI and private short-term debt can be quite sensitive to the macroeconomic environment.

All indications are that it is difficult to fully assess whether inflows to the region are of a temporary nature. This makes it difficult to design an appropriate policy response. To the extent that the private capital inflows are subject to misjudgment, countries in the region should design corrective measures, well aware that the inflows are temporary. Given that the financial sectors of countries in the region are inefficient and

that effectiveness of monetary policy remains weak, the countries are faced with a big challenge of absorbing such inflows without excessive appreciation in the domestic currency.

IV. Sustainability of capital inflows

The balance of international opinion on the sustainability of private capital inflows has undergone a virtual U-turn in the last two years. Though some authors (Devlin, Ffrench-Davis and Griffith-Jones, 1994; UNCTAD, 1994) have been warning of problems for two years, opinion in the IFls and the financial community was that capital inflows were sustainable because they reflected a fundamental revival of confidence in emerging markets and sustainable "push" factors, though their magnitude might decline over time. Even at the end of 1994 Washington sources were suggesting that a "soft landing" (i.e. a gradual decline in net inflows) was possible, unless there was a sharp rise in international interest rates or collapse in recipient country economies (Fernandez-Arias, 1994; World Bank, 1994c).

In 1995, opinion moved more towards the "hard landing" (i.e. large fall in net inflows) and "crash" (i.e. large net outflows) scenarios (see Fernandez-

Arias and Montiel, 1995, p. 28), with organizations such as the IMF (1995a) and the Bank for International Settlements (1995a) suggesting, with the benefit of hindsight, that the inflows were unsustainable.

Opinions in some African countries have undergone a similar evolution, largely in response to actual trends in inflows. Overall, the causes of inflows to Africa identified above would appear to indicate that the stabilizing influence of the lower weight of "push" factors might be offset by the higher weight of temporary/volatile "pull" factors and regional influences.

The composition of inflows to SSA makes them *a priori* less sustainable. It is generally accepted that short-term and .portfolio inflows are highly volatile (Griffith-Jones, 1995; IMF, 1995a; Reisen, 1993). It has been shown that FDI exhibits some measure of volatility (Claessens et al., 1995). If we add private transfers, the most volatile type of inflows in SSA, to the volatility ranking of Turner (1991), capital inflows to Africa have been highly volatile.

Nevertheless, until inflows actually declined sharply, opinion in some quarters was euphoric about the prospects for continued inflows, on the (untested) assumption that permanent "pull" factors were at work. Without a doubt, as in the Mexican case, there will soon be many sources telling African Governments that the inflows were "obviously" unsustainable, and identifying previously ignored economic "fundamentals" which should have indicated to anyone with reasonable intelligence that the inflows could not continue.

The key issue for African Governments is to avoid euphoria and retrospective judgements, and to focus on objective measures of the sustainability of inflows. The most convincing suggestion so far has been by Dadush et al. (1994), to the effect that net liabilities ought not to be more than 200 per cent of exports or, in dynamic form, that the change in net liabilities (measured as the ratio of the current-account deficit to exports) ought not to be more than twice the change in exports (averaged over a period of four years). This measure has been criticised for its assumption of equal weighting for all types of inflows, ignoring the higher volatility of short-term and portfolio inflows. In addition, it would be inaccurate for many SSA countries because it would include the current-account private transfer inflows. A more accurate measurement for SSA countries would be the change in net liabilities (measured as the current-

account deficit *excluding* private transfers) compared to the change in exports. In addition, to take account of different levels of volatility, it would be desirable to check short-term and portfolio inflows as a proportion of total inflows and in relation to GDP and exports. Sustainability also ought to be judged against the fact that nowadays domestic investors can far more easily denominate their holdings in foreign exchange, thereby increasing the vulnerability to outflows.

Finally, SSA Governments should be mindful of the large volume of literature indicating that inflows to developing countries (and financial inflows in general) are intrinsically volatile, having produced six crises in Latin America in the last 150 years (see Griffith-Jones, 1995). Perhaps the most prudent guideline has been provided by Williamson (1994): to regard all positive shocks as temporary, and all negative shocks as permanent. As Griffith-Jones has pointed out, if a country bases policy action on assuming that inflows are permanent, they are more likely to become temporary, as in the case of Mexico, while, if it more prudently assumes they are temporary, they are more likely to be permanent, as in the case of Chile.

V. Macroeconomic impact of private capital inflows

Many of the economies in SSA have over the past decade or so implemented wide-ranging policies intended to promote efficiency and growth. It then becomes difficult to assess whether capital inflows are a cause or effect of macroeconomic stabilization. In particular, ODA inflows have played a critical role in the reform process of a number of countries in the region. Because of such inflows, with the associated domestic financing of the budget, member countries have been able to increase both the current-account and budget deficits as a percentage of GDP without threatening macroeconomic stability. A related issue is the mis-recording of capital-account transactions in the current account as private transfers. To the extent that private transfers are large, the current-account deficit to GDP will be underestimated.

As indicated earlier, all countries in the sample received much higher private capital inflows in 1990-1993 than in the period 1986-1989 with the exception of Zambia. Private capital inflows have until recently often been seen as having largely positive effects; namely overcoming foreign-exchange and import constraints; supplementing domestic savings and investment; smoothing national expenditure by compensating for negative terms-of-trade shocks; raising the microeconomic efficiency of production, especially by reducing financial intermediation spreads and by supplying technology and skills through FDI. However, more recently, developing countries have come to realize that private capital inflows can also have negative effects, especially on macroeconomic stability, linked closely to the above positive effects. For example:

- In attempting to overcome foreign-exchange constraints, capital inflows could lead to sharp exchange-rate appreciation.

- If capital inflows are spent on imports, overcoming the import constraint can lead to rising current-account deficits.

- If spent on consumption, capital inflows can discourage domestic savings and have no effect on the size or productivity of investment.

- If financial markets are underdeveloped and performing poorly, large external inflows can reduce their intermediation efficiency still further, causing loss of monetary control and greater volatility.

- Overall, if capital inflows are procyclical, they exaggerate all the destabilizing effects of terms-of-trade changes.

This section focuses on each of these effects in turn.

A. *Effects on the exchange rate*

The single most important effect of capital inflows has been on the exchange rate. They have led to sharp appreciation in some instances and undermined efforts to improve export competitiveness. Changes in inflows have undermined exchange-rate stability, with negative effects on long-term growth (Ghura and Grermes, 1993). Their effects are hard to disaggregate from those of other stabilization measures, terms-of-trade changes and official capital inflows. However, Elbadawi and Soto (1993) have found that all types of inflows can have large short-term destabilizing effects on the exchange rate, even though short-term and portfolio inflows have no long-term effect on the exchange rate;[8] and longer-term direct investment inflows have effects largely consistent with macroeconomic equilibrium.

The private capital inflows, though predominantly short-term, have led to short-term exchange-rate appreciations in almost all countries in our sample (table 8). Kenya and Uganda experienced very sharp appreciation of their currencies in 1993/1994 and 1994/1995 at a time when private transfers and access to short-term trade credits increased markedly. The appreciation in real effective terms in both Uganda and Kenya was well over 20 per cent in 1994. Zambia experienced a depreciation in real effective terms in 1991 which was followed by an appreciation in 1992 and 1993 and a depreciation in 1994. Similarly, South Africa has experienced movements in either direction in its real effective exchange rate. In the period 1986-1989, when South Africa was a net exporter of capital, the real effective exchange rate depreciated. In 1990-1992 it appreciated again as the country became a net recipient of capital. Unlike other countries in the sample, Zimbabwe has experienced a depreciation in the real effective exchange rate throughout the period 1990-1994. This was a result of deliberate policy to guard against an appreciation in real effective terms.

B. *Effects of the balance of payments*

A second key issue is the balance-of-payments effect: price-induced increases in expenditure on imports (increasing the current-account deficit) or reserves accumulation. This is important for sustainability because, to the degree that capital inflows increase the current-account deficit through higher imports, they will automatically decline as this macroeconomic indicator deteriorates (though they will also increase fiscal revenue from tariffs); on the other hand, accumulation of reserves should increase inflows by boosting confidence. Spending on imports has also been found to lag well behind the receipt of capital inflows. S. Calvo and Reinhart (1995) suggest that small countries in Latin America have seen more reserves accumulation and less import expenditure.

The experience of the countries in our sample with respect to reserve accumulation has been mixed, making it difficult to identify a single factor accounting for observed changes therein. From table 9 it can be seen that below some countries have consistently built reserves over the period. However, some of them lost reserves due to a decrease in medium-term loans, especially following a scale-down in donor financial support. Zimbabwe lost reserves due to the prolonged drought period in 1992. The loss of reserves in Kenya and South Africa was due to a decline in official

Table 8

NOMINAL AND REAL EXCHANGE RATES OF SELECTED COUNTRIES
IN SUB-SAHARAN AFRICA

(1985 = 100)

		1986	1987	1988	1989	1990	1991	1992	1993	1994
Kenya	N	98.8	100.6	107.9	125.6	139.6	167.7	196.3	353.7	342.1
	R	...	...	...	...	103.5	108.1	100.7	128.0	100.0
South Africa	N	...	92.8	103.0	119.5	118.0	126.0	130.0	149.0	n.a.
	R	...	96.1	102.0	101.3	98.4	95.0	91.3	93.4	92.6
United Republic	N	186.9	367.4	567.4	819.4	1114.9	1252.6	1701.0	2316.0	2912.0
of Tanzania	R	...	...	...	...	396.0	382.0	438.0	497.0	497.0
Uganda	N	209.0	639.0	1584.0	3330.0	6401.0	10955.0	16922.0	17835.0	14717.0
	R	...	...	...	...	155.8	217.0	227.0	230.0	179.0
Zambia	N	251.6	283.9	264.0	416.0	932.0	1990.0	5042.0	14026.0	24813.0
	R	...	...	...	...	70.0	81.0	75.0	70.0	79.0
Zimbabwe	N	106.2	106.2	113.0	137.0	150.0	212.0	319.0	406.0	506.0
	R	...	...	...	...	100.7	126.0	128.0	132.0	139.0

Source: United Nations Economic Commission for Africa, *Economic and Social Statistics on Africa*, various issues; and IMF, *International Financial Statistics*, various issues.

Note: R denotes real exchange rates and N denotes nominal exchange rates. An increase in the index represents a depreciation.

transfers, while in Zambia and the United Republic of Tanzania this was accounted for by the decline in medium-term capital inflows. In Uganda and Zambia the drop in medium- and long-term loans was more than offset by the increase in grants. In addition, some of these countries lost reserves because of the increase in the level of imports. One key factor which has to be recognized is that the private transfers have substantially increased in Kenya, Uganda and the United Republic of Tanzania to a point that donor disbursement for balance-of-payment support is used for building up reserves.

C. Effects on investment, savings and consumption

The third main group of effects is on investment, savings and consumption, and thereby on GDP growth. In this context, it is important to note that greater expenditure on consumption will cause the real exchange rate to appreciate more rapidly, whereas investment will slow appreciation through imports of capital goods (Calvo, 1994; Khan and Reinhart, 1995). This is particularly true of investment expenditures related to FDI transactions: because these are not intermediated through the domestic financial system, they will have less effect on the real exchange rate or the financial markets. Beyond the initial division into investment and consumption, the key variables determining the GDP-effect are the type and productivity of investment, and the proportion allocated to the production of tradable.

Unfortunately, reliable savings and investment data are extremely rare in sub-Saharan countries; those that exist are usually derived as residuals from national accounts. Equally, data on import composition which might be used as a proxy is usually somewhat outdated; and data on the current account which might indicate a savings-investment gap is also misleading because it includes some capital-account inflows.[9] Preliminary calculations based on 1986-1993 data indicated ambiguous results on savings and investment behaviour in the six countries.

Table 9

EXTERNAL RESERVES OF SELECTED COUNTRIES IN SUB-SAHARAN AFRICA

(Months of imports)

	1986-1989	1990	1991	1992	1993
Kenya	1.6	0.9	0.6	0.4	2.2
South Africa	1.8	1.4	1.7	2.1	1.5
United Republic of Tanzania	0.5	2.8	2.8	4.5	2.7
Uganda	0.6	0.7	1.0	1.5	2.1
Zambia	0.8	1.4	1.4	n.a.	n.a
Zimbabwe	1.5	1.3	1.3	3.3	...

Source: See table 2.

Zambia managed to increase the rate of gross domestic investment (GDI) to GDP. This was mainly financed by ODA (see table 10). Similarly, Zimbabwe was able to marginally increase the GDI/GDP ratio. For the remaining countries, the GDI/GDP ratio fell between the two periods.

Savings as a ratio to GDP have generally decreased in the countries of our sample with the exception of the United Republic of Tanzania. Zimbabwe suffered the biggest decline of close to 12 per cent. The trends in gross domestic savings as a share of GDP indicate that growth in these countries

Table 10

SELECTED COUNTRIES IN SUB-SAHARAN AFRICA: MACROECONOMIC INDICATORS

	Current-account balance[a]		Gross domestic savings		Fiscal deficit[a]		Gross domestic investment		Inflation		Debt service	
	(as a percentage of GDP)								*(per cent)*		*(per cent of merchandise exports)*	
	1986 -1989	1990 -1993	1986 -1989	1990 -1993	1986 -1989	1990 -1993	1986 -1989	1990 -1993	1986 -1989	1990 -1993	1986 -1989	1990 -1993
Kenya	(4.8)	(1.7)	19.9	19.5	(5.7)	(5.8)	24.0	18.0	7.0	28.0	39.0	36.0
South Africa	2.9	0.2	2.7	2.2	(2.4)	(4.7)	20.0	16.0	15.6	14.5	...	...
United Republic of Tanzania	(1.5)	(16.0)	(1.4)	4.0	(5.3)	(3.9)	21.6	21.4	31.0	22.0	47.0	105.3
Uganda	(3.0)	(3.5)	3.8	0.2	(2.3)	(4.1)	16.8	14.8	170.0	30.1	55.0	77.0
Zambia	(9.4)	(10.5)	16.0	14.3	(8.0)	(5.0)	16.9	24.3	50.0	149.0	33.0	69.0
Zimbabwe	0.8	(5.8)	23.2	11.1	(6.2)	(6.0)	21.0	22.0	11.8	27.6	29.0	29.0

Source: See table 2.
　a Including grants.

has been financed mainly by foreign savings. To the extent that private capital inflows are volatile, growth is not sustainable. There is an urgent need to mobilize domestic savings to support the growth process, especially in the United Republic of Tanzania, and Uganda.

The numbers in table 10 also reveal that import demand in relation to GDP increased in the countries in the sample with the exception of South Africa. Trade liberalization combined with increased capital inflows to the six countries has increased import dependence. This is especially so in Kenya, Zambia and Zimbabwe.

D.   *Monetary and financial effects*

A potential risk of attempts to prevent exchange-rate appreciation through accumulation of reserves is the loss of monetary control, leading to an acceleration of inflation. The appropriate policy response is to sterilize the liquidity injection through open-market operations. Depending on the magnitude of the liquidity injection and depth of the financial sector, there is a great likelihood that successful sterilization can only be attained at very high interest rates. Further, the appreciation of the domestic currency, in both nominal and real terms, may not be avoided.

Increased volatility in financial markets has certainly occurred in SSA countries, but less in the stock markets than in markets for Treasury Bills and Central Bank Bills which have been attracting private capital inflows, causing speculative bubbles and high interest rates, with knock-on negative consequences for the performance of the banks' lending portfolios (Asea and Reinhart, 1995; Calvo, Sahay and Vegh, 1995; Griffith-Jones, 1995; IMF, 1995a). These can be magnified by the imbalances in the structure of assets and liabilities produced by capital inflows. The financial system acquires liquid liabilities in foreign exchange, integrated into a volatile international capital market (to add to its volatile domestic liabilities which may be made more volatile by foreign capital inflows), while its assets are neither externally protected nor liquid (Rojas-Suarez and Weisbrod, 1995).

It is difficult to separate the effects of private capital inflows from those of the wider distortions and underdevelopment of the financial sector: capital inflows only exacerbate the moral hazard and adverse risk selection already prevalent, by adding to the volume of funds requiring intermediation (Calvo, Leiderman and Reinhart, 1993). However, it is reasonable to assume that the negative effects of capital inflows on the financial system will be more pronounced in countries where the financial sector is in poor shape. If prudential regulations are binding in such circumstances, then few banks would qualify to hold wide open foreign-exchange positions overnight. This could easily trigger instability in the market as banks make efforts to reduce over-bought positions or else central banks have to remain active participants in the foreign-exchange market to promote stability, risking a loss of control over domestic liquidity.

Overall, there is strong evidence that private capital inflows to some SSA countries have been procyclical rather than countercyclical, following terms-of-trade booms (Kenya and Uganda) and exaggerating all of their destabilizing effects: "Dutch Disease" effects - in contrast to Latin America, where they have been offsetting terms-of-trade movements (Ffrench-Davis and Griffith-Jones, 1994).

The effects of such trends may be even worse in SSA countries than in other regions, because of their high degree of aid dependence: private capital inflows can reduce the capacity of SSA countries to mobilize aid inflows, especially for balance-of-payments support. In the context of liberalized foreign-exchange markets, private inflows have reduced private sector demand for donor-funded import support, leading donors to cut new pledges (Zambia and Zimbabwe). Similarly, accumulation of reserves and the apparently more healthy balance-of-payments position leads donors to question the whole rationale of fast-disbursing balance-of-payments support and to move funds to much slower-disbursing project support. This may not be appropriate, given the low absorptive capacity of the project-implementing agencies and the continuing budget constraints which would be better resolved by programme aid. The negative implications may become clear if private capital inflows reverse themselves, leading to a fall in international reserves precipitating a foreign-exchange crisis as the currency depreciates rapidly. The alternative to programme financing is direct budget support and debt relief. The local currency equivalent of a disbursement is used to support the budget as the foreign exchange boosts reserves. Apart from name, direct budget support has effects similar to those of import support. Further, it is equally difficult to sustain budget support if such inflows adversely affect economic growth.

It is for these reasons that we prefer to call the recent strengthening of the Uganda shilling a "Uganda

Disease" rather than a "Dutch Disease" (for more details of this argument, see Kasekende and Martin, 1995).

VI. Policy measures

The potential negative economic effects of private capital inflows discussed in the previous section show the need for policy measures to influence their scale and composition. The literature has concluded that no single policy measure can influence them decisively. Not surprisingly, the effectiveness of individual measures depends on the scale, nature and purpose of the capital inflows and the characteristics of the recipient economy. It is relatively easy to specify theoretical policy rules: for example, short-term volatile portfolio inflows might require some offsetting policy intervention to smooth any destabilizing effects, even though their long-term effects on equilibrium might be minimal; while long-term direct investment might be entirely consistent with long-term macroeconomic equilibrium and therefore require no corrective measures (Corbo, 1994; Elbadawi and Soto, 1994). However, given the problems with data and monitoring, many SSA Governments have had extreme difficulty in identifying capital inflows (especially their scale, composition and permanence) and therefore in deciding appropriate policy responses.

The crucial question for African countries has been whether to resist exchange-rate appreciation and, if so, how. The scope for change in exchange-rate policy has become much more limited due to the extreme degree of liberalization (to a free float) implemented in most non-CFA countries, compared to the "basket pegs", administered devaluations or band mechanisms used in other developing countries. This makes many of the conventional recommendations irrelevant: such as those for moves towards more exchange-rate flexibility, administered appreciations or depreciations, or deliberate introduction of exchange-rate uncertainty/noise to deter speculators. Some Washington-based authors have even suggested that exchange-rate policy is no longer relevant or feasible in SSA circumstances. However, given the central role of exchange-rate depreciation in the few successful adjustment programmes in SSA - notably in promoting export competitiveness - most African Governments have preferred to treat any exchange-rate appreciation as a major problem and to take measures to reverse or reduce it. (For a powerful argument of the case for making the exchange rate a key element of development policy, see Williamson, 1995.)

Furthermore, the policy response to the large capital inflows has been complicated by the current fiscal stance. With the exception of South Africa, the countries have faced budgetary problems of varying degrees. Budget deficits have varied between 1 and 13 per cent of GDP. In the case of Kenya and Zimbabwe, these have remained high throughout the first half 1990s. Uganda and Zambia have achieved significant success in controlling the budget since 1992. In the case of Uganda, the Government has made substantial repayments to the banking system. This has been achieved through strict control of Government expenditure combined with efforts to boost revenue mobilization. The countries in the sample mostly rely on the sale of financial instruments (mainly Treasury Bills) to sterilize liquidity injections. In cases where fiscal policy is expansionary, open-market operations are used to promote macroeconomic stability. Similarly, liquidity injection arising from mopping up excess foreign exchange from the market would be sterilized mainly by the sale of financial instruments. As pointed out earlier, the instrument suffers from limitation arising from the lack of depth in the financial sector. In situations where budgetary restraint is difficult and effectiveness of monetary policy instruments limited, the policy of absorbing the inflows through intervention may cause macroeconomic instability. In particular the risk of inflationary pressure is high.

In the following, three types of policy measures will be examined that have been used by countries receiving large capital inflows:

- measures to increase the demand for foreign exchange, including central-bank intervention in foreign-exchange markets; liberalization of the current account; and liberalization of the capital account;

- measures to reduce aggregate demand and offset the inflationary effects of the capital inflows or of intervening in the foreign-exchange market;

- measures to reduce the scale of capital inflows or to influence their composition in favour of investment.

A. *Measures to increase demand for foreign exchange*

Unsterilized intervention in the foreign-exchange market leads to reserve accumulation and increases the money supply. This can have secondary positive effects by reducing interest rates and making inflows less likely - but (in the absence of an accommodating increase in money demand) it may also raise inflation and thereby increase the real appreciation of the exchange rate further. Nevertheless, in the absence of monetary tools which can sterilize such large inflows, this has often been the first line of defence for low-income SSA countries.

One recommendation in the literature is for greater current-account liberalization in order to increase demand for foreign exchange. As already discussed, current-account transactions have been fully liberalized in the anglophone SSA countries which have been experiencing capital inflows. The only additional liberalization which could occur is a reduction of import tariffs. It is unlikely that this would have much effect on increasing import demand, given the existing high level of import dependence of low-income SSA countries and the low level of enforcement of tariff collection. In addition, a reduction in tariffs would be undesirable given the dependence of the budget on tariff revenue; and an increase in import demand would be undesirable, given the already high import dependence of SSA countries and the failure of adjustment programmes to effect any rationalization of import demand (these issues have been discussed in greater detail in Martin and Mistry, 1995). Thus, further current-account liberalization would not be a priority tool for most SSA countries.

Capital-account liberalization is seen as a third method of increasing demand for foreign exchange. Suggestions include full capital-account liberalization to allow capital outflows which would offset inflows; the reduction or elimination of subsidies on any inflows (e.g. incentives for foreign investment, deposit insurance or subsidized forward cover on foreign-exchange transactions); targeting gradual liberalization designed to encourage certain types of inflows or outflows (see Fischer and Reisen, 1992).

In some SSA countries, such measures might well be ineffective at this time, given the relative unimportance of inflows subject to capital-account controls or subsidies and other incentives, and the predominance of inflows coming through the porous current account and the bureaux. However, Kenya announced far-reaching measures in October 1994, intended to offset capital inflows. Residents were permitted to invest abroad and to hold accounts overseas. In South Africa and Zimbabwe there are currently active debates about capital-account liberalization. The recent trend calls for a critical

analysis (see Ffrench-Davis and Griffith-Jones, 1994) due to risks that:

- liberalization may well increase inflows (Hanson, 1992; Laban and Larrain, 1993; Mathieson and Rojas-Suarez, 1993; Williamson, 1994);

- it may also undermine the effectiveness of sterilized intervention by making domestic and foreign bonds fully substitutable;

- correct sequencing of capital-account liberalization with other measures (especially stabilization and internal financial sector strengthening and liberalization) is crucial; almost the only consistent sequencing recommendation in the adjustment literature is that capital-account liberalization should be one of the last steps in adjustment policy (see Kasekende and Martin, 1995); thus it should not be undertaken prematurely in countries with weak domestic financial systems, merely in order to influence private capital inflows.

B.   *Measures to reduce aggregate demand*

1.   *Sterilization through open-market operations*

Such sterilization has been the most popular policy in SSA countries. It has two main risks, which has provoked debate over whether it is "easy" (Reisen, 1993) or "hard" (Calvo, Leiderman and Reinhart, 1993 and 1994).

One risk is that it will perpetuate interest rate differentials and accelerate capital inflows. Frankel (1994) concludes that sterilization will increase interest rates, but to a much larger degree if the source of the problem is higher export receipts or higher money demand rather than capital inflows. The degree of increase will depend on the substitutability of Government paper and other assets, on the behaviour of the demand for money (especially its sensitivity to interest rates), and on the interest elasticity of aggregate demand. However, Fernandez-Arias and Montiel (1995) indicate that the higher interest rate effect should be only temporary. Another risk is that sterilization will increase fiscal/quasi-fiscal burdens of Government or Central Bank paper, both through larger issues of such paper and through higher interest rates than the central bank can obtain on its reserves (Calvo, Leiderman and Reinhart, 1994; Corbo, 1994). For these reasons, it has been suggested that a more realistic target than complete sterilization is to maintain the pre-inflow growth rate of real balances, as has been achieved by Chile.

As a result of the over-reliance on the treasury bill instrument to sterilize both large capital inflows and finance wide budget deficits, interest rates have increased sharply in some countries. Kenya, Zambia and the United Republic of Tanzania have suffered from this problem at different times during the early 1990s with discount rates increasing to well over 50 per cent per annum. To avoid the problem fiscal policy should be tight to ease the burden of mopping-up. Uganda offers a good example of the latter. The discount rate on Treasury Bills in that country has fallen from 40 per cent in 1990 to the current levels of between 9 and 15 per cent. The recent experience of Zambia also supports the need for fiscal restraint. Zambia has managed to reduce the discount rate on Treasury Bills from over 70 per cent in 1993 to about 20 per cent in 1994 through fiscal discipline.

2. Other methods of sterilization

There is a variety of other methods of sterilization, including an increase of the reserve ratio on bank deposits and shifting Government deposits to the Central Bank.

Increasing the reserve ratio on bank deposits (or particular types of deposits) is equivalent to a tax on the banking system (because reserve requirements are not remunerated). This can be a highly effective prudential measure to narrow spreads in financial intermediation, to reduce the money multiplier and to limit credit to the private sector (Reinhart and Reinhart, 1995). It can work particularly effectively on individual types of inflow (e.g. offshore borrowing or uncovered foreign-exchange exposure) and if used countercyclically to target the source of a boom. However, over the medium term, there is a risk that the efficiency of the financial system is reduced as borrowers may be pushed towards less efficient lenders in order to avoid the effects of reserve requirements. In addition, it requires a balanced judgement about the possible negative effects on key elements of finance such as trade finance. Kenya and the United Republic of Tanzania have used the policy of varying reserve requirements in liquidity management. However, given the current weakness in the financial sector, this policy measure tends to raise the intermediation costs further. For that reason, Uganda has avoided increasing the reserve requirements. Efforts have been made to reduce costs to commercial banks by treating a portion of vault cash as eligible reserve in addition to reducing the reserve requirement to the current level of 8 per cent. The difference in reserve requirements policy may offer a partial explanation for the far higher lending rates in Kenya and the United Republic of Tanzania compared to Uganda.

Moving Government deposits (or postal savings, social security and public enterprise funds) from commercial banks to the central bank or into Government paper (see Fischer and Reisen, 1992; Reisen, 1993; Khan and Reinhart, 1995) has also proved to be a highly effective means of sterilization. However, depending on the interest rates paid by the central bank, this could have the effect of reducing the rates paid to savers or of increasing interest rate costs to the central bank.

3. Fiscal measures

Many Washington-based authors see fiscal measures as the only long-term policy option (Corbo, 1994; Schadler et al., 1993). Similarly, the main recommendation in SSA adjustment programmes has been to tighten fiscal policy, first to guard against the inflationary impact of a possible reversal of capital inflows, and secondly to offset the effects of sterilization by reducing interest rates through lower Government borrowing, thereby discouraging capital inflows. Moreover, it has been suggested that expenditure cuts are more effective than tax rises in reducing aggregate demand (Calvo, Leiderman and Reinhart, 1993).

The policy of fiscal restraint has been used with measurable success in Uganda. The recent positive experience in Zambia and the difficulties in promoting macroeconomic stability in Kenya, Zimbabwe and the United Republic of Tanzania lend further support to fiscal restraint. Uganda has managed to absorb the large inflows without losing control over inflation and interest rates.

However, many authors have cautioned against the distortion of long-term fiscal plans in order to offset potentially temporary capital inflows. This could be especially important in those SSA countries where expenditure is already at critically low levels and the potential to increase revenue is limited. They have also indicated that fiscal measures may increase capital inflows by reducing prospects of liquidity problems for the Government and freeing funds for domestic borrowing linked to some types of capital inflows.

4.   *Measures to increase domestic savings*

Such measures are sometimes seen as a means to reduce aggregate demand, and sometimes as measures to influence the expenditure of capital inflows. Similarly, targeted sterilization measures (reserve requirements on particular types of capital inflows or borrowing) may be used to reduce aggregate demand and to influence the composition of inflows.

Most SSA adjustment programmes have recently begun to include drastic measures to boost private savings by reform of the financial sector. However, the principal mechanisms proposed have been greater competition in the financial sector by more open entry for new financial institutions, and liberalization of interest rates. There is little evidence from Africa or elsewhere that such measures have had a dramatic positive effect on private savings, and there is a high risk that other financial sector reforms may undermine prospects for higher private financial savings rates (especially the disappearance of rural bank branches and savings networks). Finally, some of the key factors in mobilizing private sector savings in other countries, such as postal savings banks, more productive social security funds, or private pensions, have barely been considered. (For more on a typical financial sector reform programme in Africa, see Martin, 1995.) Given this design of financial sector reform, it seems unlikely that measures to increase domestic financial savings will have effects large enough to counteract the effects of private capital inflows.

C.   *Measures to influence the scale and composition of inflows*

There has been heated debate over the desirability and feasibility of capital controls and taxes, with some (Dornbusch in this volume; Griffith-Jones, 1995; Williamson, 1994) believing they are an essential part of the policy arsenal; and others (Corbo, 1994, Schadler et al., 1993; Mathieson, 1993) seeing them as temporary and largely ineffective measures, which are quickly dodged through over- and under-invoicing of trade or through parallel financial and foreign-exchange markets. However, recently even conservative sources (Bank for International Settlements, 1995; IMF, 1995a) have acknowledged the positive role played in the Latin American and Asian cases by such measures as:

- extra reserve requirements on particular inflows, especially on foreign borrowing by companies

or banks or open foreign-exchange positions of the banks quantitative restrictions on inflows, for example on foreigners buying Treasury Bills (in Malaysia) or domestic bonds (Colombia);

- taxes on short-term inflows aiming at reducing the dollar returns of investments (in Brazil, Chile and Colombia);
- minimum stay periods on FDI (Colombia).

Some have tried to distinguish among measures which are good for short periods (taxes and bans) and those which are desirable for longer periods (prudential regulations such as reserve requirements), but the consensus appears to be growing that many forms of controls on capital inflows are an essential weapon in the policy arsenal, provided that they are accompanied by measures directed at demand for foreign exchange and domestic aggregate demand, and the pursuit of "sound macroeconomic fundamentals".

Given the absence of data on capital inflows in many SSA countries, it is hard to see how Governments could design appropriate controls or taxes on capital inflows. Any measures designed in the current low-information context would be more likely to risk exacerbating current distortions or speculative bubbles. In addition, the arguments used about evasion in middle-income countries with better recording systems would apply more strongly in SSA countries, making effective implementation doubtful. The same would apply to any SSA participation in a global tax. However, once more information is available, it should be possible to design carefully targeted controls and taxes.

VII. Conclusions

Where does the above analysis leave African policy-makers in deciding which policy measures to use to react to capital inflows? As in any other country, the need for policy intervention depends on the size and composition of inflows, their causes, and the perception and objective analysis of their sustainability. We have shown that the key first step for all sub-Saharan countries must be to improve recording and monitoring of inflows. For some, this means starting virtually from scratch with disaggregating data on inflows through the bureaux and monitoring private sector borrowing; for others, it is a more sophisticated process of improving the coverage of monitoring, especially of uses of inflows. However, for those countries which have abandoned all monitoring, there is concern that any attempt to record inflows would be perceived by the markets as an attempt to control and would undermine the credibility of liberalization, driving the capital inflows away or back into the parallel markets.

In order to facilitate proper analysis of capital inflows and their macroeconomic effects and in attempting to influence these through appropriate policy measures, authorities must seek to improve the recording and the monitoring systems both in their own countries and in international organizations. The intractable problem, though, is firstly, how to introduce recording and monitoring systems without driving capital inflows back to the parallel market, and secondly, how best to monitor and improve international data sources.

Nevertheless, pending improvements in the data, it is possible to see that:

- contrary to the message of global databases, several sub-Saharan countries have experienced sizable private capital inflows which are larger compared to the size of their economies than those of Latin American and Asian countries;

- the composition of those inflows (insofar as it is known) indicates that important elements (private transfers and short-term bank inflows) could be volatile; however, the prospects of maintaining private transfers are high, given an attractive macroeconomic environment;

- the causes of the inflows have been pre-dominantly "push" factors and transitory "pull" factors, and regional spillover effects in Southern African countries, rather than permanent "pull" factors, again indicating their likely unsustainability;

- perceptions and objective analyses of sustainability indicate that the inflows could be temporary but, as indicated, lack of information on the nature of investment may render them permanent; the potential volatility of the inflows makes a strong case for action to monitor them and to minimize their destabilizing macroeconomic effects.

The type of action to be taken depends on the macroeconomic effects of the inflows, compared to the current situation and the objectives of the Government.

Flows to sub-Saharan countries have consistently caused real currency appreciation, either through nominal appreciation, where stabilization policies have been tightly pursued, or through inflation, where they have not. They have sustained high import levels and permitted reserves accumulation in the countries analysed. They have caused protracted financial instability and undermined financial sector reform programmes, and they have been procyclical and have complicated aid mobilization efforts.

The current situation and objectives of the Governments are remarkably similar. All the countries studied share the objectives of improving competitiveness and reducing inflation: yet, with the possible exception of South Africa and the CFA franc zone (among those not studied), none of them would wish to use a stable exchange rate as an inflation anchor. All have relatively recently embarked on financial sector reform programmes, and are anxious to raise domestic savings from current low levels (again, South Africa is the exception with much higher initial savings levels).

Given the need to balance the objectives of competitiveness and stability, the desirable policy mix for SSA countries would be a pragmatic one drawing on the maximum number of policy levers, as in Chile, rather than relying exclusively on sterilized intervention or fiscal compression (Fernandez-Arias and Montiel, 1995; Williamson, 1995). However, as with small nations in other continents, fewer policy options are currently open to SSA Governments (S.Calvo and Reinhart, 1995) because of the following factors:

- their complete exchange-rate flexibility, and highly open current account and (through a porous current account) capital account;

- their slow progress with structural reforms, notably development of the domestic financial sector, which makes sterilization methods less effective and formal capital-account opening less desirable, for fear of exacerbating the poor health of most domestic banks;

- the poor fiscal position (in some countries), which makes sterilization costs unsustainable, or the need for prior fiscal adjustment (in others), which makes further fiscal adjustment to temporary capital inflows undesirable and politically problematic;

- the poor quality of data and of enforcement mechanisms for taxes and controls of any kind, and the unconventional nature of much of the capital (in the form of private transfers) which will make capital taxes and controls (whether national or global) less effective.

Given these factors, the priority policy measures would appear to be:

- sterilized intervention in order to minimize inflation and to accumulate reserves to guard against reversal of capital inflows;

- application of selective reserve requirements, especially on offshore borrowing and foreign borrowing by the private sector;

- fiscal tightening; despite its shortcomings, this is consistent with promoting macroeconomic stability in countries faced with high capital inflows given the relative ineffectiveness of monetary policy;

- transfer of Government and other public sector deposits from commercial banks to the central bank (although this may undermine financial stability given current weaknesses of the financial sector);

- measures to limit foreign purchases of Treasury Bills and domestic bonds;

- removal of incentives for capital inflows and selective gradual opening of the capital account (where justified, based on analysis of motives for inflows/outflows and on adjustment sequencing considerations);

- convincing donors to maintain levels of balance-of-payments and/or fiscal support in order to increase reserves and guard against future outflows.

Even this seemingly specific and limited list looks long for a typical sub-Saharan policy-maker faced with many other demands for monitoring, research and policy design and implementation. Yet, as strikingly put by S. Calvo and Reinhart (1995, p.35),

> While sound macroeconomic policies are advisable, policy-makers in *small* countries are advised to be extra cautious in protecting the domestic financial system against the vagaries of international capital inflows.

Most sub-Saharan countries are very small. Thus the problem of large unsustainable capital inflows is one they should take very seriously, devoting resources to urgent further analysis of its scale and causes, and the policy measures they can take to minimize its negative effects.

Appendix

Review of the liberalization process in selected countries in Southern Africa

Zimbabwe

The experience of Zimbabwe in liberalizing its economy is fully described by Ncube et al. (1996). The first phase of the liberalization process was started in 1990 with the objective of moving the economy from a highly regulated status to market-orientation. Imports were substantially liberalized, while surrender requirements remained in force. The current-account deficit deteriorated from $147 million in 1990 to $500 million in 1991. In the following year, Zimbabwe devalued its currency to eliminate overvaluation. Unfortunately, the economy was hit by a drought in 1992 which further widened the current-account deficit. The deficit was financed by external borrowing, enabling the Government to maintain a high level of reserves. The cover of imports increased from 4.1 months in 1993 to 5.5 months by end-December 1994 and 7 months by June 1995. The controls in foreign-exchange dealing were gradually eased in the period 1992-1994, and the Government allowed foreign investors to freely invest in the stock exchange and remit both capital and dividends, beginning July 1993. Foreign-exchange surrender requirements were also gradually eased.

Between January and July 1994, exporters were required to surrender 40 per cent of their earnings at the official rate while 60 per cent could either be sold in the interbank market or held on a foreign-currency account. The surrender requirement was abolished on July 1, 1994. The exchange rate was gradually depreciated from Zim.$2.8 in 1990 to Zim.$8.2 per US$ in 1994. An interbank foreign-exchange market was set up in January 1994, though the Reserve Bank of Zimbabwe (RBZ) remained an active participant in the market, especially during the first six months of its operation. The RBZ initially retained an official window rate but the two-tier exchange rate was finally abolished on July 1, 1994. In order to increase competition in the interbank market, the Government permitted the setting up of foreign-exchange bureaux. In February 1995 Zimbabwe became an Article VIII member of the IMF.

A key outcome of financial reform in Zimbabwe has been the surge in domestic interest rates, both nominal and real, from about 10 per cent in 1990 to

30 per cent by 1994. As a result some private sector borrowers resorted to cheaper credit lines from external sources precipitating a real appreciation of the Zimbabwean dollar.

Zambia

Zambia gradually moved its foreign-exchange regime from a controlled to a market-based system over the period 1992 to 1995. As a first step, Zambia established a foreign-exchange bureaux system in October 1992, which operated simultaneously with the official window managed by the Bank of Zambia. The dual system was eliminated in December 1993, with the setting up of the interbank system. Since then, the foreign-exchange system has been fully market-based.

In January 1994, all forms of exchange controls on both capital- and current-account transactions were eliminated. The nominal exchange-rate depreciated by over 80 per cent from Kwacha 177 per $ in 1992 to about K942 in September 1995. However, with the very high rate of inflation experienced during the period the real exchange rate actually appreciated. Zambia's import cover rose from one month in 1991 to two and a half months by 1994.

Interest rates were liberalized in September 1992 at a time when the requirements for fiscal accommodation were still high. As a result, the nominal discount rate on short- term Government paper increased sharply from 182 per cent in 1993 to 591 per cent in July 1993. The rates have since dropped to around 40 per cent. Such high interest rates undoubtedly attracted short-term capital inflows. Beginning 1994, non-residents were allowed to participate in Treasury Bills and Government Bond markets without restriction.

United Republic of Tanzania

Similar to developments in Zimbabwe and Zambia, significant progress has been achieved in decontrolling prices in the United Republic of Tanzania. The exchange and trade regime have been extensively liberalized. Import licensing has been eliminated and exporters are currently permitted to retain 100 per cent of their foreign-exchange receipts. In order to promote dealings in foreign exchange, the United Republic of Tanzania established an interbank foreign-exchange market in June 1994, and the bureaux which were set up in 1992 are permitted to participate in the interbank foreign-exchange market. This was intended to promote competition in the foreign-exchange market since only two banks were registered by then. The participation by bureaux in the interbank foreign-exchange market is to be reviewed with a view to limiting their operations to cover only "over-the-counter transactions".

The United Republic of Tanzania has made significant progress in its privatization programme. By the end of 1994, about 95 out of 371 parastatals had been divested, and 50 had been targeted for restructuring or divesture in 1995. In a further effort to provide financial support to the economic development process, the United Republic of Tanzania is preparing the ground-work for the establishment of capital markets. However, foreign investors are not yet permitted to participate in the capital market. Capital transfers to all countries are still subject to approval by the authorities.

Kenya

Kenya made substantial progress in liberalizing its trade regime during the late 1980s. However, insufficient adjustment of the exchange rate made the liberalization process unsustainable. Whenever import demand outpaced supply of foreign exchange, import licensing would be tightened as a means of matching demand and supply of foreign exchange.

The failure to sustain the reform process continued to characterize macroeconomic management in the first three years of the 1990s. In the foreign-exchange market, holders of foreign-exchange certificates were permitted to negotiate premiums in secondary market trading which created a dual system. This was followed by a revaluation and foreign-exchange rationing system which caused substantial losses to holders. Additionally, the economy was characterized by rising inflation, from 13 per cent in 1989 to a peak of 46 per cent in 1993. Furthermore, efforts to finance the widening budget deficit through sale of Government paper pushed interest rates to very high levels.

Since mid-1993, Kenya has moved very fast in stabilizing the macroeconomic environment and liberalizing the economy. Inflation was brought down to single digit levels. An interbank foreign-exchange system was started in October 1993. By end-1993, all restrictions on remittances of dividends and expatriate earnings had been lifted. In addition, residents were permitted to borrow abroad up to $1 million. In February 1994, further efforts to eliminate controls on the capital account were announced. Exporters were allowed 100 per cent retention of export proceeds, the limit on resident borrowing trom abroad was removed, foreigners were allowed to open foreign-currency accounts in domestic banks and the restrictions on domestic borrowing by foreign-controlled companies was removed. By June 1994, Kenya accepted obligations of Article VIII (Sections 2, 3 and 4) of the Articles of Agreement of the IMF.

In the financial year 1994/1995, Kenya made further progress in reforming the foreign-exchange market and liberalizing the capital account. The Central Bank of Kenya started licensing foreign-exchange bureaux in October 1994. In addition, residents were permitted to invest funds abroad including retaining funds in overseas accounts. Additionally, foreign investors were allowed to participate in the Nairobi Stock Exchange. In 1994, offshore borrowing by residents were allowed without limit, provided that interest does not exceed LIBOR plus 2 percentage points and that such borrowing is not guaranteed by the Government.

Uganda

The liberalization of the foreign-exchange and trade regime in Uganda has been extensively discussed by Kasekende et al. (1994).[10] The new Government that came into power in January 1986 took almost one and a half years in search of an appropriate policy package to address the numerous economic problems that affected Uganda. During that time, the policy regime was characterized by a high degree of uncertainty, an overvalued exchange rate and very high inflation.

Following the launch of the Economic Recovery Programme in May 1987, insufficient exchange-rate adjustment and inefficient budget management undermined the reform programme. However, since June 1990, Uganda has moved reasonably quickly to correct macroeconomic distortions. The Government implemented very tight monetary and fiscal measures, sanctioned the establishment of foreign-exchange bureaux in July 1990, launched a foreign-exchange auction system in January 1993, and replaced it with an interbank system in November 1993. Under the interbank system, all surrender requirements on exports or any other foreign-exchange inflows were removed. In addition, residents are permitted to operate foreign-currency accounts. In the period since 1990, the Government pursued an aggressive policy of attracting foreign investment. As part of this process,

Uganda enacted a new Investment Code with highly liberal provisions on repatriation of capital and dividends. Since early 1993, both nominal and real exchange rates have appreciated markedly, in part reflecting higher private capital inflows and terms of trade. In 1994, Uganda acceded to Article VIII Sections 2, 3 and 4 status of the IMF's Articles of Agreement; however, the capital account is not yet fully liberalized.

South Africa

According to Mlambo and Nell (1995), South Africa has experienced structural disruptions since 1970 that have had a profound impact on investment and the overall economic performance of the country. The Angolan war, oil price shocks in the 1970s, the worldwide recession towards the end of the 1970s, sanctions and political instability all combined have disrupted the long-run growth performance of the country.

In 1980 there was a sharp upsurge in the gold price which restored investors' confidence and paved the way for major policy transformations. By then, the political situation in South Africa had deteriorated to such an extent that foreign creditors were reluctant to extend further credit to domestic enterprises and other financial institutions. Disinvestment campaigns emanating mainly from Western nations, accompanied by stricter trade and financial sanctions, forced the Government to declare a moratorium on foreign debt in 1985. According to van der Walt and de Wet (1993) disinvestment together with the repayment of foreign debt contributed to net capital outflows of around R5 billion per annum from 1985 onward.

In addition, before 1985, the balance of payments followed a clear cyclical pattern. During an upswing in the business cycle, increased demand for imports caused the current account to move into a deficit, which in turn was financed by direct and indirect capital inflows. During a downswing, imports declined, and the current account moved into a surplus that enabled the repayment of loans. This pattern was disrupted by net capital outflows which occurred after 1985. Whereas in the past current-account deficits were financed by capital inflows, net outflows that have taken place since 1985 implied that the current account had to be transformed into a surplus.

Broadly speaking, in contrast to the period before 1985, the period thereafter saw a sharp increase in the user cost of capital for public enterprises that subsequently led to a sharp decrease in public investment.

Furthermore, it is noteworthy that because the level of savings was not enough to finance capital outflows, the significant decline in gross domestic investment as a share of GDP since 1985 eased the pressure on the current account.

Developments in the balance-of-payments constraint have had important implications for investment in South Africa since 1985. Real growth declined to a mere 0.6 percent per annum between 1985 and 1993. Furthermore, gross domestic investment as a percentage of GDP declined sharply, from an average annual rate of 28.6 per cent in the period 1970-1984 to 21.2 per cent in the period 1985-1993, with private investment falling from 15.3 to 13.6 per cent of GDP and public investment declining from 13.3 to 7.6 per cent of GDP. Surprisingly, the balance-of-payments constraint appears to have had only a marginal impact on private investment inflows.

With the breakdown of the Bretton Wood system in 1971, South Africa began to experiment with various exchange-rate systems to accommodate floating exchange rates. Following the recommendations of the 1978 Interim Report of the Commission of Inquiry into the Monetary System and Monetary Policy, South Africa opted for a dual managed floating exchange-rate system in 1979, with substantial intervention by the South African Reserve Bank. The high gold price during the 1970s and early 1980s contributed to an overvaluation of the exchange rate.

In 1983 the Reserve Bank allowed the exchange rate to be more market-determined. A direct attempt was made to drain the economy of excess liquidity with the liberalization of exchange control with the abolition of the financial rand mechanism in February 1983. Coupled with declining gold prices since 1981, political unrest and disinvestment, this contributed to a sharp depreciation of the exchange rate. Capital outflows since 1983, however, necessitated the reinstatement of the financial rand in 1985. The depreciation of the exchange rate effectively increased the cost of imported capital and subsequently depressed investment.

Political uncertainty and the concomitant macroeconomic instability that prevailed during the 1970s, and particularly after 1985, increased the risk for potential investors and consequently reduced investment.

South Africa formally accepted the obligations of Article VIII, section 2, 3 and 4 of the IMF's Articles of Agreement in September 1973.

Notes

1. Refer to Kasekende, Katarikawe and Rweikiza (1995) for a full discussion of problems relating to compiling balance-of-payments statistics in Uganda.
2. The study does not cover the experience of franc zone area. Following the change in parity of the common currency in January 1994, some of the investors expect a further devaluation which has triggered off capital outflows. Furthermore, the study does not cover the experience of Zaire and Nigeria, both of which are rich in natural resources. It would be interesting to analyse capital movements to and from these two countries given their recent developments in the economic and political environment.
3. Refer to 'Private Market Financing for Developing Countries' prepared by a staff team in the Policy Development and Review Department.
4. Of course, factors noted for other developing countries may also be partly responsible, particularly: discrepancies between source and recipient country data due to on-lending through intermediary countries; and inadequate data coverage in source countries. On the latter, see also Ffrench-Davis and Griffith-Jones (1995).
5. Similar recording of capital flows as current-account transactions has been noted in El Salvador by S. Calvo and Reinhart (1995).
6. It is also likely that there is substantial under-recording of the scale of the bureaux transactions.
7. Refer to the Centre for Research into Economics and Finance in South Africa, *Quarterly Review* October 1995, pp. 2-10.
8. These tend to be magnified by weaknesses in the financial sector. Uganda, for example, experienced turbulence in the foreign-exchange market in August 1994, partly due to panic caused by the inability of most dealers to hold wide foreign-exchange exposure levels.
9. In a number of countries in the region, bureaux transactions are not properly categorized. Certain capital-account transactions are mis-reported as current-account transactions under the line 'private transfers'.
10. Section II of the Uganda Final report as part of a wider study covering five other African Countries under the External Finance for Africa Project, managed by Oxford International Associates.

References

AGOSIN, M. (1994), "Saving and Investment in Latin America", *UNCTAD Discussion Paper,* No. 90, October, Geneva.

ASEA, P.K., and C.M. REINHART (1995), "Real Interest Rate Differentials and the Real Exchange Rate: Evidence from Four African Countries", paper to an African Economic Research Consortium Workshop, Nairobi, June.

BANK FOR INTERNATIONAL SETTLEMENTS (1994a), *Annual Report 1993/94* (Basle).

BANK FOR INTERNATIONAL SETTLEMENTS (1994b), *International Banking and Financial Market Developments* (Basle).

BANK FOR INTERNATIONAL SETTLEMENTS (1995a), *Annual Report 1994/95* (Basle).

BANK FOR INTERNATIONAL SETTLEMENTS (1995b), *International Banking and Financial Market Developments* (Basle).

CALVO, G.A. (1994), "The Management of Capital Flows: Domestic Policy and International Cooperation", in UNCTAD, *International Monetary and Financial Issues for the 1990s,* Vol. IV (UNCTAD/GID/G24/4)(New York: United Nations).

CALVO, G.A., L. LEIDERMAN, and C.M. REINHART (1991), "The Perils of Sterilisation", *IMF Staff Papers,* Vol. 38, No. 4 (December), pp. 151-174.

CALVO, G.A., L. LEIDERMAN, and C.M. REINHART (1992), "Capital Flows and Real Exchange Rate Appreciation in Latin America: the Role of External Factors", mimeo., June.

CALVO, G.A., L. LEIDERMAN, and C.M. REINHART (1993), "The Capital Flows Problem: Concepts and Issues", *IMF Paper on Policy Analysis and Assessment,* PPAA/93/10.

CALVO, G.A., L. LEIDERMAN, and C.M. REINHART (1994), "Inflows of Capital to Developing Countries in the 1990s: Causes and Effects", *Economic Perspectives* (September).

CALVO, G.A., R. SAHAY, and C.A. VEGH (1995), "Capital Inflows in Central and Eastern Europe: Evidence and Policy Options", *IMF Working Paper 95/57* (May).

CALVO, S., and C.M. REINHART (1995), "Capital Flows to Latin America: Is There Evidence of Contagion Effects?", mimeo., April.

CARDENAS, M.S., and F.O. BARRERA (1993), "Efectos macroeconomicos de los capitales extranjeros: El caso colombiano", *IDB Working Paper,* No. 147, June.

CHUHAN, P., S. CLAESSENS, and N. MAMINGI (1993), "Equity and Bond Flows to Latin America and Asia: the Role of Global and Country Factors", *World Bank IECIF Policy Research Working Paper,* No. 1160, July.

CLAESSENS, S., M. DOOLEY, and A. WARNER (1995), "Portfolio Capital Flows: Hot or Cold?", *World Bank Economic Review,* Vol. 9, No. 1 (January).

COMMONWEALTH SECRETARIAT (1995), *International Capital Markets.*

CORBO, V., and L. HERNANDEZ (1994), "Macroeconomic Adjustment to Capital Inflows: Latin American Style versus East Asian Style", *World Bank IECIF Policy Research Working Paper,* No. 1377, November.

DADUSH, U., A. DHARESHWAR, and R. JOHANNES (1994), "Are Private Capital Flows to Developing Countries Sustainable?", *World Bank Working Paper,* WPS 1160 (Washington, D.C.).

DEVLIN, R., R. FFRENCH-DAVIS, and S. GRIFFITH-JONES (1994), "Crescimentos dos fluxos de capital e desenvolvimento: Uma visão geral dos questões de política econômica" (with English summary), Pesquisa e Planejamento Econômico, Vol. 24, No. 3 (December).

DOOLEY, M.P., E. FERNANDEZ-ARIAS, and K.M. KLETZER (1994), "Recent Private Capital Inflows to Developing Countries: Is the Debt Crisis History?", *NBER Working Paper,* No. 4792 (Cambridge, Mass.), July.

DORNBUSCH, R. (1997), "Cross-Border Payments Taxes and Alternative Capital Account Regimes", in UNCTAD, *International Monetary and Financial Issues for the 1990s,* Vol. VIII (UNCTAD/GID/G24/8)(New York and Geneva: United Nations).

ELBADAWI, I.A., and R. SOTO (1994), "Capital Flows and Long-term Equilibrium Exchange Rates in Chile", *World Bank PRD Working Paper,* No. 1306, June (Washington, D.C.).

FERNANDEZ-ARIAS, E. (1994), "The New Wave of Private Capital Inflows: Push or Pull?", *World Bank IECIF Policy Research Working Paper,* No. 1312, June (Washington, D.C.).

FERNANDEZ-ARIAS, E., and P.J. MONTIEL (1995), "The Surge in Capital Inflows to Developing Countries: Prospects and Policy Response", mimeo., March.

FFRENCH-DAVIS, R., and S. GRIFFITH-JONES (1995), *Coping with Capital Surges* (New York: Lynne Rienner).

FISCHER, B., and H. REISEN (1992), "Towards Capital Account Convertibility", *OECD Policy Brief No. 4* (Paris).

FITZGERALD, E.V.K (1993), "External Finance and Economic Adjustment", paper to ISS Policy Workshop on International Capital Flows and Economic Adjustment in Developing Countries, The Hague, December.

FRANKEL, J.A. (1994), "Sterilisation of Money Inflows: Difficult (Calvo) or Easy (Reisen)?", *IMF Working Paper 94/159,* December (Washington, D.C.).

GALBIS, V. (1993), "High Real Interest Rates Under Financial Liberalisation: Is There a Problem?", *IMF Working Paper 93/7,* January (Washington, D.C.).

GHURA, D., and T.J. GRENNES (1993), "The Real Exchange Rate and Macroeconomic Performance in Sub-Saharan Africa", *Journal of Development Economics,* No. 42, pp. 155-174.

GOLDSTEIN, M. (1995), "Coping with Too Much of a Good Thing: Policy Responses for Large Capital Inflows in Developing Countries", *World Bank Working Paper,* WPS 1507, September (Washington, D.C.).

GOOPTU, S. (1994), "Are Portfolio Flows to Emerging Markets Complementary or Competitive?", *World Bank IECIF Policy Research Working Paper,* No. 1360, September (Washington, D.C.).

GRIFFITH-JONES, S. (1995), "Capital Flows to Latin America and Asia: Lessons for Eastern Europe", mimeo., Institute for Development Studies, Sussex, June.

HADJIMICHAEL, M.T., et al. (1995), "Sub-Saharan Africa: Growth, Savings and Investment 1986-93", *IMF Occasional Paper,* No. 118 (Washington, D.C.).

HANSON, J.A. (1992), "Opening the Capital Account: a Survey of Issues and Results", *World Bank FPS Working Paper,* No. 101, May (Washington, D.C.).

HERNANDEZ, L., and H. RUDOLPH (1995), "Sustainability of Capital Flows to Developing Countries: Is a Generalised Reversal Likely?", *World Bank Working Paper,* WPS 1518, October (Washington, D.C.).

INTERNATIONAL FINANCE CORPORATION (1994, 1995), *Quarterly Review of Emerging Markets,* various issues.

IMF (1994a), *Conditionality Review: Distilling the Main Messages and Directions for Future Work* (Document EBS/94/164), August (Washington, D.C.).

IMF (1994 b), *World Economic Outlook* (Washington, D.C.).

IMF (1995a), *International Capital Markets: Developments, Prospects and Policy Issues* (Washington, D.C.).

IMF (1995 b), *World Economic Outlook* (Washington, D.C.).

KASEKENDE, L., M. KATARIKAWE, and R. RWEIKIZA (1994), "The Impact of Imports on Development in Low Income Africa. Uganda Final Report", External Finance for Africa Project (Oxford International Associates).

KASEKENDE, L., and M. MARTIN (1995), "Macroeconomic Policy Research Issues: The Sequencing, Credibility and Consistency of Adjustment in Africa", paper to an African Economic Research Consortium Senior Policy Seminar, Nairobi, April.

KHAN, M.S., and C.M. REINHART (1995), "Capital Flows in the APEC Region", *IMF Occasional Paper,* No. 122, March (Washington, D.C.).

LEAPE, J. (1995), "A Review of South Africa's International Borrowing", *Quarterly Review,* Centre For Research into Economics and Finance in Southern Africa, London School of Economics, October.

LIPUMBA, N. (1994), "Africa Beyond Adjustment" (Washington, D.C.: Overseas Development Council).

MARTIN, M., et al. (1995), "Financing Investment and Production in Mozambique" (Report to the European Commission), Institute for Development Studies, Sussex, mimeo., June.

MARTIN, M., and P.S. MISTRY (1995), "Financing Imports for Development in Low-Income Africa" (Report to Sida/ Danish Foreign Ministry), mimeo., November.

MATHIESON, D.J., and L. ROJAS-SUAREZ (1993), "Liberalisation of the Capital Account: Experiences and Issues", *IMF Occasional Paper*, No. 103, March (Washington, D.C.).

McKINNON, R. (1991), *The Order of Economic Liberalisation: Financial Control in the Transition to a Market Economy* (Baltimore: Johns Hopkins University Press).

MLAMBO, K., and K. NELL (1995), "Public Policy and Private Investment in South Africa: An Empirical Investigation".

MONTIEL, P.(1995), "The New Wave of Capital Inflows: Country Policy Chronologies", mimeo., World Bank, April (Washington, D.C.).

NCUBE, M., P. COLLIER, J. GUNNING, and K. MLAMBO (1996), "Trade Liberalisation and Regional Integration in Zimbabwe", in A. Oyejide, B. Ndulu, and J. Gunning (eds.), *Regional Integration and Trade Liberalisation in Sub-Saharan Africa, Vol. 2: Country Case Studies*, AERC Collaborative Project, forthcoming.

NIEHANS, J. (1994), "Elusive Capital Flows: Recent Literature in Perspective", *Journal of International and Comparative Economics*, Vol. 3, No. 1, pp. 21-43.

OECD (1994a), *Financing and External Debt of Developing Countries* (Paris).

OECD (1994b), *Financial Market Trends* (Paris).

OECD (1994c), *Geographical Distribution of Financial Flows to Developing Countries* (Paris).

OECD (1995a), *Financing and External Debt of Developing Countries* (Paris).

OECD (1995b), *Financial Market Trends* (Paris).

OECD (1995c), *Geographical Distribution of Financial Flows to Developing Countries* (Paris).

REINHART, C.M., and S. DUNAWAY (1995), "Dealing with Capital Inflows: Are There Any Lessons?", mimeo., April.

REINHART, C.M., and V. REINHART (1995), "On the Use of Reserve Requirements in Dealing with Capital Flow Problems", mimeo., October.

REISEN, H. (1993a), "The Case for Sterilised Intervention in Latin America", mimeo.

REISEN, H. (1993b), "Capital Flows and their Effect on the Monetary Base", *CEPAL Review*, No. 51.

REISEN, H., and B. FISCHER (eds.) (1993), *Financial Opening: Policy Issues and Experiences in Developing Countries* (Paris: OECD).

ROE, A., and N.K. SOWA (1994), "From Direct to Indirect Monetary Control in Sub-Saharan Africa", plenary paper for the African Economic Research Consortium, Nairobi, mimeo., December.

SCHADLER, S., M. CARKOVIC, A. BENNETT, and R. KHAN (1993), Recent Experiences with Surges in Capital Inflows, *IMF Occasional Paper*, No. 108 (Washington, D.C.).

TURNER, P. (1995), "Capital Flows in Latin America: a New Phase", *BIS Economic Paper*, No. 44, May (Basle).

UNCTAD (1994), *Trade and Development Report, 1994* (New York and Geneva: United Nations Publication Sales No. E.94.II.D.26).

UNCTAD (1995), *Trade and Development Report, 1995* (New York and Geneva: United Nations Publication Sales No. E.95.II.D.16).

WILLIAMSON, J. (1994),"The Management of Capital Inflows", paper for IFC and the Government of India, mimeo., December.

WILLIAMSON, J. (1995), "Exchange Rate Policy and Development Strategy", plenary paper for the African Economic Research Consortium, Johannesburg, mimeo., December.

WILLIAMSON, J. (1996),"A New Facility for the IMF?", in UNCTAD, *International Monetary and Financial Issues for the 1990s*, Vol. VII (UNCTAD/GID/G24/7)(New York and Geneva: United Nations).

WORLD BANK (1993), *World Debt Tables 1993-1994* (Washington, D.C.).

WORLD BANK (1993-1995), *Financial Flows to Developing Countries* (Washington, D.C., quarterly), various issues.

WORLD BANK (1994), *World Debt Tables 1994-1995* (Washington, D.C.).

WORLD BANK (1994-1995), *Global Economic Prospects* (Washington, D.C., quarterly), various issues.

YOUNGER, S. (1992), "Aid and the Dutch Disease: Macroeconomic Management When Everybody Loves You", *World Development*, Vol. 20, No. 11, pp. 1587-1597.

MANAGING FOREIGN CAPITAL FLOWS: THE EXPERIENCES OF THE REPUBLIC OF KOREA, THAILAND, MALAYSIA AND INDONESIA

Yung Chul Park
Chi-Young Song*

Abstract

The Republic of Korea, Thailand, Malaysia and Indonesia experienced a surge in the inflow of foreign capital during the first half of the 1990s. This paper outlines the nature of capital flows in these countries and examines the process of, and the driving forces behind, their liberalization of capital account transactions. Macroeconomic effects and policy responses to capital inflows are also analysed.

Even though there is no clear evidence that the volatility in domestic financial markets increased during the period of capital inflows compared to the earlier period, the paper shows that the presence of more foreign capital can threaten the stability of financial markets for at least a short period of time. The four countries have been able to stabilize their currencies by actively intervening in the foreign-exchange market. While inflation rates increased in the first half of the 1990s compared to the second half of the 1980s, the four countries have been more or less successful in keeping the growth of the money supply and inflation under control, so that real exchange rates remained stable. However, Malaysia had to resort to direct control measures to dampen movements of short-term speculative capital and to stabilize its macroeconomy.

Sterilized intervention, which has been the main instrument of managing the inflow of foreign capital in the four countries, implies considerable costs for the economy and thus cannot serve as a measure of dealing with a continued large capital inflow, as is widely discussed in the existing literature. The paper also looks at alternative measures, such as a policy of more flexible exchange rates, allowing currency appreciation, and the encouragement of capital outflows. Implementation of a variable deposit requirement and a foreign-exchange transaction tax is also examined. The paper concludes that a currency transaction tax would be certainly one of the most effective measures in reducing movements of short-term speculative capital.

*   The authors would like to thank Gerry Helleiner, Yilmaz Akyüz and participants of the Conference on Global Capital Flows in Economic Development (organized by UNCTAD and the Jerome Levy Institute of Bard College) for their helpful comments. The authors are alone responsible for all remaining errors.

I.　Introduction

During 1990-1994 there was a surge of foreign capital inflows to developing countries in Asia. The net inflow during the period was $261 billion, more than twice that for the entire 1980s (IMF, 1995a). It represented approximately 50 per cent of total capital inflows to all developing countries.[1]

Distinct from the 1980s, much of the inflow in the 1990s was in the form of portfolio investment. While the share of portfolio investment in total net inflows was 8 per cent on average during 1983-1989, it rose to 24 per cent during 1990-1994. Net foreign portfolio investment increased from $10 billion during 1983-1989 to $63 billion during 1990-1994. Still, even in the 1990s, foreign direct investment (FDI) has been the most important source of external financing in these countries. The net inflow of FDI increased markedly, from $36 billion during 1983-1989 to $117 billion during 1990-1994, accounting for 45 per cent of the total net inflow. For comparison: in Latin America portfolio investment represented 66 per cent of the total net capital inflow during 1990-1994, while FDI represented 30 per cent during that period.

A number of developments in the Asian economies and in the industrial economies have been suggested as causes of the inflow. East Asia, including China, has been the most rapidly growing and dynamic region in the world. The higher demand for capital, arising from the need to sustain a high rate of investment, and favourable growth prospects have attracted a large amount of foreign investment to the region. Such investment has become easier as East Asian economies deregulated their domestic markets and liberalized capital-account transactions. Domestic financial reform and financial-market opening have greatly facilitated foreign investment in domestic securities. Finally, the decline in interest rates and the international diversification of the portfolios of institutional investors in the industrial countries also contributed to increased capital flows to Asia.

Capital inflows in the form of foreign direct and portfolio investment have been crucial in supporting a high rate of investment and GDP growth in South-East Asian countries such as Indonesia, Malaysia and Thailand. At the same time, however, inflows of speculative short-term capital have undermined macroeconomic stability because they have resulted in large swings in key financial variables, including the exchange rate. Some countries have therefore resorted to direct control measures to dampen short-term capital movements.

This paper analyses the experiences with the management of capital flows in four East Asian countries with different economic and institutional structures: Indonesia, Malaysia, the Republic of Korea, and Thailand. These countries have been the major recipients of foreign capital in Asia. Compared to the entire 1980s, the amount of net capital flows to the four countries doubled during 1990-1994, totalling $143 billion and accounting for about 55 per cent of total net capital flows to Asian developing countries.

Section II will examine the nature of capital flows in these countries. This is followed by an analysis of the process of and the driving forces behind capital-account liberalization. Macroeconomic effects of and policy responses to capital inflows are also analysed. We then consider some of the policy measures that have been implemented and other measures that have been under consideration for dealing with capital inflows.

II.　Trend and composition of foreign capital flows in the 1990s

A.　*Republic of Korea*

The Republic of Korea began to witness a surge in the inflow of foreign capital in 1991. The large interest-rate differential between domestic and foreign financial markets, coupled with the favourable prospects of the economy, has made the Republic of Korea one of the most attractive emerging markets, and the liberalization of the capital account triggered a massive inflow, totalling $32.1 billion during 1990-1994, more than ten times the total for the 1980s.

However, relative to the size of the economy, the magnitude of the flow to the Republic of Korea has been relatively small compared to other East Asian countries. The capital-account surplus between 1990 and 1994 averaged only 2.0 per cent of GDP, compared to 10.1 per cent for Thailand, 10.2 per cent for Malaysia, and 4.0 per cent for Indonesia. The difference is partly attributable to Korea's tighter control of capital movements, but mainly to a relatively smaller current-account deficit. In other words, the investment-saving gap of the Republic of Korea has been narrower than in the three other countries (chart 1).

Chart 1

TRENDS OF INVESTMENT AND SAVINGS, 1986-1994

(Per cent of GDP)

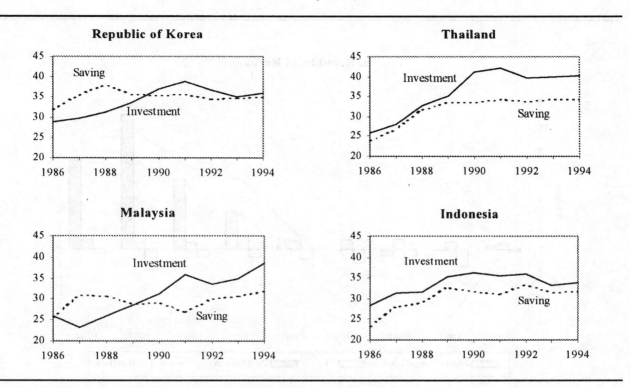

Source: IMF, *International Financial Statistics*, various issues.

In the 1990s, the capital flows to the Republic of Korea consisted mainly of portfolio investment (chart 2a). Net foreign portfolio investment increased from just $29 million in 1989 to $3.2 billion in 1991, and peaked at $11.0 billion in 1993. The cumulative amount during 1991-1994 was $27.2 billion, accounting for 88 per cent of the total foreign capital inflow during the period.

FDI was the main source of inflow in the second half of the 1980s, and it peaked in 1991. In the first half of the 1990s, the Republic of Korea became relatively less attractive to foreign corporate investment because of large increases in production costs. There was a net outflow in long-term foreign lending as loan repayments continued (see Park, 1995).

The increase in portfolio investment in the 1990s was due primarily to the softening of rules on overseas issues of securities by domestic firms and the opening of the Korean stock market. A decline in world market

interest rates resulting from the recession in the developed countries urged Korean firms and banks to mobilize cheaper foreign funds available in the international capital markets. At the same time, low interest rates in the industrial economies provided strong incentives for international investors to increase their holdings of securities in the emerging markets, including the Republic of Korea.

The opening of the Korean stock market in January 1992 accelerated the inflow, but issues of securities in international financial markets continued to be a significant portion. From the first quarter of 1992 through to the third quarter of 1995, the cumulative inflow of foreign capital related to overseas issues of securities by domestic firms and banks amounted to $19 billion, accounting for approximately 62 per cent of the total inflow of portfolio investment. The dominance was particularly pronounced during 1994-1995, when the Korean stock market performed poorly. Between October 1994 and June 1995, there

Chart 2

TREND AND COMPOSITION OF FOREIGN CAPITAL INFLOWS, 1986-1994

($ billion)

a. Republic of Korea

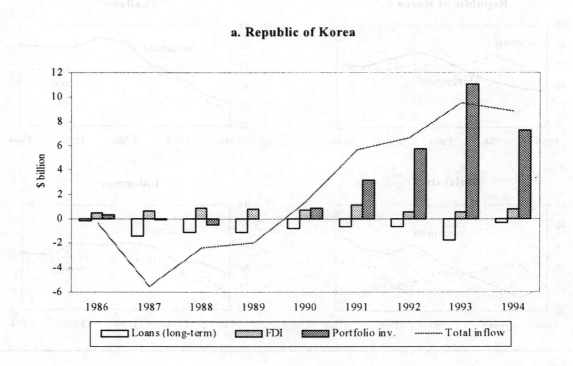

b. Thailand

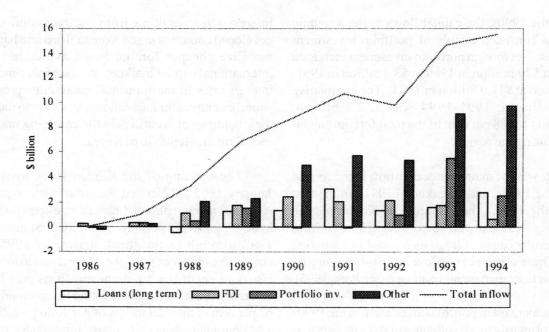

Chart 2 (concluded)

TREND AND COMPOSITION OF FOREIGN CAPITAL INFLOWS, 1986-1994

($ billion)

c. Malaysia

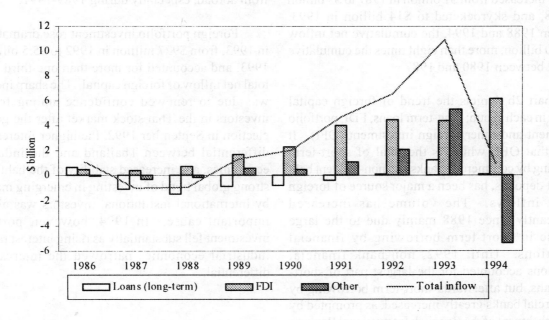

d. Indonesia

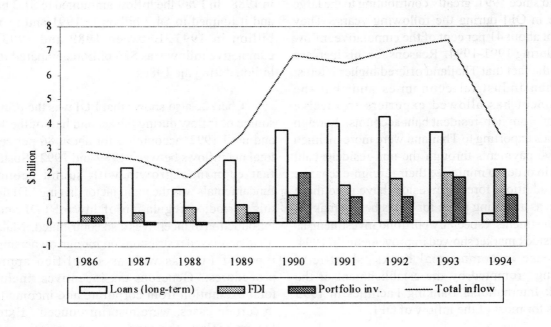

Source: IMF, *Balance of Payments Statistics*, various issues.

was a net outflow of non-resident investment in the Korean stock market of $634 million.

B. Thailand

Thailand has seen a large increase in foreign capital inflows from the late 1980s onwards. Net inflows increased from $1 billion in 1987 to $3 billion in 1988, and skyrocketed to $14 billion in 1993. Between 1988 and 1994, the cumulative net inflow was $70 billion, more than eight times the cumulative amount between 1980 and 1987.

Chart 2b depicts the trend of foreign capital inflows in each group; long-term loans, FDI, portfolio investment and other foreign investment (OFI). It shows that OFI, which is the total of short-term borrowing by commercial banks and non-resident baht account deposits, has been a major source of foreign capital inflows. The volume has increased significantly since 1988 mainly due to the large increase in short-term borrowing by financial institutions. Until 1992, non-bank financial institutions accounted for the largest part of short-term loans, but afterwards short-term borrowing by commercial banks greatly increased, as prompted by the establishment of the Bangkok International Banking Facilities (discussed in section III.B.2 below) in 1993.

It should also be noted that the volume of non-resident baht account deposits has considerably increased since 1991, greatly contributing to the large increase in OFI during the following years. They represent about 41 per cent of the cumulative inflow of OFI during 1991-1994. Reasons for this increase include the fact that Thailand offered higher interest rates than industrial economies and that the Government has allowed exporters to receive payments from non-resident baht accounts. Foreign companies exporting to Thailand were more inclined to receive payments through the non-resident baht account in order to minimize their foreign-exchange risk. In addition, foreign investors have used these accounts as a parking place for funds before making other investments, especially portfolio investment, as the Thai stock market showed improvement. In 1994, an increase in commercial banks' short-term borrowing prompted by the establishment of the Bangkok International Banking Facilities in 1993 accounts for most of the inflow of OFI.

Having reached a peak of $2.4 billion in 1990, FDI fell subsequently. An important reason is the country's poor infrastructure, which has lowered potential returns on investment. A general decline in global FDI during 1990-1991 and intense competition from developing countries such as China, Viet Nam, and India are additional causes. It should be noted that Malaysia, which has a relatively good infrastructure and a somewhat more skilled labour force, has maintained substantial FDI inflows. A high interest-rate differential boosted long-term borrowing from abroad, especially during 1989-1991.

Foreign portfolio investment rose dramatically in 1993, from $927 million in 1992 to $5.5 billion in 1993, and accounted for more than one-third of the total net inflow of foreign capital. The sharp increase was due to renewed confidence among foreign investors in the Thai stock market after the general election in September 1992, the higher interest rate differential between Thailand and the industrial economies, and increased stability of the baht. The strong global trend of investing in emerging markets by international institutional investors was also an important cause. In 1994, however, portfolio investment fell substantially as rising interest rates in industrial economies narrowed the interest-rate differential.

C. Malaysia

In Malaysia, the surge in foreign capital inflows started in 1989, following an outflow of $0.9 billion in 1988. In 1989 the inflow amounted to $1.3 billion and it jumped to $4.7 billion in 1991 and to $10.9 billion in 1993. Between 1989 and 1993, the cumulative inflow was $26 billion compared to $17 billion during the 1980s.

Chart 2c also shows that FDI was the principal source of inflow during the second half of the 1980s and until 1992, accounting for about 86 per cent of total net inflows between 1989 and 1992. Sustained fast economic growth with sound economic fundamentals was the main factor driving FDI during this period; deregulation of inward FDI and the introduction of incentives also contributed. Malaysia lifted or relaxed restrictions on foreign ownership and types of FDI, as well as simplified approval procedures. Generous tax incentives, including total exemption from corporate and income taxes in certain cases, were also introduced. External factors include the continued appreciation of the Japanese yen and rapidly rising labour costs in the Asian NIEs.

Chart 2c shows that other foreign investment, negligible until 1990, began to increase significantly in 1991, and in 1993 it exceeded FDI. For Malaysia, OFI includes portfolio investment and commercial banks' short-term external liabilities which are largely associated with their short-term borrowing and non-resident ringgit accounts. It amounted to $5.3 billion in 1993, more than two and a half times the 1992 level. It should also be noted that in 1993 there has been an unusually high entry in the capital account of $4.0 billion under errors and omissions, something that may be closely related to the inflow of foreign portfolio investment (Aziz, 1994).

The increased inflow of portfolio investment and commercial banks' borrowing was due to a large gap between domestic and foreign interest rates, the promising prospects of the Malaysian economy, and the improved performance of the domestic stock market, partly related to the privatization of several State enterprises.

In early 1994, the Malaysian Government implemented several administrative measures in order to curb the inflow of short-term speculative capital. As a result, a large net outflow was recorded under other foreign investment.

D. Indonesia

Indonesia has experienced massive inflows of foreign capital since 1990. The inflow increased from $3.6 billion in 1989 to $6.8 billion in 1990 and to $7.1 billion in 1992. In cumulative terms, it amounted to $36 billion between 1990 and 1994, compared to $25 billion in the period 1982 to 1989.

Long-term borrowing was the principal form of inflow throughout the 1980s and until 1993 (chart 2d). During 1990-1993, it amounted to $16 billion, representing about half of the total net capital inflows. While most borrowing during the 1980s was by the public sector, the level of borrowing by private firms and banks has also increased substantially since 1990. During 1990-1993, the net inflow of long-term borrowing by the private and the public sector was $10.6 billion and $3.2 billion, respectively. The corresponding figures for the period 1982 to 1989 had been $0.5 billion and $20.2 billion. The removal of the ceiling on foreign commercial borrowing by banks in 1989 and high domestic interest rates in the early 1990s were the principal factors in the increase in private borrowing. The introduction of a swap

facility with Bank Indonesia, the central bank, also helped.

Indonesia's dependence on long-term borrowing has been greater than that of the Republic of Korea, Malaysia and Thailand. The country's access to international capital markets has been limited due to the low credit rating of its domestic firms. Deregulation of inward FDI and an improved economic outlook have helped increase the flow of FDI. Still, Indonesia has not been able to secure enough FDI to fill as much of the investment-saving gap as the other East Asian countries such as Malaysia. This is attributable to poor infrastructure and low-quality labour. Accordingly, Indonesia had to rely on loans with government guarantees.

However, the loan portion of the total capital inflow fell in the 1990s, while that of FDI and portfolio investment rose compared to the 1980s. While FDI and portfolio investment made up only 12 per cent and 7 per cent, respectively, of total inflow during 1982-1989, their shares increased to 20 per cent and 18 per cent during 1990-1993. Finally, the amount of inward FDI exceeded that of long-term borrowing in 1994.

Most foreign portfolio investment in Indonesia has been made through the stock market in which foreign investors are allowed to participate since 1987. Increased portfolio investment in the early 1990s was closely related to the deregulation of domestic capital markets such as the simplification of requirements for listing on the stock exchange and the establishment of an over-the-counter market. The bullish stock market and the large interest-rate differential between Indonesia and industrial countries resulted in a large inflow of portfolio investment in 1993. Since 1993, with improved credit rating of Indonesian firms, issues of Indonesian securities in international capital markets have increased.

III. Liberalization of the capital account

A. Republic of Korea

Since the early 1960s, developments in the current account dictated the way capital controls were implemented. For example, when the current account deteriorated, restrictions on capital outflows were tightened while those on inflows were loosened.

In the first half of the 1980s, the current account continued to be in deficit although the size of the deficit was steadily decreasing. The Korean economy had difficulties in attracting foreign capital because of the high country risk relating to political instability and the continued depreciation of the Korean won. In an effort to ease the difficulties, the Government tightened regulations on capital outflows mainly by restricting overseas investments by residents, and took several measures to ease inward capital movements. In 1981, for example, foreign investors were allowed to participate in the Korean stock market through investment trust funds set up exclusively for this purpose[2] and, in 1985, Korean firms were allowed to raise capital overseas by issuing convertible bonds, bonds with warrants, and depositary receipts.

The easing led to a sharp increase in borrowing from abroad by domestic firms and banks. In 1986 the current account recorded a surplus which continued to expand until 1989. This surplus resulted from the recovery of the world economy and the rapid appreciation of the Japanese yen which improved the competitiveness of Korean exports. Foreign-exchange reserves, only $2.8 billion at the end of 1985, reached $12.6 billion a year later and $15 billion at the end of 1989. With a view to reduce what it considered excessive foreign-exchange holdings, the Government abolished all restrictions on outward foreign direct investment below $1 million and permitted residents to purchase foreign real estate for business purposes. However, commercial loans to domestic firms were not allowed, except in the case of public enterprises. Issues of bonds and depositary receipts by residents were also restricted.

In 1990, the current-account balance moved into deficit because of rising domestic wages, real appreciation of the won, and the deterioration of the world economy. The current account worsened in 1991, generating a deficit of $8.7 billion, more than four times the level of the preceding year. The amount of foreign-exchange reserves held by the Bank of Korea fell markedly. Facing difficulties in financing the mounting current-account deficit, the Government once again liberalized the capital account by amending the Foreign-Exchange Management Act (FEMA).

Under the FEMA, amended in 1991, transactions classified as capital inflows were liberalized first, although the positive list system of control - only those transactions specifically listed are allowed - remained intact. A negative list system - only those transactions specifically listed are not allowed - was adopted for current-account transactions. Residents could raise funds by issuing securities abroad under certain conditions.

Restrictions on direct investment by non-residents were almost completely lifted. Most importantly, effective from January 1992, foreign investors were allowed to invest directly in the Korean stock market, albeit with a number of restrictions, including a limitation of 10 per cent of the share that non-resident investors as a group could hold in the total equity capital of listed companies. The limit was raised to 12 per cent in December 1994 and to 15 per cent in July 1995.

As a result of these measures, capital inflows, mainly in the form of portfolio investment, began to surge in 1991. Net foreign capital inflows in 1990 amounted to only $1.3 billion, but increased to $5.7 billion in 1991 and to $9.6 billion in 1993. Net foreign portfolio investment accounted for 51 per cent of the increase in total net foreign capital inflows in 1991 and 180 per cent in 1993 (a year with negative net direct investment). During this three-year period, the cumulative total of the current-account deficit was $12.9 billion, whereas foreign portfolio investment amounted to $21.9 billion. The surge in the capital inflow resulted in a large surplus in the overall account.

A sudden increase in foreign capital inflows on top of the improvement in the current account threatened the stability of both domestic financial markets and the economy in general. Several steps were taken to liberalize outward capital movements and, thus, to reduce the overall surplus. Domestic institutional investors such as securities firms, insurance companies and investment trust companies were allowed to invest in foreign securities without any restriction, and the mode of controlling outward direct investment was changed from a positive to a negative list system in February 1994.

Even though many controls on foreign exchange and cross-border capital transactions were removed or relaxed, the foreign-exchange system was still subject to severe criticism for being too restrictive. Among other things, the rigid controls were claimed to undermine the international competitiveness of domestic firms. In response to these complaints and foreign pressure for further deregulation, the Government unveiled a new Plan for Foreign Exchange System Reform in December 1994. The Plan attempts to completely liberalize current- and capital-account transactions (with a few exceptions) and to develop an efficient domestic foreign-exchange market over a five-year period divided into three stages. It espouses a gradual liberalization process, with the actual speed of liberalization adjusted to the state of the economy. A focal point of the reform is the adoption of the negative list system in more areas. Removal of restrictions on capital outflows is given a higher priority than liberalizing inflows. Capital-account transactions closely related to investment in the real sector is deregulated prior to cross-border financial transactions (for more details, see Ministry of Finance and the Economy, 1994; and Korea Institute of Finance, 1994).

The implementation of capital-account liberalization began in February 1995, focusing on the deregulation of capital outflows. Among other things, the limit on the amount that domestic pension funds can invest in overseas securities was abolished and domestic residents were for the first time allowed to hold overseas deposit accounts.

Korean policy-makers have been reluctant to liberalize the capital account rapidly. There is considerable concern that macroeconomic stability would be jeopardized by a sudden opening-up of financial markets, while efficiency gains to the economy from liberalization are considered to be relatively small, possibly even insignificant, and would best be realized in the long run.

In a number of other countries, capital-account liberalization has increased the volatility of financial markets, including the foreign-exchange market. Furthermore, little is known as to how a small, semi-open economy such as the Republic of Korea, in a disequilibrium characterized by a domestic interest rate twice as high as that in international financial markets, would move to a new equilibrium if restrictions on capital-account transactions were removed suddenly and completely. At present, domestic financial markets are still underdeveloped and domestic financial institutions have little competitive advantage over their foreign counter-parts.

B.   *Thailand, Malaysia and Indonesia*

Unlike the Republic of Korea, these countries liberalized capital-account transactions earlier and more aggressively. Given their low saving rates, they needed a large amount of foreign capital to promote economic growth. To attract more foreign capital, they actively deregulated inward FDI and cross-border financial transactions as capital inflows decreased sharply after the Latin American debt crisis in 1982.

1.   *Foreign direct investment*

FDI flows to these countries have risen markedly since the late 1980s, attracted by strong economic performance and helped by the removal of restrictions and the introduction of incentives. While the cumulative inflow of inward FDI in Thailand was $2 billion during 1980-1987, it increased to $12 billion during 1988-1994. Total inward FDI in Malaysia was $21 between 1988 and 1994, compared to $7 billion between 1980 and 1987. For Indonesia, the numbers are $2 billion for 1980-1987 and $10 billion for 1988-1994.[3]

Thailand had lifted many restrictions on inward FDI during the 1970s, mainly through the Alien Business Law of 1972 and the Investment Promotion Act of 1977. These two acts basically espouse the negative list system. In the latter half of the 1980s, the Thai Government broadened and accelerated the liberalization process in order to attract more foreign capital, thereby helping to sustain the country's rapid economic growth. While restrictions on inward FDI in import-substitution industries were largely lifted in the 1970s, the deregulation of inward FDI in the 1980s and 1990s focused on export industries, with the expectation that the expansion of labour-intensive export industries would boost employment and help reduce the current-account deficit.

In 1991, foreign investors were allowed to own 100 per cent of firms that exported all of its output. Additional incentives for FDI in export sectors, such as tax abatement or exemption, were introduced. The Thai Government also introduced incentives for non-residents who invested in export-oriented activities outside of Bangkok. These included a five-year exemption from tariffs on imports of raw materials by foreign companies located in remote areas and exported more than 30 per cent of their output. By contrast, companies located in the Bangkok area were granted an exemption only for one year.

Foreign companies establishing in provincial areas can receive exemption from the corporate income tax for up to eight years. The maximum import tariff was reduced from 100 per cent to 30 per cent as of January 1, 1995. With the help of these deregulatory measures, annual inward FDI in Thailand increased from $0.4 billion in 1987 to $2.4 billion in 1990, declining slightly thereafter.

In Malaysia, much of the liberalization of inward FDI took place during 1985-1987. In 1985, as an incentive to encourage the transfer of advanced technology to the domestic industries, the Malaysian

Government permitted non-residents to own more than half of the capital of companies considered "high-tech". The Promotion of Investment Act of 1986 provided various incentives for foreign investment in manufacturing, agriculture and tourism. These included simplification of the investment process and raising the limit on the percentage of a joint venture that non-residents could own. Since 1987, non-residents have been allowed to wholly own companies that export at least 80 per cent of their output and to purchase domestic real estate for business purposes with funds brought in from abroad.

Starting in 1989, foreign firms could issue corporate bonds in the domestic securities market. In the same year, legislation was passed to protect the copyright of non-residents for 25 years. These measures helped increase annual inward FDI from $0.7 billion in 1988 to $2.3 billion in 1990, and to $6.1 billion in 1994.

In Indonesia, from the 1970s until the mid-1980s, the bulk of inward FDI was concentrated in the oil and gas sector. This meant ever-greater dependence of the economy on these industries. In an effort to develop a more balanced industrial structure and promote manufactured exports, Indonesia actively began to liberalize inward FDI in the non-oil-and-gas sector. In 1985, the approval process for inward FDI was considerably simplified and in the following year non-residents were allowed to establish joint ventures in the non-oil-and-gas export sector. Initially, the maximum non-resident ownership of joint ventures that exported all of their products was 80 per cent. The limit was raised to 95 per cent in 1987. More importantly, a negative list system was adopted in managing inward FDI in 1989. The minimum amount of inward FDI was gradually reduced from $1 million and was entirely abolished in 1994.

In 1994, FDI was allowed in previously barred sectors such as telecommunications, ports, railways and nuclear power. During the early 1990s, most remaining restrictions on foreign ownership were removed so that by 1994 100 per cent ownership was possible in most industries. With help of these measures, the amount of inward FDI increased from $0.6 billion in 1987 to $1.5 billion in 1991, and to $2.1 billion in 1994.

2.   Portfolio and other investment

Along with the deregulation of FDI, the three countries also speeded up the liberalization of cross-border financial transactions throughout the 1980s and early 1990s for the purpose of diversifying sources of foreign funds and encouraging the development of their domestic financial markets.

Thailand began to accelerate liberalization of cross-border financial transactions in the mid-1980s. The Government created two funds for foreign investors in Thai securities, the Bangkok Fund in 1985 and the Thailand Fund in 1986, and allowed ten more funds during 1987-1990. In 1987, in response to the foreign-ownership limit having been reached by so many companies, the Stock Exchange of Thailand established an Alien Board where foreign investors can trade such stocks among each other. In general, foreign investors are restricted from holding more than 49 per cent of the total shares of a listed Thai company, but the limit varies by industry. In the banking sector, for example, a 25 per cent limit is applied.

The Bangkok International Banking Facilities (BIBF) was launched in March 1993 with the expectation that they would lower the cost of foreign borrowing and develop Thailand as a regional financial centre. BIBF is Thailand's version of an offshore financial market, in which commercial banks with BIBF licenses are allowed to carry out lending (out-in) and other international and investment banking operations as well as traditional offshore banking (out-out). In 1993, 47 commercial banks were granted BIBF licenses. They included 32 foreign banks, 12 that already had been operating in Thailand and 20 newcomers (see Tivakul and Svetarundra, 1993; and Vichyanond, 1994).

Malaysia allowed foreign investors to participate directly in the domestic stock market in 1973, when the Kuala Lumpur Stock Exchange was established. Since 1995 foreign investors as a whole can not hold more than 30 per cent of listed shares of any one company, and those wishing to hold more than 15 per cent or 5 million ringgit worth must obtain approval from the Foreign Investment Committee.

Since 1985 foreign securities companies have been allowed to open branches and, since 1986, to invest in local securities firms. In 1987, the maximum amount of residents' overseas borrowing in foreign currency that could be raised without approval by the central bank was increased from 100 thousand ringgit to 1 million ringgit.

In 1988, foreign stock brokerage firms were allowed to increase their equity shares in local brokerage firms from 30 per cent to 49 per cent.

During 1987-1989, three investment trust funds for foreign investors were established to promote foreign participation in the local stock market. Malaysia opened the Labuan International Offshore Financial Centre in 1990.

Indonesia, in an attempt to facilitate capital inflows, embarked on active liberalization of cross-border financial transactions in the mid-1980s. Foreign investor participation in the domestic stock market was first allowed in 1987, with ownership of companies limited to 49 per cent. The Government allowed non-residents to establish joint-venture securities firms with residents in 1988.

In the same year, the Government allowed the existing branches of foreign banks to open sub-branches in six major cities (Bandung, Semarang, Surabaya, Medan, Ujung Pandang and Denpasar) outside Jakarta and permitted foreign banks to establish joint ventures with domestic banks. While there had been only one joint-venture in 1988, their number increased to 30 by the end of 1994. During the same period the number of branches of foreign banks and joint-venture banks increased from 21 to 83. In 1989, the ceiling on foreign commercial borrowing by banks was removed. In 1992, the purchase of bank shares by non-residents, initially banned, could be raised to 49 per cent while domestic firms were permitted to list up to 30 per cent of their equity on foreign stock exchanges.

It should be noted, however, that more recently there have been changes in capital-account liberalization policies of South-East Asian countries. A number of measures have been adopted to reduce the volume and volatility of short-term flows as the massive inflow of foreign capital over a short period of time was considered to be destabilizing. Malaysia and Indonesia imposed quantitative restrictions on capital inflows, while Thailand sought to deregulate outflows.

Thailand chose to liberalize outflows rather than to restrict inflows. By liberalizing foreign-exchange controls in three stages from 1990 through 1994, most restrictions on outflows were removed. Previously, the outflow of capital was tightly controlled and there was almost no restriction on inflows. The first round of the liberalization process in May 1990 focused on deregulation of current-account transactions. The second (April 1991) and third rounds (February 1994) saw most of the controls on capital outflows lifted. For example, in 1991, the Thai Government allowed the free transfer of capital up to $5 million for direct

investment and removed the requirement that repatriation of investment had to be approved. In 1994, it raised the maximum amount of capital that could be taken out of the country to Viet Nam and bordering countries to 500,000 baht (about $20,000). Among the remaining restrictions, there is the need for approval by the Bank of Thailand for the purchase of foreign securities and real estate by residents.

The Malaysian Government, in 1991, made outstanding ringgit received through swap transactions with non-residents subject to a reserve requirement. In 1992, the total amount of borrowing in foreign currency from domestic banks by a resident was limited to $1 million; previously there had been no maximum. In early 1994, the Government also implemented administrative controls to discourage the inflow of foreign capital, especially speculative short-term capital. These included prohibiting the sale of short-term money-market instruments to non-residents, commercial bank swaps, and forward transactions on the bid side with foreign customers. The first has proved to be most successful in curbing the inflow of short-term capital (IMF, 1995a).

Indonesia adopted several measures in 1991 to discourage overseas borrowing. Bank Indonesia, the central bank, reduced swap operations by lowering the limit for an individual bank from 25 per cent to 20 per cent of its capital, raising the swap premium by 5 percentage points, and announcing that future swap operations could be undertaken only at its initiative. Limits were imposed on offshore borrowing by State enterprises and commercial banks, and all State-related overseas commercial borrowing had to obtain prior approval from the Government. In the same year, a debt management team was organized to supervise foreign loan transactions.

IV. Macroeconomic aspects of capital inflows and policy responses

A. *Inflation, the real exchange rate and financial market volatility: an overview*

The effects of capital inflows on the recipient country depend on the size and composition of the inflows, the foreign-exchange rate system, developments in domestic financial markets, and the availability and flexibility of economic policy measures. Usually, a surge in capital inflows causes the nominal and the real exchange rate to appreciate

Chart 3

RATE OF CHANGE IN THE CONSUMER PRICE INDEX AND DEPRECIATION RATE OF REAL EFFECTIVE EXCHANGE RATES

(Per cent)

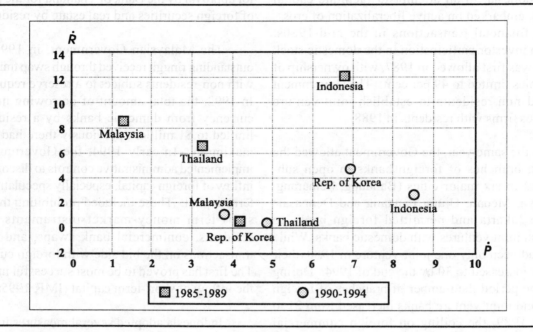

Note: $\dot{R}$ = Depreciation rate of real effective exchange rate.

$\dot{P}$ = Rate of change in the consumer price index.

The real effective exchange rates for the Republic of Korea are estimates by the Korea Institute of Finance. Those of other countries are adopted from DRI's *World Market Executive Overview*. The wholesale price index has been used to calculate real effective exchange rates of all four countries.

and the current account to deteriorate. It may also lead to an expansion of monetary aggregates, thus giving rise to increased inflationary pressure.

Chart 3 compares the average consumer price inflation and the rate of depreciation of the real effective exchange rates in the second half of the 1980s with those of the first half of the 1990s when these countries witnessed a surge in foreign capital inflow. Inflation increased in all four countries in the 1990s compared to the previous period. However, this was not necessarily a result of foreign capital inflows. Obviously, a more sophisticated and extensive econometric study is required to establish the causality between a higher rate of inflation and foreign capital inflow in these countries.

Most Latin American countries experienced an appreciation of the real exchange rate in the 1990s as a consequence of capital inflows (see Mathieson and

Rojas-Suarez, 1993). For the four Asian countries, however, real effective exchange rates depreciated, on average, in the 1990s.

The difference in the movement of real exchange rates is closely related to the composition of aggregate demand. In the Asian countries, investment as a share of GDP generally showed a rising trend during the period of capital inflows. In Latin America, investment fell and consumption rose, especially during 1990 and 1991. Differences in the behaviour of Government consumption have also been a factor (Khan and Reinhart, 1995; Leiderman, 1995; and Calvo et al., 1994). The Asian countries managed to maintain fiscal discipline in the face of rising capital inflows. Usually, public consumption is more biased than private consumption toward non-traded goods.

The stability of these countries' real effective exchange rates in the 1990s has also been greatly affected by the steep nominal appreciation of the yen against the United States dollar, coupled with stability of nominal exchange rates against the United States dollar. This brought about a sharp nominal depreciation of their currencies against the yen. Given that Japan is a major trading partner, this generated a substantial downward pressure on their real effective exchange rates. By contrast, there was only a minor influence on the real effective exchange rates of Latin American countries, as their trade with Japan is relatively less important.

The movement of foreign capital in massive amounts may increase the volatility of domestic financial markets, including the foreign-exchange market. To examine whether financial markets have become more volatile compared to the pre-capital-inflow period, GARCH variance has been estimated for exchange rates, stock returns and interest rates (see annex).

The results do not show clear evidence that exchange-rate volatility increased during the period of capital inflows compared to earlier periods. This is presumably due to the exchange-rate policies adopted: The response has been to maintain the international price competitiveness of exports by preventing a rapid appreciation of the nominal exchange rate or even inducing depreciation through intervention in the local foreign-exchange market.

The fact that the movement of the won-dollar exchange rate has become more volatile since early 1995 could be explained by the fact that the Government of the Republic of Korea refrained from intervention in the foreign-exchange market, suggesting that volatility may have been suppressed by intervention until 1994.

The rupiah-dollar rate exhibited high volatility from the second half of 1990 through the first half of 1991, because the Indonesian Government pursued depreciation of the rupiah more actively than before, as the current-account deficit increased unprecedentedly during that period. The increased volatility of the ringgit-dollar rate in early 1994 was closely related to capital flows. The Malaysian Government imposed several direct measures in early 1994 to curb the inflow of speculative short-term capital. This prompted foreign investors to withdraw investments from Malaysia. The result was a large depreciation of the ringgit over a short period of time.

Financial volatility may also rise in response to an increase in foreign participation in the stock market (Folkerts-Landau et al., 1995; and IMF, 1995a). Domestic investors in emerging markets sometimes follow the strategies of foreign institutional investors who are considered to have more advanced skills in stock investment, thereby amplifying volatility. However, there is no strong evidence that the opening of stock markets or the inflow of capital during the 1990s resulted in increased volatility (see annex chart 2). This is consistent with the results of Kim and Singal (1995) and the IMF (1995a). Indeed, the volatility of stock returns in the Republic of Korea tended to decrease after the opening of the stock market in January 1992, even though large swings remained.

However, the estimates do show that the presence of more foreign capital can weaken the stability of a stock market for at least a short period of time.[4] In late 1993 and early January 1994 massive capital inflows contributed to a rapid rise in stock prices on the Kuala Lumpur Stock Exchange, and in the first half of 1994 an outflow of foreign capital led to a rapid fall in stock prices. These resulted in an increased volatility of stock returns in Malaysia. The Thai stock market saw a sudden outflow of foreign funds (related to the Gulf War) in the second half of 1990, and the Thai and Malaysian stock markets in early 1995 witnessed quick withdrawals of foreign investment prompted by the Mexican crisis. Such flows caused an increase in volatility of stock returns (see annex charts 2b and c).

The volatility of weekly average interest rates in the Republic of Korea increased significantly in 1992 (see annex chart 3), mainly related to domestic interest-rate liberalization. In Malaysia, interest rate volatility was very high in 1986. Subsequently, the volatility decreased considerably although it sometimes showed large swings. Large volatility increases in 1990 and early 1995 are partly attributable to sudden capital outflows prompted by the Gulf War and the Mexican crisis.

Faced with a surge in the inflow of foreign capital, the four countries have sought to stabilize the exchange rates of their currencies in order to protect their export sectors. Simultaneously, they have used monetary sterilization to absorb the excess liquidity resulting from the increase in net foreign assets. Strong fiscal discipline has also been maintained, especially in Thailand.

B. Macroeconomic effects and policy responses

1. Republic of Korea

Since the mid-1960s, economic growth in the Republic of Korea has been propelled by the rapid expansion of exports and investment arising from increases in foreign demand. Reflecting this export-oriented development, the degree of openness (measured by exports plus imports as a percentage of GDP) has been very high since the mid-1980s.

Policy-makers have been very careful not to allow the competitiveness of Korean products to fall behind. Between 1990 and 1993, the foreign-exchange rate policy was geared to maintaining a weak won regardless of whether the overall balance was in surplus or deficit. As a result, the Korean won depreciated even when a large capital inflow generated an overall surplus.

The overall account recorded deficits in 1990 and 1991 because of a large current-account deficit (see table 1). This was accompanied by a depreciation of the won against the United States dollar. Since 1992, the won has been experiencing strong upward pressures as a result of large overall surpluses. Both a large increase in foreign capital inflows and the improvement in the current account have contributed to this. Despite the surpluses, the won continued to depreciate until the end of 1993, implying that the Bank of Korea actively intervened. The Bank of Korea's net foreign assets increased by $8.6 billion during 1992 and 1993, when the overall account surplus was $11.4 billion.

Since 1994, the won has shown a steady appreciation against the United States dollar. By the end of 1994 it had appreciated by 2.5 per cent compared to the end of previous year. The appreciation was mainly because of the marked appreciation of the yen against the dollar, which led to a large depreciation of the real effective exchange rate of the won. Between 1992 and the second quarter of 1995, the real effective exchange rate depreciated by 28 per cent, entirely accounted for by the appreciation of the yen. The strong yen has contributed to a sharp increase in Korean export earnings and thus meant that the central bank could let the won appreciate to a certain extent without risking erosion of the price competitiveness of Korean exporters. The large capital inflow and export expansion resulted in an overall account surplus of $2.8 billion in 1994. Although the surplus was large, so long as the yen remained strong, the Bank of Korea did not consider it necessary to intervene in the foreign-exchange market.

As to monetary policy, it appears that the Bank of Korea resorted to active sterilization to counter the effects of foreign capital inflows on the money supply. Foreign-exchange market intervention increased the holdings of foreign assets by the central bank, thereby increasing the money supply - which is the most carefully monitored intermediate target of monetary policy. To offset the increase, the monetary authorities required financial institutions to purchase monetary stabilization bonds (MSBs). Kim (1991) calculates that the Bank of Korea sterilized about 90 per cent of the increase in net foreign assets during the 1980s.

Chart 4 shows changes in the net domestic assets (NDA) and net foreign assets (NFA) of the Bank of Korea from 1986 to 1994. The amount has changed considerably even after the market average exchange rate system was adopted in 1990. This implies that the bank continued to intervene to stabilize the foreign-exchange rate. The intervention was most active during 1992-1993 because of the large increase in foreign portfolio investment. The chart also shows that changes in NFA and NDA have been inversely related to each other, suggesting that the Bank of Korea has actively engaged in mopping up increases in the money supply resulting from its foreign-exchange interventions.

Due to sterilization, money supply growth in the Republic of Korea has been kept under control. It has been decelerating continuously since 1990 and inflation has also been falling (table 1). While the Republic of Korea has avoided serious inflation, its interest rates have risen gradually since 1993 due to the crowding-out effect of the massive sterilization. The wide interest-rate gap between the Republic of Korea and the industrial economies continues to cause capital inflows.

Sterilization through sales of MSBs has other costs besides giving rise to higher interest rates: an increase in interest payments on MSBs is likely to produce inflationary pressure. Indeed, interest payments on MSBs explain about 78 per cent of the increase in the monetary base between 1990 and 1995. The Bank of Korea thus faces significant difficulties in further using sterilization to manage foreign capital inflows.

Table 1

REPUBLIC OF KOREA: ECONOMIC INDICATORS, 1987-1994

(Per cent, unless otherwise indicated)

	1987	1989	1990	1991	1992	1993	1994
GDP growth	11.5	6.4	9.5	9.1	5.1	5.8	8.4
Inflation[a]	3.0	5.7	8.6	9.3	6.2	4.8	6.2
Money supply (M2)	18.8	19.8	21.2	18.6	18.4	18.6	15.6
Interest rate[b]	12.6	15.2	16.5	18.9	16.2	12.6	12.9
Nominal exchange rate (Korean won per $)[c]	822.6	671.5	707.8	733.4	780.7	802.7	803.5
Rate of change	-6.7	-8.2	5.4	3.6	6.5	2.8	0.1
Real effective exchange rate[d] (1990=100)	113.9	99.2	100.0	103.3	111.6	119.1	124.6
Rate of change	-0.4	-8.2	0.8	3.3	8.1	6.7	4.6
Investment/GDP	29.8	33.6	36.9	38.9	36.6	35.1	36.1
Saving/GDP	35.5	35.7	35.5	35.7	34.5	34.8	35.0
Fiscal balance/GDP	0.8	0.3	0.1	-1.01	-0.3	0.1	0.2
Current account balance ($ million)	9,854	5,055	-2,179	-8,728	-4,529	385	-4,531
Current account balance as a percentage of GDP	7.4	2.3	-0.9	-3.0	-1.5	0.1	-1.2
Capital account balance ($ million)	-5,843	-3,423	3,881	4,227	8,343	6,879	9,025
Capital account balance as a percentage of GDP	-4.4	-1.6	1.5	1.5	2.7	2.1	2.4
Overall balance ($ million)	5,202	2,453	-273.9	-3,741	4,898	6,542	2,822
Foreign exchange reserves ($ million)	3,566	14,978	14,453	13,306	16,640	19,704	25,032

Source: Bank of Korea, *National Accounts,* various issues; Bank of Korea, *Monthly Bulletin,* various issues; IMF, *International Financial Statistics,* various issues.

  a   Rate of change of the consumer price index.
  b   Average annual yield on three-year bank-guaranteed corporate bonds.
  c   Annual average.
  d   Annual average; a rise in the index indicates a depreciation.

Chart 4

REPUBLIC OF KOREA: CHANGES IN NET DOMESTIC ASSETS AND NET FOREIGN ASSETS, 1986-1994

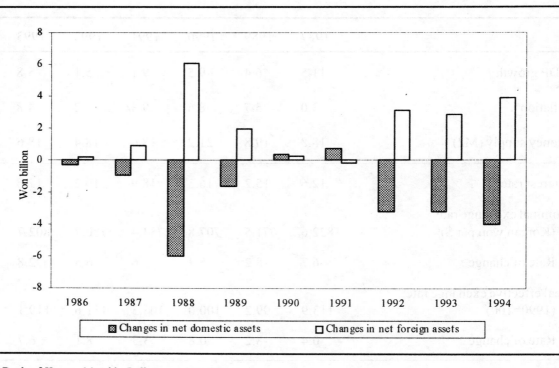

Source: Bank of Korea, *Monthly Bulletin*, various issues.

2. Thailand

Thailand has maintained fast economic growth since the late 1980s, with real GDP increases averaging 8.3 per cent annually during 1988-1994. It is often stressed that rapid growth of the Thai economy was largely due to the inflow of foreign capital beginning in 1988. The inflows played an important role in financing the high rate of investment when domestic savings were increasing slowly.

At the same time, Thailand had to deal with some adverse effects of the large capital inflow. High priority has been given to exchange rate stability (Nijathaworn and Dejthamrong, 1994; and Nijathaworn, 1995a). The baht-dollar rate has been more or less fixed since 1989. With Thailand's pursuit of export-led growth, maintaining price competitiveness for its exports has been crucial. A stable exchange rate has enabled the economy to continue to attract the foreign capital needed to maintain a high rate of domestic investment. However, the firm commitment of the Government to keep the nominal exchange rate stable has added to the burden borne by monetary sterilization to mop up excess liquidity arising from the increase in foreign assets of the central bank as a result of foreign-exchange market intervention.

Since November 1984, the baht has been linked to a multiple-currency basket while previously it had been pegged to United States dollar. This change came partly as a response to the appreciation of the United States dollar in the mid-1980s. Even though the composition of the currency basket has not been disclosed, higher weights are likely to be given to the currencies of Thailand's major trading partners, the United States, Japan, and Germany.[5] The weights are known to be adjusted according to the developments in foreign-exchange markets.

At 8 am on each business day, the Thai Exchange Equalization Fund (EEF) announces a basic exchange rate for the baht against the United States dollar. The EEF will trade unlimited amounts of the dollar with the commercial banks within a 0.02 baht band around this rate until noon. In the afternoon, the dollar is traded only in the interbank foreign-exchange market, where the rate for the baht is largely dependent on expectations of the next day's basic rate.

In setting the basic rate every day, the EEF takes into account the current state and future prospects of exports, imports and domestic inflation, along with developments in the major currencies in international foreign-exchange markets. However, most observers conjecture that the current-account balance plays a major role in deciding on the basic rate. This is reflected in the fact that the nominal rate has been extremely stable since the late 1980s. Between 1990 and 1994 the baht appreciated against the United States dollar by only 0.3 per cent annually, despite the fact that the overall account has shown a large surplus - attributable to a substantial inflow of foreign capital that more than offset the large current-account deficit (see table 2).

From the late 1980s onwards, the increase in net foreign assets has been the major source of money supply growth. This excess liquidity was partly responsible for an increase in domestic demand and high domestic inflation. The rate of change of the consumer price index rose from 2.5 per cent in 1987 to 5.9 per cent in 1990. Greater domestic demand also contributed to a deterioration in the current-account balance, which in turn reinforced Thailand's need for foreign capital. The current-account deficit as a percentage of GDP widened to 8.5 per cent in 1990, from 0.7 per cent in 1987. Although it has since moderated, it has remained above 5 per cent throughout the first half of the 1990s.

Fiscal discipline has been of great importance in managing the inflow of foreign capital (Nijathaworn and Dejthamrong, 1994; and Nijathaworn, 1995a, 1995b). The Government tightened fiscal policy in order to reduce domestic aggregate demand and inflationary pressures, as well as to lower the dependence on foreign capital by increasing national savings. The choice of fiscal policy is related to the ineffectiveness of monetary policy under a system of fixed exchange rates with free cross-border capital movements. It is also related, according to Nijathaworn (1995a, 1995b), to a policy bias (since the mid-1980s) towards strict fiscal discipline as the main medium-term means of macroeconomic stabilization. Actual government spending on investment is usually slower than budgeted expenditure, which enables the Government to achieve a fiscal surplus more easily.

The Government was able both to restrain its expenditure and improve tax revenue by enhancing the efficiency of tax collection and introducing new taxes, including a value-added tax of 7 per cent in 1992. As a consequence, the Government was able to achieve a fiscal surplus in 1988 and every year since then. Between 1988 and 1994 the average surplus was about 3 per cent of GDP. As its fiscal position improved, the Government repaid foreign debt in an effort to offset the inflow of foreign capital. The strong fiscal consolidation greatly contributed to a reduction in domestic inflationary pressure. In 1991, the fiscal surplus peaked at 4.9 per cent of GDP, absorbing more than 20 per cent of the increase in the money supply.

An important goal of monetary policy in the face of capital inflows has been monetary and interest-rate stabilization. The Bank of Thailand has used open-market operations in an attempt to control excess liquidity resulting from the increase in its net foreign assets and to reduce the volatility of domestic interest rates. This has been a tool of short-term management of excess liquidity, while fiscal policy has been used in a medium- and long-term perspective.

Frequent open-market operations have been necessary because under a system of fixed exchange rates with an open capital account as in Thailand monetary tightening is only effective in controlling liquidity and interest rates in the short run (Schadler et al., 1993). As a result, domestic interest rates were persistently higher than those of the industrial economies throughout the 1990s, providing an ongoing incentive for foreign capital to flow in (see chart 5).

Interventions in the repurchase market for Government and State-enterprise bonds and issuing central bank securities have been the main tools of monetary sterilization, which has usually been accompanied by "window guidance", through which the Bank of Thailand persuades commercial banks to restrain domestic credit. Thailand established a repurchase market in 1979 to encourage the development of a money market and to provide the Bank of Thailand with a new instrument for open-market operations (see Kittisrikangwan et al., 1994). In fact, open-market operations through the repurchase market in Thailand are effective only for very short-term liquidity management as participants prefer transactions with maturities of no more than two weeks. In general, financial institutions use the repurchase market for managing excess demand or the supply of funds with a very short time-horizon.

To overcome this, since 1987, the Bank of Thailand has issued central bank bonds with maturities

Table 2

THAILAND: ECONOMIC INDICATORS, 1987-1994

(Per cent, unless otherwise indicated)

	1987	1989	1990	1991	1992	1993	1994
GDP growth	9.5	12.2	11.6	8.1	7.6	8.9	8.5
Inflation*a*	2.5	5.4	5.9	5.7	4.1	3.5	5.3
Money supply (M2)	20.4	26.3	26.7	19.8	15.6	18.4	12.9
Interest rate*b*	9.50	9.50	12.25	13.67	8.88	8.63	8.46
Nominal exchange rate *c* (Thai bath per $)	25.72	25.70	25.59	25.52	25.40	25.32	25.15
Rate of change	-2.2	1.6	-0.5	-0.3	-0.5	-0.3	-0.7
Real effective exchange rated (1990=100)	103.5	101.8	100.0	101.0	102.6	105.6	106.1
Rate of change	7.6	-4.9	-1.8	1.0	1.5	3.0	0.5
Investment/GDP	27.9	35.1	41.1	42.2	39.9	39.9	40.1
Saving/GDP	26.9	33.7	33.5	34.4	34.2	34.2	34.4
Fiscal balance/GDP	-0.7	3.5	4.9	4.0	2.5	1.8	1.87
Current account balance ($ million)	-366	-2,498	-7,281	-7,571	-6,355	-7,047	-8,419
Current account balance as a percentage of GDP	-0.7	-3.5	-8.5	-7.7	-5.8	-5.6	-5.9
Capital account balance ($ million)	1,062	6,599	9,098	11,759	9,797	11,246	14,246
Capital account balance as a percentage of GDP	2.1	9.1	10.6	12.0	8.9	8.9	10.1
Overall balance ($ million)	945	5,029	3,235	4,618	2,925	3,907	4,169
Foreign exchange reserves ($ million)	3,906	9,641	13,247	17,287	20,012	24,078	28,884

Source: IMF, *International Financial Statistics*, various issues; Bank of Thailand, *Annual Economic Report 1994*; DRI, *World Markets Executive Overview* (fourth quarter 1995).

   a Rate of change of the consumer price index.
   b Maximum rate offered by commercial banks on three- to six month savings deposits (annual average).
   c Annual average.
   d Annual average; a rise in the index indicates a depreciation.

Chart 5

INTEREST RATES IN THAILAND AND THE UNITED STATES, QUARTERLY, 1986-1994

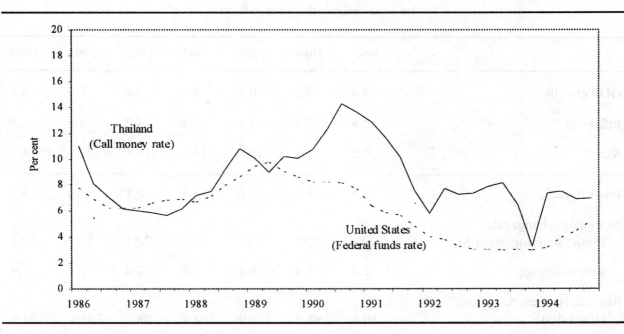

Source: IMF, *International Financial Statistics*, various issues.

between 6 and 12 months. It also established a short-term central-bank bond market in August 1995. Since then, it has also issued bonds with maturities ranging from one to six months on a weekly basis. This made the bank's injection or absorption of reserve money more effective.

The Government has also dealt with the inflow of foreign capital by deregulating the outflow of capital. In three rounds of foreign-exchange liberalization since 1990 it removed all restrictions on capital outflows, except a few that are related to portfolio and property investment. This was also accompanied by tighter prudential requirements for the financial sector with respect to capital adequacy, loan-loss provisions, and exposure to foreign-exchange risk.

As a result of fiscal discipline, monetary tightening, deregulation of capital outflows, and tighter prudential requirements, the growth of the money supply decelerated and inflation has been stable throughout the 1990s despite increasing capital inflows. The growth rate of M2 fell from 26.7 per cent in 1990 to 15.6 per cent in 1992 and to 12.9 per cent in 1994. The CPI increase went down from 5.9 per cent in 1990 to 3.5 per cent in 1993, but rose to

5.3 per cent in 1994. This rise was related to increased production costs. Continued inflows of FDI increased the demand for labour and caused the limited available infrastructure to be overcharged, leading to a rise in wages and the cost of infrastructure. The sharp appreciation of the yen against the United States dollar was also a factor. The baht depreciated by 10 per cent against the yen during 1994.

Increased foreign portfolio investment exposes Thailand's financial markets to external shocks. Foreign acquisition of Thai stocks was a major factor in the 88 per cent increase in the Stock Exchange of Thailand (SET) index in 1993, following a 26 per cent increase in 1992. Foreign investors accounted for 19 per cent of the turnover on the SET in 1993 and 20 per cent in 1994.

Thailand experienced some turbulence in its stock and foreign-exchange markets because of the Mexican crisis. In mid-January 1995, a rumour that the Government would be forced to devalue the baht due to the widening current-account deficit led foreign investors to massive withdrawals of money from Thailand. On January 12, they purchased about $5 billion in the local foreign-exchange market, driving the exchange rate against the United States dollar in

Table 3

MALAYSIA: ECONOMIC INDICATORS, 1987-1994

(Per cent, unless otherwise indicated)

	1987	1989	1990	1991	1992	1993	1994
GDP growth	5.4	9.2	9.7	8.7	7.8	8.3	8.7
Inflation[a]	0.8	2.8	3.1	4.4	4.7	3.6	3.7
M2	7.2	16.1	12.8	14.5	19.1	22.1	14.7
Interest rate[b]	6.5	6.6	6.8	7.3	8.1	7.4	5.5
Nominal exchange rate[c] (Malaysian ringgit per $)	2.52	2.71	2.71	2.75	2.55	2.57	2.62
Rate of change	-2.4	3.4	0.0	1.7	-7.4	1.1	1.9
Real effective exchange rate[d] (1990=100)	89.6	98.7	100.0	104.4	98.0	102.1	105.4
Rate of change	9.2	-0.9	1.3	4.38	-6.1	4.2	3.2
Investment/GDP	23.2	28.6	31.3	35.9	33.5	35.0	38.5
Saving/GDP	31.1	29.0	29.1	26.8	30.1	30.8	32.0
Fiscal balance/GDP	-7.7	-3.3	-3.0	-2.0	-0.8	0.2	-0.5
Current account balance ($ million)	2,575	315	-870	-4,183	-2,167	-2,809	-4,147
Current account balance as a percentage of GDP	8.1	0.8	-2.0	-8.9	-3.7	-4.4	-5.9
Capital account balance ($ million)	-1,537	1,330	1,786	5,623	8,743	10,798	1,511
Capital account balance as a percentage of GDP	-4.9	3.5	4.7	11.9	15.1	17.4	2.1
Overall balance ($ million)	1,119	1,230	1,953	1,238	6,615	11,343	-3,157
Foreign exchange reserves ($ million)	7,055	7,393	9,327	10,421	16,784	26,814	24,888

Source: IMF, *International Financial Statistics,* various issues; Bank Negara Malaysia, *Annual Report 1994;* DRI, *World Markets Executive Overview* (fourth quarter 1995).

    a Rate of change of the consumer price index.
    b Average annual yield on long-term Government bonds.
    c Annual average.
    d Annual average; a rise in the index indicates a depreciation.

Chart 6

INTEREST RATES IN MALAYSIA AND THE UNITED STATES, QUARTERLY, 1986-1994

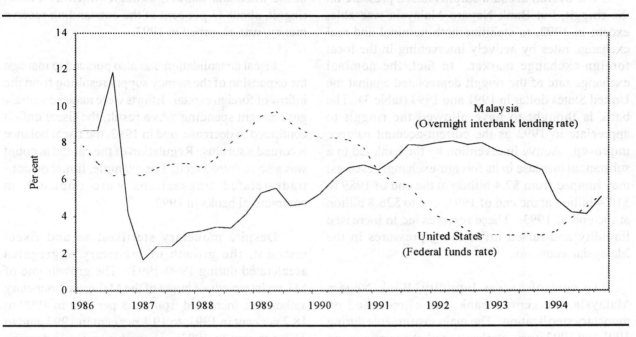

Source: IMF, *International Financial Statistics*, various issues.

the interbank market down by 4.5 per cent, to 26.3 baht per dollar. The SET index fell by 5 per cent on January 12 and 13.

The EEF began to intervene by selling unlimited amounts of United States dollars at a fixed rate of 25.04 baht per dollar. A baht-dollar swap facility was also introduced by the Bank of Thailand in an attempt to gain the confidence of foreign investors. Ultimately, the panic subsided and the foreign-exchange and the stock market stabilized. A sustained crisis was avoided because Thailand's economic fundamentals were basically sound, especially as compared to Mexico. Nonetheless, careful attention should be paid to the fact that a rumour was able to temporarily destabilize the Thai economy.

3. Malaysia

Malaysia has maintained a real GDP growth rate between 7 and 9 per cent since 1987. This rapid growth has been due largely to a rapid increase in investment, with foreign capital providing an important source of financing. According to the estimates by Bank Negara Malaysia (1995), a 1 per cent increase in real FDI and foreign borrowing

resulted, respectively, in 0.111 per cent and 0.056 per cent growth in real GDP during 1970-1993.

Faced with a substantial foreign capital inflow, until early 1994, the Government mainly used sterilized intervention in the foreign-exchange market to avoid negative consequences for the economy.

Since 1975, the ringgit has been pegged to a basket of currencies of Malaysia's major trading partners - principally the United States, Japan, Singapore, Germany, the United Kingdom, and the Netherlands. Bank Negara Malaysia has intervened frequently in the interbank foreign-exchange market to maintain the ringgit-dollar exchange rate within a target range. It is widely believed that the bank's target rate has been determined by the movement of an undisclosed multiple-currency basket.

During 1990-1993, despite a large current-account deficit, the overall account maintained a surplus as a result of the huge inflow of foreign capital (see table 3). In particular, during 1991-1993, the interest-rate differential between Malaysia and the rest of the world began to widen (see chart 6). At the same time, the market expected the ringgit to appreciate, as it was considered significantly undervalued; this resulted in a pronounced increase in the inflow of foreign capital during this period.

The overall account surplus raised pressure on the ringgit, but Bank Negara Malaysia was able, except in 1992, to stabilize both nominal and real exchange rates by actively intervening in the local foreign-exchange market. In fact, the nominal exchange rate of the ringgit depreciated against the United States dollar in 1991 and 1993 (table 3). The bank is thought to have allowed the ringgit to appreciate in 1992 as the current-account balance improved. Active intervention by the bank led to a substantial increase in its foreign-exchange reserves: they jumped from $7.4 billion at the end of 1989 to $10.4 billion at the end of 1991, and to $26.8 billion at the end of 1993. These reserves led to increased liquidity and raised inflationary pressures in the Malaysian economy.

To control excess liquidity, Bank Negara Malaysia, the central bank, has often relied on monetary sterilization. The main instruments during 1991 and 1992 were interbank-market operations and changes in the statutory reserve requirement. The bank tried to absorb excess liquidity by taking out loans with maturities of less than 3 months in the interbank market. To restrain lending by banks, it raised the reserve requirement from 6.5 per cent to 7.5 per cent in 1991, and to 8.5 per cent in 1992. Additional measures were adopted to contain domestic credit expansion. In 1991, the bank added foreign loans related to swaps and foreign borrowing from offshore financial markets to the list of liabilities subject to reserve requirements. Also, it required deposits of the Employee Provident Fund, which holds about 20 per cent of financial assets in the country, and those of the Government to be transferred from private banks to the central bank. Overall, Bank Negara Malaysia absorbed 24 billion ringgit from the banking sector through sterilization measures in 1992, equivalent to 90 per cent of the outstanding stock of reserve money.

However, monetary sterilization resulted in a rise in domestic interest rates until early 1993, leading to a widening gap between domestic and foreign rates. The high interest-rate differential and the buoyant performance of the Malaysian stock market attracted additional foreign capital, especially in the form of portfolio investment, thus necessitating further sterilized intervention. In an effort to increase the coverage and effect of sterilization, Bank Negara Malaysia introduced the Bank Negara Bill and the Malaysia Savings Bond in 1993. During that year, it absorbed 6 billion ringgit and 1.4 billion ringgit, respectively, with these instruments. Nonetheless, the principal sterilization measure was still intervention in the interbank market, through which 27 billion ringgit, about 45 per cent of the outstanding reserve money, was absorbed in 1993.

Fiscal consolidation was also pursued to manage the expansion of the money supply resulting from the inflow of foreign capital. Efforts were made to restrain government spending. As a result, the fiscal deficit continued to decrease, and in 1993, the fiscal balance recorded a surplus. Regulation of the capital account was also re-introduced. For example, limits on non-trade-related transactions were imposed on commercial banks in 1992.

Despite monetary sterilization and fiscal restraint, the growth of monetary aggregates accelerated during 1990-1993. The growth rate of M3, an intermediate target of the Malaysian monetary authorities, increased from 12.8 per cent in 1990 to 18.2 per cent in 1991, to 19.1 per cent in 1992, and to 23.5 per cent in 1993. The net increase in foreign assets held by Bank Negara Malaysia accounted for 64 per cent of the increase in M3 in 1992 and 75 per cent in 1993. M2 was also increasing (see table 3).[6]

Prices rose faster in the early 1990s than in the 1980s. Between 1990 and 1993, the annual increase in the consumer price index averaged 4.0 per cent, although it began to moderate in 1993. The comparable figure for 1985-1989 was only about 1.4 per cent. Given that the growth rate of the Malaysian economy had exceeded the potential rate, rapid monetary growth resulting from the inflow of foreign capital raised inflationary pressure further. While the potential growth rate is estimated by Bank Negara Malaysia (1995) to be 7 to 8 per cent, the Malaysian economy has actually grown by more than 8 per cent since 1988 (except in 1992). Also, the increase in inward FDI raised wages and the costs of other inputs, exacerbating inflationary pressures. In the first half of the 1990s Malaysia witnessed a sharp rise in asset prices. The stock market has been bullish, partly due to significant foreign portfolio investment. In 1993, the Kuala Lumpur Composite Index rose by 98 per cent, generating concern about a speculative bubble.

The inflow of foreign capital destabilized the economy and led to a loss of monetary control by the central bank (Aziz, 1994). More importantly, the increase in the inflow of short-term speculative capital,

Table 4

CHRONOLOGY OF ADMINISTRATIVE MEASURES TO CONTAIN
CAPITAL INFLOWS IN MALAYSIA IN 1994

	Measures	Date Implemented	Date Lifted
(1)	Increase in statutory reserve requirement of commercial banks, finance companies and merchant banks		
	8.5 per cent → 9.5 per cent	January 3, 1994	
	9.5 per cent → 10.5 per cent	May 16, 1994	
	10.5 per cent → 11.5 per cent	July 1, 1994	
(2)	Inclusion of all funds sourced abroad in the eligible base for computing statutory reserve requirement and liquidity requirement	January 16, 1994	
(3)	Placement of limits on non-trade-related external liabilities of banking institutions[a]	January 17, 1994	January 20, 1995
(4)	Prohibition of sales of short-term monetary instruments by residents to non-residents[b]	January 24, 1994	August 12, 1994
(5)	Transfer of ringgit funds of foreign banking institutions held in commercial banks' non-interest bearing foreign vostro accounts to Bank Negara Malaysia	February 2, 1994	May 16, 1994
	Inclusion of vostro balances in the eligible liability base for reserve and liquidity requirement	February 16, 1994	August 16, 1994
(6)	Prohibition of commercial banks' swaps and outright forward transactions on the bid side with foreigners[c]	February 23, 1994	January 20, 1995

Source: Bank Negara Malaysia, *Annual Report 1994*.

a Non-FDI-related external liabilities are also subject to ceilings.

b The restriction was applied to highly liquid instruments, including Bank Negara Bills, Treasury Bills, Malaysian Government securities, Cagamas Bonds and Notes, BA and negotiable instruments of deposit with a remaining maturity of one year or less. From February 7, 1994, private debt securities with a remaining maturity of one year or less (except convertible bonds) were also subject to the restriction.

c This measure was intended to prevent overseas investors from establishing a speculative long forward position of the ringgit when it was expected to appreciate.

especially in 1993, made the financial markets vulnerable to a reversal in the flow. All these effects prompted Bank Negara Malaysia to implement six administrative measures in January and February 1994 to contain the inflow, particularly of speculative short-term capital (see table 4). These included the prohibition of short-term money-market instrument sales to non-residents, a ban on commercial bank swaps unless trade-related, and tight restrictions on forward transactions with foreigners. Liabilities included in computing statutory reserves and liquidity requirements were expanded to cover foreign-currency deposits, foreign-currency borrowing from foreign banking institutions, and interbank borrowing. Also, the statutory reserve requirement was raised to 9.5 per cent (it was raised again in May and July 1995).

There was an immediate response from the foreign-exchange and stock markets. The ringgit depreciated rapidly due to an outflow of foreign capital. By the end of February 1994, it had depreciated against the United States dollar by 3.3 per cent from the end of the previous year. The Kuala Lumpur Composite Index, after recording a new high of 1,314 points on January 5, 1994, quickly fell below the 1,000 level, losing 954 points on March 21, 1994.

From the second quarter, however, the ringgit and stock prices began to stabilize. For the rest of the year, the ringgit displayed an upward trend against the United States dollar and the Composite Index rose steadily. The markets reflected the improved soundness of the Malaysian economy rather than the inflow of speculative funds: high economic growth and fiscal consolidation continued.

The moderation of inflation in 1993 prompted Bank Negara Malaysia to reduce monetary sterilization in 1994. This led to a fall in domestic interest rates while international rates were rising, narrowing the differential between Malaysia and the industrial countries. Lower interest rate together with administrative measures discouraged the inflow of foreign funds and encouraged the outflow of foreign capital invested in the Malaysian securities.

Finally, in the second half of 1994 a net outflow of foreign capital was recorded as short-term speculative funds moved elsewhere. This resulted in a deceleration of the expansion of M3, which had grown by 23.5 per cent in 1993, to only 13.1 per cent in 1994. Consumer price inflation also moderated; it peaked at 4.4 per cent in February 1994, falling to 3.0 per cent in June 1994. Also, in the second half of 1994, as the economy showed signs of stabilization, Bank Negara Malaysia lifted some of the administrative measures (see table 4).

The use of administrative measures is controversial. It is often argued that such measures should be used rarely and only temporarily, as they lead to distortions in the long run and damage a country's reputation. However, direct controls, coupled with a policy of low interest rates, were considered helpful in curtailing destabilizing short-term flows of foreign capital and restoring economic stability in Malaysia (IMF, 1995a). It should be noted, however, that this was possible only against the background of the sound economic fundamentals of the Malaysian economy.

4. Indonesia

Rapid economic growth of Indonesia in the 1990s benefitted from the inflow of foreign capital. However, there were also adverse effects such as accelerating money supply growth. During 1990 and 1991, the economy showed signs of overheating due to a rapid expansion of demand caused by a substantial inflow of foreign capital (Bank Indonesia, 1994). Consumer price inflation rose from 6.4 per cent in 1989 to 7.8 per cent in 1990, and to 9.9 per cent in 1991. There was also a deterioration in the current account resulting from increasing imports: the deficit widened by $3.2 billion between 1989 and 1991, and the ratio of the deficit to GDP rose from 2.5 per cent to 4.4 per cent (see table 5).

The inflow of foreign capital increased domestic liquidity and foreign-exchange reserves held by Bank Indonesia. Like in the Republic of Korea and Malaysia, the Government attempted to absorb the excess liquidity mainly through monetary sterilization. It also increased prudential requirements for commercial banks and imposed some direct controls on credit expansion. Despite the difficulties in macroeconomic management, the first priority has always been given to maintaining a weak rupiah in order to enhance the international competitiveness of exports (other than oil and gas which account for a quarter of total exports.) The central bank has intervened in the interbank foreign-exchange market to maintain this policy.

Since 1978, the rupiah has been pegged to a basket of the currencies of Indonesia's major trading partners; previously, it had been pegged to the United States dollar. Every business day at 3 pm, Bank Indonesia announces a selling and a buying rate for the rupiah against the United States dollar. The rates are applied to commercial banks' settlements on the same day as well as to swap transactions and export-draft rediscounting with the central bank. In 1994, the band was widened from 20 to 30 rupiahs. The market rate of the rupiah against the dollar is determined in the interbank foreign-exchange market, with its level reflecting expected changes in central bank rates. Normally, it fluctuates within the band set by the central bank the previous day.[7]

Table 5

INDONESIA: ECONOMIC INDICATORS, 1987-1994

(Per cent, unless otherwise indicated)

	1987	1989	1990	1991	1992	1993	1994
GDP growth	4.9	7.5	7.2	7.0	6.5	6.5	7.3
Inflation[a]	9.3	6.4	7.8	9.4	7.5	9.2	8.5
Money supply (M2)	22.4	39.8	44.2	17.0	20.2	22.0	20.2
Interest rate[b]	17.50	18.58	18.53	21.18	21.13	16.35	12.99
Nominal exchange rate[c] (Indonesian rupiah per $)	1,643.9	1,770.1	1,842.8	1,950.3	2,129.9	2,087.1	2,160.8
Rate of change	28.2	5.0	4.1	5.8	4.1	2.8	3.5
Real effective exchange rate[d] (1990=100)	100.0	100.8	100.0	104.7	108.4	111.5	114.3
Rate of change	34.1	-4.0	-0.8	4.7	3.5	2.9	2.5
Investment/GDP	31.4	35.2	36.1	35.5	35.9	33.2	34.3
Saving/GDP	28.1	32.7	31.7	31.1	33.4	31.5	31.8
Fiscal balance/GDP	-1.0	-2.1	0.4	0.5	-0.6	0.5	0.6
Current account balance ($ million)	-2,098	-1,108	-2,988	-4,260	-2,780	-2,016	-2,790
Current account balance as a percentage of GDP	-2.8	-1.2	-2.8	-3.7	-2.2	-1.3	-1.6
Capital account balance ($ million)	3,481	2,918	4,495	5,697	6,129	5,772	3,839
Capital account balance as a percentage of GDP	4.6	3.1	4.2	4.9	4.8	3.7	2.2
Overall balance ($ million)	630	495	2,251	1,528	2,070	594	784
Foreign exchange reserves ($ million)	5,483	5,357	7,353	9,151	10,181	10,988	11,820

Source: IMF, *International Financial Statistics,* various issues; Bank of Indonesia, *Financial Statistics,* various issues; DRI, *World Markets Executive Overview* (fourth quarter 1995).

    a Rate of change of the consumer price index.
    b One-year time deposits rates in commercial banks(end of period).
    c Annual average.
    d Annual average; a rise in the index indicates a depreciation.

The main factor Bank Indonesia considers in setting its official rate has been the inflation differential between Indonesia and its major trading partners (*Bank Indonesia Annual Report*, 1992/1993; and *Euromoney*, 1995). Given that inflation has been persistently high in Indonesia relative to the industrial economies, the nominal exchange rate of the rupiah has persistently depreciated even when the overall balance was recording a surplus due to the large inflow of foreign capital (see table 5). The nominal exchange rate of the rupiah showed a steady depreciation of about 4.0 per cent annually against the United States dollar between 1990 and 1994, while the inflation differential between Indonesia and the United States was 4.8 percentage points. Also, the rupiah depreciated sharply against the Japanese yen in the same period. Consequently, the real effective exchange rate of the rupiah was fairly stable.

The policy to stabilize the exchange rate has been aimed at containing short-term capital inflows. A persistent depreciation of the rupiah's nominal exchange rate can keep the domestic effective interest rate (interest rate minus expected depreciation rate of the rupiah) lower than it would have been when the currency appreciates. This helped reduce the incentive for foreign capital inflows.

However, the policy aimed at maintaining exchange-rate stability in the face of a massive inflow of foreign capital has led to an increase in the money supply, making the change in net foreign assets an important determinant of the change in money supply. This outcome led Bank Indonesia to pursue monetary sterilization continuously. To absorb excess liquidity, Bank Indonesia relies mainly on sales of short-term central bank securities, Bank Indonesia Certificates (Sertifikat Bank Indonesia, SBI). These were first issued in February 1984. Initially such certificates were issued with maturities of 6 months or less, but since February 1991 longer maturities have also been issued. The bank issues SBIs in daily auctions, with maturities ranging from 7 to 360 days, depending on the state of domestic liquidity. The bank also absorbs liquidity by selling money-market securities (Sural Berharga Pasar Uang, SBPU) to commercial banks. SPBUs are short-term private securities traded in the money market, including promissory notes issued by banks and their customers and bills of exchange. Bank Indonesia sells SPBUs from its portfolio in auctions whenever there is a need to withdraw liquidity.

Monetary sterilization was stepped up as the money supply increased dramatically in 1990. This led to an increase in the sales of SBIs and SBPU in the following two years. Net sales of SBIs increased to 9.4 trillion rupiahs in 1991 and 9.6 trillion rupiahs in 1992, compared to net repayments during 1989 and 1990 (see chart 7). As a result, the ratio of outstanding SBIs to M1 increased from 6 per cent in 1990 to 42 per cent in 1991, and to 72 per cent in 1992. Net sales of SBPUs also began to rise in 1992. The sterilization helped moderate the growth rate of money supply. M2 growth fell from 44.6 per cent in 1990 to 17.0 per cent in 1991.

Bank Indonesia used several additional methods to control excess liquidity. It would raise the discount rate on export drafts, and impose direct controls on banks to contain credit expansion. For example, a portion of State-enterprise deposits in commercial banks were transferred to the central bank in 1991. Several measures to restrict the inflow of foreign capital were implemented in the course of 1991, as discussed earlier.

These measures and monetary sterilization were more or less successful in moderating domestic demand in 1992. The consumer price index rose by only 7.5 per cent during the year, almost 2 percentage points less than in 1991, and the current-account deficit was reduced by $1.4 billion. However, the inflation rate rose again to 9.2 per cent in 1993, and to 8.5 per cent in 1994. One factor was the decision by the Government to reduce industrial subsidies, which led to the rise in administered prices of a number of commodities produced by State enterprises. These included cement, fertilizers and oil-based fuels.

Rapid growth of the money supply was also an important source of inflation (Asian Development Bank, 1995). Since 1993, Bank Indonesia has done less sterilization in order to reduce the burden of interest payments on SBIs (see chart 7). Higher inflation can also be attributed to the persistent depreciation of the nominal exchange rate of the rupiah. Especially the sharp depreciation of the rupiah against the Japanese yen resulting from the steep appreciation of the yen in international foreign-exchange markets, together with Indonesia's policy of maintaining a weak rupiah, caused prices of imported goods from Japan to balloon. From the end of 1992 through the end of 1994, the rupiah depreciated by 33 per cent against the yen, but the share of Japanese goods in Indonesia's total imports remained at approximately 30 per cent. This implies that exchange-rate stabilization had some destabilizing macroeconomic effects.

Increased issues of central bank securities in the early 1990s tended to raise their discount rates, thus

Chart 7

INDONESIA: NET SALES OF SBI AND SBPU, AND THE SBI DISCOUNT RATE

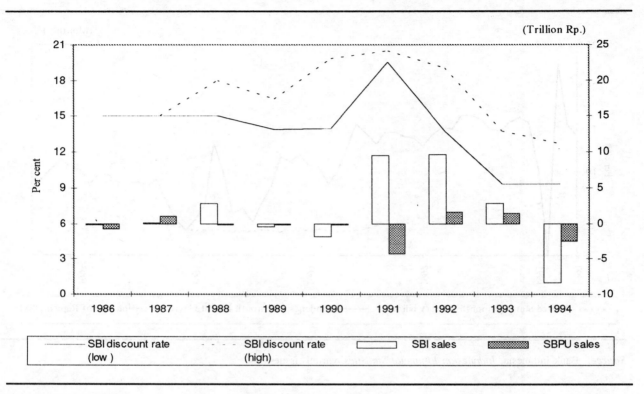

Source: Bank Indonesia, *Indonesian Financial Statistics*, various issues.
Note: SBI discount rate: left scale, SBI and SBPU sales: right scale; for further explanations, see text.

leading to higher interest rates in the Indonesian economy and to a further widening gap between domestic and international rates. In March 1992, the Government permitted foreign investors to purchase up to 49 per cent of the shares of domestic private and State-owned commercial banks listed on the Indonesian stock markets. Previously, they had not been allowed to buy shares of banks. The larger interest-rate differential, coupled with the development and deregulation of the domestic capital market, provided a strong incentive for foreigners to invest in Indonesian securities. As a result, the inflow of foreign portfolio investment - which is presumed to be short-term and speculative - rose sharply.

In an attempt to reduce the inflow of short-term capital, Bank Indonesia began to lower the discount rates of SBIs in 1992 and continued to maintain nominal depreciation of the rupiah. Nonetheless, Indonesia's effective rate of returns (domestic interest rate minus depreciation rate of the rupiah) remained high relative to returns available in industrial countries

(see chart 8). In addition, institutional investors' world-wide rush into emerging markets contributed to a flood of foreign portfolio investment, especially after mid-1993. The proportion of foreign ownership of shares on the Jakarta Stock Exchange rose from 24.0 per cent in fiscal year 1992/1993 to 31.0 per cent in fiscal year 1993/1994.[8] Accordingly, the economy became vulnerable to a sudden outflow of foreign capital.

The Mexican crisis in December 1994 shook Indonesia's foreign-exchange and capital markets. Rumours of rupiah devaluation linked to the size of Indonesia's large foreign debt (about $87 billion in 1994, the equivalent of about eight times the value of foreign-exchange reserves at the end of 1993) triggered a withdrawal of funds. On December 22, 2 days after the Mexican Government devalued its currency by 15.3 per cent, strong demand for the United States dollar caused the rupiah to depreciate rapidly against the dollar in the interbank market. On January 13, 1995, the exchange rate of the rupiah rose to 2,223

Chart 8

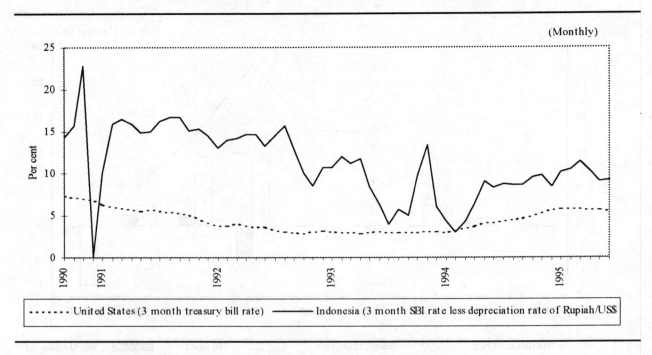

INTEREST RATES IN INDONESIA AND THE UNITED STATES

Source: Bank Indonesia, *Indonesian Financial Statistics*, various issues.

against the United States dollar, 5 rupiah above Bank Indonesia's selling rate. Compared to December 22, 1994, the rupiah had depreciated by 1.7 per cent. In the eleven months before the crisis, the average rate of depreciation had been only 0.3 per cent a month.

To restore exchange-rate stability, Bank Indonesia intervened by selling $580 million in spot, forward, and squaring transactions. Simultaneously, it raised its official discount rate by 50 basis points. These measures helped restore confidence that the rupiah would not be devalued further, so that demand for the dollar subsided.

The Indonesian stock market suffered a net outflow of foreign investment and falling stock prices in early January 1995. By the end of January 1995, these had reversed, but the net inflow was slower than prior to the Mexican crisis. Ownership by non-residents of shares listed on the Jakarta Stock Exchange fell from 31.8 per cent at the end of March 1994 to 28.9 per cent a year later. A bearish sentiment has continued since the crisis. Moreover, interest rates have shown a rising trend as Bank Indonesia increased the discount rate for SBIs, in part to prevent another major exodus of capital.

V.   Policy alternatives for managing capital inflows

To mitigate negative effects of surges of capital inflow, it is essential to enhance the soundness and robustness of the economy. Still, sudden such surges can threaten the stability of financial markets and the economy at large, so that policy measures, at least on a temporary basis, are required.

The key policy measure, especially in response to sustained large *in*flows, to stabilize both the exchange rate and the money supply has been sterilized intervention. However, sterilization through issuing central bank securities or increases in reserve requirements has shortcomings, particularly when used over longer periods. It results in quasi-fiscal costs as long as the interest rate on central bank securities is higher than that on foreign-exchange reserves.[9] Also, interest payments on these securities increase the money supply and, as a result, can contribute to inflation, which in turn causes an appreciation of the real exchange rate. In addition, sterilization may produce a vicious circle, as further capital inflows may be caused by the widening differential between domestic and international interest rates. Thus, in the long run, it is not a capable measure of dealing with a continued large capital inflow.

A surge in capital flows - a sharp change in the direction and level of liquid speculative capital - has a potential for destabilizing domestic financial markets. In the current world financial environment, the distinction between short-term and long-term capital has partly lost its meaning. Rather, it is the speed and ease with which capital in various forms can flow that is relevant. This is partly a function of the type of asset (or liability) and partly a matter of the controls and rules applied to it by regulators in a specific market, such as restrictions on the movement of certain types of capital. In liberalized financial markets, portfolio investment is generally quite liquid. The Republic of Korea, Thailand, Malaysia, and Indonesia have experienced substantial inflows of this kind of foreign capital since the early 1990s.[10]

This section takes up policy measures that have been used or considered to deal with undesired consequences of continued capital inflows. These include both macroeconomic policy measures and direct capital controls.

A. *Macroeconomic policies*

1. *Flexible exchange rates*

In the face of capital inflows, all four countries have acted to maintain, or even depreciate, their exchange rates, in order to help the price competitiveness of their exports. They have largely succeeded: their currencies have been stable or, in the case of Indonesia, even depreciated against the United States dollar. At the same time, they have experienced a large current-account deficit (see tables 1 to 3, and 5).

A policy of flexible exchange rates implies that the exchange rate is allowed to fluctuate according to market conditions. Given that the four countries studied here have a large overall surplus due to the massive inflow of foreign capital, a flexible-exchange-rate policy would result in an appreciation of their domestic currency. By allowing appreciation, they can reduce the burden of sterilization discussed earlier. Also, unless appreciation is not expected to be persistent, the magnitude of capital inflows might be reduced through a rise in the expected rate of depreciation.

Flexible exchange rates would also help reduce inflation by lowering import prices. Because these countries depend heavily on Japanese-produced industrial equipment and intermediate goods, the appreciation of the yen against the dollar resulted in higher domestic prices through simultaneous depreciation of the domestic currency against the yen. Although by the end of 1995 the yen had weakened against the dollar from its record levels in early 1995, the problem of having a principal market for exports (the United States) different from a principal source of imports (Japan) remains. In an effort to mitigate the effect of the yen rate on domestic prices, the Malaysian Government allowed an appreciation of about 4 per cent against the United States dollar during the second quarter of 1995 (Wuchikomi et al., 1995).

When the capital inflow is fully absorbed through appreciation of the nominal exchange rate, the real exchange rate also appreciates, and this leads to a large current-account deficit. If a country adopts a single policy variable such as the money supply or the exchange rate to absorb the impact of capital inflows, it is likely to experience side effects that are considered undesirable. It is thus better to employ both monetary and exchange-rate policy to maintain sustainable growth with price stability. In any case, the integration of the domestic economy into the world economy makes it more difficult to manage exchange rates and the money supply separately.

Fiscal policy is also a useful tool in dealing with capital inflows. Increasing the budget surplus can mitigate both inflationary pressure and appreciation of the real exchange rate. Moreover, because a reduction in Government expenditure has the same effect as a decrease in demand for loanable funds, it can lower interest rates. Thailand provides an example for the successful use of this approach.

However, due to the heavy demand on the Government for investment in infrastructure and social services it is very difficult to have a large budget surplus in these countries. Furthermore, fiscal policy is generally designed on the basis of medium- and long-term considerations, which makes it too slow to allow timely intervention in dealing with short-term speculative capital inflows.

2. *Encouraging capital outflows*

Increasing capital outflows can play an important role in dealing with inflows. All the countries under consideration have lifted restrictions on capital outflows to reduce, directly and indirectly, the volume or the potential adverse effects of the capital inflow. However, the size of outflows is still negligible relative to that of inflows in all four countries. The main reason is the reluctance of domestic residents to invest abroad. This is particularly true for portfolio investment, because of lower returns and lack of requisite investment skills by domestic financial institutions.

However, central bank swap arrangements could be used to provide additional incentives for domestic residents to make portfolio investments abroad. When the accumulation of foreign reserves exceeds a desired level, the central bank sells a part of the reserves to domestic financial institutions in exchange for domestic currency. The buyers are required to invest the acquired funds abroad for a specified period. At the end of the period, the central bank reimburses the buyers for any loss resulting from the interest-rate differential between the domestic and foreign markets, as well as any loss from changes in the exchange rate. Germany used this method to stabilize the money supply in the 1970s, and the Philippines, Malaysia, and Singapore have also used it. Since pressure on the money supply from the foreign sector is transferred abroad during the swap period, a swap can contribute to stabilizing the domestic money supply and interest rates without new issues of central bank securities.

B. *Direct management of capital inflows*

Employing a mix of monetary, fiscal, and exchange-rate policies, together with encouraging capital outflows may not always be sufficient to counter surges in capital inflows. The authorities may then consider the introduction of a tax on foreign-exchange transactions or direct control measures such as limitations on the amount of domestic currency foreigners can purchase, restrictions on external borrowing by banks, and an increase in the reserve requirements.

1. *Variable deposit requirement*

Imposing a variable deposit requirements (VDR) on incoming capital, i.e. differentiating reserve levels according to the specific type of a capital inflow and particular circumstances, reduces the volume of inflows. VDRs are similar to compensatory balances on loans as a way of raising effective interest rates. More specifically, they work as an implicit levy on

capital transactions which, by increasing their cost, decreases demand.

A VDR is more market-efficient than quantitative restrictions but, because it limits domestic firms' access to international financial resources, it has to be implemented carefully. To the extent that FDI is a long-term investment in real productive capacity and contributes to economic development it should not normally be discouraged. VDRs on portfolio investment are difficult to impose for practical reasons. This leaves only foreign borrowing by residents as an area where a VDR might be used.

The reserve ratio can be adjusted according to the volume of capital inflows, but should be kept constant across maturities. It is also straightforward to determine the ratio that fully absorbs the interest-rate differential between home and abroad. It is:

$$R' = \frac{R_x}{1-D} + E_x$$

where R' is the effective interest rate on foreign borrowing, R_f the foreign interest rate, D the reserve ratio, and E_x the expected rate of depreciation during the borrowing period.

Substituting the domestic interest rate for the effective rate, i.e. making it as expensive to borrow abroad as domestically, allows the equation to be solved for the reserve ratio (D). Required reserves would be deposited in non-interest bearing foreign-currency accounts at the central bank until the loan is repaid.

Because a VDR hinders access to foreign financial resources that can enhance the competitiveness of domestic banks and firms, its use should be limited to periods of heavy capital inflow caused by a rapid appreciation of the exchange rate or a substantial increase in interest-rate differentials. In such cases, VDRs have been shown to be effective, at least in the short run.

Australia used this method when experiencing a surplus in its overall account coupled with a current-account deficit in the early 1970s. A rapid rise in domestic interest rates due to a restrictive monetary policy generated expectations of an exchange-rate appreciation and thus led to massive capital inflows. When the Government imposed a non-interest-bearing reserve requirement on all foreign borrowing exceeding A$10,000, inflows were reduced. The reserve ratio, initially 25 per cent, was adjusted depending on the size of inflows.

Equally, Malaysia made an effort in January 1995 to curb the inflow of short-term capital by making foreign-currency borrowing from foreign banking institutions subject to a reserve requirement. This is a variant of the VDR, with a single reserve ratio being imposed, regardless of the volume of foreign borrowing. The requirement, coupled with other restrictions on capital inflows implemented in early 1994, contributed to reducing the amount of incoming foreign capital.

In the Republic of Korea, the legal framework for imposing a VDR is in place, but it has never applied in practice. Its effects on capital inflows would undoubtedly be quite small because foreign borrowing by residents has not been important compared to FDI and foreign portfolio investment. The Government continues to directly restrict borrowing from abroad by domestic firms and financial institutions. However, when this restriction is relaxed, the volume of such borrowing is expected to rise rapidly.

On the other hand, a VDR would be fairly effective in curtailing capital flows into Indonesia and Thailand, where foreign borrowing by residents has accounted for a large portion of capital inflows. However, the Thai Government would probably be reluctant to use a VDR because Thailand has promoted itself as a regional financial centre, and such a move might jeopardize such a development.

2. A levy on foreign-exchange transactions

Transaction taxes are used in a number of financial markets: for example, by stock exchanges in the Republic of Korea and Japan, although the rates are very low. Foreign-exchange transaction taxes, both explicit and implicit, as a means of deterring short-term speculative capital flows have been extensively analysed (Dornbusch, 1997; Eichengreen and Wyplosz, 1993; Eichengreen et al., 1995; Felix, 1995; Frankel, 1995; Garber, 1995; Garber and Taylor, 1995; and Kenen, 1995). An explicit levy on foreign-exchange transactions has been widely debated within the industrial economies and international organizations such as the United Nations and the IMF, but so far has not been introduced in any country. A currency transaction tax can be implemented worldwide. However, the case for or against a global tax is beyond the scope of this study. In this section, only the practicality as well as desirability of imposing

the tax unilaterally by an individual country is examined. There is also the question of whether the tax should be imposed on foreign-exchange transactions related to the current account. Such a tax increases costs for those trading goods and services and thus might cut into the competitiveness of exports. To avoid this problem, the tax should perhaps be confined to capital-account transactions, in particular, non-resident investments in domestic stocks, bonds, and other short-term financial instruments. The tax also would have to include financial derivatives because they can mimic conventional financial instruments.

In general, the tax could be levied when foreign investors buy and sell domestic currency in connection with their trading in these financial instruments. Since foreign investors have to exchange foreign currencies for domestic currency at domestic financial institutions, administration of the tax would not be as difficult as it might appear. Moreover, in many countries including the Republic of Korea, foreign investors have to register and invest through designated financial institutions, and hence find it much more difficult to avoid the tax than otherwise. It should be noted, however, that a tax that may be effective in some countries may not work in others because of differences in the financial and foreign-exchange system.

There are several ways to handle a transaction tax: it can be imposed on the seller or the purchaser of the domestic currency, or both. For foreign-exchange transactions, round-trip taxes are more effective. The tax rate can be varied according to the degree of capital-market openness and the level of short-term capital flows. It should be noted that the impact of such a tax is related to the length of the investment period. For example, when a 2 per cent round-trip tax is imposed (1 per cent for each buy and sell), the annualized decrease in return on investment is around 0.2 per cent over a 10-year period, but for a day-trade the decrease is about 124,600 per cent at an annual rate.

An implicit levy requires foreign investors to make non-interest-bearing deposits at the central bank when they sell foreign currencies for domestic currency. Examples include Italy during the 1970s and Spain in 1992.[11] Unlike an explicit tax, an implicit tax hampers long-term investments if the deposit period is as long as the investment period. This can be mitigated by having the same deposit period for all transactions, one just long enough to decrease the returns on short-term investments to the point where they become unattractive. Care must be taken in deciding the reserve ratio, as it will discourage long-term investment if it is too high, while too low a reserve ratio will not accomplish the purpose.

Even if a comprehensive and clean currency transaction tax system is introduced, financial markets sooner or later are likely to find ways to evade the tax. One of the most likely ways to do so is to increase cross-border transactions that do not go through the local foreign-exchange market. To prevent this, a tax system in which cross-border payments as well as the purchase or sale of foreign exchange is taxed can be implemented, as suggested by Dornbusch in this volume. However, the cost of administering such a system may be too high to make it a realistic. As Dornbusch points out, it will also increase offshore clearing of inflows and outflows, which lowers the effectiveness of the tax system. Moreover, even this system cannot prevent financial markets from evading the tax by developing complicated derivatives.

A foreign-exchange transaction tax increases transaction costs, which in theory should discourage the movement of short-term speculative capital. However, many observers doubt their effectiveness. It is sometimes argued that empirical studies have failed to demonstrate a relationship between transaction costs and volatility in domestic financial markets. This implies that a foreign-exchange transaction tax would not decrease the volatility of exchange rates or security prices (Schwert, 1993; Hakkio, 1994; and IMF, 1995b).

Even if it works, the tax has shortcomings. By decreasing the return on domestic securities, it makes them less attractive to foreign investors, and, to the extent that the tax reduces liquidity (the volume of transactions), it could make the foreign-exchange market more volatile. In addition, it raises equity problems if it is applied only to transactions by non-residents. A foreign-exchange transaction tax is also inconsistent with the aim of countries like the Republic of Korea, Thailand, and Malaysia to become international financial centres, something that requires liberalization and internationalization of the domestic financial market.

Nonetheless, a transaction tax might have positive effects if applied flexibly, with the tax rate being adjusted to the amount of short-term capital flows. It will help lengthen the investment horizon of foreign investors and shift foreign participants in domestic financial markets from trading to investing. Even though it may not be able to reduce the volatility

of stock or bond prices, it can at least manage the pace of capital flows. The revenue can be used to enhance the stability of the foreign-exchange market.

The use of a foreign-exchange transaction tax could mitigate the reluctance of developing countries to open their financial markets (Dornbusch, 1997). The Korean Government plans to liberalize capital-account transactions more aggressively in the future. With a tax in place, albeit at a zero rate in normal times, it could tell opponents of liberalization that it has a weapon against speculators.

Malaysia implemented direct controls on capital inflows in 1994 as the increased inflow of short-term speculative capital undermined the stability of its economy and financial markets. These might not have been necessary if a currency transaction tax had been applied.

As was explained in section IV, Thailand and Indonesia experienced turbulence in their financial markets due to a sudden outflow of foreign capital prompted by the Mexican crisis. It is, however, expected that they are opposed, or at least reluctant, to impose a transaction tax because they feel it would reduce the amount of capital available for their economic development. In these countries, the need for foreign capital to finance a high rate of domestic investment will continue for some time in the future. Rather than inviting difficulties in external financing, Thailand and Indonesia are willing to accept some volatility in capital movements as long as foreign capital, whether short-term speculative or not, is contributing to economic development. These countries also feel that imposing a currency transaction tax will cause damage to their financial markets, which are still in an infant stage of development, and may lead to retaliation by industrial countries which are major investors in these countries.

VI. Conclusions

The Republic of Korea has gradually headed into capital-account liberalization and its progress is expected to accelerate. This process, if well managed, will contribute to the development and globalization of the domestic economy as well as to greater efficiency of the domestic financial market. The inflow of foreign capital has been crucial to supporting a high rate of investment and output in Indonesia, Malaysia and Thailand. In fact, except for the Republic of Korea, it appears that all three East Asian countries are prepared to accept all types of foreign financing, regardless of their maturities, as long as foreign capital is needed to sustain rapid growth.

The ongoing liberalization of capital-account transactions, the growing need for foreign capital, and favourable growth are likely to combine in attracting a large amount of capital to the East Asian economies. However, at times, such a growth-oriented policy may suffer from an increase in the volatility of short-term capital flows, which may disturb domestic financial markets and macroeconomic stability, as it has in Malaysia. Faced with the instability problem, Malaysia had to resort to direct control measures to dampen short-term capital movements.

Maintaining the soundness and robustness of the domestic economy may be the most efficient way to offset any negative effects of speculative short-term capital, but when there is a surge of capital inflows, Governments of the four countries are likely to consider measures to influence the level and characteristics of capital inflows, such as taxes on short-term bank deposits and other financial assets, reserve requirements against foreign borrowing, prudential limits on banks' offshore borrowing, and limits on consumption credit as suggested in IMF (1995a). While it has shortcomings, the currency transaction tax would be certainly one of the most effective measures in reducing volatile short-term speculative capital movements.

Notes

1   Asian developing countries include Asian NIEs, ASEAN and other Asian countries except Japan.
2   The Korea International Trust was the first fund designed specifically for foreign investors. It was established in 1981 by the Hankuk Investment Trust Corporation. The Korea Fund, organized under United States law and listed on the New York Stock Exchange, was launched in 1984. Others followed, including the Korea Europe Fund (based in Guernsey and listed in London) in 1987 and the Korea Asia Fund (based in the Cayman Islands and listed in Hong Kong and London) in 1991.
3   Japanese firms have been the most active foreign investors in these countries. The sharp appreciation of the yen vis-à-vis other major currencies after the Plaza Accord in 1985 drove many Japanese firms to move production facilities to South-East Asian countries to take advantage of their lower wages and natural resource costs. Japan accounted for 40 per cent of total inward FDI in the three countries during 1990-1992.
4   Foreign investors held 10.0 per cent of listed stocks in the Republic of Korea by the end of 1995, 13.0 per cent in Malaysia by the end of 1994, and 28.9 per cent in

Indonesia in March 1995. In Thailand, foreign investors accounted for about 20 per cent of the total turnover in 1994.
5   According to *Euromoney* (1995), the weights are 80-85 per cent for the United States dollar, 8-15 per cent for the yen, and 4-10 per cent for the Deutsche mark.
6   M3 in Malaysia is M2 plus all private sector deposits with finance companies, merchant banks and discount houses.
7   As of April 1995, the Indonesian foreign-exchange market was composed of 112 foreign-exchange banks and 9 brokerage companies. Commercial banks are subject to limits on their foreign-exchange position. As of early 1996, a bank's overall position is limited to a weekly average of 25 per cent of its paid-up capital.
8   The Indonesian fiscal year ends on March 31.
9   For Latin American countries these costs have been estimated by Leiderman (1995) to amount to between 0.25 and 0.50 per cent of GDP.
10   UNCTAD (1995) pointed out that one important factor in determining vulnerability to sudden swings in capital flows is the extent to which residents issue and hold foreign-currency-denominated assets at home. It appears that the four countries studied in this paper are not very much exposed to this kind of vulnerability since they still apply strong restrictions on issuing and holding such assets. Furthermore, since domestic markets for foreign-currency-denominated assets are not well developed in these countries, acquisition of such assets by residents is very limited. Thus, residents of these countries obtain most foreign-currency-denominated assets abroad rather than at home.
11   When the September 1992 European currency crisis hit, Spain, in an attempt to avoid a realignment of the peseta, imposed an implicit levy on the purchase of foreign currencies by domestic financial institutions. (This is in the opposite direction than the levy considered here.)

References

ASIAN DEVELOPMENT BANK (1995), *Asian Development Outlook* (New York: Oxford University Press).

AZIZ, Z. (1994), "Capital Flows and Monetary Management: the Malaysian Experience", paper presented at the Eleventh Pacific Basin Central Bank Conference, Hong Kong, October 31 - November 4.

BANK INDONESIA, *Annual Report,* various issues.

BANK INDONESIA, *Indonesian Financial Statistics,* various issues.

BANK INDONESIA (1994), "Indonesia's Experience in Managing Capital Inflows", mimeo. (Research Department).

BANK OF KOREA, *National Accounts,* various issues.

BANK OF KOREA, *Monthly Bulletin,* various issues.

BANK OF KOREA, *Balance of Payments,* various issues.

BANK NEGARA MALAYSIA (1995), *Annual Report 1994.*

BANK OF THAILAND (1995), *Annual Economic Report 1994.*

CALVO, G., L. LEIDERMAN, and C. REINHART (1994), "Capital Inflows and Real Exchange Rate Appreciation in Latin America: The Role of External Factors", *IMF Staff Papers,* Vol.40, pp. 108-151.

DORNBUSCH, R. (1996), "Cross-border Payments Taxes and Alternative Capital-Account Regimes", in UNCTAD,

International Monetary and Financial Issues for the 1990s, Vol. VIII (UNCTAD/GID/G24/8)(New York and Geneva: United Nations).

DRI (1995), *World Markets Executive Overview*, Fourth Quarter.

EICHENGREEN, B., and C. WYPLOSZ (1993), "The Unstable EMS", *Brookings Papers on Economic Activity*, No. 1.

EICHENGREEN, B., J. TOBIN, and C. WYPLOSZ (1995), "Two Cases for Sand in the Wheels of International Finance", *Economic Journal*, Vol. 105, pp. 162-172.

EUROMONEY (1995), *The 1995 Guide to Emerging Currencies*.

FELIX, D. (1995), "The Tobin Tax Proposal", *Futures*, Vol.27, No.2, pp. 195-208.

FOLKERTS-LANDAU, D., G. SCHINASI, M. CASSARD, V. NG, C. REINHART, and M. SPENCER (1995), "Effects of Capital Flows on the Domestic Financial Sectors in APEC Developing Countries", in M. Khan and C. Reinhart (eds.), "Capital Flows in the APEC Region", *IMF Occasional Paper*, No.122.

FRANKEL, J. (1995), "How Well Do Foreign Exchange Markets Function: Might a Tobin Tax Help?", paper presented at the UNDP Meeting on Proposals for an International Currency Transaction Levy, New York, October 10.

GARBER, P. (1995), "Issues of Enforcement and Evasion in a Levy on Foreign Exchange Transactions", paper presented at the UNDP Meeting on Proposals for an International Currency Transaction Levy, New York, October 10.

GARBER, P., and M. TAYLOR (1995), "Sand in the Wheels of Foreign Exchange Markets: A Special Note", *Economic Journal*, Vol. 105, pp. 173-180.

HAKKIO, C. (1994), "Should We Throw Sand in the Gears of Financial Markets?", *Economic Review*, Federal Reserve Bank of Kansas City, Vol.79, No.2, pp. 17-31.

IMF (1995a), "Financial Transaction Taxes", mimeo.

IMF (1995b), *International Capital Markets: Developments, Prospects, and Policy Issues* (Washington, D.C.), August.

IMF, *Balance of Payments Statistics*, various issues.

IMF, *International Financial Statistics*, various issues.

KAHN, M., and C. REINHART (1995), "Macroeconomic Management in APEC Economics: The Response to Capital Inflows", in M. Kahn and C. Reinhart (eds.), "Capital Flows in APEC Region", *IMF Occasional Paper*, No.122, pp. 15-30.

KENEN, P. (1995), "The Feasibility of Taxing Foreign-Exchange Transactions", paper presented at the UNDP Meeting on Proposals for an International Currency Transaction Levy, New York, October 10.

KIM, E.H., and V. SINGAL (1994), "Opening Up of Stock Markets: Lessons from and for Emerging Markets", *Papers on Policy Issues*, Korea Institute of Finance, No. 6.

KIM, K. (1991), "A Study on the Effectiveness of the Sterilization Policy in an Open Economy: the Case of Korea", *Studies in Financial and Monetary Economics*, Vol.28 (in Korean).

KITTISRIKANGWAN, P., M. SUPAPONGSE, and J. JANTARANGS (1994), "Monetary Policy Management in Thailand", in *Papers on Policy Analysis and Assessment*, Economic Research Department, Bank of Thailand.

KOREA INSTITUTE OF FINANCE (1994), *Foreign Exchange System Reform in Korea* (in Korean).

KOREA MINISTRY OF FINANCE AND THE ECONOMY (1994), *The Plan for Foreign Exchange System Reform* (in Korean).

LEIDERMAN, L. (1995), "Policy Lessons from Latin America's Experience with Capital Inflow", in R. Dornbusch and Y. C. Park (eds.), *Financial Opening: Policy Lessons for Korea* (Seoul: Korea Institute of Finance and International Center for Economic Growth).

MATHIESON, D., and L. ROJAS-SUAREZ (1993), "Liberalization of Capital Account: Experiences and Issues", *IMF Occasional Paper*, No.103.

NIJATHAWORN, B. (1995a), "Central Banking Policies in Thailand", paper presented at the Sixth APEEM Meeting, Bangkok, Thailand, August 17-18.

NIJATHAWORN, B. (1995b), " Capital Flows, Policy Response, and the Role of Fiscal Adjustment: The Thai Experience", paper presented at a World Bank Seminar on Managing Economic Reform under Capital Flow Volatility, Washington D.C., May 30 - June 2.

NIJATHAWORN, B., and T. DEJTHAMRONG (1994), "Capital Flows, Exchange Rate and Monetary Policy: Thailand's Recent Experience", in *Papers on Policy Analysis and Assessment*, Economic Research Department, Bank of Thailand.

PARK, Y.C. (1995), "Korea's Experience with Managing Foreign Capital Flows", paper presented at the UNDP Meeting on Proposals for an International Currency Transaction Levy, New York, October 10.

SCHADLER, S., M. CARKOVIC, A. BENNETT, and R. KAHN (1993), "Recent Experiences with Surges in Capital Inflows," *IMF Occasional Paper*, No.108.

SCHWERT, G. (1993), "Stock Market Volatility", *Journal of Financial Services Research*, Vol.46, pp. 23-24.

TIVAKUL, A., and P. SVETARUNDRA (1993), "Financial Innovation and Modernization of the Thai Financial Market", paper presented at the OECD Workshop on Financial Innovation and Modernization of Financial Market, Paris, December 2-3.

UNCTAD (1995), *Trade and Development Report 1995* (New York and Geneva: United Nations Publication, Sales No.: E.95.II.D.16).

VICHYANOND, P. (1994), "Thailand's Financial System: Structure and Liberalization", *Research Monograph*, No.11 (Bangkok: Thailand Development Research Institute).

WUCHIKOMI S., M. MURAKAMI, and Y. HAGIWARA (1995), "Foreign Exchange Rate Policy and the Role of the Yen in East Asian Countries", *Bank of Tokyo Quarterly*, Autumn, Research Department (in Japanese).

Annex

Estimates of financial market volatility in the Republic of Korea, Thailand, Malaysia and Indonesia, 1985-1995

Annex chart 1

GARCH VARIANCE OF WEEKLY EXCHANGE RATES

a. Korean won / US dollar
(January 1986 to December 1995)

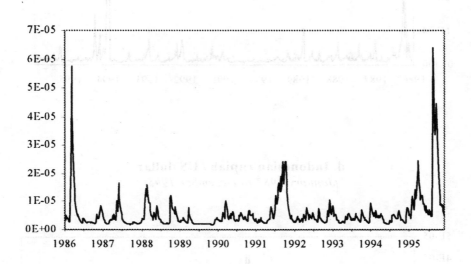

b. Thai bath / US dollar
(January 1986 to December 1995)

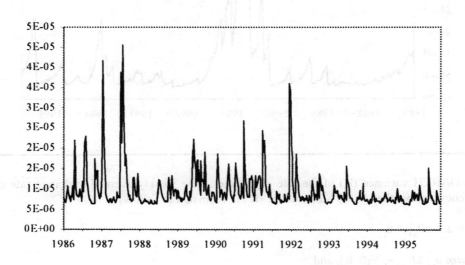

Annex chart 1 (concluded)

c. Malaysian ringgit / US dollar
(January 1986 to December 1995)

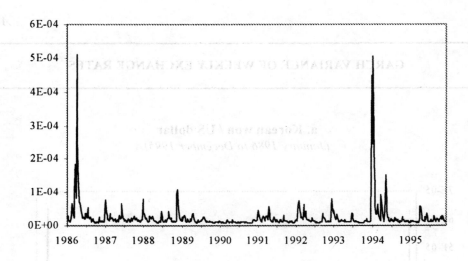

d. Indonesian rupiah / US dollar
(January 1987 to December 1995)

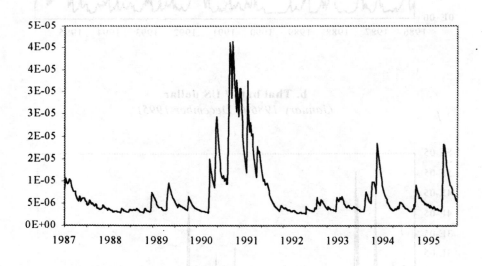

Note: The GARCH variance (h_t) of the rate of change in the weekly average exchange rate of the local currency against the United States dollar (R_t) is estimated as follows:

$$R_t = a + bR_{t-1} + u_t$$

where $u_t / \Omega_{t-1} \sim N(0, h_t)$, and

$$h_t = w + \alpha u^2_{t-1} + \beta h_{t-1}$$

GARCH VARIANCE OF WEEKLY STOCK RETURNS

a. Republic of Korea
(January 1986 to December 1995)

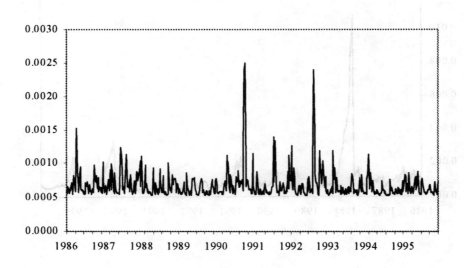

b. Thailand
(January 1987 to December 1995)

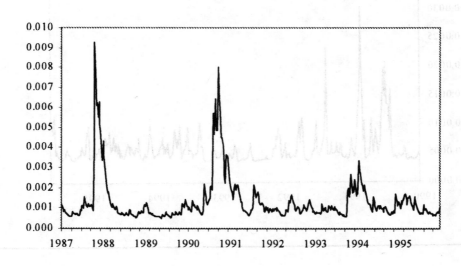

/...

Annex chart 2 (concluded)

c. Malaysia
(January 1986 to December 1995)

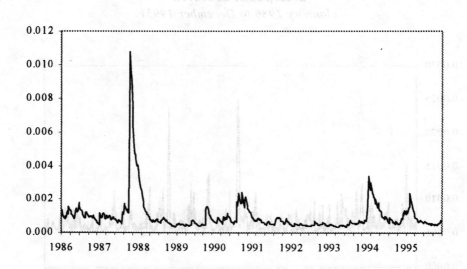

d. Indonesia
(April 1990 to December 1995)

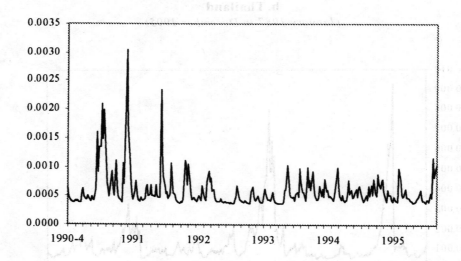

GARCH VARIANCE OF INTEREST RATES

a. Republic of Korea
(Three-year corporate bond yield)
(January 1989 to December 1995)

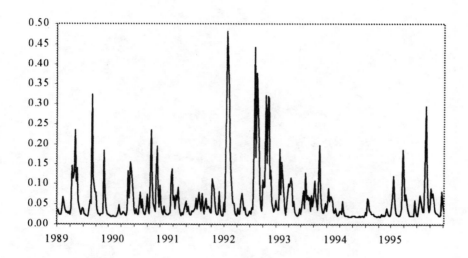

b. Malaysia
(Weighted average of three-year interbank rate)
(August 1985 to December 1995)

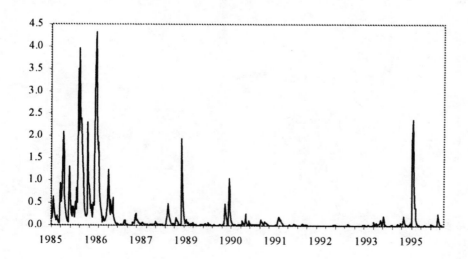

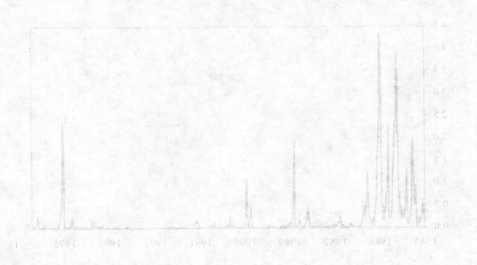

THE NEW CONDITIONALITIES OF THE INTERNATIONAL FINANCIAL INSTITUTIONS

Devesh Kapur

*Habit is habit, and not to be flung out of the window, but coaxed
downstairs a step at a time*

Mark Twain, quoted in a speech by Barber Conable, former President
of the World Bank, to World Resources Institute, 1987.

Abstract

In recent years the international financial institutions have seen a secular increase in the
scope of their agenda and activities. Their burgeoning agenda has coincided with a
corresponding increase in their conditionalities, both implicit and explicit. This paper seeks
to understand the causes for these developments that began at the end of the 1980s. It examines
the principal elements of the new agenda, in particular those related to the environment,
"governance" and public expenditures, and the conditionalities underpinning them.

Conditions related to the environment have had their strongest impact at the project level
while IDA-borrowers have been required to prepare national environmental action plans as a
condition of lending. Governance-related conditions have been introduced in four areas: public
sector management, accountability, legal frameworks, and information and transparency issues.
Both environment and governance conditionalities have coalesced on the issue of
"participation", which has expanded from a condition for project lending, to the formulation
of country assistance strategies. The new emphasis on public expenditure reviews, scrutinizing
both current and capital expenditures, is now informing lending conditions on the level and
distribution of borrower Governments' social expenditures as well as "non-productive"
expenditures.

Finally, the paper examines the implications of the new agenda for both the borrowers and
the institutions themselves. While there are sound reasons underlying the "new" agenda,
implementation will prove problematic given that these issues are relatively subjective,
discriminatory and politically charged. For the international financial institutions themselves
the excessive complexity of conditions attached to their lending is likely to have an adverse
impact on the demand for loans as well as on project performance.

I. Introduction

Since the end of the 1980s, the international financial institutions (IFIs) have seen a dramatic increase in the scope of their agenda and activities. Their burgeoning agenda has been parallelled by a corresponding increase in conditionalities on their lending, both implicit and explicit (Gibbon, 1993; Nelson, 1993). This paper examines the growth of the agendas and conditionalities of the IFIs by focusing particularly on the World Bank. Trends in the Bank have tended to set the pace for other multilateral development banks with the exception of the European Bank for Reconstruction and Development (EBRD).

The paper first places the growth of the agendas and associated conditions in a historical context, focusing on the first expansionary wave that began in the early 1980s with the launching of structural adjustment lending. We then analyse the reasons that led to a second expansionary phase starting at the end of that decade. Third, we examine the principal elements of this new agenda, in particular those related to the environment, "governance" and public expenditures, and the conditionalities underpinning them. Finally, the paper examines the implications of the new agenda, for both the IFI borrowers and the institutions themselves.

II. The Bank follows the IMF: adjustment lending and formal conditionality

At the beginning of the 1980s many developing countries economies were faced with deepening economic problems. Some of the problems were caused by external shocks - notably post-war lows in commodity prices and high real interest rates (triggered in turn by the second-oil shock and economic policies in the developed countries), others by the cumulative effects of internal policy choices. Two additional transformations - political changes in major developed countries, most notably in the United States and the United Kingdom, but also Germany and Canada, and new intellectual currents in the economic profession - drastically altered the milieu in which the IFIs operated.

It was in this climate that the World Bank launched its programme of structural adjustment lending. Although the Bank's decision to add an additional lending instrument in 1979 slightly preceded some of the above events, its evolution was markedly influenced by them, as well as by the onset of the debt crisis in middle-income countries in 1982.

Contrary to later interpretations, structural adjustment lending did not mark the beginning of the Bank's policy-influencing role. From its inception, the World Bank has identified its contribution to development with improving borrower policies as much as with lending (Brookings Institution, forthcoming). It played that policy role in various ways: studies and economic research; discussions with officials from borrowing countries; technical expertise transmitted through project lending; and a combination of policy dialogue and informal conditionality backed by the threat of restricting the volume of its lending. Its capacity to influence policies was undermined in the 1970s, in part by its own desire to multiply the level of lending, and in part because borrowers could resort much more easily to other sources of finance.

Structural adjustment lending, launched in 1979, differed in two important respects from the Bank's past lending modalities: (1) the distinctness with which it was anchored in balance-of-payments problems of borrowers; and (2) the explicitness and detail of conditionalities. Conditionality in the form of loan covenants has always been a key element of World Bank loans. But structural adjustment lending introduced a much greater formalism in conditionalities, as well as greater commitment than in the previous decade to enforce them.

The initial emphasis on balance-of-payments problems in the early 1980s led the Bank to focus its lending conditions on fiscal and trade policies, and on the productive sectors, especially agriculture (but also to some degree on energy and industry). But as the 1980s advanced, several trends developed. The scope of objectives attached to adjustment lending expanded steadily, and so did the volume of Bank resources devoted to adjustment lending. While the emphasis on fiscal policies remained unchanged, trade-related conditions and those specifically targeted at productive sectors, waned. At the same time, there was an increasing emphasis on conditionalities related to public institutions and regulations, and to reforms of state-owned enterprises and the financial sector (table 1).

The World Bank has always paid considerable attention to institutional issues of development and public sector management. The shift in the 1980s was rationalized principally in terms of economic efficiency criteria: for most of the decade, lending

Table 1

ADJUSTMENT LENDING CONDITIONALITY BY AREA OF POLICY, 1980-1991

(Per cent)

	1980 -1983	1984 -1987	1988 -1991
Macro/fiscal	22	21	21
Public enterprise	10	14	16
Public institution/regulation	8	9	12
Financial sector	6	10	14
Trade	18	16	10
Social sector	1	0	3
Energy and industrial sectors	16	10	8
Agricultural sector	18	18	12
Other sectors	2	1	3
Total	100	100	100
Memo items:			
Total number of adjustment operations	41	91	124
Average number of conditions per operation	32	39	56

Source: Calculations by the author.

conditions were restricted to a narrow economic sphere despite a steady expansion in the conditionality agenda. But increasingly the Bank's conception of what constituted the economic sphere began to broaden and nibble at the boundaries of what could, under different criteria, be seen as part of the social and political domain. It could be argued that the procedural elements of structural adjustment lending almost made this inevitable - if some worthy goals could be included under the conditionality umbrella, why could this umbrella not be expanded into a tent, incorporating more and more worthy causes? However, the fact that the IMF managed for long to limit its conditionality agenda leads one to conclude that matters of timing (the coincidence of adjustment lending with external changes) and differing institutional objectives may explain why the Bank did not similarly restrict its agenda.

III. The new agenda

At the end of the 1980s, a combination of long-term trends and immediate political events converged into a reorientation and further expansion of the Bank's agenda. A major stimulus was the World Bank's Long-Term Perspective Study on sub-Saharan Africa, which had been prompted by the persistence of the continent's development crisis and the disappointing results of structural adjustment lending (World Bank, 1989). By explicitly relating sub-Saharan Africa's economic predicament to a "crisis of governance" in that region, the study marked the first time that the World Bank publicly articulated "governance" as a central issue that needed to be addressed. Previous Bank studies on Africa had been criticized for the lack of consultation with experts from the region. By contrast, this study had been prepared with considerable consultations with African experts who strongly urged the Bank to address this issue. In addition to traditional influences (staff and donors), the Bank's new agenda came to be increasingly influenced by non-governmental groups both in borrowing and donor countries, but especially the latter reflecting the power of single-issue politics in the richer countries.

A second stimulus came from criticism of the World Bank's record on poverty and the environment. Although ostensibly separate issues, the two coalesced in the minds of some of the Bank's most vocal critics. It was argued that the Bank's structural adjustment agenda had shortchanged the poor by crowding-out lending for poverty-oriented projects and conditionalities that focused excessively on public expenditures (due to their emphasis on reining-in fiscal deficits), resulting in cuts in social-sector spending. The Bank changed tack, first by instituting projects with social safety-net features and then by ratcheting up its lending for social sectors (table 2). The last, coupled with a perceived need to address the composition of public expenditure to address fungibility issues, especially in countries where external finance was a significant fraction of Government budgets, would soon take the Bank into the deeper waters of public expenditure reviews.

The environmental critique of the Bank's operations had been fuelled by several well-publicized problems related to projects in Indonesia and Brazil, and later in India. This critique, however, quickly expanded from narrow ecological concerns to "human rights" of forcibly relocated people, and to the modalities employed by the Bank and its borrowers

Table 2

WORLD BANK LENDING COMMITMENTS BY SECTOR, 1950-1995

(Per cent)

	Infra-structure [a]	Social sectors [b]	Programme and adjustment [c]	Other [d]
1950-1959	64	...	19	17
1960-1969	64	4	5	27
1970-1979	36	12	4	46
1980-1989	32	15	18	34
1990-1995	27	26	23	24

Source: World Bank commitment data.
   a   Transportation, telecommunications, power, energy.
   b   Education, environment, human resources, population, health and nutrition, water supply and sanitation, urban development.
   c   Debt reduction, import rehabilitation, sector adjustment, structural adjustment.
   d   Agriculture, finance, industry, mining and other extractive activities, multi-sector, public sector management, tourism, unclassified sectors.

in designing and implementing projects, leading to questioning the development priorities of the Bank and its borrowers. Gradually, the environmental agenda expanded from assessments of the environmental impact of individual projects to environmental action plans on the country level, and further to broader issues that increasingly overlapped with those under the "governance" rubric - such as beneficiary "participation", "transparency" and "accountability".

It could be argued that these changes simply reflected deeper underlying developments, both within the borrowing countries and in the external environment. There can be little doubt that in many borrowing countries, the processes and institutional structures of Government had visibly deteriorated over previous decades. Senior officials of many borrowing countries have been pressing their counterparts in the IFIs, privately to be tougher in their approach to conditionality as to enhance their bargaining strength in constraining the machinations of their political superiors. Local NGOs and intellectuals, frustrated by their Governments' frequently perverse policies and practices, and their own political weakness, have increasingly sought external allies to leverage their cause. It is noteworthy that the perceived lack of

redress of local groups vis-à-vis their Governments, and the spill-over of this frustration to IFI-funded projects has occurred as much in countries with democratically elected Governments as in others. Examples include the Narmada project in India, which served as a catalyst for pressures that led to the setting-up of the World Bank's inspection panel, and the Arun dam project in Nepal, which was the first to receive the attention of this panel. More recently, in the case of the Rondonia project in the north-east of Brazil, local NGOs have been urging the World Bank to require the State Government of that province to take certain actions. The Ghazi Barotha Hydro Power project in Pakistan is yet another, albeit less charged, example.

Externally, the profound international changes in Eastern Europe and the subsequent collapse of the Soviet Union seemed to vindicate the unequivocal superiority of a liberal-market democratic system as a way of organizing human affairs. But other developments, while less immediately visible, added to the constellation of forces affecting the IFIs. Perhaps the most important among them was a relative weakening of the principals involved in running the IFIs, the nation States. State sovereignty, deemed paramount at Bretton Woods, had been weakening due to a multitude of factors, including the increasing globalization in trade and capital flows, the decline of political parties, the rise of NGOs, and the information revolution. In international legal financial circles, chinks began to appear in the hitherto secure concept of "sovereign immunity". It was a matter of time before these forces would impinge on the IFIs.

The impact of these changes was felt almost immediately in the creation of the EBRD in 1991, where for the first time political goals were specifically incorporated in the charter of an IFI. This new institution was explicitly committed to transforming the economic systems of countries in Eastern and Central Europe, on the basic condition that borrowing members were committed to the "fundamental principles of multiparty democracy, the rule of law, respect for human rights and market economics".

Greater attention to - loosely defined - "governance" issues also emerged in other multilateral fora. The preamble to the Lome-IV convention included several paragraphs on human rights, and UNDP redefined its mission as "capacity building" and launched a new *Human Development Report*, which called attention to the question of governance.

At the World Bank, changes were leveraged through IDA replenishments which, since the early 1980s, had increasingly become the Achilles heel of its autonomy. The IDA Deputies, in reaching agreement on IDA-9 in 1989, linked the replenishment to the following conditions: (1) country assistance strategy (CAS) papers for IDA countries should be discussed by the Board of Governors of the World Bank; (2) assessments of environmental impact should be instituted; and (3) the Board should have a greater say in tranche releases of Structural Adjustment Loans. Although these requirements were initially meant to apply to IDA borrowers, they soon spilled over to IBRD. The fact that some of the Bank Group's largest (and most powerful) borrowers are IDA-blend countries means that strict boundaries are difficult to maintain.

Pressures for CAS discussions by the Bank's Board also came from within the Board itself in the context of IBRD lending for debt and debt-reduction operations. Instead of the existing project-by-project involvement, the Board was determined to monitor lending at a strategic level. The CAS emerged as the vehicle for discussions of country-lending strategy against the background of a country's external environment, its policies and performance. For IDA countries it became a requirement that country

assistance strategies specifically incorporate governance issues addressing the capacity and willingness of borrower Governments to carry out much-needed reforms. More recently, project-level covenants like resettlement have been gradually incorporated into a broader policy dialogue woven into a CAS.

In examining how the new agenda has emerged, it must be noted that concerted protests by borrowing-country Executive Directors in the IFIs have been rare. While it may perhaps reflect a realization that much of the new agenda is theatre, it also reflects the beliefs of finance ministries in the functionality of these changes as well as regional variances in the receptivity to these changes. The stark contrast between Latin America and Africa in the implementation of privatization and the vanguard position of the Inter-American Development Bank among the regional development banks on issues related to the governance agenda, undoubtedly reflect as much the preferences of the region's borrowers, as the consequences of IFI conditionality. Moreover, borrower-country Board members acting on a presumption that "what goes around comes around" keep their reservations muted on conditionalities linked to loans to other countries, allowing a "divide-and-rule" strategy to work.

For many countries the principal forum in which an increasing range of political issues is raised by donors is at the meetings of donor consultative groups, chaired by the World Bank. This reflects a renewed moral activism by richer countries and their desire to use development assistance as an instrument for political change. As stated earlier, there are good reasons for the richer countries to adopt a more interventionist stance on issues of political process. It is less clear, however, whether the activism born of moral indignation and dwindling resources has the patience to engage in a considered deliberation on the difficult issues of institutional competence, differences in political practices and relative priorities (van Arkadie and Mule, 1995). We now turn to some of the new lending conditions that have grown out of this activism.

Environmental conditionality

Environmental concerns were first formally integrated into World Bank operations by an "operational manual statement" in 1984 (OMS 2.36, "Environmental Aspects of Bank Work"). At the time the Bank's approach was to adopt "guidelines" rather than "standards" or "requirements", reflecting a belief that approaches needed to be tailored to local circumstances.

As a result of the conditions of the IDA-9 agreement, formal processes and methods for environmental impact assessment were put into place in 1989 by an "operational directive"(OD 4.00), and revised in 1991 (OD 4.01).[1] These outlined specific procedures for the environmental assessment of Bank operations and related types of environmental analysis. Bank policies regarding borrower requirements on several other environment-related issues were tightened in the early 1990s. While some had a narrow technical focus (dam safety, agricultural pest control), others had sector-wide (forestry, water resources management) or social (involuntary resettlement, indigenous peoples) repercussions. The decline of World Bank lending for traditional investment projects in agriculture, infrastructure and industry (table 2), means that the new environmental requirements apply to less than half of Bank lending.

The IDA-9 agreement also required that all IDA-recipients complete national environmental action plans (NEAPs) by the end of the IDA-9 period, i.e. 1993. A new operational directive on National Environmental Action Plans (OD 4.02) was issued in 1992. Subsequently, environmental action plans were initiated for those IBRD countries (such as Brazil, Mexico and Indonesia) where global environmental interests were perceived to be at stake. By now, NEAPs have been undertaken for many IBRD countries.

In theory, NEAPs were the responsibility of the borrowing country. In practice, for many IDA-only countries struggling to maintain rudimentary governmental activities, the artificial deadlines for yet another externally mandated requirement ensured that there would be limited borrower ownership of NEAPs. The reports would be written with the help of external consultants, to meet the formal requirements as much as a genuine process reflecting country-wide concerns.

Governance conditionality

In November 1990, at a consultative group meeting for Kenya chaired by the World Bank, donors took the unprecedented step of linking aid to Kenya to economic *and political* reform in that country. Although the event was a milestone in establishing governance issues on the agenda of donors and the IFIs, as noted above, the shadows cast by governance issues had been lengthening for some time before then.

Since then, various facets of governance issues have emerged as an integral part of the agenda of official finance, especially concessional finance. Donors have been divided, reflecting confusion and contradiction between stated principles and commercial and strategic interests. Some have been advocating tough action, others have preferred a behind-the-scenes approach, while still others have witnessed significant internal differences due to divergent views of foreign and aid ministries.

In the early 1990s the Bank decided to raise the profile of governance in CAS presentations to its Board, without specifying which type of issues would be raised. Discussions of governance began to be required in the CAS of IDA countries. But for these countries the principal fora for pressure on the broadening agenda are the consultative groups and consortia where the World Bank plays an important formal and informal role. In practice, the salience of the issue has varied enormously, with East Asia and sub-Saharan Africa representing the two extremes. Dependence on official external finance and economic outcomes have been at least as important as the intrinsic objective reality of governance-related issues in the degree of pressure brought to bear on individual countries.

The swiftness with which the term "governance" has captured centre-stage in the economic development lexicon is, in part, due to the remarkable properties of the term. It has a "motherhood" quality to it - no one could ever be against "good governance"; it is elastic - it can be stretched to include yet more additions to the agenda. It is also plastic, rendering it able to reflect the concern *du jour*.

With these caveats, governance has been loosely equated with the term "good Government" and for the IFIs is deemed to have four principal components: sound economic policies; competent public administration; open and accountable Government; and respect for the rule of law. Inherent in this were the requirements of a liberal democratic State: a limited role for the State (and relatedly) an economy guided principally by market forces and open to international exchange; with supportive elements of popular participation, accountability of rulers and the strengthening of an autonomous civil society.

The IFIs' articulation of governance issues was formalized in two reports by the World Bank (World Bank, 1991a, 1991b). In trying to keep their actions on governance within the bounds laid down by their articles, the IFIs have attempted to view governance in instrumental terms - as the grease that enables the engine of development to work more smoothly, thereby allowing their interventions to be more effective. To this end, the aforementioned reports identified four aspects of governance as germane to the World Bank's purposes of fostering economic development: public sector management; accountability; the legal framework; and information and transparency. Concerned that the Bank's involvement not cross the mandate of its Articles, the Bank's legal counsel attempted to limit the institution's concern with governance to the "contribution it makes with social and economic development and not with the form of the political regime" and emphasized the need for judgements based on country traditions and circumstances. For this reason the Bank has tried to maintain that in the area of human rights its Articles mandate it to focus on economic, social and cultural rights (one of the two United Nations covenants on human rights) and not on political and civil human rights (the other United Nations covenant on this issue).

Some parts of the governance agenda as enumerated above have long been integral to the World Bank's operations. Examples include improved public sector management and greater accountability through better audit systems and more open procurement procedures. The IFIs' efforts in advancing "transparency" and "accountability" aspects of the governance agenda are, to a considerable extent, repackaging and formalization.

Part of the governance agenda is directed at the issue of corruption. The IFIs, and the World Bank in particular, have since the mid-1980s attributed governmental corruption (largely) to competition for scarce State resources. This increasingly complemented the efficiency rationale in the advice and pressures emanating from the IFIs that pressed for a shift in the boundary between the public and the private sector in favour of the latter. Such a shift, it was argued, would reduce pressures on the governmental apparatus and reduce patronage possibilities. Lending conditionality reflected this belief, emphasizing State enterprise reform and deregulation in the 1980s, and adding civil service reform (often leading to civil service retrenchment) and privatization at the end of the decade and into the 1990s.

Despite much rhetoric, the emphasis on privatization is a phenomenon only of the 1990s. The far greater extent of privatization that occurred in Latin America relative to Africa, is a reflection more of the beliefs of Governments than of differences in pressure applied by the IFIs. One reason for the more forceful stance in the 1990s was the budgetary impact of continued losses of parastatals. Initially, when privatization became an explicit part of Bank conditionality, the institution tried to specify the number of enterprises concerned and to identify those that were to be sold. As it became apparent that such conditionalities put Governments in the unfavourable position of a fire sale, the Bank modified its views from the earlier insistence of selling assets within a specified time frame. Lately, the conditionalities related to privatization appear to have again become more specific. While a much cited example - privatization of the sniffing dog service of the customs agency in Jamaica - is by no means the rule, it is indicative of the level of detail lending conditions can sometimes reach down to.

A major mechanism deployed by the IFIs to promote the accountability aspect of governance has been to push for decentralization. This has been pressed through changes in budgetary processes driven by a long-held belief that moving the locus of decision-making to where resources are spent results in greater accountability. This reflects a swing-back of the pendulum from earlier thinking in public administration reform, when local Governments were often seen as particularly corrupt and inept, and captured by local elites. This view implied that many social reform programmes required external, i.e. central, intervention to prise open atavistic structures. In fact, this belief is inherent in the current centralized decision-making - whether in the IFIs or the central Governments -, which is seen in certain international circles as the only way to persuade borrower Governments to undertake necessary reform measures. The move may also run against efforts to reduce governmental bureaucracies. Some Governments were centralizing to husband scarce skills and also to curb the growth of duplicative bureaucracies at various levels of Government.

The IFIs' interest in participation was initially prompted not by the governance agenda *per se*, but by the soul-searching that followed major reviews of their portfolios. The World Bank's review in 1992 (widely known as the "Wappenhans Report") stressed the importance of "ownership" to ensure better implementation. This was interpreted to mean that Bank projects needed to include a wider constituency than simply borrower Governments in their design and implementation. The justification for stressing participation due to its positive role in development effectiveness and better portfolio performance was soon complemented by two other factors: participation was seen as a worthwhile goal in and of itself; and it had repercussions on the aid climate, given the strong attachment to the issue of many of the Bank's non-borrowing constituencies. As a result, requirements were put into place to ensure that affected groups were duly consulted; new information disclosure policies were instituted (this last, in turn, was a condition of accepting concessional funds for the Global Environment Facility); more recently an independent inspection panel has been created at the World Bank, where groups directly affected by Bank projects can file grievances. This issue has already placed more rigorous demands on borrowers to consult with local NGOs, a requirement that is likely to be tightened further if a new staff directive currently under process is implemented. The "participation" aspect of the governance agenda has been strongly pushed by Northern NGOs; while it is likely to result in better outcomes for the Bank's investment projects, it has most certainly empowered Northern NGOs' considerably in the IFIs' decision-making.

An outgrowth of the new agenda is the importance given the legal framework. The degree of World Bank involvement in this area represents an important departure from its past. To a certain extent this change is a logical outcome of changes in economic systems of many IFI borrowers. The Bank's push for a greater role for market forces, as well as opening up to foreign investment, while contentious at the beginning of the 1980s, had become less so by the end of the decade. As new members used to a command system operating with administrative orders joined the Bank, their move to a market system required a different legal system that could underpin transactions in a market economy, ranging from commercial codes to contract and property laws.

The evolution of legal systems in societies reflect complex interactions in societal forces and values and convictions. The Bank's legal counsel made it clear that successful legal reform could not be imposed from the outside and could not be rushed through. Countries needed to conduct broad consultations and extensive debates. The limited expertise of the IFIs on this subject was another concern. While much lending has been at the request of borrower countries, and has taken the form of technical assistance loans (for training of law officials in business law and commercial transactions; compliance, enforcement and settlement mechanisms; administrative steps to reduce the time to resolve business disputes, etc.), changing specific laws is common in adjustment loan conditionality, and conditionality requiring broader changes in legal codes are not uncommon.

Conditionality with respect to public expenditure

Throughout its history the World Bank has always paid attention to Government budgets. The Bank would examine the budgetary feasibility and priorities of a Governments' investment programmes by undertaking public investment reviews. These reviews focused essentially on capital expenditure. By the mid-1980s, with adjustment lending growing rapidly, overall Government expenditure came under greater scrutiny, due to fungibility concerns arising from, (1) the budgetary support aspects of adjustment lending, (2) the large share of external financing in many Government budgets and, (3) a greater focus on poverty alleviation. Many observers expressed concern that in their haste to meet fiscal targets (budget deficits), Governments were cutting those expenditures that were essential for long-term development (for instance, expenditures on operations and maintenance and non-wage expenditures in social sectors), rather than "unproductive non-developmental" expenditures driven by short-term political exigencies. This led to closer examination of Government expenditure, now including also current expenditure, and as a result public expenditure reviews emerged as an integral part of the Bank's analytical arsenal.

Once "unproductive" expenditures began to be closely scrutinized, it was matter of time before these concerns spilled over to military expenditure. The easing and then the end of the cold war gave this politically sensitive issue a new impetus, with expectations of a large "peace dividend". In April 1991 a communiqué of the Development Committee explicitly raised concerns on "excessive" military expenditure. The Bank's legal counsel made it clear that the determination of an appropriate level of military expenditure for a member country was typically based on security and political considerations falling outside the Bank's legally authorized power, let alone its competence. However, the legal counsel also made it clear that there were several spheres - risk-management analysis, research, adjustment lending operations, and the Bank's involvement in public expenditures - where the institution could pursue the allocation of public expenditure for non-productive purposes. Although the IFIs do not overtly address the issue, an unstated reason for focusing on military expenditure by the donor community is to reduce the political power of the military establishment in many impoverished nations.

The Bank has been addressing the issue through country dialogue and IDA allocations. In some cases, it has undertaken operational work at the request of Governments, ranging from defense industry conversion (Argentina) to demobilization of armies (Uganda). The Bank and the Fund began to share data on both military debt and military expenditure. Through public expenditure reviews (PERs), the two institutions began jointly to address the issue indirectly. World Bank conditionality would mandate increases in allocations to development expenditures with the expectation that, with the Fund simultaneously insisting on overall budget ceilings, military expenditures would be squeezed.

More recently, the principal impetus for PERs and resultant conditionality has been the Bank's poverty agenda. A staff operational directive on poverty reduction (OD 4.15) issued in December 1991, directs staff to prepare and periodically update poverty assessments which assess the consistency between Government policy and the reduction of poverty. These requirements (amplified in the Bank's Poverty Reduction Handbook), call, amongst other things, for country poverty assessments to review public expenditures and institutions to identify possible reallocations of resources that will expand the access of the poor to physical and social infrastructure.

PERs grew rapidly at the turn of the decade due to the demands of the Special Program for Africa at the time. As non-wage operations, and maintenance expenditure and military expenditure came under greater scrutiny, conditionalities on social sector spending in adjustment loans increased rapidly (from 7 per cent of adjustment operations in the early 1980s to about one third of all adjustment operations).

The PER-poverty reduction nexus was strengthened following the Social Summit in Copenhagen in 1995 which, inter alia, called for the Bretton Woods institutions to ensure budgetary transparency and accountability in the use of public resources in order to increase the quality and effectiveness of social expenditures. In a paper for the Development Committee, the institutions have enthusiastically supported this idea. Although the Social Summit had many recommendations that covered all countries, the selectivity of focus of the Bretton Woods institutions simply reflects the absence of any influence on policies of non-borrower Governments. World Bank structural adjustment programmes will include greater conditionality to protect, or increase, social sector spending, especially on basic services, and the Fund will pay greater attention to this subject in the context of surveillance and its economic and financial programmes. The two institutions have set up a joint task force to ensure greater collaboration on public expenditure issues, and a handbook on public expenditure management is being prepared.

Despite a seemingly simple concept, PERs require substantial effort and skill. Although the IFIs have initiated training programmes to improve Government capacities in this area, in smaller countries the capacity continues to be weak. In these countries PERs are done mostly by the IFIs or consultants made available to the country, casting doubts on cherished notions of "ownership". However, in some cases (Ghana for example), after a few rounds of PERs countries have gradually assumed ownership of these reviews.

As an auditing exercise the informational content of a good analysis of public expenditure is important in and of itself, both for budget management and, if put in the public domain, to guide public debate on the issue. But, as has been the case in the past, PERs appear to have emerged as the latest "magic bullet" on the poverty front. Based on PERs, loan conditions of IFIs, for instance on health expenditures, now extend to the level and composition of spending as well as budget management processes, including ceilings on wage expenditure, floors on medicines, share of drugs, etc..

Even if PERs were of high quality, the relationship between public expenditure and poverty alleviation is quite complex, and the often strong conclusions implied by the degree of lending conditionalities are questionable. In reality, data problems are severe. Internal reviews have indicated that many PERs lack even basic data on the functional and economic composition of expenditure, major programmes, private-sector provision, etc., that would be important for informed decision-making.

IV. Implications

It must be emphasized that in an era of shrinking development aid, with no signs of reversal, the "new" lending conditions of the IFIs are here to stay, given the strength of pressures in this direction within the IFIs, groups from non-borrowing members, and also from groups within the borrowing countries themselves. They do, however, point to a broader predicament facing multilateral institutions which are emerging as the instrument to implement multilaterally what countries are unwilling or unable to do on a bilateral basis. The current discussions seeking to link international trade with labour standards is simply another aspect of a broader trend on social assessments and associated conditionalities.

The new lending conditions pose an inherent dilemma for the IFIs: the difficulty in reconciling laudable goals with questionable means. Putting aside the question of the *desirability* of the new development goals, there remain basic questions about *how* the IFIs should relate to them. Should the IFIs be the major instruments of seeking these goals, and if so, how important should conditionality be to this role? Does the clamour for using IFI lending conditions to achieve new goals reflect a certain naiveté on the ability and utility of conditions to meet these goals?

How will these new conditionalities work? Compliance will remain problematic. The IMF has been applying formal conditionality for decades. Even though the Fund's agenda has been quite restricted, and confined to issues that are highly measurable, Fund conditionality has worked only to a limited extent. The World Bank's new agenda has a much wider span; many of the new issues require more subjective judgements. If we combine this with the reality that they are more strongly applied to weaker Governments which are already struggling, and further combine it with financial exigencies, for instance problems of rescheduling multilateral debt, one wonders what real compliance will be. Loan conditionalities follow a sort of "Laffer curve"; beyond a certain extent additional conditionality can become self-defeating. Judgements on an optimum degree of conditionality are difficult. Where the track record on meeting conditionalities in the past has been weak, non-lending (or up-front actions) may be desirable. Yet, here again, it should be stressed that even extreme economic sanctions have worked poorly in pressuring countries to change. Non-lending where reforms have not occurred may simply hasten the collapse of States (e.g. Liberia and Somalia), rather than promote reform.

Alternatives to IFI conditionality to advance these goals exist in principle - for instance, so-called "development agreements", organized and overseen by representatives of donors, recipients and third parties, that would call for reciprocal action by donors (in terms of long-term financial commitments) in return for recipients implementing an agreed development strategy (Adams, 1991).[2] However, it is unclear how such alternatives might work in practice.

A troubling aspect of the new agenda and associated conditionalities is the fact that despite attempts to limit the intrusion of IFIs into issues that are indubitably those of domestic politics (most notably by the Bank's legal counsel and by the borrowers), the new agenda is inexorably dragging the IFIs in. The separation of such issues may have been a fiction in the past but the distinction was functionally important for the IFIs.

In many countries the World Bank has begun to engage parliamentarians in the policy debate. Is this appropriate? Should IFI staff limit action to technical dialogue and policy advice to Government officials even if asked by the Government to help in parliamentary persuasion? The limited degree of economic literacy and the resultant confusion on economic policy debates means that in pushing for ownership and participation, it is to be expected that the staff of IFIs engage in activities of broader outreach. This approach does, however, carry the risk that politicians could be tempted to associate the IFIs with the Government, leaving them exposed if matters don't work out.

In certain countries where recent peace accords have tried to put an end to internal strife (e.g. Guatemala and Angola), the IFIs have made their lending conditional to the Government sticking to the peace accord, arguing that issues of violence and lack of security matter to their lending when they are material to a Government's capacity to execute an economic programme or are material to the economy in general. But since human-rights violations have been written into the peace accords, the IFIs position that their lending be linked to the Government's commitment to the peace accords have willy-nilly led them to tread into matters of human rights violations.

The widening scope of conditionality, in part, mirrors the IFIs new lending agenda, as seen in the case of the World Bank (table 2). For instance, in so far as the World Bank is lending more for social sectors than in the past, it should not be surprising to see the emergence of new conditions that pertain to this sector. However, the expanding agenda is also resulting in goal congestion (Naim, 1996) and is fundamentally at odds with the message of the IFIs in the 1980s - that in order to function more efficiently, Governments needed to restrict their burgeoning agendas to make them bureaucratically more manageable. If burgeoning agendas are detrimental to the cause of well functioning Governments, are they not likely to have similar adverse effects to the cause of well functioning IFIs - which are after all simply inter-governmental organizations?

In recent years it has been apparent that the performance of projects funded by the World Bank has been adversely affected by the excessive complexity arising from ever increasing operational guidelines, directives and other documents that are directly applicable institution-wide to the preparation, appraisal, implementation and evaluation of investment operations. Increasing complexity of the IFIs' lending guidelines results in inadequate compliance and not infrequently substitutes for careful project preparation and borrower ownership. There is also the question of institutional comparative advantage. There is a danger that the evangelical fervour for the "new" agendas and conditions may be crowding out and undermining the core economic analytical strengths and economic conditionalities of these institutions. The IFIs lending record suggests that projects aimed at changes in areas where political and social resistance was the strongest have been most prone to failure. Performance has been particularly weak in technical assistance projects, the problems being related to the public sector management aspects of governance. It may still be important for the IFIs to push for lending and conditions in these difficult areas - but there must be a greater tolerance for failure.

For the borrowers, the new agenda has substantially raised the transaction costs of borrowing from the multilateral development banks. This is an important reason why, despite the financial attractiveness of IBRD loans, demand for it has been stagnating, while demand for (and supply of) private capital has dramatically escalated in the first half of the 1990s. For this reason, and also because larger borrowers are likely to be able to fend off many of these conditionalities, the application of the new conditionalities will bite mostly on those borrowers whose demand elasticity for Bank loans is low - mainly IDA-only countries. Thus, in practice the IFIs may emerge as more discriminatory than they already are.

The perceived intrusiveness of the new agenda and associated conditionalities also imply a greater contentiousness in their implementation - leaving the IFIs potentially exposed to greater divisiveness due to a lack of consensus on goals but even more on the means to advance those goals. There are also potential moral-hazard problems in the IFIs involvement in these areas, arising from the asymmetry in the burden of risk. Borrower Governments will have to face the

political and financial risks while the IFIs will remain largely insulated from these.

Many of the terms of the new agenda are sufficiently imprecise, giving a much stronger presumption of what these concepts imply to different groups than the reality. The greater subjectivity of these issues means that to decide where the IFIs should draw the line between the economic, social and political dimensions of governance will be difficult and more easily subject to short-term pressures and the proclivities of staff and management. The complexities of the issues also mean that to reach balanced judgements requires deep country-specific knowledge. However, the staffing incentives within these institutions inherently discourage the building-up of area expertise.

In taking on political issues, the IFIs have taken on aspects of a politician's garb - where smooth, well articulated and confident positions that reflect the perceived demands of the pressure groups at hand, overwhelm issues of substance that may matter more for their borrowers. There is also a sharp time-inconsistency problem inherent in the new agenda. Taken as a package, the "model" driving the agenda is a liberal democratic one. Even if the model is accepted, the institutional underpinnings of liberal democratic States have taken centuries to evolve. That patience is no longer apparent. IFIs want to see concrete results within a few years, a time scale orders of magnitude faster than the pace of institutional change in the rich countries.

It must be clearly understood that the door through which new conditionalities have been entering into the agendas of the IFIs is the periodic replenishments of their concessional windows (IDA, GEF, FSO, ESAF, ADF). The borrowing countries have yet to grapple with the reality of increasing trade-offs between accepting "soft" financing from IFIs and the fact that this will necessarily come with more and more strings attached.

In light of the above, it is important that a continuing watching brief on developments in this sphere be maintained. This could be done by exchanging experiences in a systematic manner across countries as well as across different IFIs. However, in focusing on formal conditions, one should not lose sight of informal conditionalities or pre-conditionalities, whereby loans are not brought forward in the first place. The consistency of evolving conditions with the IFIs' articles and their implications for future IFI lending also need more careful examination.

Notes

1   Prior to 1992 staff instructions were incorporated in "Operational Directives" (ODs) and "Operational Manual Statements" (OMSs). Since 1992, new instructions are issued in the form of "Operational Policies" (OPs) and "Bank Procedures" (BPs), complemented by "Good Practice" (GP) statements.

2   Other variations of this include "Development Contracts" first formulated by the Norwegian Foreign Minister, Thorvald Stoltenberg, in 1989.

References

ADAMS, F. 1991), "Toward a concept of Development Agreements", mimeo.

BROOKINGS INSTITUTION (forthcoming), *A History of the World Bank*, (Washington, D.C.: The Brookings Institution).

GIBBON, J. (1993), "The World Bank and the New Politics of Aid", *European Journal of Development Research*, Vol. 5, No. 1 (June).

NAIM, M. (1996), "From Supplicants to Shareholders: Developing Countries and the World Bank", in G.K. Helleiner (ed.), *The International Monetary and Financial System: Developing Country Perspectives*, (New York: St. Martin's Press).

NELSON, J., and S. EGLINTON (1993), "Global Goals, Contentious Means: Issues of Multiple Aid Conditionality", *ODC Policy Essay*, No. 10 (Washington, D.C.: Overseas Development Council).

VAN ARKADIE, B., and H. MULE (1995), "Some Comments on Recent Trends in Donor Conditionality", mimeo.

WORLD BANK (1989), "Long-Term Perspective Study on Sub-Saharan Africa" (Washington, D.C.).

WORLD BANK (1991a), "Issues of 'Governance' in Borrowing Members - The Extent of their relevance under the Bank's Articles" (Washington, D.C.).

WORLD BANK (1991b), "Managing Development: The Governance Dimension" (Washington, D.C.).

NOTES ON MDB CONDITIONALITY ON GOVERNANCE

Aziz Ali Mohammed

Abstract

The paper examines the tensions resulting from the application by the Multilateral Development Banks (MDBs) of conditions for promoting good government in borrowing countries. The "governance conditionality" covers, inter alia, promoting the rule of law and accountability to citizens; curbing corruption; protecting legitimate private sector activities and interests; and encouraging participatory approaches to decision-making.

While borrowing Governments remain anxious to improve their governance credentials, their willingness to accept MDB conditions in these areas is circumscribed by the backlash effects of being perceived as acceding to the dictate of external agencies. The public reaction is stronger for two reasons: first, it is harder to prove that governance conditions bear directly on the successful outcome of particular projects and programmes and, second, prescriptions in these areas are seen as falling outside the "core" competencies of the MDBs and as being inconsistent with their non-political mandates.

For their part, the MDBs confront several difficulties in applying governance conditionality: how to avoid being pushed into the domestic political arena; how to monitor compliance of conditions that inevitably call for subjective judgements; how to prevent a weakening of governmental authority when calling for participation of non-governmental organizations, especially if they are foreign-based. There are issues of non-discriminatory treatment among borrowing members and there is also an issue of even-handedness as between creditor and debtor Governments, especially when applying conditions relating to the two-sided area of corruption.

In order to minimize the tension emerging from governance conditionality, the paper advances a few ideas, emphasizing in particular the need to be highly selective in targeting efforts to areas that offer the promise of tangible results in a reasonable period of time, and, after these areas have been selected in agreement with the borrowing Government, to commit substantial resources for capacity-building.

I. Introduction

The April 1996 Communique of the Inter-governmental Group of Twenty-four addressed the governance issue, among others, in the following words:

> Ministers had reservations about whether the Multilateral Development Banks could be an appropriate source of policy advice in the area of promoting good governance and civil society - issues that fall within the jurisdiction of borrowing Governments. Given the mandates of the Multilateral Development Banks, the conditions attached to financial assistance should be directly relevant to the success of the programs they support and performance should be judged on the basis of objectively measurable criteria. Ministers expressed serious concerns about the use of environmental, governance, human rights, labour standards, or other issues to further protectionist interests in industrial countries.[1]

In a statement to the Development Committee on April 23, 1996, the G-24 Chairman expressed concern about "conditions that are increasingly applied by the Multilateral Development Banks (MDBs) in such diverse areas as governance, human rights, the distribution of public expenditures, legal system reforms". He mentioned two factors bearing on his concern that conditions applied by MDBs relating to governance "may fail to produce results". The first was "that countries are required to show results in a fraction of the time that advanced nations took decades, if not centuries, to achieve". The second was a "growing sense that what is being asked is the application of a model that may be appropriate for some of the major shareholders of the Bretton Woods institutions but is inappropriate for many developing countries". He added that "even when developing-country Governments are willing to accept the conditions, their ability to implement them is put at risk by widespread resistance on the part of domestic public opinion".

There is a dilemma emerging for both member-Governments and the MDBs as they grapple with the governance issue. The MDBs are responding to an increasing recognition of the importance of good governance for the successful outcome of their lending operations; they are also cognizant of the growing resistance in their principal shareholder countries to providing concessional resources for disbursement in countries where Governments are seen by them as not fully accountable to their citizens, where decision-making processes are opaque, and where a high degree of corruption is tolerated. For their part, borrowing Governments are concerned, indeed anxious, to improve their governance credentials, especially as they move toward increasing reliance on private sector initiative and market-based financing of infrastructure and other investment activity previously in the domain of the State sector. Their willingness, however, to accept governance conditionality in their transactions with the MDBs is circumscribed by a "backlash" generated by a public perception that the borrowing Governments are acceding to the "dictate" of external agencies, rather than relying on their own initiatives to reinforce good governance.

This note is an attempt to respond constructively to the dilemma. After reviewing the evolution of MDB interest in governance conditionality (section II), the note illustrates some of the elements that contribute to stronger "backlash" effects in the governance area (section III). It next enumerates some of the difficulties that MDBs confront when applying conditions for good government (section IV), and in their light, it proposes a few ideas that might reduce the problems involved for both MDBs and borrowing Governments (section V).

II. Development of the "new conditionalities"

MDB conditionality has traditionally been applied in the form of loan covenants to specific projects and has been justified as bearing directly on the projects' success. This justification could be extended to environmental conditions, when these began to be applied from the mid-1980s, on the basis that the development process can be sustainable only if the environment is protected. Even when structural adjustment lending gained a substantial share of MDB lending in the late 1980s, its broader conditionality usually applied to the promotion of macroeconomic stability in the context of fostering balance-of-payments viability. Since such conditions had long been a staple of IMF conditionality, it was possible to justify their use by the MDBs, especially when they became part and parcel of the process linked to the formulation of Policy Framework Papers, in which the Bretton Woods institutions worked together to establish the terms and conditions of structural adjustment loans.

However, a transformation from macroeconomic into governance conditionality had begun when MDB reviews of investment programmes were extended into public expenditure reviews, and then into public expenditure ceilings as part of fiscal deficit reduction programmes. Such an overall ceiling, when joined to a condition protecting a "core" investment programme, became in effect, a ceiling on so-called "non-productive" expenditures. With growing IMF/MDB insistence, during the early 1990s, on the desirability of reducing military and on enlarging social sector expenditures, the manner in which macroeconomic conditionality was applied, could be construed as a subtle means of influencing sovereign decisions on the allocation of domestic public spending.

The emphasis on governance became more explicit after the establishment of the European Bank for Reconstruction and Development (EBRD) in 1990: its charter prescribed in its preamble that borrowing members were committed to the "fundamental principles of multiparty democracy, the rule of law, respect for human rights and market economics"[2]. While these desiderata were meant to apply to the EBRD's clientele of erstwhile centrally planned socialist countries in Eastern and Central Europe and the former Soviet Union, it was not long before such conditions began to appear in the context of financial relations with developing countries. The Lome-IV Convention, for instance, incorporated several references to human rights in its preamble, and UNDP and other United Nations fora (especially after the Copenhagen Social Summit of March 1995) began to advocate "good government" issues in their work.

Finally, the Report of the Task Force on Multilateral Development Banks[3] emphasized the importance of "more effective government and the emergence of a strong civil society". It asserted that there is a strong relationship between "good public sector policy" and "economic efficiency" and defined good policy as including the "rule of law, protection of legitimate economic activities and interests, a government's accountability to its citizens, effective measures to curb corruption, a participatory approach to development, easy access to important information and services, and sound decision making, reflecting the actual needs of the people". The Report concluded that the MDBs should help create and maintain such an environment "while being at once sensitive and determined". In commenting on the Report, the World Bank stated that "the Bank is now actively promoting good governance, not only in traditional public administration areas but in strengthening legal systems, helping Governments improve their public communication capacity on difficult economic development issues, increasing participation, and

responding to many government requests for help on decentralization"[4].

III. Backlash effects

The incorporation of "good government" conditions in MDB lending operations was designed to remove deficiencies in the borrowing country that were seen as retarding the development effort. However, this type of conditionality attracted strong reaction from the general public and, in particular, from vested interests that were beneficiaries of such deficiencies, especially when these had persisted for any length of time. This reaction was stronger than for the traditional conditionalities applied by the MDBs for two reasons. First, it was harder to prove that these conditions bear directly on the successful outcome of particular projects or programmes; second, they were regarded, as implied in the above-mentioned G-24 Ministerial communique, as falling outside the "core" competencies of the MDBs and their legal mandates.

Anti-government campaigns launched by interested groups are more apt to attract general support if there is an element of truth to the charge that, but for a governance condition laid down by an external lending agency, a project would have moved faster and/or could have been completed at lower cost, if the Government had simply followed its own agenda of good governance. For instance, participation in decision-making by all "stakeholders" is a governance condition that would typically be attached by an MDB, when supporting a large-scale construction or land resettlement project, where private land has to be acquired on payment of compensation. Generally, the value of land increases once the Government decides to undertake a project in a particular area. Some astute buyers start acquiring the land in advance and others try to bargain for exorbitant prices. Consultations with all stakeholders may thus unnecessarily push up the cost of specific development projects.

Similar difficulties can arise when MDBs seek to bring in non-governmental organizations (NGOs) into their project preparation process. In many instances, NGOs can serve a valuable countervailing social interest by empowering weaker elements in the society against the overbearing influence of rent-seeking local elites. However, in many developing country contexts, NGOs can, just as easily, become instruments, advertent or otherwise, in the hands of the same elite interests when opposing some government initiative or the other. It is easier to attack an MDB for giving ear to foreign NGOs. The MDB finds it particularly difficult to avert the intervention of a foreign NGO when an Executive Director from a donor or creditor country presses the claims of its national NGOs in respect of a project or programme that the MDB intends to bring to its Executive Board for approval. Oftentimes, NGOs in industrial countries tend to be single-issue advocates and their ability to bring influence to bear on their Governments to apply conditions on bilateral assistance programmes is extended to MDBs when these agencies seek funding for concessional resources from legislative bodies in donor countries.

The governance conditionality advocated by foreign NGOs can raise sensitive foreign and domestic policy and security issues and create obstacles to implementation inside the borrowing country, for example if those officials that traditionally negotiate with the MDBs are seen to be trespassing beyond their traditional jurisdictions by accepting conditions that permit foreign interests to use their clout with the MDBs to interfere in sensitive domestic issues. Often such NGOs seek to superimpose their own cultural values on societies subscribing to different ethical and spiritual values. Consequently, such governance conditions are seen as imposing the ideological or cultural preferences of advocacy groups in the industrial countries on borrowers, thereby inviting the charge that the MDBs are being made to serve as instruments of rich-country paternalism, especially in their dealings with poorer member-countries, who must depend on the concessional windows of the MDBs for funding. Great care has to be exercised by the MDBs to ensure that the participation of NGOs, whether foreign or local, does not encroach upon areas of responsibility assigned to State institutions under the respective constitutional arrangements of borrowing countries or intrude into the development of direct relations between Governments and their own civil society organizations, including local NGOs.

IV. Difficulties in applying governance conditionality

Managing their interaction with the NGO community is not the only, or even the most pressing, issue confronting the MDBs in applying governance conditionality. A fundamental question is the non-political mandate of the MDBs and how to reconcile that mandate with the application of conditions that are likely to push them into the domestic political arena.[5] An example is MDB conditionality in "post-conflict" situations (e.g. Angola, Guatemala, Nicaragua) that requires the Government to adhere to the terms of a peace accord. Since the protection of human rights is typically written into such accords, the MDBs become embroiled in domestic disputes when political opponents charge that their rights are being violated by the Government, in contravention of the terms of the peace accords.

Another difficulty arises because monitoring compliance with governance conditions inevitably calls for subjective judgements on the part of the MDBs much beyond what they have had to deal with in the past. Deciding where and how to draw the line between the technical and political dimensions of governance conditions requires the staff to reach unambiguous conclusions about, what often are, ambiguous situations or outcomes. Moreover, the making of balanced judgements on complex situations requires deep country-specific knowledge, a requirement that runs directly counter to staffing incentives[6] that typically discourage the build-up of in-depth area expertise. In any event, the need to make judgements that cannot always be supported by strictly objective criteria opens MDB staff to the charge of accommodating the proclivities of their managements or the ideological biases of the major shareholders of the MDBs.

Working on governance issues entails a broadening of MDBs' contacts beyond normal governmental (executive) channels. This means not only extending attention to elements of the administrative machinery beyond the usual circle of the officials in planning and finance ministries, but also to other organs of the State, i.e. with the judiciary (in the case of legal reforms) or with parliamentarians (where deadlines for legislative enactments are involved). Such contacts carry risks that politicians would associate the MDBs with the Government in power, leaving them exposed to attack when governments change.

There is here a deeper risk as well for the MDBs: conditionality calling for transparency and participatory proceedings might involve bringing in unelected - and sometimes unrepresentative groups - into decision-making processes, thereby tending to further weaken governmental authority in countries where such authority tends to be weak already.

Next, there is the issue of non-discriminatory treatment among borrowing members. The governance agenda substantially raises the political cost of borrowing from the MDBs. This might partly explain why demand for the non-concessional loan and guarantee products of the IBRD has been stagnating, even while the demand for private capital has escalated in the first half of the 1990s. For this reason, as well as the fact that larger borrowers are better able to finesse the implementation of many of the new conditions, the application of such conditions affects mostly smaller and poorer countries that have little or no access to private sources of capital and require highly concessional terms for their foreign borrowing.

The resulting discriminatory treatment of MDB borrowing members has two serious implications: the loan portfolio of the MDBs tends increasingly to be skewed away from stronger towards weaker borrowers, thereby affecting the creditworthiness of the institutions. Second, the governance conditions are applied mostly to Governments that are already struggling to govern and the conditions erode their credibility at home if they are suspected of accepting the conditions strictly out of financial exigency rather than from any conviction as to their appropriateness under the prevailing circumstances. This loss of credibility feeds back into the "backlash" problem.

Finally, there is a question of even-handedness as between creditor and debtor Governments when applying conditions relating to corruption, a pre-eminent governance issue. While many of the causes of corruption inhere in domestic conditions, corruption in the award of contracts for the supply of foreign goods and services always involves two parties; the corruptor is apt to be a supplier, typically located in an industrial country, sheltering under a "tied" aid arrangement or the domestic procurement requirements of a national export-credit agency. In such cases, the application of an anti-corruption condition only on the procurement process in the borrowing country raises issues of legitimacy and fair dealing. The MDBs are seen to have little power over foreign suppliers offering bribes to buyers in the borrowing countries, despite their insistence on internationally competitive bidding regulations, since presumably all suppliers would have made similar allowances for the payment of "marketing commissions" in their quotations.[7] This is another aspect of discriminatory treatment of members that risks compromising the moral position of MDBs in applying governance conditionality [8]; at the least, it makes it possible for interested parties in the borrowing country to manipulate public opinion against the MDBs by raising questions about the legitimacy of their role in the governance area on the plausible ground that the MDBs practice a "double standard" in their dealings with their members.

While the rest of this paper largely addresses the issue of interaction between MDBs and borrowing Governments, it is important for the MDBs to recognize that corruption is a two-sided matter and they must be prepared to press donor/creditor Governments to take steps to deal with corrupting elements among their own suppliers, contractors and other intermediaries. The MDBs finance a large range of investment activities in developing countries and their procedures for procurement and their internal controls must be constantly strengthened in respect of projects financed by them.[9]

V. Suggestions for reducing backlash effects

A certain tension is emerging in the relationship between MDBs and borrowing Governments that needs to be handled carefully in order to achieve the "good government" objectives that borrowing Governments assuredly share with the MDBs.

At one extreme is a position that MDBs should not be dealing with member-countries that countenance widespread corruption in their business dealings with suppliers or investors, domestic or foreign and that tolerate, or practice, other forms of misgovernance. Apart from its unworkability [10], this posture would foreclose the possibility of influencing the course of reform in many situations. Governments are rarely monolithic entities, and there are contending forces within each of them; the influence of the external agency is exercised primarily through alliances (not necessarily overt but implicit) with domestic groups that are seeking to improve governance, and to strengthen their hands by the promise of external funding, if the counsels of the reformers are accepted. To withdraw altogether from dealing with certain Governments thus becomes a counsel of despair, rather than a pragmatic way of pursuing "good government" objectives, except in the most extreme of situations.

In seeking these objectives, it is essential for the MDBs to be highly selective in targeting efforts to areas that offer the promise of yielding tangible results in a reasonable period of time. This requires a fairly deep understanding of the governance situation in each country and a willingness to adapt the conditionality to the individual country situation, rather than seeking uniformity of content or prescription across member-countries. Once these areas are selected in agreement with the authorities of the borrowing Government, the MDBs must be willing to commit substantial resources, by way of both technical and financial assistance, for capacity building and other improvements in the selected sectors, and to allow sufficient time for results to emerge.

Past efforts have been made by MDBs in extending technical assistance in areas such as public administration, privatization of State-owned enterprises and the reform of tax and financial systems, with varying degrees of success. It is important to derive lessons from these transactions to find what succeeds and what fails and why. Where independent evaluations are made, as they are in a number of World Bank project and programme areas, it is important to disseminate them widely, not only in the countries to which they relate but also in countries confronting similar problems. Most such reports are now written only in English (and sometimes in French or Spanish); in many cases, these languages are accessible only to the local elites. A broader audience would be reached by making translations available in one or more local languages (e.g. Swahili in East Africa, Urdu/Hindi in the Indian sub-continent) at a cost that would be a tiny fraction of the cost of the initial evaluation and then pricing them for sale at marginal cost.

In some countries, it might be valuable to focus even more narrowly than hitherto, for example on improving direct tax administration in countries where extensive tax evasion prevails, by providing resources for installing computerized systems of cross-checking returns and providing training in their use. Ideological preconceptions in the taxation area are often transmitted through technical assistance provided by MDBs using consultants from the advanced countries. Excessive emphasis on progressive systems of income, capital gains and wealth taxation often results in foisting complicated tax codes that provide much scope for tax avoidance on the part of higher income groups, able to mobilize high-priced accounting and legal talent. The outcome is often contrary to that intended: a much greater degree of social inequity results as tax-evaded income is typically spent on conspicuous consumption, rather than invested, or invested unproductively in real estate where poor urban land valuation and registration arrangements make it easier to conceal assets paid for from evaded incomes. A greater attention to presumptive methods of direct taxation and a willingness to accept the lessons learnt in developing country environments by local officials might well provide more effective assistance in the governance area than reliance on prescriptions offered by experts from the advanced countries.

Another approach would be to work with lower levels of Government in a typical area of corruption, involving the transfer of property rights in urban plots of land and zoning for commercial land uses: the gains to those able to acquire land rights or zoning variances through State action tend to be enormous, given the fact that in most of the larger cities in the developing world, land values tend to match, if not exceed, those in many developed countries. Funding for machinery at the municipal level to register mutations and transfers of property rights, and to ensure speedy access to land records and zoning approvals, might be a constructive method of tackling a major area of misgovernance.

It is notable that many Governments have regulations on the books for exercising budgetary discipline over spending, for competitive bidding on procurement contracts, for proper auditing of fiscal transactions, etc.. It is lack of full compliance with such regulations more often than their absence, that creates some of the governance problems in the public sector, especially in the management of State enterprises. In many instances, a more effective way of improving governance, even if an indirect one, would be to insist on more traditional economic or technical conditions relating to such matters as closer monitoring of compliance with expenditure controls; procurement regulations; more transparent procedures for the sale of State land and the privatization of State enterprises; quicker finalization of final budget accounts and the prompt publication of audit reports. Loan conditions that support better compliance would have greater public acceptability (and less danger of public misapprehension) if tied to existing regulations and laws already "on the books", instead of requiring new legislation to fulfil MDB conditions.

Finally, a corollary of this would be the exercise of utmost caution on the part of MDBs in claiming credit for the application of governance conditionality. They must remain ever mindful of their non-political mandates and not allow any "public relations" concerns of their own, or of their industrial country shareholders, into appearing to be acting in discriminatory ways, especially in relation to their smaller and poorer member-countries that depend on concessional funds for their development.

Notes

1 Communique of the Ministers of Intergovernmental Group of Twenty-Four, *IMF Survey*, Vol. 25, No. 9 (May 6, 1996).

2 Quoted by D. Kapur in "The New Conditionalities of the International Financial Institutions", in this volume. Much of the discussion in section IV of this note draws on the same paper.

3 *Serving a Changing World*, Final Report of the Development Committee Task Force on Multilateral Development Banks (DC/96-01, 03/08/96).

4 Comments of the Multilateral Development Banks on the Task Force Report (DC/96-6, 04/12/96).

5 To take the World Bank Group as an example, the IBRD Articles of Agreement stipulate that "the Bank and its officers shall not interfere in the political affairs of any member; nor shall they be influenced in their decisions by the political character of the member or members concerned. Only economic considerations shall be relevant to their decisions..."(Article IV, Section 10). In addition to identical language in the IDA Charter, there is another stipulation that it pay "due attention to considerations of economy, efficiency and competitive international trade *and without regard to political or other non-economic influences or considerations*" (Article V, Section 1(g); italics supplied). While not strictly germane to this paper on the MDBs, it is notable that the IMF Guidelines on Conditionality stipulate that "... in helping members to devise adjustment programmes, the Fund will pay due regard to the domestic social and political objectives, the economic priorities and the circumstances of members..."(Guideline # 4, Decision # 6056-(79/38).

6 These incentives emphasize "broadening" rather than "deepening" expertise through an expectation that promotion depends on staff being mobile across country as well as functional departments.

7 Moreover, the cost of giving bribes can usually be written off as marketing expenses under the tax regimes of many industrial countries; the OECD has recently adopted recommendations for disallowing tax deductions for bribes.

8 Another example of asymmetry arises in relation to drug trade, which is fuelled by effective demand originating in major industrial countries. Countries that have climatic conditions suitable for growing coca or the geographical location that makes them conduits for transmitting drugs from producing to consuming centres have become subject to the wholesale corruption of their law enforcement bureaucracies by the drug trade. To apply anti-corruption, legal and judicial reform conditions to transactions in such countries, without being able to do anything at all in the countries where the profits of the drug trade originate, can only intensify hostility to MDB conditionality in the governance area.

9 The World Bank has tightened its procurement and loan procedures in recent days and is working on a comprehensive strategy to deal with problems of corruption in concert with member-Governments.

10 Unless the country is a brand-new member, the MDB would ordinarily be in the midst of a series of transactions, on some of which it would be disbursing funds and others in respect of which it might be receiving repayments of principal as well as interest service on all outstanding loans (and commitments).

A MULTILATERAL DEBT FACILITY

Global and National

Matthew Martin*

Abstract

In July 1995, a World Bank Task Force proposed a Multilateral Debt Facility (MDF) to resolve the debt problems of Highly Indebted Poor Countries (HIPCs). Its misinterpretation alarmed many, by wrongly suggesting that it would need $11 billion of scarce aid money immediately to cancel debt up-front and, thus, undermine the financial integrity of the Bretton Woods institutions.

As the World Bank report was being completed, the Government of Uganda was establishing, at its July 1995 Consultative Group meeting, its own Uganda Multilateral Debt Fund (UMDF), with many similar aims and characteristics, in order to reduce its own multilateral debt problem. It has been successfully implemented and attracted large amounts of donor aid funding.

This report examines the case for HIPC multilateral debt relief and the best ways to achieve it. First, it argues the case for multilateral debt relief, based on the debt overhang in debtor economies, and the additionality in some circumstances from using aid for this purpose. Second, it assesses how many countries need relief, finding that a maximum of 31-33 countries may need relief if debt sustainability is comprehensively and realistically assessed. Third, it confirms the availability of sufficient funds for multilateral debt relief, provided that the IMF, the World Bank and bilateral donors all share the burden of its financing. Fourth, it stresses the need (building on the lessons of the MDF proposal and the UMDF) for both global and national coordination, through a global Trust Fund, normal national Consultative Group and Round Table meetings, and country-specific multilateral debt funds in order to ensure the optimal sustainability of financing for HIPC development.

* This paper draws heavily on my experiences as external debt advisor to the Government of Uganda. I am most grateful to the Government of Uganda for its confidence and for the pleasure of working with officials so committed to the welfare of their people; and to the Government of Sweden (and earlier the Governments of Austria, Denmark, the Netherlands and Switzerland) for funding the work which led to the establishment and success of the Ugandan Multilateral Debt Fund. I am also most grateful to my fellow members of the Commonwealth Advisory Group on Multilateral Debt, many developing country and OECD Government policy-makers and officials, senior staff of the Bretton Woods Institutions and NGOs for their input, and to Nils Bhinda for research assistance.

Introduction

A misleading front-page article in the *Financial Times* of 14 September 1995, leaking an internal World Bank Task Force report, provoked a loud debate about whether it was feasible to establish a $11 billion Multilateral Debt Facility, to cancel the debts owed by Heavily-Indebted Poor Countries (HIPCs) to the IMF, the World Bank and regional development banks.

The three main concerns raised in that debate have been:

(1) Do the HIPCs really need $11 billion of up-front multilateral debt stock reduction?

(2) Where can the money be found, given declining aid budgets, without diverting funds from other developing countries and other development needs in the HIPCs themselves?

(3) Will cancelling the stock up-front undermine the financial integrity of the international financial institutions?

These questions were entirely misdirected. As this paper will show, the Multilateral Debt Facility (MDF) never intended to cancel stock up-front. Instead, it was a cleverly crafted mechanism which was to pay around $11 billion of multilateral service as it fell due over 15 years, thereby avoiding moral hazard for creditors and debtors, and protecting the financial integrity of the international financial institutions (IFIs), while overcoming the problem of the "debt overhang" of the HIPCs. As a result, sufficient funding is available to make HIPC debt sustainable if the multilateral institutions, other creditors and donors share the burden.

At the Annual Meetings of the IMF and World Bank in October 1995, the Interim and Development Committees asked the Bretton Woods institutions to undertake an extensive analysis of the HIPCs' debt problems to assess whether current initiatives are sufficient to resolve them and, if not, to develop appropriate new strategies. Such analysis is continuing and, in that context, this paper aims to answer four key questions:

(1) Why do HIPCs need multilateral debt relief?

(2) How many HIPCs need multilateral debt relief?

(3) Where can the money be found without reducing flows to other developing countries?

(4) What mechanism will best give relief without damaging the Bretton Woods institutions or developing countries?

I. The case for multilateral debt relief

The case for multilateral debt relief revolves around two issues:

• Would multilateral debt relief have positive effects on the debtor economy?

• Is direct multilateral debt relief in some circumstances a better use of concessional funds than new aid (in other words, is a dollar of debt relief worth more than a dollar of aid)?

If the answer to each of these questions is positive, the international community should provide direct relief on multilateral debt, rather than continuing with the current practice of refinancing multilateral debt service with new concessional loans. This section deals with each question in turn.

A. The effect of debt on the economy

The case for relief of any type of debt rests on two of effects:

• the "debt overhang" effect - the impact of the stock of debt (measured either in its nominal $ amount or at its "present value" - i.e. adjusted for the concessionality of the stock);

• the "liquidity" effect - the impact of the stream of debt service "crowding out" investment.

If the "liquidity" effect predominates, it can be overcome by current methods of dealing with multilateral debt - providing new loans to pay service. Therefore the debate over whether to introduce new mechanisms for multilateral debt relief revolves around the strength of the "debt overhang" effect. Recent literature suggests seven reasons why a debt overhang has negative effects:

(1) Almost all recent econometric analysis finds strong negative effects of the debt overhang on growth and investment, with the correct direction of causation, including several studies for Africa. It also finds large positive effects of lifting the debt overhang in the Brady countries in Latin America (see box 1).

ECONOMETRIC EVIDENCE ON THE DEBT OVERHANG

In the early 1990s there has been a great deal of econometric analysis of the effects of the debt overhang on growth and investment. Almost all studies find strong negative effects on growth and investment. Several qualifications of these findings have been raised, but closer inspection reveals their flimsiness:

- The direction of causation is untested. Most major studies, including several focussing on HIPCs or sub-Saharan African (SSA) countries, do show the correct direction of causation, by testing the effect of prior debt positions on subsequent macroeconomic developments;

- The size of the effect is not always very strong. Almost all of the major recent studies find large, statistically significant negative effects on investment and growth, including those focusing on HIPCs and SSA (see below).

- It is unclear whether the negative effect of debt is through overhang or liquidity. However, all studies which separate the two effects (Greene and Villanueva, 1991; Kumar and Mlambo, 1995; Savvides, 1992) find that overhang is far more important than liquidity.

- Many of the studies focus on middle-income countries rather than HIPCs. It is true that HIPCs have not been studied enough, but six major studies which find strong effects cover HIPC and SSA countries (Cohen, 1993 and 1995; Hadjimichael et al., 1995; Kumar and Mlambo, 1995; Oshikoya 1994; and Savvides, 1992).

- Few studies disentangle debt from other factors. Of course, it is extremely difficult to disentangle debt from other policy and exogenous influences on growth and investment. However, almost all of the major studies cited above control for several other factors or include them in their regressions, and find debt to be among the strongest explanatory variables.

- Few studies distinguish private and public investment. The latter can be severely distorted by aid flows. Greene and Villanueva (1991), Kumar and Mlambo (1995) and Oshikoya (1994) do.

The only major recent study which fails to find a significant negative effect is IMF (1995). However, as pointed out by Woodward (1996b), its statistical analysis is "simplistic" and "anything but rigorous", and its results are invalidated by the distortionary effects of exchange-rate changes and aid flows on investment. It contains three of the methodological problems raised above - failure to test causation, failure to go beyond correlation and test other variables which might affect growth and investment, and failure to test overhang and liquidity separately. Its "examples" of cases which prove there is no necessary connection between debt overhang and poor performance are either distorted by other factors or actually prove the debt overhang hypothesis. IMF (1995) also cites no other studies in support of its findings and ignores a large proportion of the literature discussed above. Using the same data, Woodward (1996b)conducts more rigorous analysis, and finds strong, statistically highly significant negative effects of debt on investment and growth.

There is, therefore, robust econometric evidence that the debt overhang is a major constraint on investment and growth in HIPCs. In the light of such evidence, the IMF, the World Bank, the Paris Club and commercial creditors have supported debt-overhang reduction through the Naples and Brady terms and the IDA Commercial Debt Reduction Facility. Naturally, debt reduction must be combined with measures to eliminate all of the other constraints - but it would make a major contribution to HIPC development.

(2) The debt overhang has deterrent effects on private investment by reducing the credibility of government policy and enhancing uncertainty. Investors feel, regardless of the scale of policy reform implemented, that there is a risk that gains from investment may be taxed away through fiscal measures, foreign-exchange controls, or higher interest rates, to ensure the availability of funds for external debt service. This has been confirmed in many surveys of domestic investors by investment promotion agencies and private sector promotion studies in the HIPCs, which list debt high among the factors undermining Government credibility.

(3) It also has deterrent effects on public investment. The amount of resources available for public investment in human capital and infrastructure, which is a crucial complement to private investment, depends on unpredictable negotiations with creditors and donors, and on IFI assessment of compliance with adjustment criteria. Perceptions of this dependence and likely reduced public investment adds to uncertainty among private investors.

(4) The debt overhang leads to a distortion of fiscal policy and reserves management. It creates uncertainty and a perceived need to "ring-fence" debt service when the Government is designing fiscal and reserve management policy. As a consequence, fiscal policy may neglect longer-term priorities (overcompressing other types of expenditure, or overtaxing) or reserves may be held in excessively liquid form, making reserve management less efficient.

(5) The debt overhang can have deterrent effects on policy reform or lead to a loss of programme "ownership" due to the feeling among even the most committed debtor policy-makers that creditors are doing too little to respond to policy reform, and that gains from reform go to pay debt, forcing them into continuing aid dependency (and diverting aid away from non-debt-distressed countries). This has been shown conclusively to undermine the sustainability of adjustment. In contrast, debt relief allows policy-makers to show international endorsement and put the debt problem behind them, generating political stability and support for further reform.

(6) The existence of a debt overhang reduces access to foreign investment and international financial markets. There is ample evidence from the investors themselves that the debt overhang is a deterrent to foreign private capital flows to the HIPCs. All creditworthiness and ratings analyses on which foreign investors rely include strong negative debt elements. Those running portfolio investment funds for Africa or attempting to promote investor interest in HIPC privatisations assess the existence of a debt overhang as a key negative influence. Some incentives, such as export-credit guarantees, are directly cut as a consequence of a debt overhang. In addition, the flows of "foreign private capital" to some HIPCs cited in some recent studies (IMF, 1995) are illusory: they consist largely of capital flight repatriation, unrecorded exports or workers' remittances (see Kasekende et al. in this volume).

(7) Frequently repeated debt and adjustment negotiations imply high transactions costs. They absorb much time of the few senior economic officials in most HIPC Governments, diverting them from economic policy formulation and implementation. HIPCs in sub-Saharan Africa have held over 10,000 sets of negotiations in the last 10 years (Killick, 1995 and 1993; Martin 1991).

On the other hand, only two major arguments have been raised against debt stock relief:

First, it is argued that "debt is not the only problem" for debtor countries, and that advocates of relief are ignoring the importance of the policy environment. This is highly offensive to those developing country policy-makers (for example in Uganda) which have been implementing massive policy reforms and are arguing that the supply response to those reforms is being hampered by debt overhang. As the Brady experience showed, lifting the overhang at an early stage is essential to improving the supply and foreign capital responses to policy reform. The econometric evidence (see box 1) reinforces this view by controlling for many other policy factors. Of course, HIPCs require many other measures if they are to attract sustained flows of foreign private capital, but action on debt is among the top priorities.

Second, it is said that, if the "short-leash" procedure of current refinancing is ended, there is a "moral hazard" for the debtor of non-repayment, irresponsible new borrowing or poor economic policies by the debtor, in the absence of adequate sanctions. However, it is easy to design eligibility criteria which overcome this problem. Assuming that a precondition for multilateral debt relief would be the implementation of an adjustment programme, the strictness of current conditionality and the tying of large proportions of aid to IMF approval certainly constitute "adequate sanctions". Their effectiveness in generating high will to pay have been demonstrated conclusively in the last 10 years, when the multilateral institutions have been paid at the expense of all other creditors, especially non-OECD Governments. In addition, the "tranching" of relief proposed in the MDF document (paying a proportion of annual service as it falls due) would guarantee that the short-leash could be maintained. The true moral hazard is in the other direction: that Government ownership of adjustment programmes and will to pay will be reduced by the perception that good performance is not being rewarded by a loosening of the leash or by sufficient debt relief. As Uganda found in 1995 when its Naples terms excluded further reduction on the debt it had rescheduled in 1992, and deferral of service on post-cut-off date debt, good performance is rewarded by being told that you need less relief! The issue of creditor and debtor moral hazard will be taken up again in section IV below.

What does the debt overhang effect imply for solutions? It is important to remember that, while efforts to reduce the overhang will also help the liquidity problem, refinancing with new loans, to help the liquidity problem, will worsen the overhang problem by increasing the debt stock due to the need to refinance interest payments. In this light, especially as the overhang appears to be the main problem according to the econometric evidence, steps should be taken which will impact positively on both by tackling the overhang. It is these arguments which have made the "debt overhang effect" the basis for all recent initiatives on debt reduction - the Naples Terms, the IDA commercial debt reduction facility, and especially the Brady deals for Latin America. The same arguments apply even more strongly to multilateral debt, because the fact that it will have to be paid on schedule makes it a much "harder" overhang than other debt which can be reduced.

B. The question of additionality

Having demonstrated the effects of the debt overhang on the debtor economy, there is one more critical question: is debt relief a better use of aid budgets in some circumstances than new aid? In other words, can a dollar of debt relief be worth more than a dollar of aid? One of the main concerns about multilateral debt relief has been whether its funding will be additional, or whether it will divert funds from aid for low-income countries (both highly indebted and less indebted). As a senior World Bank official put it in December 1995: "... one dollar of debt relief means one dollar less aid: there is no such thing as a free lunch".

This "additionality" issue is particularly critical for those developing countries which might not qualify for multilateral debt relief, but use bilateral aid or funds from IDA or the Enhanced Structural Adjustment Facility (ESAF) as an important source of reserves or balance-of-payments support. It has been accentuated by the awareness that real aid levels were cut in 1991-1993 and stagnated in 1994, reaching their lowest average levels for 20 years as a proportion of GNP of DAC member countries (OECD, 1996), and by the difficulties experienced in the recent and current negotiations to replenish ESAF, IDA and the African Development Fund. In the context of scarce bilateral aid resources maximum value from each dollar is necessary.

Strictly speaking, of course, no funding is additional. There is always a competing use for the money or a risk from using extra money. A few would still argue that SDR issues and IMF gold sales are not additional, because they carry risks. The key dilemma about additionality is therefore whether the advantages of using a particular source of funds for a particular purpose outweigh the disadvantages (or the advantages of using the funds for another purpose).

This paper suggests that there is "additionality" from multilateral debt relief, for three reasons:

- In some circumstances, a dollar of debt relief is worth more than a dollar of aid, by generating higher aid commitments and accelerating disbursements (see sub-section 1 below).

- Coordinated debt relief can enhance this additionality compared to the current procedure of ad-hoc refinancing with loans or grants (see sub-section 2 below).

- There are "additional" funds in the multilateral institutions themselves which can be used without diverting aid budgets (see section III).

1. Additionality of debt relief

Many donors and HIPC recipient countries have come to see in the early 1990s that in many circumstances a dollar of debt relief will provide more money than a dollar of new aid, because it will increase both the commitments and the disbursements of bilateral aid:

On commitments, some donors (notably Switzerland, Sweden, the Netherlands and Norway, and the World Bank in the "Fifth Dimension") have earmarked funds which they use only for debt relief and not for ESAF/IDA/ADF contributions or other balance-of-payments support. These reflect high levels of political support for debt relief in their countries, based on the correct perception that the debt overhang is a key barrier to development in highly-indebted low-income countries, and that debt relief is more valuable than other forms of aid because removing the overhang improves growth prospects for debtors and payment prospects for creditors. These have recently amounted to $200 million a year and, according to consultations with these donors, they are expected to continue at the same or higher levels in the future.

On disbursements, many donors find that debt relief or direct budget support are the most efficient forms of aid (see Martin and Mistry, 1996). The alternatives are import support, project aid, technical assistance, or emergency relief.

Many donors have major problems disbursing import support, reflecting the liberalization of foreign-exchange and import systems in low-income countries. Such support is sold to private importers, which pay counterpart funds to the government budget to purchase the goods. Given the administrative complexities and restrictions (procurement procedures, tying to exports of a particular supplier country, excessive documentary requirements, multiple bank accounts, delay in approvals and disbursements), private demand for this aid has dwindled as importers have become more able to use their own foreign-exchange earnings or funds borrowed or purchased on the free foreign-exchange markets - because it provides much less value for money. Donors have had to incur growing administrative costs in a desperate struggle to get the funds disbursed. When they do not succeed, these funds are frequently lost to the recipient country, to the donor's fast-disbursing aid budget, or even to the overall aid budget.

Many donors have similar problems disbursing project aid, with growing pipelines of undisbursed project aid in many countries which have tried to switch away from balance-of-payments support. In order to get project-aid funds disbursed (and avoid losing them from future budgets), donors are incurring huge administrative costs for project design and monitoring, or for reinforcing absorptive capacity in line ministries and project executing agencies.

Recipient Governments also have to find additional funds to pay the recurrent and local currency project costs, something that is often impossible given the need for fiscal restraint. In addition, in spite of some improvements through public investment programmes and sector programmes, the procurement of goods and personnel for project aid remains largely ill-coordinated and non-competitive, reducing its efficiency and value for money - partly because recipients rarely lead project design and/or implementation.

Technical assistance and emergency aid are far less subject to disbursement delays, but they are also less efficient. In spite of recent efforts to improve coordination and replace technical assistance with capacity-building, most of this aid remains non-transparent. The valuation of goods and services supplied is often exaggerated or unavailable to the recipient, who also has virtually no control over the design of the programmes, and the development impact of the aid is often short-lived or non-existent.

In contrast, direct donor support for multilateral debt relief, reserves or the budget is virtually free of restrictions, making it fungible for maximum efficiency. Its valuation and use are entirely transparent. It requires no commitments of budget funds for recurrent costs, and virtually no expenditure on complementary capacity building or technical assistance. It is disbursed immediately, with no administrative restrictions, and on a predictable schedule - and for that reason reduces the donor and recipient transaction costs necessary for disbursement. Under the design proposed in section IV below, the debtor would have firm control over its own debt-relief strategy, fully coordinated with all creditors and donors. For all of these reasons, such support provides greater value for money without increasing aid budgets.

2. *Enhanced additionality through organized and coordinated debt relief*

Because many donors already see debt as a key barrier to development in the HIPCs, the judgement between a dollar of debt relief and a dollar of aid has already been made in many countries. Aid is already being massively diverted to ad-hoc financing (explicit or implicit) of debt service, causing huge "subtractionality" because resources could be spent on more desirable development purposes. This occurs in one of three ways:

(1) By obliging other creditors to provide more debt relief:

- in the case of more concessional debt relief by the Paris Club; almost all Club creditors fund this relief by raiding their aid budgets;
- commercial debt buy-backs through the IDA facility; these have diverted IBRD net income and donor aid funds;
- relief from non-OECD official creditors (bilateral Governments and multilateral institutions such as the OPEC Fund or the Arab Bank for Economic Development in Africa (BADEA)), which obviously has a direct cost to other developing countries.

(2) By accrual of arrears to all other creditors: Total HIPC arrears at the end of 1994 were $75 billion. They doubled in the period when multilateral debt became a burden and refinancing was tried (1990-1994). Arrears to most Paris Club Governments imply additional aid diversion to fund budgetary losses; arrears to commercial creditors result in provisions and tax write-offs, reducing fiscal revenues for spending on aid. Developing countries which are creditors of the HIPCs - and the multilateral institutions which they fund (e.g. OPEC Fund, Arab Monetary Fund) have suffered even more directly, with a much higher proportion of stock in arrears than their OECD counterparts, because debtor countries had to give priority to paying the IFIs (see Martin et al., 1996a).

(3) By diverting aid to refinance multilateral debt service, through either:

- (mainly) diversion of balance-of-payments aid to pay multilateral debt service, either directly or indirectly - again diverting aid from other developing countries;
- (secondarily) new lending by the IMF or World Bank; Killick (1995) has found strong evidence that past refinancing strategies (and future continuation of such strategies) divert huge amounts of IFI lending towards debt-distressed countries;
- (thirdly) the "fifth dimension", which pays IBRD interest of borrowers which have become IDA-only, and diverts "IDA reflows" and donor aid for co-financing.

All of these methods imply high immediate financial costs for developing countries. There are several ways to quantify the costs of only the refinancing element.

The most comprehensive is to include payments to soft windows of the IFIs; contributions of balance-of-payments support for debt-related adjustment programmes through (for example) the Special Programme of Assistance (SPA) for Africa; and direct contributions to pay arrears and current service to the multilateral financial institutions. The Commonwealth Secretariat (Killick, 1995) has estimated this diversion at around $9 billion a year, nearly a quarter of bilateral aid.

A narrower calculation adds untied balance-of-payments/debt relief aid to the HIPCs, which is genuinely fungible to use for paying multilateral debt, to funds for non-bilateral debt relief. Based on donor documents, this averaged $850 million a year in 1990-1995.

The narrowest approach includes only aid used for multilateral debt relief or the payment of arrears. It is impossible to quantify this precisely, due to donor confidentiality. However, it has absorbed large amounts of balance-of-payments support from some donors (especially France), and smaller proportions of other donors, such as Belgium (Rwanda), Canada (Guyana, Haiti, Nicaragua, Rwanda), the European Union (Uganda), Germany (Nicaragua, Niger), Denmark (Uganda), Japan (Haiti, Viet Nam), Norway (Nicaragua, Zambia), the United Kingdom (Zambia), and the United States (Bolivia, Guinea-Bissau, Haiti, Nicaragua, Niger, Rwanda, Sao Tomé and Principe). Latin American countries have even made small contributions for Haiti and Nicaragua. A survey for this paper of three like-minded donors, which conduct frequent ad-hoc multilateral debt operations (the Netherlands, Sweden and Switzerland), combined with documents on support groups and the "fifth dimension", indicates that $1.8 billion ($360 million a year) was provided in 1991-1995 for direct multilateral debt relief.

This leads to the conclusion that current procedures involve huge "subtractionality" for both the debt-distressed and non debt-distressed developing countries, as aid is diverted away from development purposes to fund the debt relief, arrears and debt service of the debt-distressed.

Current procedures also imply major non-financial costs for debt-distressed countries and other developing countries, in terms of the efficiency, accountability and administrative costs of aid, which dramatically reduce its actual and perceived quality. The MDF paper pointed to contamination of the IDA portfolio and reduction of the quality of policy dialogue, caused by the need to disburse "defensive" loans rapidly, to refinance multilateral service and maintain positive net transfers. The haphazard ad-hoc way in which bilateral aid is diverted at the last minute to pay multilateral service also undermines its quality. These practices have received wide publicity in donor countries, discrediting the quality of aid, and accentuating pressure to cut aid budgets.

The ad-hoc payment of individual maturities of service also has huge staff time costs for debtors and donors, in negotiation and disbursement efforts, financial costs through interest on arrears (estimated at over $500 million during 1990-1995), and reduced transparency of aid. It also provides no predictability of multilateral service, allowing arrears which necessitate excessive reserves, provisioning, and contingency funds in the Bretton Woods institutions, and sour relations between them and policy-makers in the countries concerned - leading to delays in commitments and/or disbursements.

The effects of current refinancing procedures on creditors and donors are a mirror-image of the "overhang" effect on debtors. The "overhang" effect on creditors and donors distorts their planning and actions, and imposes on them huge transaction costs and uncertainties. There is a need to remove the debt overhang from the creditors, by organized and coordinated global debt relief, which will:

- avoid distortionary "defensive" lending by the international financial institutions and thereby improve the quality and development results of their policy dialogue and financing;

- reduce the administrative and financial trans-action costs of aid flows, by coordinating negotiation and disbursement procedures, and avoiding arrears or double-payments;

- enhance the predictability of multilateral debt servicing and reduce arrears, thereby improving IFI financial management and their relations with country policy-makers;

- improve the reputation of aid flows by changing public perception in donor countries from one where non-transparent aid diversion for ad-hoc refinancing undermines public support for aid, to one where transparent use of aid for multilateral debt relief provides a sustainable solution to the HIPC debt problem and increases public support.

In sum, coordinated debt relief would allow the aid commitments earmarked for debt relief to be fully disbursed; increase disbursements and value for money from each dollar committed, compared to other types of aid; reduce the transaction costs for all sides (by using additional resources such as IMF gold and by increasing value for money from existing commitments); free some bilateral money for other recipients or for project aid; and enhance the predictability and reputation of aid flows. In addition, for the most heavily indebted poor countries, the debt overhang is a critical barrier to their recovery and development. Obviously, a balance must be maintained between aid for debt relief and aid for the many other priorities in the development programmes of the HIPCs - which can only be achieved if multilateral debt relief is agreed as part of an overall assessment of external financing needs and in a development-oriented forum such as a Consultative Group or Round Table meeting. In these respects, and particularly if the IMF and the World Bank share the burden of relief, additionality is available and there can be "a free lunch" for all involved from using concessional resources for coordinated debt relief.

II.   How much debt relief is needed?

Any assessment of the need for multilateral debt relief should be based on country-by-country debt-sustainability analysis for HIPCs, based on transparent and objective standards - not on stylized global scenarios. Such analysis should include sustainability indicators and macroeconomic forecasts, as well as debt relief and assumptions of new finance.

A.   *Sustainability indicators*

1.   *External viability*

Normal sustainability analysis uses as the overall basis of judgement that at the end of the projection period chosen the country will be "externally viable". This requires that, firstly, balance-of-payments equilibrium can be achieved without resorting to exceptional financing, through either donor balance-of-payments support, adjustment lending or debt relief; and that, secondly, the level of indebtedness is such as to ensure that future debt-service problems will be unlikely, and a country will be able to service its debt without resorting to rescheduling.

These standards have been accepted inter-nationally for many years, and are used to judge external viability in decisions over new IMF loans. Yet, using them to assess the needs for debt relief would show only that around 39 of the 41 HIPCs will need exceptional financing (balance-of-payments support, IMF ESAF and debt relief) for the next 10-15 years, and virtually none of them will have a level of indebtedness far enough below the critical levels after 10 years to assure that future debt service problems are unlikely. More detailed analysis is clearly needed.

2. *Choice and critical level of sustainability indicators*

The Fund and the Bank currently use two main indicators of sustainability: the present value of the debt/export ratio and the debt-service/export ratio. Both are well-accepted, the only issue is their critical level. Several studies have identified the levels which have proved to be unsustainable in the past (for example World Bank, 1994a). The critical levels after debt relief should be a ratio of present value of debt to exports of 200 per cent and a ratio of debt service to exports of goods and services of 15 per cent. It is important to recall that the need for multilateral debt relief is determined by assessing sustainability after all other relief - comparable ratios before relief are higher.

There is a powerful case for adding fiscal ratios to the critical indicators, in equal ranking with export ratios. There are two types of fiscal burden[1], the liquidity burden and the fiscal overhang.

Using a recent IMF Occasional Paper on Official Financing (IMF, 1995) as the basis for the analysis, it can be seen that the indicator of the fiscal liquidity burden in HIPCs should be debt service compared to budget revenue excluding grants, and that the critical level of this indicator is probably the same as for exports - 15 per cent.

The fiscal overhang is an important indicator for the fiscal burden because a high debt stock has a powerful effect on distorting the planning of expenditure, revenue effort and domestic financing (in those countries which require domestic financing of a deficit) towards ensuring that debt is payable, and towards trying to reduce aid dependence rapidly. When one sees the low levels of expenditure as a percentage of GDP in Uganda, and the revenue effort which (though low as a proportion of GDP) is crippling many private sector companies, or the inflationary domestic borrowing necessary partly to

sustain debt service in other countries, this effect is clear. More testing should be conducted to identify the critical ratio of fiscal overhang.

The four primary indicators should be supplemented with secondary indicators of debt sustainability. These should be used to decide on eligibility for debt relief in borderline cases. They include foreign-exchange reserves below six months of import cover, the pace and variability of economic growth, continuing fiscal or balance-of-payments financing gaps, and dynamic indicators of debt sustainability (e.g., if the present value of debt is growing faster than exports, GDP or budget revenue).[2]

On the other hand, grant inflows and private transfers should not be taken into account in assessing debt servicing capacity. First, around 70 per cent of aid flows to the HIPCs are not available as "free foreign exchange" for spending on debt service or supporting the budget or reserves. Their foreign exchange and local currency are earmarked for projects or for technical assistance. Secondly, the levels of present value or debt service compared to exports plus grants and transfers that in the past have proved critical and unsustainable (i.e. requiring arrears accumulation or debt relief) would be much lower than the levels of present value to exports (200 per cent) and debt service to exports (20 per cent) mentioned above. This would imply that roughly the same number of HIPCs were in an unsustainable situation. Thirdly, the flows cannot be relied upon to continue into the future - and should not, given the risks of aid dependence and the volatility of private transfers.

3. *Time horizon*

A third issue is the time horizon to use in judging sustainability. Current procedures provide relief to those countries which have unsustainable current ratios, or averages of the three most recent years.[3] The IMF and the World Bank have recently begun to use a much longer horizon, classifying countries as "sustainable" if their ratios become sustainable before 1999; "possibly stressed" if they are sustainable by 2004; and "unsustainable" if ratios remain unsustainable after 2004. They argue that projected ratios should be used in order to incorporate improvements due to economic reform.

However, ten years is far too long a time horizon. The horizon chosen should depend partly on the importance ascribed to debt overhang effects. If overhang is the key burden, its rapid removal is essential; after 10 years it will have had pernicious long-lasting effects which will be near-impossible to reverse. Moreover, expecting the debtor country to absorb all of the risks to which it is vulnerable over 10 years appears to be saying that creditors will penalize with lower debt relief any debtors which perform well enough in the next 5-10 years to extricate themselves from the overhang. This risks giving debtors a perverse incentive to perform less well.

Another reason for a shorter time horizon is that margins of error on projections compound themselves over time, with small changes in assumptions having major effects on sustainability. For example, while a 4 per cent export growth rate over ten years would result in a 50 per cent cumulative rise, a 7 per cent growth rate would produce a doubling of exports.

Finally, all creditors should provide relief at the same time, in order to allow the country to "exit" definitively from rescheduling and reach debt sustainability, and to maximize the positive effects of removing the overhang for countries with a good economic policy track record.

Taking into account all of these factors, the time horizon should be set consistent with the projected date at which the country will receive Paris Club "exit" treatment under the Naples Terms, which will occur within a minimum three years and maximum five years for almost all countries.

B. Macroeconomic forecasts

1. The need for realism and growth

Macroeconomic forecasts in adjustment programmes and Policy Framework Papers have in the past proven to be systematically over-optimistic with regard to the prospects for export growth (IMF, 1993; Martin and Mistry, 1994). They have also tended to project import levels and elasticities, and fiscal expenditures/growth rates which are inadequate to produce rapid growth, and reserves which are insufficient to protect against high vulnerability to external shocks. Any country-specific projections must carefully avoid overoptimism on exports and excessive compression of imports.

Export growth rates should not be dramatically higher than recent performance, even if devaluations

have just occurred (e.g. in the CFA zone) or are expected, until the effects of devaluation are demonstrated. High recent growth rates in other countries should not necessarily be expected to continue; they should be scaled down to reflect the ending of price and production effects of temporary commodity booms (e.g. coffee for Kenya and Uganda), initial liberalizations or the ending of wars (e.g. Mozambique).

Import elasticities should match those which have been shown to be necessary for sustained growth. In countries without stable elasticities, or with no track record of adjustment, they should be set at least at 1. More detailed analysis of sectoral or commodity elasticities, and of the relationship between imports and growth, should be pursued urgently, as should improvements in import data (Martin and Mistry, 1996).

In addition, forecasts should target per capita real GDP growth, investment/GDP and domestic savings/GDP ratios and realistic incremental capital-output ratios, which are fully compatible with self-sustaining long-term growth, and should fully integrate debt overhang effects on growth and investment.

2. Alternative macroeconomic scenarios and probability/sensitivity analysis

The margin of error for any forecast is inevitably large, particularly given the risk of unexpected shocks. As a result, the forecasts of sustainability should be subjected to sensitivity and probability tests of the vulnerability of the projections to a set of indicators of vulnerability identified for each country, to judge the risk of unexpected deviations. A list of such indicators should include:

*   Drought: for many HIPCs, droughts should be factored into any projections, because they have a devastating impact on the economy several times in each decade. This could be argued especially for economies in Southern Africa, the Sahel and the Horn of Africa.

*   Policy slippage: there must be allowance for likely delay in implementing "satisfactory policies" due to internal or regional conflict, political instability or elections. In addition, the effects of the debt overhang on policy slippage should be incorporated.

*   Export price and production shocks: countries are most vulnerable to these shocks if they have a high concentration of exports in 2-3 main

products - and projections should take account of the effects of price rises or falls on incentives and production levels.

• Import price shocks: countries are vulnerable to changes in import prices insofar as they depend on imports of food or oil.

• Shortfalls in aid or private capital flows: countries are vulnerable to changes in the amounts or terms of flows to the degree that their imports, budget, investment or GDP depend on them. Where such flows are important, debt sustainability analysis should expand into full-fledged "external finance sustainability analysis" (Martin et al., 1996b).

• Domestic debt burdens: the sustainability of external debt should be intimately linked to that of domestic debt, not least because of their combined effects on the budget, which have major implications for fiscal capacity to service external debt (Martin et al., 1996b).

Such analysis is time-consuming, especially because it must not just mechanically project debt sustainability indicators, but must be fed through comprehensive appropriate models to show interactions. Yet it is particularly necessary because there is no evidence that negative and positive shocks cancel each other out over time: sensitivity analysis of recent projections indicates persistent optimism about supply response and aid flows.

The question in any sensitivity analysis should be not "is it possible that our projections may be optimistic?", but "by what factor should we scale down our projections to allow for the higher likelihood of negative shocks and our proven past overoptimism?". The best approach is to combine all factors to which countries are vulnerable into worst-case and best-case scenarios, assess their probability based on the last 5-10 years of adjustment, weight them accordingly, and adjust the baseline scenario according to the weightings. This may sound a complex task, but is one routinely used by analysts in international financial markets.

C. Debt relief and new finance assumptions: burden-sharing and synchronization

The third element in debt sustainability analysis is assessing the contribution which each creditor will make to relief and new financing, and whether all creditors are sharing the burden. This is particularly important because HIPCs have a somewhat diverse debt composition - with some owing most to the Paris Club, some to the Bretton Woods institutions, and some to non-OECD creditors such as Russia. This must not become an excuse for dividing countries up into groups for which action by X creditor or groups of creditors will be crucial to debt sustainability. Rather, it must be a reason for maximizing coordination and equitable burden-sharing among all creditors and donors.

There are three main components of this calculation: the percentage of debt reduction, the terms of new financing, and the timing of relief and new financing pledges.

1. The percentage of debt reduction

It will be vital to ensure that the Bretton Woods institutions both make a substantial contribution, because they are critical to sustainability in a number of countries (IBRD to Cameroon and Côte d'Ivoire, IDA to Burundi, Niger, Uganda and Rwanda and the IMF to Burundi, Guyana, Sudan, Uganda and Zambia). Equally, the regional development banks are important for some countries (AfDB/ADF for Burundi, Guinea-Bissau, Rwanda and Sao Tomé and Principe, and IDB for Bolivia, Guyana and Nicaragua). For some Sahel countries, the Arab and OPEC financial institutions are critical (Martin et al., 1996a).

As already discussed, current Paris Club policy will provide 67 per cent service relief to HIPCs with a good track record within two to three years, and 67 per cent stock relief within five to six years. This broad principle will need to be interpreted with maximum generosity for most countries - including action on post-cut-off date and previously rescheduled debt - if the Club is to share the burden appropriately. In addition, there is likely to be some delay in establishing the track record to qualify for both service and stock relief, which could in itself delay multilateral relief. In early 1996 there has been active discussion of prospects of moving to 80 or 90 per cent reduction. If it occurs, it may somewhat lessen the need for multilateral relief; but it should not be made a precondition for such relief.

Non-OECD official creditors (especially Russia, which accounts for around 50 per cent of debt owed to them by HIPCs) have not provided relief on terms comparable to the Paris Club. If they are to do so, new mechanisms will have to be designed (Martin et al., 1996a). Russia is critical to sustainability for Angola, Ethiopia, Madagascar, Mozambique, Nicaragua and Viet Nam, as are Trinidad and Tobago for Guyana, and Arab creditors for Mauritania, Somalia and Sudan. Its absence will increase the need for multilateral relief, by making Angola, Ethiopia, Guyana, Madagascar and Viet Nam unsustainable.

Commercial creditors have completed or are preparing buy-backs at secondary market prices or lower (implying reduction of over 85 per cent), funded by the IDA Commercial Debt Reduction Facility and cofinancing grants from bilateral donors. However, Côte d'Ivoire and other middle-income countries such as Cameroon and Nigeria may have major problems getting such high discounts on their commercial bank debt restructurings. In addition, other debtors may be somewhat less sustainable because not all commercial creditors will participate in their IDA debt reduction facility buy-backs.

Overall, there is no guarantee that non-OECD official creditors will share the burden. Better coordination through existing fora (Consultative Groups and Round Tables with special sessions on debt) will be essential to success (see also section IV below).

2.   *The terms of new financing*

Some creditors and donors will need to share the burden by providing new financing as well as or instead of debt relief. Therefore, assumptions on new financing also need to be highly realistic.

If projections for exports, imports and reserves are realistic, gross financing needs may well rise for many countries during the next ten years. If this is not compatible with projected trends in financial flows to the HIPCs, more debt relief may be needed. Particular caution should be taken when projecting trends in domestic or foreign private investment. Recent data give no reason for projecting sharp rises in most countries, indicating a potential need for greater relief. Aid flows are likely to decline, with no compensating switch from loans to grants. As the debt overhang falls, there will be strong pressure to resume lending to HIPCs. Moreover, the projected rising multilateral share of aid is likely to increase the share of loans unless IDA agrees to provide grants to HIPCs. Such trends would also raise relief needs.

It will be vital to identify gross financing needs realistically, to be cautious on non-debt flows (grants and foreign investment) and on the potential for increasing domestic savings, and to define clearly the grant element of loans which is appropriate for HIPCs. It is also important to ensure that the terms of all new loans (especially some "less concessional" such as ESAF or BADEA) are made much more concessional accordingly. An appropriate grant element would at least match the debt reduction percentage (85-90 per cent). Ideally, HIPCS would receive only grants while their debt is unsustainable.

3.   *The timing of debt relief and new financing*

The sequencing of debt relief and new financing will also be a critical issue for ensuring burden-sharing and maintaining the preferred-creditor status of the multilateral financial institutions. A sequencing recently suggested in Washington is as follows: A debtor would first obtain its service treatment of 67 per cent by the Paris Club and comparable treatment from all non-multilateral creditors. Next, it would spend three further years proving its adjustment track record to qualify for 67 per cent stock treatment by the Paris Club. It would then reach a "decision point" at which a comprehensive sustainability analysis would be conducted and discussed in a coordinated forum and, if stock treatment by all non-multilateral creditors were insufficient for sustainability, multilateral creditors would offer relief on service. After another three years, if its position was still not sustainable, a country would receive comprehensive stock treatment, including 90 per cent reduction by all non-multilaterals, and service relief or stock prepayment by multilaterals.

It is not clear that such a sequencing is necessary to protect the preferred-creditor status of the multilateral financial institutions; this will be achieved by the requirement for prior stock reduction by other creditors. As also argued on the grounds of debtor sustainability in section II.A. above, the multilateral financial institutions should provide relief within a minimum three years - otherwise the Paris Club will not be able to ensure debt sustainability and allow a debtor to qualify for "exit" rescheduling. A more desirable sequencing would be that the multilateral financial institutions provide service relief (and limited stock relief through prepayment) from the moment when a country qualifies for Paris Club stock treatment.

D. How many countries need debt relief?

Using the four primary indicators suggested earlier, and assuming that any one critical indicator is sufficient to be eligible for multilateral debt relief (which should be the standard), table 1 divides countries into sustainable and unsustainable. It shows that 32 countries are unsustainable for three years, and 27 for at least five years.

Taking into account macroeconomic projections and burden-sharing leads to some adjustments in the list. Given the excellent growth prospects of Equatorial Guinea, this country should probably be included in the sustainable countries. Angola, by contrast, should be added to the unsustainable list if Russia fails to provide relief that is comparable to the Paris Club. High growth prospects also probably offset the risk of less relief from Russia for Viet Nam, leaving its position as sustainable.

This indicative exercise implies that, depending on the time period chosen, and the view of the relative probability of high growth and less relief from Russia, between 31 and 33 countries have unsustainable debt positions after the maximum possible debt relief has been provided - around three-quarters of the HIPCs. This analysis does not attempt to correct for the effects of optimistic export or aid growth rates or overcompressed import elasticities, to look at secondary indicators beyond those relating present value and debt service to exports and fiscal revenue, or to incorporate other major downside risks such as drought or policy slippage. As such, it probably represents a somewhat optimistic picture.

Of course, this number will probably be reduced by the likely stringent eligibility criteria for multilateral debt relief, designed in order to avoid moral hazard for debtors, and to ensure burden-sharing among creditors: these issues have been discussed above and will be taken up again in the next section. Nevertheless, it is clear that a significant number of countries have a problem: new mechanisms for multilateral debt relief are necessary.

III. Funding multilateral debt relief

One of the key current issues in the debate over multilateral debt relief is whether there are sufficient funds available and adequate aid flows to both HIPC and non-HIPC low-income countries.

A. How much money is needed?

The first question is how much money is needed to fund relief on multilateral debt which would be sufficient to make debt burdens sustainable. The *Financial Times* article cited at the beginning of this paper vastly exaggerated the funding needs by presenting the $11 billion as being due immediately, whereas it was the entire amount of debt service which would have been paid over 15 years if all HIPCs were immediately eligible for relief.

The true annual funding needs for multilateral debt relief are relatively small, because the fund will pay the service of countries as they gradually become eligible, with two preconditions (proof of need and prior Naples stock treatment). Until they become eligible, countries will pay their own debt service. Unfortunately, data are not available to estimate costs based on the assessment of eligible countries in section II.D. Using the 24 countries in the MDF paper (including "arrears" countries), and optimistic projected dates for Naples stock treatment, the estimated cost is:

- $400 million a year in 1997, when the first three countries will be eligible (Bolivia, Nicaragua, Uganda);[4]
- $500 million in 1998, when one or two more countries will become eligible;
- rising to $850 million in 2000-2001, by which time another ten countries will have become eligible;
- $1.4 billion from 2002, when another six countries will be eligible, to 2006;
- $200 million in 2006-2010, as the present value of multilateral service falls.

Kenya and Myanmar are not rescheduling and so will not be eligible. The total maximum cost of relief in the next 15 years would therefore be around $11 billion.

However, three unrealistic assumptions underlie these calculations of maximum needs: that countries will implement adjustment entirely on schedule - which, as discussed in section II.B., is extremely unlikely; that eligibility is interpreted as flexibly as in the MDF paper; if criteria are less realistic and comprehensive, the number of eligible countries and resources needed would fall sharply; that as much multilateral debt relief is needed as assumed in the MDF paper; if the Paris Club or non-OECD creditors

Table 1

CLASSIFICATIONS OF HEAVILY INDEBTED POOR COUNTRIES, ACCORDING TO DEBT SUSTAINABILITY

Country	Classification	Explanation
Angola	?	Less debt relief from Russia
Benin	U	Fiscal burden for > 3 years
Bolivia	U	Export burden > 5 years, Fiscal > 3 years
Burkina Faso	U	Fiscal and Export burden for > 3 years
Burundi	U	Fiscal and Export burden for > 5 years
Cameroon	U	Fiscal and Export burden for > 5 years
Central African Republic	U	Fiscal for > 5 years
Chad	S	- - - -
Congo	U	Fiscal and Export burden for > 5 years
Côte d'Ivoire	U	Fiscal and Export burden for > 5 years
Equatorial Guinea	?	Fiscal/Export > 5 years outweighed by growth prospects
Ethiopia	U	Export > 5 years, Fiscal > 3, less debt relief from Russia
Ghana	S	- - - -
Guinea	U	Fiscal and Export > 3 years
Guinea-Bissau	U	Fiscal and Export > 5 years
Guyana	U	Fiscal and Export > 5 years, less debt relief from Trinidad and Tobago
Honduras	U	Export >3 years, Fiscal >5
Kenya	U	Fiscal and Export >3
Lao People's Democratic Republic	S	- - - -
Liberia	NYD	- - - -
Madagaskar	U	Fiscal and Export > 5 years, less debt relief from Russia
Mali	U	Fiscal > 5 years
Mauretania	S	- - - -
Mozambique	U	Fiscal and Export > 5 years
Myanmar	U	Export >5 years
Nicaragua	U	Fiscal and Export > 5 years
Niger	U	Fiscal and Export > 5 years
Nigeria	NYD	- - - -
Rwanda	U	Fiscal and Export > 5 years
Sao Tomé & Principe	U	Fiscal and Export > 5 years
Senegal	U	Fiscal > 5 years
Sierra Leone	U	Export > 3 years, Fiscal >5 years
Somalia	U	Fiscal and Export > 5 years
Sudan	U	Fiscal and Export > 5 years
Tanzania	U	Fiscal and Export > 5 years
Togo	U	Fiscal > 3 years
Uganda	U	Export > 5 years, Fiscal > 3 years
Viet Nam	S	Less Relief from Russia outweighed by growth prospects
Yemen, Republic of	S	- - - -
Zaire	U	Fiscal and Export > 5 years
Zambia	U	Fiscal and Export > 5 years

Totals

U	31-33	Export or Fiscal Burdens not Sustainable after 3 years
S	6-8	Export and Fiscal Burdens Sustainable after 3 years
NYD	2	No data available

Note: S = sustainable; U = unsustainable; NYD = not yet determined due to lack of data; ? = status unclear, see text.

increase relief to 80 per cent or more, funding needs will fall.

Being more realistic on these issues will reduce needs in the medium-term by at least 30 per cent, to around $7 billion - but the higher figure is used here in order to be conservative.

B. What are the potential funding sources?

The second issue is to identify the potential sources of the funding for an MDF, bearing in mind the need for maximum additionality as discussed above. The bulk of funding should come from the multilateral financial institutions themselves. Each institution has funds which are "additional", in the sense that, *ceteris paribus*, their use will not reduce lending capacity below projected levels. Given that the case for using these funds productively is gaining ground, the discussion is now revolving around what to use them for: in particular, whether they are needed to maintain the existing concessional lending capacity (ESAF and IDA) of each institution, or can be spared for multilateral debt relief.

1. The IMF: gold sale, investment or pledges[5]

Some have suggested that there are arguments of principle against using IMF resources for more concessional loans or debt relief. On closer inspection, these appear flimsy:

- "It would undermine prospects for future IMF quota increases"; these depend on many other factors in which HIPC debt would be insignificant - and for some OECD countries serious efforts to resolve the HIPC problem might even improve their image of the Fund.

- "It might weaken Fund conditionality"; such "moral hazard" arguments have already been dismissed - and many have suggested that the debt overhang gives debtors more leverage over the Fund (which is forced to refinance service or incur arrears) than vice versa.

- "The IMF should not be a development lending institution or breach uniformity of treatment for all its members"; both have already happened due to SAF and ESAF.

- "Not all ESAF-eligible countries need relief"; appropriate eligibility criteria dispose of this.

- "Such small IMF contributions will not solve the problem of the most severely-indebted

HIPCs"; obviously they will be supplemented by World Bank and bilateral donor funds.

The second issue is whether the IMF has any additional resources. Among its $52 billion of reserves the IMF currently has a gold stock of 100 million ounces, worth about $40 billion at current market prices. A portion of these could be sold, with the proceeds either used directly for debt relief; invested with the income on the investment used for debt relief; or pledged as reserves to protect against the contingent risks of ESAF and the Rights Accumulation Programme, releasing reserves totalling $3 billion from the "ESAF Reserve Account" and the "Special Contingency Account II " (SCA2), for multilateral debt relief. The technical case for sale, investment or pledging has been made conclusively (see Killick, 1995; and Woodward, 1996b, for details).

Using gold would not undermine the sound financial base underpinning the monetary nature of the IMF. Sales of the requisite dimensions would reduce IMF reserves by only around 10-15 per cent and, as the gold stock is valued by the IMF at $35 an ounce, such sales would even increase the paper value of the Fund's reserves. Such sales would reduce the value of members' reserves by only 0.3 per cent. Gold investment or pledging would have even less effect. Investment of the proceeds would maintain the value of the reserve capital, and almost certainly produce a better return than continued holding of gold; and pledging would not touch the capital at all.

There would be no significant effect of small sales, or especially of pledging, on the world market price of gold, and therefore no damage to the value of the remaining gold reserves.

It is therefore entirely feasible to sell a small proportion of the gold and either spend or invest the proceeds, or to pledge the gold as security for lending. These were, after all, virtually the same arguments which convinced the IMF Board to sell 33 per cent of its gold in 1976, at a price of only $125 an ounce, and to spend half of the proceeds on the Trust Fund. The same gold has eventually been recycled, and supplemented by donor contributions, to create SAF and ESAF.

The third issue is whether gold should be used to contribute to multilateral debt relief. Until recently, some have argued that any gold is needed to ensure that ESAF can become "permanent". However, each of the three assumptions underlying this argument is invalid:

First, there is no ESAF financing gap in 1998-2000. The assumption of such a gap springs from highly optimistic projections that ESAF funds will be disbursed by 1998: because ESAF repayments do not begin until 2000, there will be no funds to lend in 1998-2000, and low amounts in 2000-2005. More realistic calculations, based on past trends and bearing in mind the current problems with programmes in many countries, indicate that current funds will last until 2000, and will be sufficient to maintain lending capacity thereafter.

Second, the assumption of constant share for ESAF in funding eligible countries' (growing) finance needs is simplistic, because commitments and disbursements depend on a myriad of factors. In addition, if current ESAF terms continue, it is undesirable for the HIPCs, because it will increase debt which is now among the least concessional available for HIPCs. ESAF will (and probably should) not continue to fund the same proportion of HIPCs' financing needs as in recent years.

Third, it is not true that there are no other funds for the ESAF loan capital. Even if donors provide no more loan capital, the Fund could draw minimally on its general resources, or use the SDR 0.6 billion available from the Special Disbursement Account, at no cost to its capacity to lend to other countries. It will then have enough money (with ESAF repayments) to fund commitments 20 per cent higher in nominal terms than in the last five years, without needing to use gold for the capital.

On the other hand, money is needed to fund the interest subsidy on the ESAF loans. The interest subsidy for the current ESAF was funded entirely by donor contributions, but in the current aid climate, many are now refusing to contribute. The most likely combination of funds, therefore, appears to be around 50 per cent from the IMF's resources and 50 per cent from donor contributions. The IMF has several options for its share: however, direct use of resources from the Reserve Account or Second Special Contingent Account would reduce funds available for ESAF lending or Rights Accumulation Programmes, and is therefore not advisable. Instead, most favour sales or pledges of gold. To fund 50 per cent of the interest subsidy, the Fund would need to sell or pledge only around 3.8 per cent of its gold reserves (3.8 million ounces, worth $1.52 billion), or to invest only around 6.8 per cent of its stocks or 6.8 million ounces.

IMF gold is therefore certainly available for multilateral debt relief. Two main proposals exist:

- lengthening the grace and maturity of ESAF (and extending its interest rate subsidy), as proposed above all by United Kingdom Chancellor Clarke; calculations by the Fund indicate that it would require only 2.7 million ounces of gold sales/ pledges (or 4.8 million ounces invested) to fund all of the additional interest subsidy needed;

- contributing directly to multilateral debt relief, by providing grants to fund debt service as it falls due (either through a Multilateral Debt Facility or a new IMF account); if the Fund were to make a contribution of $100 million a year, it would have to sell only 0.25 million ounces of gold every year over 14 years - a total of 3.5 per cent of the gold stocks.

The combined cost of funding 50 per cent of the interest subsidy, doubling the grace and maturity of ESAF, and contributing $100 million of grants each year to multilateral debt relief for the next 14 years would therefore be $4 billion or 10 per cent of the IMF's gold reserves if gold is sold and/or pledged; and $6.04 billion or 15.1 per cent if gold is invested. All three measures can and should be taken.

However, if a choice among the three options, i.e. the interest subsidy, doubled grace and maturity, or grant contributions, is needed, a direct grant contribution to multilateral debt relief is certainly preferable, because it would reduce the debt overhang - and is needed, as discussed in section III.C. below. Longer grace and maturity for ESAF would reduce the debt overhang only marginally and very gradually, by softening its terms. Merely establishing a permanent ESAF would make no additional contribution to debt relief, because the Fund would only be refinancing service on ESAF loans with new loans on ESAF terms.[6] As a result, if the IMF's contribution is limited to establishing a permanent ESAF, many donors are beginning to ask three questions:

- Is a new contribution to the ESAF interest subsidy fund, for lending on short grace and maturity, a good use of our aid? Some donors have already decided not to contribute.

- If it makes no grant contribution, should the IMF have any role in the governance and decisions on eligibility of any global Trust Fund or country-specific funds established?

- Should IMF debt service be eligible for payment out of any Trust Fund resources or country-specific funds?

2.   The World Bank: IBRD net income, IDA reflows and reserves[7]

The World Bank has several potential sources of funding, all of which (unless stated otherwise below) are usable without any damage to the financial integrity of the World Bank, the fundamental determinants of which are its callable capital base, and the confidence of its members in its financial management. Neither the debt crisis of the early 1980s nor the Mexican crisis of 1994 had any significant effect on the Bank's borrowing costs, and their potential cost to the Bank's portfolio was around 10 times greater than HIPC debt reduction needs. Early resolution of the HIPC debt problem would even improve market perception of the Bank's financial management.

On March 19, 1996, donors agreed that the next replenishment of IDA (IDA-XI) would be at a level of $22 billion over three years, maintaining its lending capacity in real terms. However, in spite of extra efforts by some donors, notably Japan, new donor contributions were disappointing. As a result, considerable amounts of the World Bank's projected resources will have to be diverted to IDA-XI, reducing considerably the funds available for multilateral debt relief:

(1)   IBRD net income
For many years, a proportion of the net income of the IBRD on its investments and loans has been transferred to IDA in order to supplement its lending capacity.[8] Recently, this transfer has been running at around $300 million a year. However, most of this income will be needed to supplement IDA lending in FY1997, 1998 and 1999, though it should be available thereafter. Fortunately, in FY1995, the Bank made windfall net earnings of $850 million. Around $350 million of this has been used for Rwanda and Bosnia, but $500 million remains for debt relief.

(2)   IDA reflows
As a result of the disappointing donor contributions to IDA XI, all IDA reflows will be needed to supplement IDA in 1996-1999, leaving none to use for multilateral debt relief. Reflows will increase dramatically during 2000-2010, freeing IBRD net income and some reflows for multilateral debt relief purposes but, unless donors substantially increase pledges to IDA XII, only $100 million a year of reflows will be available.

(3)   Interest subsidy account
This account was established in 1975 to subsidize interest rates on IBRD loans for the poorest IBRD borrowers. In 2001 the full amount of $154 million will be available either to refund to donors, or to use for other purposes (World Bank, 1995a).

(4)   Reserves and provisions
IBRD specific provisions have been made against the risk of default by countries in non-accrual status. They could therefore be used only marginally, as an offsetting contribution to a Multilateral Debt Trust Fund as payments were made to clear debts of countries in non-accrual status. However, IBRD reserves, at around 14 per cent of existing loans in addition to specific provisions, are commonly regarded by financial market analysts as excessive. Their reduction to around 12 per cent would pose no threat to the financial credibility of the IBRD, especially if they were used for a purpose which increased the certainty of multilateral debt service payments - though their use would deprive the IBRD of some additional income derived from investing the reserves. Careful use of provisions and especially reserves would indeed enhance Bank creditworthiness (for more detail, see Commonwealth Secretariat, 1996; Killick, 1995; and Mistry, 1995).

Now that the IDA-XI negotiations are over, it is obvious that the World Bank can spare some funds - though less than hoped - for multilateral debt relief, without reducing concessional lending through IDA. It is also important to note that the MDF proposal had a positive effect on the IDA-XI replenishment, transforming the image of the World Bank in the development community, and allowing some bilateral donors to increase pledges. Multilateral debt relief will also have positive future effects, by ending the distortion of the IDA portfolio through extra large fast-disbursing "defensive" loans to help pay debt service; by guaranteeing reflows to IDA, making its lending projections more secure; and by allowing higher growth from debt relief, which in the longer term could reduce the demands of some countries on IDA resources.

Finally, the IDA negotiations also agreed on the possibility of providing grants to the most debt-distressed IDA borrowers. This is an important step, and any resulting reduction in recycling of funds for new IDA lending will be more than offset by the rapid rise in reflows in the early part of the next century.

However, it will make only a small and very gradual contribution to slowing the rise of the debt overhang - direct grant contributions to multilateral relief are needed as well.

3. Other multilateral creditors

It is less clear how other multilateral creditors might contribute to debt relief.

Among the Multilateral Development Banks, while the Inter-American Development Bank (IDB) has sufficient reserves and net income to contribute in the same way as the World Bank for the few Latin American HIPCs which are affected, the African Development Bank (AfDB) currently needs to use its net income to supplement its insufficient reserves, and has virtually no concessional reflows or new concessional lending capacity. Donors will need to bear in mind when deciding on contributions to multilateral debt relief that the African Development Fund (ADF) also needs an adequate replenishment, and may wish to use part of their pledges to ADF for a Trust Fund to prepay AfDB loans with grants.

The European Union is rapidly expanding its capacity to provide grants to low-income countries, and has three instruments available to it in order to make a contribution. First, it could convert any outstanding loans to HIPCs into grants. Second, it could use its substantial arrears of STABEX disbursements in some countries for multilateral debt relief grants provided that they were agriculture-linked. Third, for countries which can not absorb import support (as discussed in 1.2), it should switch its Structural Adjustment Funds to either direct budget support, reserves support or debt relief support.

The financial condition of other "non-OECD" multilateral institutions (where the financial contributors are non-OECD Governments) such as the Arab Fund for Economic and Social Development (AFESD), the Arab Monetary Fund (AMF), BADEA, the Central American Bank for Economic Integration (CABEI), the Islamic Development Bank and the OPEC Fund varies considerably. Several different methods will be needed for them to make an appropriate contribution within their abilities (Martin et al., 1996a).

4. The availability of bilateral aid funds

The arguments for using bilateral aid funds for multilateral debt relief have already been presented in section I.B. above. It is extremely difficult to quantify most of the donor funds which would be available, partly because such items as direct budget support might, through the fungibility of non-project aid, be regarded as providing resources to pay multilateral debt service. Ultimately, burden-sharing should be judged in the context of contributions to the overall non-project financing needs of the HIPC country. Nevertheless, it is possible to identify several sources of funds:

- **Earmarked funds**
  A survey of three of the four major donors which currently earmark funds for multilateral debt relief has indicated that they plan at least to keep these funds constant at the recent level of $200 million a year, and possibly to maintain or increase them in real terms - especially because allocating them to multilateral debt relief might allow them to be disbursed more rapidly. Nevertheless, it is safest to assume only nominal or real maintenance of these funds;

- **Freed funds**
  Three types of funds which have until now been diverted to multilateral debt relief or new lending should be freed as a contribution of the international financial institutions to debt relief:
  - the approximately $160 million a year of bilateral funds which have been paying multilateral debt service without being earmarked for such a purpose;
  - the funds which donors contributed to the ESAF interest subsidy at its last replenishment (around SDR1 billion or $1.5 billion); and
  - the funds which were "locked out" of the recent IDA replenishment. As predicted in the MDF document, some donors had their intended higher pledges to IDA-XI "locked out" by insistence on burden-sharing with a lower United States contribution; these funds may therefore be available for multilateral debt relief, through either pledges to the MDF or extra bilateral aid.

However, given the pressure on bilateral aid budgets, the apparent "non-fungibility" of some donor funds (for example, many ESAF and IDA contributions come from Ministries of Finance, which for political reasons resist the idea of using these funds for multilateral debt relief), and the view among some donors that project aid is more important than non-project aid, even the most optimistic observer should include only the first type of freed funds in any calculation of financing available.

- *Faster disbursement*

As already discussed in section I.B., switching funds from import support or project aid to debt relief or budget support would in most HIPCs dramatically increase disbursement speeds. For those donor countries where non-disbursement results in loss of the funds for the recipient country, and in loss of overall aid budget due to criticism of low recipient capacity to absorb aid, faster disbursement might produce genuine additional resources for individual recipient countries and for overall aid budgets. However, such additionality is likely to be small and is impossible to quantify - so is not included below.

C. *Overall financial calculations*

Table 2 summarizes the funds available for multilateral debt relief, in three scenarios.

Scenario I is the most pessimistic, including only IBRD net income (including windfall), IDA reflows and the interest subsidy account; and highly conservative assumptions about donor funding: that funds already earmarked by three donors for debt relief ($200 million) will be available at the same *nominal* level;

Scenario II reflects a higher contribution by the bilaterals. It adds to Scenario I the assumptions that the remaining non-earmarked bilateral aid ($160 million a year), which is now being used directly for multilateral debt relief, will continue to be used for this purpose; and that all of these aid funds will be maintained in *real* terms.

Scenario III adds an IMF contribution, through gold sales/pledges/investment to provide grants of $100 million a year for relief.

All the scenarios are conservative in their assessment of available resources, by excluding:

- income earned on any Trust Funds established;
- qualitative/transaction cost-saving/disburse-ment-increasing effects on aid;
- donor funds freed by use of IMF gold to fund 50 per cent of the ESAF interest subsidy, or funds locked out of IDA;
- IBRD reserves;
- contributions from other multilateral creditors.

The results are striking. Based on the maximum MDF needs explained in section II.B.1., the World Bank resources and donor contributions in Scenario I (a 64/36 burden-sharing between the Bank and the bilaterals) would cover needs only for the first four years. With Scenario II, the maximum realistic contribution from bilateral aid (a 44/56 burden-sharing between Bank and bilaterals), there is still a financing gap from 2003 through 2008. It is only with an IMF contribution of $100 million a year (around 10 per cent of total funding, compared to its 28 per cent share of the present value of HIPC debt) that the necessary relief can be funded: the gap in 2005-2007 could be closed by ploughing back the investment earnings on the Trust Fund into the Fund itself. If the IMF does not make a contribution, the World Bank will have to draw on its reserves to ensure sufficient funding. The surplus of funds in 2008-2010 indicates that all sides could afford to reduce their contributions after this period, freeing more funds for other concessional flows.

The funds needed for HIPC multilateral debt relief are therefore available - if the IFIs make a significant contribution. It would be desirable to maximize the use of their "most additional" funds - IMF gold and World Bank reserves - in order to free more bilateral aid for other development purposes. Both gold and reserves could be used without damaging the financial integrity of the institutions - but one or the other would be sufficient to fund relief needs, in addition to IBRD net income and IDA reflows (which are acceptable sources if they do not reduce IDA lending). Finally, we will need to design creative mechanisms to allow other multilateral institutions to contribute without reducing new aid flows, and to ensure that bilateral aid freed by multilateral contributions does not disappear from aid budgets.

IV. What are the best mechanisms?

In 1995-1996, attempts to resolve the multilateral debt problem have focussed around two routes: a global Multilateral Debt Facility (MDF), proposed by the World Bank in July 1995, and a Uganda Multilateral Debt Fund (UMDF), proposed in December 1994 and established in July 1995. This section examines their costs and benefits - not as either/or options but to learn how to combine the two into the best possible mechanism for relief.

However, both have been subject to one major criticism: the concept of setting up a new Facility or

Table 2

FUNDING MULTILATERAL DEBT RELIEF
($ million, annual amounts or averages)

	1996	1997	1998	1999	2000	2001	2002	2003	2004	2005	2006	2007	2008	2009	2010	Total 1996 -2010
Maximum MDF needs [a]	0	400	500	600	850	850	1400	1400	1400	1400	1400	200	200	200	200	*11000*
Scenario I - Maximum World Bank contribution and earmarked bilateral aid remaining constant in nominal terms																
Total funds available	700	200	200	400	600	754	600	600	600	600	600	600	600	600	600	*8254*
World Bank total [b]	500	0	0	200	400	554	400	400	400	400	400	400	400	400	400	*5254*
IBRD net income (1996 = windfall)	500	0	0	150	300	300	300	300	300	300	300	300	300	300	300	*3950*
IDA reflows	0	0	0	50	100	100	100	100	100	100	100	100	100	100	100	*1150*
Interest subsidy account (2001 only)						154										*154*
Earmarked bilateral aid (constant in nominal terms)	200	200	200	200	200	200	200	200	200	200	200	200	200	200	200	*3000*
Gap/carryover	*700*	*500*	*200*	*0*	*-250*	*-346*	*-1146*	*-1946*	*-2746*	*-3546*	*-4346*	*-3946*	*-3546*	*-3146*	*-2746*	*-2746*
Scenario II - Greater bilateral aid (remaining constant in real terms) and part of "freed" aid used																
Total extra funds available	160	171	182	193	205	217	230	243	256	270	284	298	313	329	345	*3696*
"Freed" aid contributed	160	160	160	160	160	160	160	160	160	160	160	160	160	160	160	*2400*
All aid constant in real terms [c]	0	11	22	33	45	57	70	83	96	110	124	138	153	169	185	*1296*
Gap/carryover	*860*	*831*	*713*	*706*	*661*	*782*	*212*	*-345*	*-889*	*-1419*	*-1935*	*-1237*	*-524*	*205*	*950*	*1296*
Scenario III - IMF contribution																
IMF gold sales	100	100	100	100	100	100	100	100	100	100	100	100	100	100	100	*1500*
Gap/carryover	*960*	*1031*	*1013*	*1106*	*1161*	*1382*	*912*	*455*	*11*	*-419*	*-835*	*-37*	*776*	*1605*	*2450*	*2450*

Source: MDF Proposal Document and donor surveys.

a MDF proposal projections are postponed for one year because the facility is assumed not to be ready for disbursements until 1997, and adjusted for the projected date of Paris Club stock treatment.

b Projected World Bank contributions are adjusted for fiscal years.

c Projections of real constant aid allow for 3 per cent nominal growth per year.

Fund. Why, many ask, do we need to set up a new Facility or Fund, with associated expenditure of political will during the negotiations, and inevitable administrative costs when funds are available and already being used for multilateral debt relief? Why can we not just improve the use and scope of existing mechanisms? The next section deals with that question.

A. The need for coordination and burden-sharing

Without a coordinated framework, "existing mechanisms" - and the definition of their desirable use and scope - will continue to be considered piecemeal by each international financial institution and other creditor groups. More specifically, a coordinated solution is critical because:

- it offers an unique opportunity to judge the sustainability of a debtor's debt burden in a way which involves all creditor groups and to get away from the approach which has exacerbated the debt overhang in the last decade (of judging the measures which are feasible from the point of view of each creditor group and implementing them regardless of their effect on debtor sustainability);

- only a coordinated solution is likely to involve the debtor Government fully in assessing its own debt sustainability;

- there is also a need to judge the relative importance of elements of the debt overhang by taking into account whether it is essential for any particular creditor to be paid - and therefore the impact of poor coordination on other creditors; as already discussed, the IMF and World Bank have to be paid - at great cost to debtors and (in arrears or relief) to other creditors;

- the African Development Bank has virtually no resources of its own; therefore the international community cannot leave it to cope with its problems alone, if an excessively drastic cut in its new lending capacity for the rest of the decade is to be avoided;

- creditors and donors acting in separate fora (Paris Club and Consultative Group/Round Table meetings), on the basis of assessments of financing needs provided by different institutions (IMF, World Bank, UNDP) on the basis of different considerations, and at different times, have failed to fulfil debtors' genuine financing

needs for development (see Martin and Mistry, 1994);

- the comparability of debt relief and burden-sharing on new money discussed in section II.C. above requires a comprehensive overall framework for analysis and forum for decisions.

B. A global Multilateral Debt Facility

The World Bank Task Force proposed a global Multilateral Debt Facility (MDF) last July (World Bank, 1995a). This proposal has achieved a great deal in getting the Bretton Woods institutions and their shareholders to analyse country-debt sustainability in a more comprehensive and realistic way, in raising the profile of multilateral debt on the international agenda, and in enhancing the World Bank's reputation on debt issues. The core elements of the proposal are:

- comprehensive assessment of debtor countries' debt sustainability;

- concerted action on all components of a nation's debt to achieve debt sustainability, ending the previous fragmented approach and encouraging greater relief by all groups;

- payment of multilateral debt service as it fell due, over a specified period of time;

- commitment up-front to make the payments, in order to reduce the debt overhang effect;

- funding from a combination of IMF, World Bank and bilateral donor resources;

- a separate Trust Fund facility to catalyse maximum contributions from all sides;

- eligibility based on a track record of good adjustment performance and prior stock reductions by creditor Governments and commercial lenders.

The MDF was carefully designed to answer two criticisms levelled at multilateral debt relief, by protecting the financial integrity of the international financial institutions (IFIs) and by guarding against moral hazard for debtors and creditors.

(1) Protecting the financial integrity of the international financial institutions

As discussed in section III.B., there are many sources of IMF and World Bank financing for multilateral debt relief which would not damage their financial integrity. The MDF went further in protecting this integrity by proposing a facility at "arms-length" from the Bank, to avoid "self-entanglement". The facility would be financed and governed jointly with other funders, and cover service to several IFIs (with no direct or indirect link between the amount of money due to any one IFI and its payments into the Facility), in order to reduce the public perception of any one IFI paying itself to forestall a debt write-down. It also proposed a cut-off date (loans contracted after this date would not be eligible for relief). There was to be no question of writing off or writing down any debt.

The "Fifth Dimension" shows that an arms-length approach may be unnecessary. It is paying interest on IBRD loans, using mainly World Bank resources, and could therefore have been perceived as "non-arms length". However, because it was carefully explained to the markets, confined to 20 countries which do not borrow from IBRD, and with clear eligibility criteria, it had no negative effect on IBRD borrowing costs. The MDF will only expand payment of service to cover other multilateral financial institutions, with equally clear eligibility criteria, and again for countries which do not borrow from IBRD. Discussions with City institutions indicate that there will be no negative effect on IBRD borrowing costs: many suggest that if the IFIs design an orderly strategy and process for countries to move to debt sustainability, it will strengthen their financial integrity, and rather reduce IBRD borrowing costs.

To ensure burden-sharing among the multilateral financial institutions and bilaterals, it would be desirable to create a Trust Fund into which both bilaterals and multilateral financial institutions could contribute. If this has positive "arms-length" spin-offs, so much the better: but it will also be desirable to give donors the maximum flexibility for contributions by allowing country-specific funds.

(2)   Guarding against moral hazard
As already discussed in section I, debtor moral hazard of poor economic policies, due to lower commitment to adjustment and less programme ownership, is far greater under the current system of refinancing than with any well-designed system of multilateral debt relief. The MDF is such a system, eliminating "moral hazard" of poor economic policies by insisting on an excellent track record of compliance with adjustment programmes.

The second debtor "moral hazard" of "non-payment" can be dealt with much more effectively in the context of adjustment programmes which are based on comprehensive assessment of debt sustainability: the IFIs will be much more able to judge the reason for non-payment (will or ability) and act accordingly. In any case, non-payment is unlikely to occur when relief makes the burden sustainable.

The third debtor risk, of replacing one type of debt with another, by irresponsible new borrowing, is also dealt with firmly: the MDF proposes to require that all new medium- and long-term borrowing be on "appropriately concessional terms". However, many will feel that this phrase needs more precise definition.

As for creditor moral hazard, the first type, of providing less debt relief, will be prevented by insisting on burden-sharing among all creditor groups - indeed on prior stock reductions by bilateral and commercial creditors. The risk that this will not be forthcoming has already been discussed in section II.C. It is highly likely that the MDF, with global backing and support from the IFIs, will be able to push strongly for greater burden-sharing but, in some cases, this may be more successfully achieved by assisting creditors and debtors to design innovative relief mechanisms, or by leading the way with multilateral relief.

The second type, of "throwing good money after bad" through defensive lending, will be eliminated by the arms-length, transparent nature of the MDF. Again, it should be remembered that this is a dominant characteristic of the current refinancing system.

Thus the MDF proposal should not lead anyone to worry about the preferred-creditor status or financial integrity of the IFIs, the borrowing costs of the IBRD, or debtor or creditor moral hazard. On all these grounds, it is a vast improvement over the current refinancing procedure.

However, four elements of the MDF proposal should be of concern to developing countries and to donors who are considering contributions:

*   The proposed *control of its Trust Fund* by a Steering Group of contributing donors, with no representation from developing countries or independent experts; and the Bank's day-to-day

control over the precise terms and conditions for disbursements to eligible countries.

- The *assessment of debt sustainability and design of the facility* entirely by IMF and World Bank staff. In spite of laudable efforts by the Bank (and to a much lesser degree the Fund) to consult on the issues, developing country policy-makers (and even creditor Governments and other independent sources) have been largely excluded from the assessment and design process. Neither the Fund nor the Bank has a monopoly on good ideas: nor are they - as the creditors who are being analysed - entirely impartial. Assessment of country sustainability and future changes in the design of the facility should be assigned to a group with wider membership from the international community.

- The suggestion that a *critical mass of financing* (around $1-1.2 billion) will be needed - of which 50 per cent must come from non-World Bank sources - before a Facility can be established. The funds available from both the World Bank and bilaterals will be mainly on the same annually-disbursed basis as for the Fifth Dimension. While the World Bank windfall net income and some bilateral up-front funds could create a fund of around $600-700 million, a larger critical mass would require the IMF to sell gold up-front to pay into the MDF, or to free other resources for MDF by gold pledges.

- Ensuring the maximum *catalytic effect* on bilateral and IMF contributions to the MDF, and on aid in general. As discussed in 3.2, the global political will and publicity underlying implementation of an MDF might catalyse a 50 per cent contribution from bilateral donors. However, this might be offset by (misplaced) worries about the large amounts apparently required, and by the divergence of donor interests in different debtor countries. As a result, the MDF would need to allow maximum flexibility for donors, both on the timing of contributions and on the possibility of cofinancing or parallel financing of the kind now used in the Fifth and Sixth Dimensions. Similarly, the IMF may feel unable to go beyond small annual payments and/or softening the terms of ESAF.

C. The Uganda Multilateral Debt Fund

Uganda has a particularly heavy multilateral debt burden: around 80 per cent of the debt stock at the end of 1995 and 70 per cent of debt service in the next ten years. It has also done everything possible to reduce other types of debt, including a commercial debt buyback and Paris Club Naples stock treatment, and has an excellent adjustment track record. As a result, at the Uganda Consultative Group in 1994, the Government of Uganda, donors and the World Bank agreed to analyse Uganda's multilateral debt and identify ways to reduce the burden. The Governments of Austria, Denmark, the Netherlands, Sweden and Switzerland commissioned a study by independent and Ugandan officials, which resulted in a proposal for a "Uganda Multilateral Debt Fund" (UMDF), which was subsequently incorporated in a revised National Debt Strategy for Uganda (see Martin, 1995; Government of Uganda, 1995a, 1995b, 1995c).

In many ways, this proposal was similar to the later Multilateral Debt Facility. It was based on a comprehensive assessment of Uganda's debt sustainability and part of a comprehensive strategy designed to achieve comparable terms of debt relief from all creditors through a coordinated approach at the Consultative Group. It envisaged the payment of a proportion of multilateral debt service as it fell due, in order to bring service down to a sustainable level and reduce the overhang effect. Donors were to pay the equivalent of the debt service up-front (at least at the beginning of each financial year) into a Uganda Multilateral Debt Fund, and to make a commitment in principle to sustained future support of this fund. It also requested similar contributions by the IMF and World Bank, but without success.[9] Moreover, the UMDF proposal envisaged the establishment of a separate fund to catalyze maximum contributions from all sides and it was based on Uganda's excellent track record of adjustment performance, especially specific commitments on fiscal and reserves management (and new borrowing limits - see below), and prior stock reductions by the Paris Club and commercial lenders.

The proposal also used the same method to protect the financial integrity of the IFIs. It was an entirely "arms-length" Fund, because it was managed by the Government of Uganda, subject to discussions at quarterly meetings of local donor representatives, and at annual Consultative Groups; because it was financed entirely by donors other than the IFIs; and because it covered service due to all IFIs (IMF, World Bank and AfDB). However, it did not apply a cut-off date for relief.

Similarly, strong mechanisms were incorporated to avoid debtor moral hazard. The UMDF proposal was based on Uganda's excellent track record of compliance with adjustment programmes, and contributing donors have made clear that their payments are contingent on continued efforts. In addition, management of the funds by Uganda has encouraged further progress on reserves and fiscal management and new borrowing, and deepened the dialogue with donors on these issues. Its success in reducing debt to sustainable levels has allowed Uganda to pay all debt service to the Paris Club and other essential creditors, avoiding Ugandan need for more relief. Its more efficient method of paying multilateral creditors has avoided even transitory arrears. The UMDF proposal goes further than the World Bank MDF in avoiding accumulation of new debt. The Government of Uganda has undertaken no new borrowing from the AfDB hard window, no new borrowing (with the exception of ESAF and a tiny emergency ceiling for non-concessional borrowing) except on IDA-comparable terms; and no new borrowing of any kind except for purposes for which grants are not available, and until prospects for grants have been fully explored. In other words, the UMDF has proven the MDF's theory that debtor moral hazard is avoidable.

However, the UMDF has been only partly successful in avoiding creditor moral hazard. Uganda has been unable to get all its remaining commercial and non-OECD creditors to share the burden of debt relief, because fragmented negotiations have continued for creditors not present at the Consultative Group (Paris Club stock treatment and IDA commercial debt buy-backs had already occurred). Moreover, the UMDF has taken the pressure off the multilateral financial institutions to lend defensively - though it was never a country in which either IFI indulged in this practice to a large degree, because its adjustment track record merited continued large lending. On the whole, the UMDF has shown the need for the MDF to act strongly against creditor moral hazard.

There were also some crucial differences with the Multilateral Debt Facility proposal, which should make it more attractive for members of the Group of Twenty-four.

The fact that the UMDF was managed by the Government of Uganda, rather than funders, had several advantages:

- Interest accrued to the UMDF account in the period before multilateral service fell due, increasing the role of contributions to the fund in paying multilateral service.[10]

- It encouraged the Government of Uganda to continue its efforts to improve its policies on reserves management, fiscal and new borrowing policy.

- It has given the Government of Uganda the leading role in continuing to assess the evolution of Uganda's debt burden, dramatically improving its debt management.

- It has given donors more freedom to take independent decisions to pay funds into the UMDF, and at times which are convenient to them (some operate on calendar years, others on fiscal years), thereby mobilizing more funds.

- It has given the Government of Uganda, donors and IFIs an equal say in conditions for disbursements, and a full opportunity for each contributing donor and IFI to raise its own questions about the use and management of the funds and budgetary savings.

The assessment of debt sustainability and design of the fund was conducted by Uganda, but extensively discussed at all stages with donors and the Bretton Woods institutions (local offices and headquarters). The assessment - shared by donors and the Bretton Woods institutions according to their statements in donor meetings in Kampala - was that Uganda's multilateral debt was "unsustainable". The UMDF also required a much more limited "critical mass" of funds - only pledges in principle from three major donors of around $30 million - to launch the Fund. The establishment of a separate UMDF has had a catalytic effect way beyond expectations, due to flexibility in payment methods and timing. It has generated pledges from five donors to cover more than two-thirds of multilateral service (including the IMF), which are paid at the start of the calendar year, and with commitments in principle to funds in future years. Donors have also been allowed to make parallel contributions if they cannot pay into the MDF, though only one has chosen this option. Coordination has been successfully achieved using the normal annual Consultative Group meeting, at which donors announced pledges and non-Paris Club creditors announced relief, to maximize the catalytic effect; and local quarterly meetings called by the Government of Uganda, with donors and Bretton Woods institutions to discuss technical issues, amounts and debt-related economic policy.

There are three lessons to be learned from the experience with the Ugandan Multilateral Debt Fund. First, it has reduced Uganda's multilateral debt service to sustainable levels - but in the absence of IMF or

World Bank contributions, this diverts bilateral donors' aid from other uses. Second, analysing its burden and strategy, debating the issues with donors and IFIs, and managing the UMDF, has been highly positive for the Government of Uganda. The responsibility for debt management was transferred to the Government, which improved its structures for debt management. Third, the UMDF has allowed multilateral service to be paid on schedule through coordinated management by the Government. This has dramatically reduced the transaction costs of debt overhang, allowed improvements in planning, and further reinforced government commitment and ownership.

One important issue is what these lessons imply for other HIPCs. It is true that donors have been exceptionally keen to fund Uganda's MDF because of its high proportion of multilateral debt, and its excellent adjustment track record. However, provided that a global coordination mechanism exists to establish clear criteria of need and adjustment track records for other countries, similar success should be expected for other HIPCs.

D. Lessons for optimal debt relief mechanisms

The above comparison of global and country-specific funds shows that both will be needed in order to catalyse the maximum multilateral debt relief funding, protect IFI financial integrity and guard against debtor and creditor moral hazard. The key features of an optimal debt relief mechanism emerge clearly from comparing the two methods, as summarised in table 3:

(1) Design and management
Debt sustainability analysis (both initial and continuing) should be led by the debtor country, assisted by independent analysts where necessary, and consulting the IFIs and donors throughout, in order to improve debt management capacity.

The design of the global Trust Fund facility should involve full consultation of the debtor Governments identified as potentially eligible, to ensure that it is tailored to their needs.

While the design of disbursement conditions and terms for the global Trust Fund should be undertaken in Washington, those for bilateral donor contributions to the country-specific funds

should be freely negotiated by the debtor Government and the donor.

Management of the country-specific fund should, where considered feasible by donors in view of a Government's fiscal and reserves management record, be consigned to the debtor Government, to encourage further improvements in debt, fiscal and reserves management. Alternatively, a fund could be held off-shore while debtor capacity improves.

(2) Debt relief method
While up-front stock reduction would be a preferable payment method, payment of service as it falls due (with a commitment to pay for the foreseeable future) can be highly positive in reducing many of the effects of the debt overhang.

Payment coordination needs to be maximized by a country-specific fund and interest should accrue preferably to the fund of the individual debtor, rather than to the global account of an MDF, in order to maximize the effective relief for the debtor.

(3) Funding
The IFI contribution from the Trust Fund could be paid into the country-specific fund. A critical mass of global contributions to a Trust Fund should not be stressed, settling instead for a mass of indications of contributions sufficient to fund the relief needed. For maximum catalytic effect, it would be desirable to leave (as with the IDA commercial debt reduction facility) donors the choice either to pay money into a global Trust Fund or to provide cofinancing or separate grants.

(4) Financial integrity of the international financial institutions
An arms-length facility and a cut-off date would be desirable for burden-sharing but not essential to protect IFI financial integrity.

(5) Moral hazard
It is relatively easy to avoid debtor moral hazard through an adjustment track record. If country-specific funds are established, it is more possible and necessary to examine the debtor's reserves and fiscal policies (without intrusive conditionality).

Debtor moral hazard of non-payment can be overcome by sufficient relief (see UMDF) and

Table 3

COSTS AND BENEFITS OF DIFFERENT MECHANISMS

	World Bank MD facility	*Uganda MD fund*
1. Design and management		
Debt sustainability nalysis *(initial and continuing)*	Comprehensive by IMF/World Bank	Comprehensive by Uganda/IFIs/donors
Design of facility	By IMF/World Bank tailored to global consensus	By Uganda/IFIs/donors tailored to Uganda needs
Design of disbursement conditions and terms	By IFIs, monitored by funders	By Uganda, in conjunction with funders/IFIs
Management of facility *(and disbursement terms)*	By funders/IFIs	By Uganda, monitored by funders/IFIs
2. Debt relief method		
Payment method	Service as falls due +limited prepayment	Service as falls due +limited prepayment
Payment coordination	Improved through Uganda/MDF	Total through Uganda
Interest accrual	To central MDF	To Uganda MDF account
3. Funding		
IFI contribution	Proposed IMF/World Bank will free bilateral aid	None therefore bilateral aid diversion
Donor pledges	Up-front US$1-1.2bn for "critical mass"	Up-front US$30 million for "critical mass"
Catalytic effect	Highly positive Positive: global will and publicity Negative: donor doubt about large amounts and interest in different recipient countries	Proven highly positive Negative: lack of global will and publicity Positive: donors find small amounts and have interest in Uganda
4. IFI financial integrity		
Arms-length	Entirely	Entirely - but no cut-off date
Cut-off date	Yes	No
5. Moral hazard		
Debtor adjustment	Adjustment track record	Adjustment track record +Uganda-specific policies on fiscal/reserves
Debtor non-payment		
Debtor new borrowing	"Appropriately concessional"	IDA-only except ESAF/ emergency+priority grants
Creditor burdensharing	More likely success: through facility with IFI support	Less successful: concerted only through Government strategy
Creditor defensive lending		
6. Coordination mechanism		
International mechanism	Not specified	Consultative group
In-Country mechanism	Not specified	Local Government-led donor meetings

Source: Government of Uganda, 1995a, 1995b; World Bank, 1995a.

new borrowing conditions should be specified precisely as on the Uganda model.

For multilateral debt relief to work effectively, the mechanism should consist both of a global Trust Fund and of country-specific multilateral debt funds. The global Trust Fund will achieve coordination at a global level, keeping pressure on donors and IFIs to contribute to multilateral debt relief, and on other creditors to provide comparable debt relief terms, will conduct periodic global analysis to ensure balance in the uses of concessional funds between debt relief and other purposes, and will conduct continuing analysis of relative burdens for different debtors.

Country-specific multilateral debt funds will add a guarantee of debtor leadership in assessing its own debt sustainability and improving its debt management and associated macroeconomic policies - in full cooperation with the IFIs and interested donors; and full flexibility for donor decisions on the amounts and timing of contributions to individual funds, catalysing maximum donor contributions.

Finally, the fora for coordinating the global and country-specific elements should be the normal annual Consultative Group and Round Table meetings. These would be expanded to include a special session on debt and external financing, where the debtor Government and IFIs would present their agreed assessment of the debtor's debt sustainability and external financing needs, including debt relief and non-project aid. Donors and IFIs would then pledge non-project aid, including grants for the country-specific multilateral debt fund, and non-OECD creditors would announce comparable relief. The annual Consultative Group would be supplemented at a local level by quarterly meetings of the Government, interested donors and multilateral creditors, to discuss policy, administrative and procedural details. This two-tier structure has worked extremely well in the Ugandan case, providing all sides with ample opportunity for consultation, and further improving Government management and ownership of debt and related macroeconomic policies.[11]

V. Conclusion: the need for urgent action

In the first quarter of 1996, the Executive Boards of the IMF and World Bank have agreed that there is a debt overhang effect, and that a significant number of countries have a multilateral debt problem, which requires a new and comprehensive solution. This conclusion therefore concentrates on key issues in the design of such a solution.

(1) The MDF framework can lift the debt overhang

The debt overhang effect has been clearly demonstrated. The arguments presented in Section I have been the basis of bilateral and commercial debt relief for a decade, and are an even sounder basis for relieving multilateral debt, because it must be paid. They also demonstrate that refinancing using loans (such as ESAF or IDA) will fail to reduce the overhang, and that their is more money - and especially greater value for money - to be had for some recipients and from some donors, by providing aid for coordinated multilateral debt relief.

The solution proposed in the MDF - guaranteeing to pay service with grants as it falls due - should have a major impact on removing the effects of the debt overhang. It will therefore encourage foreign and domestic private investment and public investment, improve fiscal and reserves planning, enhance Government commitment to and ownership of economic policy reform; dramatically reduce the transaction costs of negotiations for creditors and debtors; and allow supply response to adjustment policies. In addition, it incorporates effective ways to avoid moral hazard for debtors and creditors. For maximum effect, it should also incorporate prepayment of the least concessional multilateral debt to reduce the present value of the debt stock.

(2) Sustainability analysis must be realistic and comprehensive

The analysis conducted for this paper reveals that the maximum number of countries which will need multilateral debt relief is between 31 and 33. This is higher than recent analysis from Washington (between 8 and 20), but both numbers are sufficient to require new mechanisms. As with all of the wide range of numbers for affected countries cited in the last 18 months, these are based on indicative preliminary analysis. Final analysis underlying the decision of eligibility and the amount of relief provided must be entirely realistic and comprehensive, in the following ways:

- expanding the core sustainability criteria to put fiscal capacity on an equal basis with foreign exchange capacity;

- using levels of such criteria which fit with the thresholds identified in the literature - 20 per cent debt service and 200 per cent present value;
- using secondary indicators such as reserves levels, balance-of-payments and fiscal financing gaps, and dynamic indicators of the change of present value to check impending problems;
- reducing the period for judging sustainability to three years for a possible problem, and five years for a definite problem, to correspond with the likely period for Paris Club "exit treatment";
- ensuring that the baseline macroeconomic scenario is realistic on export growth prospects and on the levels of imports, reserves and investment needed for sustained growth, and includes per capita growth levels sufficient to reduce poverty dramatically;
- conducting formal sensitivity and probability analysis of alternative macroeconomic scenarios based on likely risk factors (such as drought, insecurity, export and aid trends) and, given the systematic optimism in past projections, stressing the downside risk;
- being entirely realistic about the prospects for debt reduction by other creditors (especially non-OECD Governments and institutions) and new official and private flows, and designing creative mechanisms to ensure that all external financiers .share the burden both in terms of the amount of debt relief or new money, and its timing.

(3)   There is enough money if all parties contribute

Indicative estimates of the funding needs of multilateral debt relief over 15 years range from a minimum of $7 billion to a maximum $11 billion. These amounts are available without diverting existing aid flows, underfunding IDA or ESAF, or threatening the financial integrity of the IFIs, provided that the burden is fairly shared among all relevant parties:

- The World Bank should use a small amount of IBRD net income, its recent windfall net income gains and the Interest Subsidy Account (and if possible in later years a tiny amount of IDA reflows), in order to contribute around $350 million a year, around 40 per cent of MDF needs.

- The IMF should sell or pledge 10 per cent of its $40 billion of gold reserves, or invest 15 per cent. This would provide enough resources to fund a $100 million annual grant contribution to multilateral debt relief (around 10 per cent of MDF needs, compared to its share of 28 per cent

of HIPC multilateral debt in present value terms), and 50 per cent of the interest subsidy of a permanent ESAF with doubled grace and maturity.

- Bilateral donors should pledge around $360 million a year (maintained if possible in real terms), in direct contributions to a global Trust Fund, co-financing and parallel financing. This would fulfil approximately 50 per cent of the MDF needs, and would represent only a maintenance of their recent direct funding levels for multilateral debt relief.

(4)   Mechanisms must be global and country-specific

The principles of the World Bank's MDF have already been tested at a country level by the Uganda Multilateral Debt Fund, with highly positive results in avoiding any damage to the financial integrity of the international financial institutions and minimizing risks of debtor and creditor moral hazard.

For maximum effectiveness, any initiative needs a global Trust Fund *and* country-specific funds:

- The global Trust Fund would ensure synchronization, burden-sharing and transparency by all creditors, to avoid creditor moral hazard; maximize contributions from donors and the international financial institutions; analyse the most urgent global needs for concessional funds and the relative burden on different debtors; establish a cut-off date and take any other measures necessary to maintain the arms-length nature of relief; establish broad preconditions for relief such as a good adjustment track record and precisely specified new borrowing conditions, to avoid debtor moral hazard; and ensure consistency, transparency and consultation of all sides in the design of country funds.

- Country-specific funds would maximize debtor initiative in assessing its debt sustainability and negotiating disbursement conditions and terms; ensure total coordination of payments to avoid any duplication or transitory arrears; and give donors and the international financial institutions maximum flexibility to contribute in ways (and at times within the year) which suit them, provided that they make an up-front commitment to act. Where justified by donor confidence in the debtor's reserves and fiscal management, the debtor Government could manage the fund itself, in order to improve its reserves and debt management procedures and ownership. In other cases, it could be held offshore and managed jointly by the debtor and IDA.

The global and country-specific funds would best be coordinated at meetings of creditors, donors, international financial institutions and the debtor in the normal Consultative Group/Round Table meetings, supplemented with quarterly meetings of Government, international financial institutions and donors in the debtor country, in order to deal with interim administrative and policy issues. This model has worked extremely well in Uganda, allowing full consultation of all sides and further improving Government management and ownership of debt and related macroeconomic policies.

A significant number of HIPCs need the debt overhang lifted from their economies; funds are available without reducing aid flows to other developing countries or flows to HIPCs for other development purposes; and excellent mechanisms can be designed drawing on the ideas of the MDF and the operations of the Uganda Multilateral Debt Fund. There is no technical reason why the international community should not take decisive action on comprehensive multilateral debt relief for the HIPCs.

Notes

1   In assessing the fiscal burden, the question arises if service payments - notably to the IMF - should be included. Such payments are the direct responsibility of the central bank. A critical factor to consider is that the losses sustained by most central banks due to IMF debt service are eventually passed on to their Treasuries when they have to recapitalize central banks. Excluding IMF debt service from the calculation might make a few more countries sustainable, but might be unrealistic.

2   Excellent preliminary work on fiscal gaps and dynamic fiscal debt sustainability is presented in Appendix II of IMF (1995).

3   These have been the basis for the categories of debt distress used by the World Bank (such as Severely Indebted Low Income Countries - SILICs) and for qualifying for Paris Club debt reduction (Highly Indebted Poor Countries - HIPCs).

4   No estimate is made for 1996 because relief is unlikely to be available until 1997.

5   SDR allocations are not discussed here because their assignment to multilateral debt relief on grant terms would require large amounts of subsidy/transfer of OECD allocations, which is highly unlikely. Nor is a new IMF quota increase - which should begin to be discussed in 1996 and will in the longer term provide larger resources for the Fund.

6   Some have suggested that ESAF itself represents a sharp rise in the concessionality of IMF lending, and is equivalent to significant debt relief. This is an irrelevant argument for most HIPCs, which have been borrowing on ESAF terms for several years. As at April 1995, total non-ESAF lending to HIPCs was only SDR1.7 billion. Of this, SDR1.1 billion is owed by four "arrears" countries, and will be refinanced on ESAF terms under the Rights Accumulation Programme. Another SDR342 million will have been repaid to the Fund by end-1996. Only SDR176 million will be outstanding by the end of 1996, representing recent lending to Cameroon, Congo and Viet Nam, for which refinancing on ESAF terms would enhance concessionality. Viet Nam (SDR133 million) is unlikely to qualify for multilateral debt relief. Therefore by renewing the ESAF on current terms, the Fund would effectively be softening the terms of only SDR43 million of debt.

7   More details of these funding sources are provided in the draft MDF paper.

8   There is a valid doubt as to whether the Bank should be making large amounts of net income out of its IBRD borrowers and transferring the funds to other purposes. However, this long-accepted practice is not expected to end.

9   However, Norway prepaid the World Bank's remaining IBRD stock up-front during the discussions of a UMDF. Without this generous action , various donors and the World Bank would have continued to make contributions to the Fifth Dimension for Uganda.

10   The original proposal (Martin, 1995) had suggested paying the ESAF into the Fund in order further to increase debt servicing capacity: the compound interest earned on the ESAF Funds (net of interest payments to the IMF) would effectively have doubled the period before which Uganda had to use any of its own resources to pay the IMF (ie equivalent to the Clarke proposal).

11   One suggested alternative is a one-off "Super CG", where representatives of major creditors would participate. However, organizing such a meeting for each debtor country would add to transaction costs, reduce the role of aid agencies which are paying for the multilateral debt relief and which can take a more development-oriented view of debt sustainability, and duplicate the work of the Paris Club in coordinating the policies of OECD Treasuries and export-credit agencies. A one-off meeting would also not provide sufficient flexibility for re-assessing country needs annually in the light of new economic developments.

References

COHEN, D. (1993), "Low Investment and Large LDC Debt in the 1980s", *American Economic Review*, Vol. 83, No. 2 (June).

COHEN, D. (1995), "The Sustainability of African Debt", mimeo., Ecole Normale Superieure, Paris.

COMMONWEALTH SECRETARIAT EXPERT GROUP (1996), "Note on The Multilateral Debt Problem", mimeo., 3 February (draft).

EURODAD (1995), *World Credit Tables: Creditor-Donor Relations from Another Perspective*, 1994-1995 edition (Brussels).

GOVERNMENT OF UGANDA (1995a), *A Strategy for Reducing the External Debt of Uganda*, 15 July.

GOVERNMENT OF UGANDA (1995b), Proposal for a Multilateral Debt Fund, 15 July.

GOVERNMENT OF UGANDA (1995c), Speech by Mr. Mayanja-Nkangi, Minister of Finance and Economic Planning, Uganda, to the Commonwealth Finance Ministers' Meeting, Jamaica, 5 October.

GREEN, Reginald H. (1996), "Debt Burden Reduction, Lending, Concessional Finance: Relative Cost Effectiveness Permutations and Combinations", paper to DCN, February.

GREENE, J., and D. VILLANUEVA (1991), "Private Investment in Developing Countries", *IMF Staff Papers*, Vol. 38, No. 1 (March), pp. 33-58.

HADJIMICHAEL, M. et al. (1995), Sub-Saharan Africa: Growth, Savings and Investment, 1986-93, *Occasional Paper*, No. 118 (Washington, D.C.: IMF), January.

HARDY, Chandra (1995), "The Case for Multilateral Debt Relief for Severely-Indebted Countries", in UNCTAD, *International Monetary and Financial Issues for the 1990s*, Vol. VII (UNCTAD/GID/G.24/7) (New York and Geneva: United Nations), pp. 27-40.

IMF (1993), "Review of Experience Under ESAF-Supported Arrangements", *Occasional Paper* (Washington, D.C.).

IMF (1995), "Official Financing for Developing Countries", *Occasional Paper* (Washington, D.C.), December.

KASEKENDE, Louis; Damoni KITABIRE, and Matthew MARTIN (1997), "Capital Inflows and Macroeconomic Policy in Sub-Saharan Africa", in UNCTAD, *International Monetary and Financial Issues for the 1990s*, Vol. VIII (New York and Geneva: United Nations).

KILLICK, Tony (1993), "Enhancing the cost-effectiveness of Africa's negotiations with its creditors", in UNCTAD, *International Monetary and Financial Issues for the 1990s*, Vol. III (UNCTAD/GID/G.24/3) (New York: United Nations).

KILLICK, Tony (1995), "Solving the Multilateral Debt Problem: Reconciling Relief with Acceptability", Report to Commonwealth Secretariat, September.

KUMAR, M., and K. MLAMBO (1995), "Determinants of Private Investment in Sub-Saharan Africa: an Empirical Investigation", mimeo., IMF, Washington, D.C..

MARTIN, Matthew (1991), *The Crumbling Facade of African Debt Negotiations: No Winners* (London: Macmillan).

MARTIN, Matthew (1995), (with Susan Lukwago and Nils Bhinda), "A Sustainable Proposal for Reducing the Burden of Uganda's Multilateral Debt", Report to the Government of Uganda and 6 major donors, 3 February.

MARTIN, Matthew (1996a), (with Alison Johnson and Nils Bhinda) "Sharing the Burden: Reducing Africa's Debt to Non-OECD Official Creditors", mimeo., UNCTAD, Geneva, February.

MARTIN, Matthew (1996b), (with Alison Johnson and Nils Bhinda), *ESAIDARM/USAID New Borrowing Workshop Manual*, materials on External Financing Sustainability.

MARTIN, Matthew, and Percy S. MISTRY (1994), "How Much Aid Does Africa Need?", report by Oxford International Associates to SIDA/DANIDA/Ford Foundation/S.G.Warburg.

MARTIN, Matthew, and Percy S. MISTRY (1996), "Financing Imports for Development in Low-Income Africa", report by External Finance for Africa/Oxford International Associates to SIDA/Government of Denmark.

MISTRY, Percy S. (1994), *Multilateral Debt: An Emerging Crisis?* (The Hague: FONDAD), February.

MISTRY, Percy S. (1995), "The Multilateral Debt Problem: Lurching Towards Resolution?", paper presented at OXFAM Seminar, September, London.

O'CALLAGHAN, Gary (1993), "The Structure and Operation of the World Gold Market", *Occasional Paper*, No. 105 (Washington, D.C.: IMF).

OECD (1996), *Development Cooperation*, 1996 Report (Paris).

OSHIKOYA, T. (1994), "Macroeconomic Determinants of Domestic Private Investment in Africa: An Empirical Analysis", *Economic Development and Cultural Change*, Vol. 42, No. 3 (April), pp. 573-596.

OVERSEAS DEVELOPMENT INSTITUTE/ALL-PARTY PARLIAMENTARY GROUP ON OVERSEAS DEVELOPMENT (1994), *Africa's Multilateral Debt: A Modest Proposal* (London).

SAVVIDES, A. (1992), "Investment Slowdown in Developing Countries During the 1980s: Debt Overhang or Foreign Capital Inflows", *Kyklos*, Vol. 45, No. 3.

WOODWARD, David (1996a), "IMF Gold Sales as a Source of Funds for Multilateral Debt Reduction" draft paper for EURODAD *World Credit Tables*, forthcoming.

WOODWARD, David (1996b), "Debt Sustainability and the Debt Overhang in Highly-Indebted Poor Countries: Some Comments on the IMF's View", draft paper for EURODAD *World Credit Tables*.

WORLD BANK (1994a), *Reducing the Debt Burden of Poor Countries*. Development in Practice Series, November.

WORLD BANK (1994b), *World Debt Tables*, 1993/1994 edition (Washington, D.C.).

WORLD BANK (1995a), *The Multilateral Debt Facility*, draft internal document, 21 July.

WORLD BANK (1995b), *World Debt Tables*, 1994/1995 edition (Washington, D.C.).

FROM PLAN TO MARKET:
THE WORLD DEVELOPMENT REPORT 1996

AN ASSESSMENT

Peter Murrell*

Abstract

This essay assesses the World Development Report 1996 *(WDR), which examines the post-socialist economic transition. The overall assessment is that the WDR is of high quality, with a clear structure, thoughtful discussion of difficult issues, and skilful exposition. The WDR has two distinct parts, the first examining liberalization, stabilization and enterprise reform, the second discussing broader reforms. In the first part, the accumulated experience of transition is central; the second contains a more general discussion, because lessons from transition are less complete on these longer-term reforms.*

The essay compares the WDR's conclusions with the standard policies advocated by the World Bank, showing that the highlighted conclusions do not endorse those policies. The WDR contains material that could be used to challenge those policies, for example its treatment of China and its acknowledgment that partial, gradual reforms can work well.

The WDR's conclusions are affected by the questions it asks and does not ask, for example when it poses two stark, idealized alternatives, a rapid programme and partial and phased reforms. This distinction is problematic when the notion of rapid reform is taken to be synonymous with reforms producing good results. The focus on fast reforms aimed at long-term goals implies relatively little attention to the reduction of short-run inefficiencies.

The WDR presents a new analysis, leading to the strong policy prescription that for most transition countries faster liberalization is better. This essay concludes that this analysis has too many problems to be used to advocate the desired policy prescription.

This essay's disagreements with the WDR's judgments centre on the nature of the trade-offs in the short run and on how to react when first-best policy is foreclosed. While the WDR supports the prevailing policy stance of the World Bank on these issues, it does so weakly and not without citing counter-evidence.

---

*   The author was a member of a panel of outside experts that commented on various drafts of the *World Development Report*. His role on that panel was that of an outside commentator, the same role as in the writing of this paper. He gratefully acknowledges the comments from Gerry Helleiner on an earlier draft.

I. Introduction

Consider an academic or an official of a multilateral organization making new acquaintance with a country, considering the reform of its institutions and policies. This country, Ruritania, let it be said, is ripe for criticism. Monetary policy is loose, the central bank having legal, but not actual, independence. The trade regime, although more liberal than a few years ago, still suffers from numerous controls and interventions, fostering corruption. Local officials administer ad-hoc price controls and place constraints on the flow of goods between regions. With a large share of industrial wealth still owned by the State but State control diminishing, insiders are grabbing assets at bargain prices. The financial system is weighed down by non-performing loans made at the Government's behest. The rule of law is a sideshow in economic calculus.

Ruritania is obviously ripe for the "shock-therapy, neo-liberal" surgery that has been advocated by the IMF, the World Bank, and a large number of influential academics over the last few years. This surgery has been especially prominent in the advice given to countries that have been emerging from communism, which are the focus of the *1996 World Development Report* (World Bank, 1996; henceforth *WDR* or *Report*).

But wait. Shouldn't our adviser ask how Ruritania is faring in pursuit of economic progress, before advocating a large change fraught with risks? China is one such Ruritania, with an unparalleled record of economic performance over the last eighteen years. If our adviser compared China's institutions and policies against the standard menu advocated by the World Bank and the IMF and then advocated sweeping reforms on the basis of that comparison, surely there would be a risk of killing the goose that is laying the golden egg. As the experience of China shows, implementing the standard profile of policies and institutions is not a necessary condition for economic success in the process of economic transition.[1]

Shouldn't our adviser also ask whether the policy-makers of Ruritania have tried to apply the shock-therapy, neo-liberal treatment in the past? Russia is one such Ruritania, with a record of economic performance over the last five years that seems unimaginably bad compared to expectations in the late 1980s. Russia's reform experience shows that an attempted implementation of the standard reform policies is hardly a sufficient condition for economic success.[2]

China and Russia, in their own ways, signal the deep gaps in our understanding of the bases of success and failure in economic transition, and indeed in economic development in general. China has been profoundly successful by adopting gradual liberalizing policies buttressed at every stage by elements of the old policy-making regime. To what extent has the success of China been dependent on the combination of the old and the new and to what extent has the old allowed the new to proceed and function effectively? How can China have succeeded so dramatically with so few elements of the institutional profile that are usually considered so crucial for economic success? These are two of the most important questions facing those studying the transition. The *WDR* is to be complemented in challenging the reader to think of these questions, even if it does so implicitly rather than explicitly. But there is a cost in terms of the consistency of the *WDR*'s message and that of its sponsor. The message that countries should quickly implement neo-liberal reforms, which has been at the heart of World Bank advice for the countries in transition, appears in the *WDR* but in an equivocal manner. This equivocation, prompted it seems most of all by Chinese experience, constitutes an important departure, a point that will be discussed in section III below.

In Russia, the standard shock-therapy reform was initiated in 1992 and then suffered almost immediate retrenchment. Economic and policy developments in subsequent years were very much affected by this initial burst of reform, especially by the destruction of the central administration that was a component of this reform. In considering the applicability of the standard reform model for countries such as Russia, there is the fundamental question of why the initial burst of policy moves was not sustained in that country. In what way did the initial burst of neo-liberal, primarily destructive policies, set in train the events of subsequent years? The *WDR* eschews analysis of this question, implicitly preferring to view the progress of liberalization in subsequent years as independent of the events of 1992. This approach raises serious questions concerning the *WDR*'s most determined effort to sustain elements of the shock-therapy, neo-liberal message, when the *Report* examines the relation between liberalization and economic success. This issue will be discussed in section IV.

Section II describes the structure and content of the *WDR*. Section III.A contains an evaluation of the

WDR's conclusions, examining how the *Report* draws back from endorsing the policies that have been advocated by the World Bank in the last years. In section III.B the evidence in the *Report* that could be used to mount a criticism of those policies will be reviewed. Section IV discusses analytical features of the *WDR*, focusing on the questions that the *WDR* addresses and the methods employed in examining the effects of liberalization.

II. A summary and general evaluation of the *WDR 1996*

The *WDR* is a work of high quality whose consistent organization, clear discussion of difficult issues, and skilful exposition all serve to make a document that is more often persuasive than not. The presentation of statistical information in particular is balanced and evocative. Future researchers will be able to use the lode of information that was prepared for the *Report* and that will appear in background papers. The range of issues discussed is impressive, in light of the obvious space constraints. On many of these issues the *WDR* offers convincing analyses.

A. Structure

The coverage of the *WDR* follows a pattern that is fairly standard in the literature on transition. The four chapters in its first half, entitled "The Challenge of Transition", deal with those aspects of policy that were most easily conceptualized at the beginning of transition and that were prime candidates for early policy moves - liberalization, stabilization, and enterprise reform, the latter heavily focused on privatization.[3] It is these chapters that have most to say about the results of the policies implemented in the transition countries. They contain much information and the most controversial elements of analysis, to be discussed in section IV.B below.

The second part of the *WDR*, "The Challenge of Consolidation", examines a broader range of reforms, most of which involve institutional construction that can take a decade or more to complete. There is discussion of the development of legal institutions, the building of financial systems, the changing role of Government, the reform of health and education, and the opening to the world economy.

This structure is both conventional and reasonable, with one caveat addressed in the next paragraph. Given that the avowed aim of the *WDR* is to examine the actual experience of transition (page 5), relatively more space might have been devoted to the subjects of chapters 1 and 2, liberalization and stabilization, since there is so much more transition-country experience on these issues than on the topics examined in later chapters.

What could be missing from this seemingly comprehensive picture? As is standard in Western analyses of transition processes, the structure follows almost directly from what Western advisers would like to achieve in terms of policies and institutional creation. The problem when adopting this standard approach is that it forces one to conceive of the transition process as simply destruction of the old and construction of the new, rather than a process of transformation in which much remains, much mutates, and much dies (Stark, 1992). This structure makes it difficult to ask which existing features of the economies and societies have helped to ameliorate problems at the beginning of the transition and which traditional structures have acted as functional substitutes for the vitally needed institutions that can only be created in decades. The Chinese case brings these questions to the fore and the *WDR* prompts us to pose them, but the *Report*'s structure ensures that they will not be answered. We learn about the elements of Chinese reforms that are consistent with the standard menu, not about the aspects that are very different.[4]

This weakness in the *WDR* is not a reflection of this document alone. The *WDR* is a product of the discipline of economics and of the way in which academic economists and multilateral institutions study and interact with developing countries and their policy-makers. It reflects such disparate factors as the decline of area studies in academia and the perceived bureaucratic need to keep officials of multilaterals at a distance from their client countries. Given these factors, perhaps there is no alternative to the approach of the *WDR* at present, but it is important to be aware of the limitations that this approach imposes.[5] The simple fact is that economists are usually not intellectually equipped and often not philosophically predisposed to analyze the unique features of a society, in order to advocate changes that fit well into the existing structures.

B. Style

The style of the *WDR*'s analysis varies across its different chapters. There are three distinctive types of literature on the transition: normative, descriptive, and positive (Murrell, 1995), the relative importance of which has changed as transition progresses. On the fall of communism, *normative* papers were the most common. Such papers seek lessons on the strategy or tactics of reform that follow from the economics literature, usually relying on examples from Western economies or advanced middle-income countries such as Chile. A significant part of the *WDR* is devoted to such normative analyses, in which the policy lessons have not been generated by, or tested upon, transition experience. This is especially the case in the latter half of *WDR*. In such areas as the reform of legal institutions, the functioning of Government, and the development of financial systems, the lessons of transition are highly incomplete, simply because not enough time has elapsed.

The second type of literature is a *descriptive* one, portraying the progress of policy, of institutional reforms, and of the paths of major economic variables. This is an important aspect of the *WDR* and it is well carried out. The tables and figures are informative and the reader is given a large number of important anecdotes that help to suggest the flavour of developments. Chapters 3 and 4, on privatization and social welfare, are especially strong in this regard.

To provide such description, there is a pressing need to collect information beyond that readily available from the authorities. This is not only because available data is of poor quality, but also because dramatic changes are occurring in variables not usually reported by Governments, such as the degree of freedom to engage in market activity. In this respect, the authors of the *WDR* have done a significant favour for researchers by constructing a consistent series charting the progress of economic liberalization in the transition countries. Summary statistics appear in the *WDR* and a background paper contains more detailed information, presenting three separate measures that chart the changing level of economic freedoms in internal markets, in foreign trade, and in ease of private sector entry across all the transition countries during 1989-1995.[6] These data are very important research tools and they will be used, and misused, by researchers many times in the future.[7] Other examples of new data summarized briefly in the *WDR* and appearing in background papers are those on the growth of financial institutions

(Claessens, 1996) and on trade and trade arrangements (Kaminski et al., 1996).

A final style of discussion, which might be called *positivist*, aims to advance knowledge, and policy advice, by analyzing transition processes themselves. Indeed, this type of discussion should be the fulcrum of the *WDR*, since: "This report is devoted to exploring the experience of the economies in transition, to identifying which approaches work and which do not, and to pinpointing the critical elements of success" (page iii).

In fact, it is only in the first half of the *WDR* where the accumulated experience of the transition economies is dominant, when the focus is on liberalization, stabilization, enterprise reform (particularly privatization), and the effects of these measures on living standards and labour markets. The *WDR* is simply too ambitious in claiming that it is "devoted to exploring the experience of the economies in transition". On many aspects of reforms it is just too early to verify, modify, or refute existing knowledge using transition experience.

Even for early reforms such as liberalization and stabilization, key pieces of information are still to be generated. One central question concerns the extent to which the effectiveness of different reforms varies with starting conditions. A comprehensive answer to this question must reflect the timing of recovery in the countries with the worst starting conditions - the poorer, more isolated, former Soviet republics. But, this recovery was starting only as the *WDR* went to press. Similarly, although chapter 3 says much that is useful about the workability and the immediate effects of privatization schemes, the importance of privatization must lie in its effect on economic performance, something that will only show up in the data after several years.

In sum, the *WDR* should be regarded as an early analysis of the experience of transition. The *Report* is preliminary since it will take a decade or more for the full effects of early reforms to be clearly evident and for major institutional reforms to be completed. This is not to say that publication of this *WDR* is premature. The analysis of transition processes is already having some effect on views of the workability of different reforms. Nevertheless, another *WDR* on the same topic will be needed in ten years time.

III. The perspective on transition, explicit and implicit, of the *WDR*

The *WDR* is necessarily a political and bureaucratic document. It emanates from a large, high-profile organization and is written by a committee. It navigates a sea of criticism and comment, carrying careers through the surf, confronting waves of entrenched bureaucratic interests and conventional wisdoms, leaving in its wake discarded ideas and individuals. Therefore, the reader looking for the work's true significance must often dig below the surface, to examine what is missing from the *Report* and to highlight information included in the document that has not been emphasized. The dog that does not bark is as important as the one that does.

In the case of the *WDR*, it is especially important to compare conclusions against expectations, the latter based on the typical transition-economy policies advocated by the World Bank. For the last seven years, the World Bank has tended to side with the "all-out approach" or the "fast as possible on all fronts" strategy, adopting a neo-liberal endpoint as the over-riding goal.[8] This has implied an approach in which an abstract endpoint, say free trade or the absence of subsidies, is an objective to be reached as soon as politically feasible, without consideration for the phasing of such moves from an economic point of view. It has implied an emphasis on the destruction of the old institutions with no consideration of their possible functionality in the short run, as bridging elements of a transition strategy. The World Bank has tended to support a "constructivist" point of view, to use Hayek's term, implying a deep faith in the workability of institutions designed by technocrats, even distant technocrats, as when laws are written in Washington for countries emerging from the dark years of communism. In all of this, the potential risks in radical reform are downplayed (Fanelli et al., 1992).

In comparing the *WDR* to the policy perspective summarized in the previous paragraph, two features stand out. First, the highlighted conclusions of the *WDR* do not amount to the same policy perspective. Certainly, there are interpretations of those highlighted conclusions that could provide sustenance for those who look to the *Report* for a justification of the types of reforms that the World Bank and the IMF have pushed in the past. But this is hardly surprising, given the bureaucratic and political nature of the generation of this *Report*. What is surprising is that a reasonable interpretation of those highlighted conclusions could underpin policies of a very different tenor. Second,

there are facts and arguments in the *WDR* that might be used as the basis of a challenge to the intellectual underpinning of the World Bank's past policies. This challenge is not directly made in the *WDR*. Nevertheless, there are hints of a change in world view. These two features of the *Report* are examined separately in the next two sub-sections.

A. *Explicit conclusions of the* WDR

Is the *WDR* a clear endorsement of the shock-therapy, neo-liberal approach, with which the World Bank has tended to align itself in the past six years? No, "The Report's core message is that firm and persistent application of good policy yields large benefits" (page 5). Good policy includes "extensive liberalization" and "determined stabilization" (page 5), but the speed and scope implied by the adjectives in these phrases is left open to interpretation. We learn that "decisive and consistent reform pays off" (page 9) and that "constancy in reforms has been vital for restoring growth and containing inflation" (page 19). But only those who wanted to keep central planning, or were of inconstant temperament, could disagree. Even in chapter 2, which comes closest to supporting the all-out approach, there is retreat in the conclusions, which simply state that "countries that liberalize markets and preserve economic stability are rewarded" (page 43). Tito, Kadar, and Gorbachev might have said the same thing.

The final chapter of the *WDR* offers seven "Lessons of Experience", which are the definitive compilation of its findings. Let us examine each in turn, commenting on their implications for the philosophies of reform and the policies that the *WDR* endorses.

(1) Consistent policies, combining liberalization of markets, trade, and new business entry with reasonable price stability, can achieve a great deal - even in countries lacking clear property rights and strong market institutions.

We might note that "liberalization of markets, trade, and new business entry" does not imply an absence of central government intervention, say, into the affairs of State enterprises, nor a move to free trade in a few months, as advocated by some. "Reasonable price stability" does not imply that countries should aim to bring stabilization down from high levels in a very short time, as has been implicit in many IMF-guided first attempts at stabilization. Since the *WDR* buttresses this conclusion by reference to China and Viet Nam, it can hardly be construed to endorse a shock-therapy, neo-liberal approach.[9]

(2)   Differences between countries are very important, both in setting the feasible range of policy choice and in determining the response to reforms.

This conclusion admits an immediate corollary - that policy choices should be calibrated to the characteristics of the country in question. Because the response to specific reforms will be determined by country characteristics, the optimal package of reforms must, under weak conditions, differ across countries. A policy-maker could certainly regard this conclusion as being an invitation to argue that his or her country should not be faced by the standard set of conditionalities.

(3)   An efficient response to market processes requires clearly defined property rights - and this will eventually require widespread private ownership.

The word "eventually" implies a retreat from an endorsement of rapid privatization. Indeed, this conclusion does not even endorse privatization itself, since its policy implications are consistent with the processes that are occurring in China, and to some extent in Poland, where new private sectors are creating widespread private ownership through superior growth.[10] Indeed, "widespread private ownership" does not imply much about the size of the residual State sector.

(4)   Major changes in social policies must complement the move to the market - to focus on relieving poverty, to cope with increased mobility, and to counter the adverse inter-generational effects of reform.

This conclusion results from the *WDR*'s candid assessment of the effects on poverty and re-distribution of the first years of liberalization and stabilization. It is a conclusion that will raise few objections. If its implications were followed, then major reforms in World Bank policy would be required. "Major changes in social policies" would need to become as important in conditionality as a balanced budget.

(5)   Institutions that support markets arise both by design and from demand.

The *WDR* has an effective discussion of the way in which laws and institutions arise from the interplay of State action and the demands of citizens and powerful economic actors. It argues that laws cannot be simply transferred from foreign quarters, but must be calibrated to the needs and institutions of the recipient society. This conclusion easily fits within schools of legal development that have very different perspectives, including the "law and economics" and "law and society" schools (Posner, 1972; Friedman, 1977). The conclusion does, however, remove the ground from under the many scholars and development practitioners who have plied their trade in transition countries in the past few years by presenting textbook laws for adoption, without talking to the citizens or enterprises that would be subject to these laws.

(6)   Sustaining the human capital base for growth requires considerable reengineering of the education and health delivery systems.

Given that the education and health-care delivery systems of the communist countries were so intimately tied to their economic and political systems, it would be hard to find a dissenter from this nevertheless important conclusion.

(7)   International integration can help to lock in successful reforms.

The integration of the reforming countries into the world economy and more generally into the international arena of intellectual, technological and informational exchange is a central aspect of transition. On this there is little disagreement. The *WDR*'s statement of its conclusion leaves open a number of questions: what is the appropriate speed of economic opening, whether a phased opening could serve other goals of transition, what is the degree of opening that is the goal, and what dimensions of opening are most important.[11] These are all questions that might have different answers for different countries.

In sum, we have seen that the highlighted conclusions of the *WDR* do not endorse the central tenets of the strategies that the IMF and the World Bank have advocated for countries in transition in the last six years. Of course, the *WDR* does not explicitly acknowledge this. Nevertheless, policy-makers receiving World Bank aid, and subject to conditionality, can certainly hope that the present *WDR* represents the beginning of a process of intellectual adjustment within the World Bank. In the following sub-section, it will be argued that the *WDR* contains information that provides the seeds for such adjustment.

B. The elements of a criticism of past transition policies

Suppose one reads the *WDR* with a desire to collect evidence to criticize the "shock-therapy, neo-liberal" approach to reforms. Could one find such evidence? The following provide some examples.

1. What is "all-out reform"?

When the *WDR* makes its ambivalent case for "all-out reform", the meaning of that term is usually left ambiguous.[12] However, Viet Nam's reforms are characterized as "bold" and not phased or gradual (box 1.4, page 21). Vietnamese reforms began in 1986 in a limited fashion, but with many elements that later proved very beneficial during the stage of more intense reforms. Inflation took six years to fall below the IMF's favourite target of 10 per cent a year. After ten years of reform, the extent of liberalization in Viet Nam is still below that of 16 of the 26 countries in Central and Eastern Europe and the Newly Independent States (figure 1.2, page 14). The State sector was restructured by the Government itself, rather than being simply liberalized at the beginning of reforms.[13] During the last ten years, the size of Viet Nam's State sector increased as a proportion of a rapidly growing economy. If Vietnamese reforms fit the World Bank's definition of "bold and not phased or gradual", then there is a much wider spectrum of reform programmes that fit under the World Bank's philosophical umbrella than many reforming Governments - and economists - previously thought.

2. The case of China

The *WDR*'s treatment of China and its explicit acknowledgment that partial, gradual reforms can work, and work very well, is important. Admittedly, the *Report* does try to argue that those types of reforms could not have worked in most countries. However, this argument is mainly based on political considerations and questions relating to the degree of governmental capacity. Thus, more narrowly economic arguments are implicitly downplayed in the choice between the "all-out approach" and phased or gradual reforms.

More importantly, at several points the *WDR* suggests that the phasing of reforms and the reliance on the old instruments has improved economic performance in China. For example, the partial controls present during the gradual liberalization served a coordinating function, limiting disruptions. Gradualism contributed to success (page 25). Even as late as 1994-1995, administrative controls helped the process of stabilization (page 35). Moreover, "With ... the ability to impose direct controls, the Chinese Government was able to liberalize along a dual-track process without seriously undermining macroeconomic balance (page 143)".[14] Had the authors of the *WDR* possessed the philosophical bent to examine the institutional features of these aspects of policy, one suspects that much important information could have been conveyed to policy-makers in other countries.

Of course, part of the Chinese success is due to fortunate structural features of the economy. For example, Sachs and Woo (1994) focus on the relatively small scale of State industry, the relative shallowness of Chinese planning, the structural linkages to export markets, etc. The *WDR* takes a balanced approach to this debate, associating China's success both with the character of its reforms and structural advantages. This is in contrast to Sachs and Woo, who emphasize the limitations of China's reforms, leaving the reader with the improbable notion that there is nothing remarkable about a period of economic policy which has produced a leading candidate for the most successful episode of economic development in history. A more balanced approach than in Sachs and Woo, complementary to that in the *WDR*, can be found in Walder (1995) and its accompanying symposium, which offers some economic lessons of the Chinese transition.

3. The costs of transition

The *WDR* does not shrink from discussing the exceedingly large costs of transition, while not highlighting them. Chapter 4 argues that the output declines have contributed greatly to poverty. If the World Bank's prime goal is the reduction in poverty and if the existing policy approach has been accompanied by such immense increases in poverty, then surely there must be a need to re-think the present policy approach.

Such a re-evaluation might begin by examining East Germany's "instant" transition, which is regarded as being as close to the "all-out approach" as has occurred (page 9). In East Germany, "Transition has relegated an entire generation to the economic sidelines" (box 1.1, page 10). It is absolutely transparent that these two observations constitute a damning criticism of the "all-out approach", at least for any country that did not have a big brother to provide an instant welfare State.

On the costs of transition, one should also mention the important comment that unemployment has not been a major contributor to restructuring (page 73). This information should be stressed since many believed, and still believe, that the level of unemployment would actually be a barometer of the progress of reforms. This comment constitutes an important change in perspective on the cost-benefit ratios of differing reforms.

4.   The old and the new

"In all regions growth has largely resulted from the lifting of restrictions on new entry and a surge of previously repressed activities" (page 22). Thus, there is an absence of large gains from the old State sectors of the economy, upon liberalization and stabilization. This observation reflects on the effectiveness of different policies toward these sectors. At the heart of the "shock-therapy, neo-liberal" approach is the advocacy of the complete liberalization of the old State sector at the beginning of reforms, followed by swift privatization (Lipton and Sachs 1990a, 1990b). The contrasting point of view would emphasize the costs of rapid change and of the withdrawal of direct control mechanisms in a sector that has been created in a non-market environment (Kornai, 1989; McKinnon, 1992; Murrell, 1992a).

If there has been a collapse of the old State sector due to absent institutions and distorted incentives (page 27), if direct controls help macroeconomic balance (page 143), and if privatization produces few effects quickly (page 55), then a rapid push to reform the old State sector has an exceedingly low benefit-cost ratio, compared to that derived from facilitating the growth of new sectors, which will eventually challenge the State sector. Hence, past policies might have focused more on increasing contestability and facilitating entry, rather than concentrating on revamping the old State sector and destroying the accompanying administrative mechanisms. There might have been more differentiation between policies for the new and for the old, recognizing that measures imposing high adjustment costs on old sectors are exactly the ones that most encourage the development of the new sectors.

This point does enter the *WDR* in minor ways. The many examples of Chinese policies constitute one such example. Another lies in the equivocation (page 50) on the need for the type of fast, desperate privatization that has often been advocated in the past. Indeed, when the *WDR* endorses workers' control of enterprises as a stop-gap transitional measure (page 50), it comes close to acknowledging this overall point of view.

5.   Top-down and bottom-up

Chapters 5 and 6 emphasize a balance between a bottom-up process and a top-down process in the development of important aspects of reforms. The attention and the plaudits given to China in the *WDR* would lead to the same conclusion. This is a point that is of immense importance to the tenor of policy. It leads attention away from a focus on the central levers of power and away from the design of large-scale programmes for social reconstruction. It leads toward the necessity of understanding the complex institutional structure that always exists at ground level and toward attempts to complement this structure, rather than simply trying to subvert it to create an ideal. It leads the policy-maker to focus on the present structure, rather than an ideal endpoint.

IV.   The analysis

The *WDR* is not a new piece of analysis; that is not its aim and should not be. Rather it is a summary and interpretation of existing research and factual information. However, there are two areas where analytical judgments do affect conclusions. The first lies in the questions that the *WDR* chooses to ask and on which it hangs its discussion of evidence. The second analytical choice centres on the way in which the *Report* examines the effects of liberalization. In this area, the *WDR*, and particularly one of its background papers (de Melo et al., 1996), adds a piece of original empirical work to the literature. This empirical work is important because it provides the one case in which the *WDR* comes closest to giving a resounding endorsement to the types of policies that the World Bank has advocated in the last few years. The following two subsections examine each of these areas of analysis.

A.   Are the right questions addressed?

1.   Two not-so-stark alternatives

The *WDR* begins by asking the reader to consider two stark, idealized alternatives - a "rapid, all-out programme" versus "partial and phased reforms" (page 9), emphasizing that these alternatives greatly simplify reality. Important elements of the *Report* are framed in terms of the comparative properties of these two alternatives.

In dealing with complex economic systems, there is a vital need to use such simplifying concepts. For example, the distinction between gradualism and shock therapy, even though murky, has probably helped policy-makers to frame issues and aided academic debate. Thus, the objection is not to the use of simple alternatives, but rather to question whether they are employed in a analytically satisfactory and consistent manner in the *WDR*.

The difficulty with discussing the speed of reform is that this is a highly ambiguous concept unless one qualifies the essential components of direction.[15] Stalin, after all, was no slouch in matters of economic reform. In narrowly defined areas of policy, such as the liberalization analyzed in the *WDR*'s chapter 2, this problem is not so important. (Although, as the foregoing discussion of the Vietnamese case shows, the boundaries of what is deemed a fast reform might be quite flexible.) But in broader matters the notion of speed becomes quite problematic. This is especially the case when conclusions about one aspect of reform, for example on liberalization, are used to buttress conclusions about the overall speed of all reforms (page 143).

In using the term "rapid reform", there is a natural tendency to employ it in a way that becomes synonymous with "implementing reforms that produce good results". This occurs, for example, in the *WDR*'s approving characterization of Viet Nam's dirigiste State sector reforms as radical and in the endorsement of a "jail" for large loss-making enterprises (box 1.4, page 21 and pages 47-48). The point here is not to argue that these particular policies were ill-advised, but rather that there is paradox in treating these policies as if they were perfectly consonant with a programme whose underlying philosophy is the speediest possible liberalization.

2. The long run versus adjustment in the short run

Economics provides its most powerful policy lessons when they are framed in the context of a long-run idealized world rather than in a second-best short run. Thus, the economist's advice on reforms usually concentrates on the endpoint of policy rather than the

very special problems of adjustment that arise when the foundations of a system are changing. That advice is a catalog of how to destroy one system and build another, rather than an analysis of how to function in, and to move through, a transitional State when elements of both systems are in existence. The *WDR* does not escape from this problem, although it is no worse than the average work in this respect.

This focus on the endpoint does mean that there are some missed opportunities to examine important questions. For example, the *Report* argues that early in transition some changes can be quick while others are slow, resulting in large inefficiencies at the early stages of reform (page 9). However, the *Report* largely ignores addressing how these inefficiencies might be ameliorated. According to the *WDR*, China has been successful in this respect, but the policy-maker interested in knowing how China accomplished this success will not learn very much from the *WDR*. One wonders how a policy-maker, faced with enormous short-run political pressures, would react to a report that does not decide to devote any space to a detailed discussion of policies that might ameliorate declines in national income that have ranged from 20 to 50 per cent.

Similarly, the analyses of enterprise behaviour and stabilization are centred on the medium term rather than the short run. For example, studies which point out that enterprise behaviour is highly dysfunctional in the first years of rapid reform (Pinto et al., 1992; Berg, 1994a) are ignored in favour of studies that show adjustments occurred later (Pinto et al., 1993; Berg, 1994b).

This focus on the implementation of policies for the long run also has the effect of distracting one's attention from what should be the ultimate objective of policy, improving economic welfare as soon as possible. The successful implementation of policy sometimes becomes the goal, ignoring the gestation periods for the effects of policies. Thus, when the Czech Republic's mass privatization programme is pronounced the most successful to date (page 56), one might question the criteria being employed to evaluate policies since the consequences of that programme on human welfare can hardly be known as yet.

3. The old and the new in the short run

The focus on the long run discourages the policy-maker from looking at the short run with a pragmatic eye. The long-run view simply encourages policy-makers to think of old institutions as targets for destruction, not asking, for example, whether the old instruments of direct intervention could supplement standard stabilization tools during the first years of sharp change.[16]

The focus on the long term also takes the policy-maker's attention away from the question of whether there any reasons to differentiate between the liberalization of the new private sector and the liberalization of the State sector, in the short run. In fact, as explained above, the *WDR* gives empirical information that would encourage such differentiation, the old State sector having contributed so much less to the recovery in Eastern Europe than the new private sector. But the unwillingness to differentiate in policy between these two sectors means that questions are never posed on the trade-offs between encouraging the new and reforming the old. To the extent that there is limited governmental capacity, acknowledgment of the differences between these sectors, would allow policy-makers to best allocate that capacity.

4.   The contrast between extremes versus trade-offs at the margin

When the *WDR* comes to strong conclusions, it is often through analyses that are implicitly driven by contrasts between countries at the opposite ends of the reform spectrum, between the Ukraines and the Polands. Such analyses are appropriate if the goal is to convince policy-makers that they should not follow the Ukrainian model, a worthy objective, but not an ambitious one. The more challenging questions arise when examining trade-offs at the margin within a package of coherent reforms: whether a country such as Poland lost much by delaying privatization; whether Russia could have gained by slowing down its privatization; which residual price controls (all countries had them) were beneficial and which were costly; which old State structures have slowed adjustment and which have helped.[17]

In the same vein, the *WDR* emphasizes how important it is to get inflation down to reasonable levels, without suggesting that there are trade-offs in the speed of adjustment. The *Report* suggests that growth is inconsistent with an annual rate above 40 per cent, but that there should be a lower target in the long run. However, a policy-maker might like to receive information on how quickly he should aim to reduce a high rate of inflation to the 40 per cent level.

5.   The interaction between starting conditions and choice of policy

The *WDR* acknowledges that starting conditions should affect the character of reforms, but devotes little effort to examining the relationship between starting conditions and the nature of reforms to be undertaken. Should the targeted inflation rate in the first year of stabilization vary with the existing rate? If price liberalization results in local officials controlling prices (Murrell et al., 1996), should the centre adapt its policies on price liberalization? Should the amount of control on the State sector in the first two years of reforms be related to the amount of control existing when reforms begin? Should an incompetent and corrupt administrative structure be reformed and used or simply destroyed? If there is a low level of trust in government is it worth forsaking economically important but unpopular policies in order to increase that level of trust? Is a badly drafted law that absorbs local knowledge better or worse than a well-drafted one that is easily misunderstood by those without any familiarity with Western legal concepts? These are the real choices that arise in transition.

6.   Trade-offs

As indicated above, the question of trade-offs in transition policy is not one that is very prominent in the *WDR*. Of course, short-run trade-offs are very difficult to understand and to analyze. This is why the "fast as possible" policy is so beguiling: that policy allows one to ignore decisions that are so agonizingly difficult. Yet these are the very decisions that policy-makers must confront everyday. Thus, any work on transition that offers advice to policy-makers should necessarily be able to suggest an answer when the policy-maker asks: "I have 1000 competent officials. Where should I allocate them?". This involves questions of whether to focus on privatization or legal issues or social welfare policies or governmental administration. The *WDR* ignores addressing this question. In the present neo-liberal climate, the result is that social protection is largely forgotten and that the quality of governmental administration is ignored.

On trade-offs implicit in more detailed policies, the *WDR* does do a better job. In particular, chapter 3 gives important insights into the relative costs and benefits of the various methods of privatization. Similarly, chapter 6 gives the reader a sense of the difficult choices to be made in reforming financial systems.

B. The analysis of liberalization

As befits a work of synthesis, the *WDR* contains few elements of original research. However, chapter 2 is an exception in that it introduces new data, indices of the progress of liberalization, which are used in a regression framework to drive the *Report*'s strongest conclusion, and the one that is most supportive of the World Bank's general stance over the last few years. This is the policy prescription that for most transition countries faster liberalization is better. The present sub-section examines this and other elements of the analysis in the *WDR*.

1. The method

The *WDR*, and supporting background papers, examine the effects of the speed and the degree of liberalization on economic performance.[18] The methodology involves using an "average liberalization index for 1989-95", which measures the average degree of economic freedom in the various transition countries over that time period. This measure is related to growth rates in the periods 1989-1995 and 1994-1995. A significant relationship between growth and the liberalization index appears.[19] Although the underlying data for this index has three components - relating to the degree of freedom to engage in domestic transactions, to establish new firms, and to engage in international trade - the analysis in the *WDR* does not differentiate between these three aspects of liberalization.

The logic of using a multi-year average measure of the degree of economic freedom to explain growth is impeccable: firms will take time to adjust to the new policy environment, and the more time this environment has been in place the more permanent it will seem, thus encouraging firms to make costly adjustments. Unfortunately, this logic leads the researcher into an almost intractable problem given available data - it is difficult to differentiate between several hypotheses, all of which would cause the measured degree of economic freedom to be correlated with growth rates. This point arises from the fact that the average liberalization index used by the *WDR* actually embodies four separate pieces of information:

- the extent of pre-1990 reforms, because countries that enjoyed greater economic freedom before the fall of communism would score fairly high even if policy remained unchanged;

- the date at which the communist regimes fell,

because more extensive reforms only became possible at that date. Thus, Poland would naturally score higher on this index than Estonia because the latter's reforms began later, even though they were probably deeper. This means, unfortunately, that the average liberalization index could be a proxy for many other factors. For example, it is surely no coincidence that the anti-communist revolutions occurred first in those countries closest to Western Europe, but these countries are likely to perform better purely because of locational advantages.

- the speed of reforms. However, this index does not reflect this factor as strongly as one would like given the interpretation that the *WDR* hangs on the use of this index. For example, a country that went from central planning to complete economic freedom instantaneously on January 1st 1990 would only score 16 per cent less than a country that made this policy move in phases over the three years beginning in 1990.

- the depth of liberalizing reforms.

While it is obviously correct to argue that the first two factors are highly pertinent in explaining variations in economic performance across countries, these two factors have little connection to the major conclusions that the *WDR* draws from the use of the average liberalization index.[20] They weaken any attempts to use the index to conclude that: "Stronger ... liberalization spells a smaller output decline - and a stronger recovery" (figure 2.2, page 28).

There is a further, deeper, statistical problem in this analysis. The statistical analysis does not examine the issue of simultaneity: in which direction does causality flow? Does causality flow from faster liberalization to better performance or from better initial conditions to better performance to the sustaining of initial attempts at liberalization? A number of countries - Bulgaria, Russia, Kyrgyzstan, and Mongolia, for example - retreated somewhat on rather ambitious reforms after the depth of economic crisis was observed. This implies that there might be a statistical relation between economic performance and liberalization produced by the fact that countries with better initial conditions would have experienced lesser declines and might have had less of a tendency to reverse or slow down reforms.

Thus, we return to the important case raised in the opening of this essay, exemplified by Russia, where an initial attempt at fast liberalization and destruction of the old system led directly to a chaotic policy environment, in which the tenor of policy could neither be characterized as conforming to the all-out approach or to a systematic, gradualist reform. In two ways the *WDR* ignores the issues raised by this case. First, the statistical analysis of liberalization ignores the resultant simultaneity problems, preferring instead to view policy as exogenous. Second, the policy advice stemming from this statistical analysis effectively side-steps the issue of how to deal with countries that have not been able to implement the "all-out approach" to liberalization. What policy-makers in reforming countries need most is probably not further "proof" that the all-out approach is the best, but rather thoughts on what to do when that approach is not available to them.

2.   The adequacy of the evidence

It is common for economists to affect a greater degree of confidence in their prescriptions than the underlying evidence really justifies. The *WDR* is typical in this respect, rather than being either comparatively cautious or rash. Nevertheless, there are a number of places in the *Report* where an observer might disagree with the judgments on the available evidence. Let me cite a few examples.

There is quick dismissal of the possibility that the character of stabilization programmes might have led to declines in output (page 26). This is still surely the subject of legitimate debate, given the influential voices that have raised counter-claims (Berg and Blanchard, 1994; Calvo and Coricelli, 1992). It is a fact that the production levels of State industry in Poland dropped by 31 per cent in the month that its big-bang stabilization programme was introduced. There is a similar coincidence of the onset of determined stabilization and fall in production in several other countries. Although one could side with the *WDR* in assuming that factors not connected with stabilization were the prime culprits, a balanced assessment would certainly acknowledge that the evidence is hardly decisive.

The *WDR* concludes that "Establishing essentially free trade ... early on yields a particularly large return in these countries ..." (page 32). Apparently the evidence is not quite so clear. Summers (1993, p. iii), in developing lessons for Russia from a World Bank conference on the recessions in Eastern Europe, gave the following advice: "It was a mistake for Poland to move so fast to one of the world's freest trade regimes - for two reasons. The first is

the need for fiscal revenues. The second is the need for more time to manage change at the enterprise level".

On the issue of change at the enterprise level, the *WDR* emphasizes that there has been a "substantial adjustment" even by State enterprises (page 142). But this summation ignores parts of the picture that are very important for deliberations on reform policy. First, it ignores the fact that during the first two or three years of newly liberalized regimes the behaviour of State enterprises has been quite dysfunctional, showing a lack of responsiveness to the new circumstances, with large drops in productivity. Second, there is some indication that there is a non-linear relation between change and adjustment, too rapid a regime change causing firms to become less responsive to the new environment (Estrin et al., 1995; Ickes et al., 1995). Lastly, it is simply not clear that State enterprises are performing better on average than they did before reforms began. Hence, a reasonable picture of enterprise response to the new conditions would mention a period of non-adjustment and an aggregate decline in performance, followed by patchy recovery.

The key result, to date, on the performance of large privatized enterprises is that very few differences can be observed between privatized enterprises and non-privatized ones (Brada, 1996). The major difference is between new private firms and enterprises that are presently or formerly State-owned. This observation has very important consequences for deliberating on the role and configuration of privatization policy (Murrell, 1992a). This evidence is mentioned in the *WDR* (page 55), but not given its due weight. The *Report* is happier to cite methodologically problematic evidence showing the effects of privatization than equally problematic evidence that shows no effect (page 49). It is no inconsistency to hold the position that privatization is an important policy tool and simultaneously think that the effects of privatization will show up mainly in the long run. In the interests of keeping policy-makers well informed, this position seems the most reasonable one to take, given existing evidence.

V.   Conclusions

As is normal when reviewing a new work, more importance has been given to mentioning disagreements than agreements. But that tone should not be allowed to obscure the extent to which the reviewer finds himself in agreement with much of the *Report*. There are large swathes of the content of the *WDR* with which a large majority of economists can readily agree. In transition policy, there is virtual unanimity on the need for decisive and extensive liberalization, for monetary and fiscal policies consistent with reasonable rates of inflation, for undertaking policies that ensure that most of economic activity is eventually carried out in the private sector, and for developing an institutional framework that supports capitalism and free markets. As section III above makes clear, the highlighted conclusions of the *WDR* centre on those areas of policy where there is much agreement between economists. Thus, one can readily agree with "the Report's core message ... that firm and persistent application of good policy yields large benefits" (page 5).

The differences with the judgments of the *WDR* centre on what to do in the near term, on the nature of the trade-offs in the short run, and on how to react when application of first-best policy is foreclosed either by politics, or by the absence of suitable administrative mechanisms, or by the lack of skilled personnel who understand and are sympathetic to the mechanisms of a market economy. These are the areas in which economics, as a policy science, is the weakest and therefore where economists are most likely to find disagreements with each other. Unfortunately, these are exactly the areas that are most important to policy-makers.

In approaching these short-run issues, there are two, dissonant trends evident in the *WDR*. The first, and the most expected, is the analysis that aims to support the "all-out approach", which the World Bank has favoured in its policy advice over the last six years. The above discussion has tried to show that the support in the *WDR* for that approach is quite equivocal. Section III.A points out that conclusions highlighted by the *WDR* are too general to act as a buttress for the "all-out approach". Section III.B lists elements of the *Report*'s discussion that are inconsistent with the approach. Section IV.B argues that the *WDR*'s analysis in support of the all-out approach has too many methodological problems to be anything but suggestive of possibilities.

The second trend is the presence of evidence within the *WDR* that can be used to sustain a criticism of the World Bank's past policy advice for the transition countries. This evidence is clearly laid out, even if its implications are left implicit. Nevertheless, the *WDR* comes close to becoming a critic of the institution that has sponsored it.

These conflicting trends within the *WDR* might be understood as the result of two conflicting forces. First, there is the inertia behind the support for the shock-therapy, neo-liberal message. This support has been buttressed to some extent by the turnaround in Eastern Europe and the Baltics, a turnaround so welcome that it has made it easier to forget the years of deep economic crisis that followed the first reforms. Second, there is the contrasting evidence that emanates from the post-Soviet world, particularly from the CIS countries, and from China and Viet Nam. While it is clear that China's success is partly due to special, non-replicable conditions, it is equally clear that the Chinese reforms could not have worked at all if the shock-therapy, neo-liberal paradigm was the only means to understand transition processes. The *WDR* is to be congratulated in endeavouring to deal with the profound implications of Chinese success.

It remains to be seen, however, whether the *WDR* is a harbinger of deep changes in the perceptions of the workability of different reform policies.

Notes

1. Viet Nam also provides such evidence. Uzbekistan, which the *Report* largely ignores, hints at being an important data point in this respect. But at least another five years are needed to make any reasonable judgment on the effects of that country's reforms.

2. China and Russia score very closely on the measures of economic freedoms that were created as part of the background work for the *WDR* (de Melo et al., 1995). Hence, these countries would look equally problematic to the adviser. The difference between these two countries then lies in the route by which they reached the present levels of economic freedom and the institutional and policy aspects not captured in these measures.

3. The discussion of a fourth subject matter, social welfare and labour markets, centres on the consequences of these early reforms, particularly of liberalization and stabilization.

4. The interested reader can begin to gain insights into the distinctive aspects of the Chinese case by reading the essays by Jefferson and Rawski, Perkins, and Yusuf in the Spring 1994 issue of the *Journal of Economic Perspectives*.

5. For example, Murrell (1996) and its accompanying symposium suffer the same problem.

6. De Melo et al. (1996). The construction of such data is obviously a problematic exercise in itself, involving an uncomfortable amount of retrospect and judgment, something which is not to the taste of many economists. However, in the judgment of this reviewer, this is a valuable exercise, certainly improving upon loose qualitative statements of the policy stance of countries, providing the research community with a set of explicit numbers that can be used and debated.

7. See Fischer et al. (1996), and Aslund et al. (1996) for early examples.

8   World Bank (1991). In practice, there has been much variation within the World Bank on the types of programmes pursued in different transition countries. This author's impression, based on limited evidence, is that policies typically attributed to the World Bank are advocated most fervently by its top officials, who, being removed from the messy realities of everyday decisions, are able to function in a more abstract realm. Thus, the radical neo-liberal policies are present much more in the basic elements of conditionality than in both the monitoring of that conditionality and the narrower microeconomic programmes.

9   The paragraphs explaining this conclusion do contain one sentence in support of the standard prescription "... for the bulk of these economies ... faster and more consistent reform is better" (page 143). However, it is clear that the authors of the *WDR* allow a very broad interpretation of what is a "faster and more consistent reform".

10   Letting the private sector challenge the State sector by superior economic performance is the essence of an evolutionary, non-shock-therapy approach to transition (Murrell, 1992b).

11   Chapter 2 (pages 29-32) does advocate quick trade liberalization for a majority of transition countries, but the authors of the *Report* have chosen not the make this a part of their conclusions.

12   The ambiguous meaning of such terms as "shock therapy", "all-out reform", or evolutionary reform is a significant problem in discussing reform policy, a problem that this present essay does not escape. This problem is inherent in discussing a multi-dimensional choice, within a single term. This problem is well illustrated by trying to classify Kornai (1990) into an existing camp. Kornai's analysis is coherent and compelling, but not classifiable in the terms used in this paper. Thus, Kornai has in the past been characterized as both shock therapist and gradualist. Murrell (1993) argues that these terms are best seen as denoting an overall philosophy of reform, rather than specific policies.

13   The inter-relation between the Government and the State sector at the beginning of reforms is one crucial difference between the main competing models of reform. Contrast Lipton and Sachs (1990a, 1990b) and McKinnon (1992).

14   This use of the old direct measures to help in macroeconomic adjustment is also one of the crucial differences between the main competing models of reform; see Murrell (1992a).

15   To be sure, the *WDR* is not alone in this respect, most broad analyses of transition processes leave us with such inconsistencies.

16   This point is particularly important since standard stabilization tools are less effective when markets are poorly developed (Ickes and Ryterman, 1995).

17   The *WDR* does confront this type of question in some instances, for example, whether a country should immediately adopt completely free trade or whether delay can help adjustment (page 32). But it is not clear that it really come to grips with the question of trade-offs in trade liberalization. See section II.B.2 below.

18   One measure of the importance of this contribution of the *WDR* is that it has already spurred research by influential authors, Fischer et al. (1996) and Aslund et al. (1996), using the very data constructed for the *WDR*.

19   The word "liberalization" is somewhat of a misnomer, one that has the potential for confusion. Liberalization denotes change, while the liberalization index measures the degree of economic freedom, rather than changes in the degree of economic freedom. Thus, for example, the United States would score very high on this index even though it has not liberalized significantly in the last years. This point, although semantic, is important in interpreting results.

20   An analysis in one of the background papers does go some way toward blunting criticisms such as these, by introducing initial conditions into the regressions in which growth is related to liberalization. But that analysis cannot completely negate such criticisms, since the average liberalization index cannot be purely a measure of the speed and scope of reforms. The index is not the correct one to examine the hypothesis that the *WDR* uses it for.

References

ASLUND, Anders, Peter BOONE, and Simon JOHNSON (1996), "How to Stabilize: Lessons from Post-Communist Countries", paper presented at the Brookings Panel on Economic Activity, March 28-29.

BERG, Andrew (1994a), "The Logistics of Privatization in Poland", in Olivier J. Blanchard, Kenneth A. Froot and Jeffrey D. Sachs (eds.), *The Transition in Eastern Europe: Volume 1, Country Studies* and *Volume 2, Restructuring* (Chicago and London: The University of Chicago Press).

BERG, Andrew (1994b), "Does Macroeconomic Reform Cause Structural Adjustment? Lessons from Poland", *Journal of Comparative Economics*, Vol. 18, No. 3 (June).

BERG, Andrew, and Olivier J. BLANCHARD (1994), "Stabilization and Transition: Poland, 1990-1991", in Olivier J. Blanchard, Kenneth A. Froot and Jeffrey D. Sachs (eds.), *The Transition in Eastern Europe: Volume 1, Country Studies* and *Volume 2, Restructuring* (Chicago and London: The University of Chicago Press).

BRADA, Josef (1996), "Privatization is Transition: Or is it?", *Journal of Economic Perspectives*, Vol. 10, No. 2 (spring).

CALVO, Guillermo, and Fabrizio CORICELLI (1992), "Stabilizing a Previously Centrally Planned Economy: Poland 1990", *Economic Policy*, No. 14 (April).

CLAESSENS, Stijn (1996), "Banking Reform in Transition Countries", mimeo., World Bank (March).

DE MELO, Martha, Cevdet DENIZER, and Alan GELB (1996), "From Plan to Market: Patterns of Transition", mimeo., World Bank (April).

ESTRIN, Saul, Alan GELB, and Inderjit SINGH (1995), "Shocks and Adjustment by Firms in Transition: A Comparative Study", *Journal of Comparative Economics*, Vol. 21, No. 2 (October).

FANELLI, José M., Roberto FRENKEL, and Lance TAYLOR (1992), "The World Development Report 1991: A Critical Assessment", in *International Monetary and Financial Issues for the 1990s*, Vol. I (UNCTAD/GID/G24/1)(New York: United Nations), pp. 1-29.

FISCHER, Stanley, Ratna SAHAY, and Carlos VEGH (1996), "Stabilization and Growth in Transition Economies: Early Experience", *Journal of Economic Perspectives*, Vol. 10, No. 2 (spring).

FRIEDMAN, Lawrence M. (1977), *Law and Society: An Introduction* (Englewood Cliffs, N.J.: Prentice Hall).

ICKES, Barry, and Randi RYTERMAN (1995), "The Organization of Markets and Its Effect on Macroeconomic Stabilization", mimeo., World Bank.

ICKES, Barry, Randi RYTERMAN, and Stoyan TENEV (1995), "On Your Marx, Get Set, Go: The Role of Competition in Enterprise Adjustment", mimeo., World Bank.

JEFFERSON, Gary H., and Thomas RAWSKI (1994), "Enterprise Reform in Chinese Industry", *Journal of Economic Perspectives*, Vol. 8, No. 2.

KAMINSKI, Bartlomiej, Zhen Kun WANG, and L. Alan WINTERS (1996), "Foreign Trade in the Transition: The International Environment and Domestic Policy", *Studies of Economies In Transformation*, No. 20 (Washington D.C.: World Bank).

KORNAI, Janos (1990), *The Road to a Free Economy* (New York: Norton).

LIPTON, David, and Jeffrey SACHS (1990a), "Creating a Market Economy in Eastern Europe: The Case of Poland", *Brookings Papers on Economic Activity 1*, Vol. 1.

LIPTON, David, and Jeffrey SACHS (1990b), "Privatization in Eastern Europe: The Case of Poland", *Brookings Papers on Economic Activity*, Vol. 2.

McKINNON, Ronald (1992), *The Order of Economic Liberalization: Financial Control in the Transition to a Market Economy* (Baltimore: Johns Hopkins University Press).

MURRELL, Peter (1992a), "Evolution in Economics and in the Economic Reform of the Centrally Planned Economies", in Christopher C. Clague and Gordon Rausser (eds.), *Emerging Market Economies in Eastern Europe* (Cambridge, Mass.: Basil Blackwell).

MURRELL, Peter (1992b), "Evolutionary and Radical Approaches to Economic Reform", *Economics of Planning*, Vol. 25, No. 1.

MURRELL, Peter (1993), "What is Shock Therapy? What Did it Do in Poland and Russia?", *Post-Soviet Affairs*, Vol. 9, No. 2 (April-June).

MURRELL, Peter (1995), "The Transition According to Cambridge, Mass.", *Journal of Economic Literature*, Vol. XXXIII, No. 1 (March).

MURRELL, Peter (1996), "How far has the transition progressed?" *Journal of Economic Perspectives*, Vol. 10, No. 2 (spring).

MURRELL, Peter, Karen Turner DUNN, and Georges KORSUN (1996), "The Culture of Policy-Making in the Transition from Socialism: Price Policy in Mongolia", *Economic Development and Cultural Change*, forthcoming.

PERKINS, Dwight (1994), "Completing China's Move to the Market Economy", *Journal of Economic Perspectives*, Vol. 8, No. 2 (spring).

PINTO, Brian, Marek BELKA, and Stefan KRAJEWSKI (1992), "Microeconomics of Transformation in Poland: A Survey of State Enterprise Responses", *Working Paper*, WPS 982 (Washington D.C.: World Bank).

PINTO, Brian, Marek BELKA, and Stefan KRAJEWSKI (1993), "Transforming State Enterprises in Poland: Evidence on Adjustment by Manufacturing Firms", *Brookings Papers on Economic Activity*.

POSNER, Richard A. (1972), *Economic Analysis of the Law* (Boston: Little, Brown).

SACHS, Jeffrey, and Wing T. WOO (1994), "Structural Factors in the Economic Reforms of China, Eastern Europe, and the Former Soviet Union", *Economic Policy*, No. 18 (April).

STARK, David (1992), "Path Dependence and Privatization Strategies in East Central Europe", *East European Politics and Societies*, Vol. 6, No. 1 (winter).

SUMMERS, Lawrence H. (1993), "Foreword", in Mario I. Blejer, Guillermo A. Calvo, Fabrizio Coricelli and Alan H. Gelb (eds.), *Eastern Europe in Transition: From Recession to Growth?*, World Bank Discussion Papers, No. 196 (Washington D.C.).

WORLD BANK (1991), *World Development Report 1991: The Challenge of Development* (New York: Oxford University Press).

WORLD BANK (1996), *World Development Report 1996: From Plan to Market* (New York: Oxford University Press).

WALDER, Andrew G. (1995), "China's Transitional Economy: Interpreting its Significance", *The China Quarterly*, No. 144 (December).

YUSUF, Shahid (1994), "China's Macroeconomic Performance and Management During the Transition", *Journal of Economic Perspectives*, Vol. 8, No. 2 (spring).

UNITED NATIONS CONFERENCE ON TRADE AND DEVELOPMENT

Palais des Nations
CH-1211 GENEVE 10
Switzerland

International Monetary and Financial Issues for the 1990s

Volume V (1995)

United Nations Publication, Sales No. E.95.II.D.3
ISBN 92-1-112371-2

Göran Ohlin
The Negative Net Transfers of the World Bank
Louis Emmerij
A Critical Review of the World Bank's Approach to Social-Sector Lending and Poverty Alleviation
Nguyuru H.I. Lipumba
Structural Adjustment Policies and Economic Performance of African Countries
Robert Wade
The East Asian Miracle: Why the Controversy Continues
Alfred Maizels
The Functioning of International Markets for Primary Commodities: Key Policy Issues for Developing Countries
Donald R. Lessard
Effective Use of Financial Markets for Risk Management by Developing Countries: An Overview

Volume VI (1995)

United Nations Publication, Sales No. E.95.II.D.7
ISBN 92-1-112375-5

Manuel R. Agosin, Diana Tussie and Gustavo Crespi
Developing Countries and the Uruguay Round: An Evaluation and Issues for the Future
Dani Rodrik
Developing Countries After the Uruguay Round
Ann Weston
The Uruguay Round: Unravelling the Implications for the Least Developed and Low-Income Countries

Volume VII (1996)

United Nations Publication, Sales No. E.96.II.D.2
ISBN 92-1-112394-1

John Williamson
A New Facility for the IMF?
Ariel Buira and Roberto Marino
Allocation of Special Drawing Rights: The Current Debate
Chandra Hardy
The Case for Multilateral Debt Relief for Severely Indebted Countries
Azizali F. Mohammed
Global Financial System Reform and the C-20 Process
Raisuddin Ahmed
A Critique of the World Development Report 1994: Infrastructure for Development
Dipak Mazumdar
Labour issues in the World Development Report: A Critical Assessment
Ann Weston
The Uruguay Round: Costs and Compensation for Developing Countries

Other selected UNCTAD publications

Trade and Development Report, 1995
United Nations Publication, Sales No. E.95.II.D.16
ISBN 92-1-11-2384-4

Part One   Global Trends

   I   The World Economy: Performance and Prospects
   II   International Financial Markets and the External Debt of Developing Countries
        Annex: Impact of the Naples Terms

Part Two   Rethinking Economic Policies

   I   Convergence of Growth, Inflation and Unemployment in the North
   II   The Invisible Hand, Capital Flows and Stalled Recovery in Latin America
   III   Systemic Risk and Derivatives Markets: Selected Issues

Part Three   Unemployment and Interdependence

   I   The Issues at Stake
   II   Trade, Technology and Unemployment
   III   The Labour Market, Capital Formation and Job Creation
   IV   Policies for Full Employment
        Annex I: A Simulation Model of North-South Trade and Unemployment
        Annex II: The Dynamics of Service Sector Employment
        Annex III: Disguised Unemployment in the North

Trade and Development Report, 1996
United Nations Publication, Sales No. E.96.II.D.6
ISBN 92-1-112399-2

Part One   Global Trends

   I   The World Economy: Performance and Prospects
   II   International Capital Markets and the External Debt of Developing Countries

Part Two   Rethinking Development Strategies: Some Lessons from the East Asian Experience

   I   Integration and Industrialization in East Asia
   II   Exports, Capital Formation and Growth
   III   Responding to the New Global Environment

Annex   Macroeconomic Management, Financial Governance, and Development: Selected Policy Issues

****

United Nations Publications may be obtained from bookstores and distributors throughout the world. Consult your bookstore or write to United Nations Sales Section, New York, or to the Editorial Assistant, UNCTAD, Palais des Nations, CH-1211 Geneva 10, Switzerland (Tel. 41-22-907.5733; Fax. 41-22-907.0274).

UNCTAD Series on East Asian Development: Lessons for a New Global Environment

No. 1   Yilmaz Akyüz
          New trends in Japanese trade and FDI: Post-industrial transformation and policy challenges

No. 2   Tun-jen Cheng, Stephan Haggard and David Kang
          Institutions, economic policy and growth in the Republic of Korea and Taiwan Province of China

No. 3   Yoshihisa Inada
          The economic impact of regional integration with special reference to APEC

No. 4   K.S. Jomo
          Lessons from growth and structural change in the second-tier South-East Asian newly industrializing countries

No. 5   S.C. Kasahara
          The role of agriculture in the early phase of industrialization: Policy implications from Japan's experience

No. 6   Gabriel Palma
          Whatever happened to Latin America's savings? Comparing Latin American and East Asian savings performances

No. 7   V.R. Panchamukhi
          WTO and industrial policies

No. 8   Robert Rowthorn
          East Asian development: The flying geese paradigm reconsidered

No. 9   Ajit Singh
          Savings, investment and the corporation in the East Asian Miracle

No. 10   *UNCTAD Secretariat Report* to the Conference on East Asian Development: Lessons for a New Global Environment, held in Kuala Lumpur (Malaysia), 29 February to 1 March 1996.

****

Papers of the *UNCTAD Series on "East Asian Development: Lessons for a New Global Environment"* may be obtained from the Editorial Assistant, UNCTAD, Palais des Nations, CH-1211 Geneva 10, Switzerland (Tel. 41-22-907.5733; Fax. 41-22-907.0274).

UNCTAD Discussion Papers

No. 94, January 1995	XIE Ping	Financial services in China
No. 95, January 1995	William W.F. CHOA	The derivation of trade matrices by commodity groups in current and constant prices
No. 96, February 1995	Alexandre R. BARROS	The role of wage stickiness in economic growth
No. 97, February 1995	Ajit SINGH	How did East Asia grow so fast? Slow progress towards an analytical consensus
No. 98, April 1995	Z. KOZUL-WRIGHT	The role of the firm in the innovation process
No. 99, May 1995	Juan A. DE CASTRO	Trade and labour standards: Using the wrong instruments for the right cause
No. 100, August 1995	Roberto FRENKEL	Macroeconomic sustainability and development prospects: Latin American performance in the 1990s
No. 101, August 1995	R. KOZUL-WRIGHT & Paul RAYMENT	Walking on two legs: Strengthening democracy and productive entrepreneurship in the transition economies
No. 102, August 1995	J.C. DE SOUZA BRAGA M.A. MACEDO CINTRA & Sulamis DAIN	Financing the public sector in Latin America
No. 103, September 1995	Toni HANIOTIS & Sebastian SCHICH	Should governments subsidize exports through export credit insurance agencies?
No. 104, September 1995	Robert ROWTHORN	A simulation model of North-South trade
No. 105, October 1995	Giovanni N. DE VITO	Market distortions and competition: The particular case of Malaysia
No. 106, October 1995	John EATWELL	Disguised unemployment: The G7 experience
No. 107, November 1995	Luisa E. SABATER	Multilateral debt of least developed countries
No. 108, November 1995	David FELIX	Financial globalization versus free trade: The case for the Tobin Tax
No. 109, December 1995	Urvashi ZUTSHI	Aspects of the final outcome of the negotiations on financial services of the Uruguay Round
No. 110, January 1996	H.A.C. PRASAD	Bilateral terms of trade of selected countries from the South with the North and the South
No. 111, January 1996	Charles GORE	Methodological nationalism and the misunderstanding of East Asian industrialization
No. 112, March 1996	Djidiack FAYE	Aide publique au développement et dette extérieure: Quelles mesures opportunes pour le financement du secteur privé en Afrique?
No. 113, March 1996	Paul BAIROCH & Richard KOZUL-WRIGHT	Globalization myths: Some historical reflections on integration, industrialization and growth in the world economy
No. 114, April 1996	Rameshwar TANDON	Japanese financial deregulation since 1984
No. 115, April 1996	E.V.K. FITZGERALD	Intervention versus regulation: The role of the IMF in crisis prevention and management
No. 116, June 1996	Jussi LANKOSKI	Controlling agricultural nonpoint source pollution: The case of mineral balances
No. 117, August 1996	José RIPOLL	Domestic insurance markets in developing countries: Is there any life after GATS?
No. 118, September 1996	Sunanda SEN	Growth centres in South East Asia in the era of globalization
No. 119, September 1996	Leena ALANEN	The impact of environmental cost internalization on sectoral competitiveness: A new conceptual framework
No. 120, October 1996	Sinan AL-SHABIBI	Structural adjustment for the transition to disarmament: An assessment of the role of the market
No. 121, October 1996	J.F. OUTREVILLE	Reinsurance in developing countries: Market structure and comparative advantage
No. 122, December 1996	Jörg MAYER	Implications of new trade and endogenous growth theories for diversification policies of commodity-dependent countries
No. 123, December 1996	L. RUTTEN & L. SANTANA-BOADO	Collateralized commodity financing, with special reference to the use of warehouse receipts

****

Copies of *UNCTAD Discussion Papers* may be obtained from the Editorial Assistant, UNCTAD, Palais des Nations, CH-1211 Geneva 10, Switzerland (Tel. 41-22-907.5733; Fax. 41-22-907.0043/0274).